INVESTING IN PEOPLE,
SECOND EDITION

INVESTING IN PEOPLE, SECOND EDITION

Financial Impact of Human Resource Initiatives

Wayne Cascio

John Boudreau

This book is the product of an alliance for the Society for Human Resource Management (SHRM). With more than 250,000 members, SHRM is the world's largest professional association devoted to human resource management.

FT Press offers excellent discounts on this book when ordered in quantity for bulk purchases or special sales. For more information, please contact U.S. Corporate and Government Sales, 1-800-382-3419, corpsales@pearsontechgroup.com. For sales outside the U.S., please contact International Sales at international@pearson.com.

Company and product names mentioned herein are the trademarks or registered trademarks of their respective owners.

Printed in the United States of America

First Printing December 2010

Pearson Education LTD.
Pearson Education Australia PTY, Limited.
Pearson Education Singapore, Pte. Ltd.
Pearson Education North Asia, Ltd.
Pearson Education Canada, Ltd.
Pearson Educación de Mexico, S.A. de C.V.
Pearson Education—Japan
Pearson Education Malaysia, Pte. Ltd.

ISBN-10: 0-13-707092-6

ISBN-13: 978-0-13-707092-3

Vice President Publisher
Tim Moore

Associate Publisher and Director of Marketing
Amy Neidlinger

Acquisitions Editor
Megan Colvin

Editorial Assistant
Pamela Boland

Operations Manager
Gina Kanouse

Senior Marketing Manager
Julie Phifer

Publicity Manager
Laura Czaja

Assistant Marketing Manager
Megan Colvin

Cover Designer
Alan Clements

Managing Editor
Kristy Hart

Project Editor
Jovana San Nicolas-Shirley

Copy Editor
Krista Hansing Editorial Services, Inc.

Proofreader
Water Crest Publishing, Inc.

Indexer
Lisa Stumpf

Senior Compositor
Gloria Schurick

Manufacturing Buyer
Dan Uhrig

Library of Congress Cataloging-in-Publication Data

Cascio, Wayne F.

Investing in people : financial impact of human resource initiatives / Wayne F. Cascio, John W. Boudreau. -- 2nd ed.

p. cm.

ISBN-13: 978-0-13-707092-3 (hardback : alk. paper)

ISBN-10: 0-13-707092-6

1. Human capital--Accounting. 2. Labor costs--Accounting. 3. Employees--Training of. 4. Personnel management. I. Boudreau, John W. II. Title.

HF5681.H8C37 2011

658.3--dc22

2010036551

From Wayne Cascio:

*To my parents, Frank and Joan Cascio, who invested
so much of themselves in me.*

From John Boudreau:

*To my family, who continually inspire me to see
the wonderful potential in people.*

Contents

Acknowledgments

Published books represent more than the words that authors write, for they typically are products of the collective efforts of many people, and this one is no exception. We would like to thank Professor Carolyn Youssef and the inaugural class of the Ph.D. program in human capital management at Bellevue (Nebraska) University for their many helpful comments on material in the first edition of the book. In addition, we sincerely appreciate the enthusiastic encouragement and guidance that we received throughout the project from former Acquisitions Editor Jennifer Simon, Assistant Marketing Manager Megan Colvin, and Project Editor Jovana San Nicolas-Shirley of Pearson Education. We also deeply appreciate the support provided by the Society for Human Resource Management (SHRM) for the development of the software (accessible at http://hrcosting.com/hr/) that accompanies the book, and we thank our software developer and updater, John Jarrard, for the high-quality software that he developed and continues to maintain. Of course, any omissions or errors are the responsibility of the authors alone.

About the Authors

Wayne Cascio holds the Robert H. Reynolds Chair in Global Leadership at the University of Colorado Denver. He has authored more than 150 journal articles and book chapters and 24 books. In 1999 he received the Distinguished Career award from the HR Division of the Academy of Management. He received an honorary doctorate from the University of Geneva (Switzerland) in 2004, and in 2008 he was named by the *Journal of Management* as one of the most influential scholars in management in the past 25 years. In 2010 he received the Michael R. Losey Human Resources Research Award from the Society for Human Resource Management. His work is cited regularly in the business press. Dr. Cascio is a Fellow of the National Academy of Human Resources, the Academy of Management, and the American Psychological Association. Currently he serves as a senior editor of the *Journal of World Business*.

John Boudreau is Research Director at the Center for Effective Organizations and Professor of Management and Organization in the Marshall School of Business at the University of Southern California. He is recognized worldwide for breakthrough research on the bridge between superior human capital, talent, and sustainable competitive advantage. He is a strategy, human resource management, and talent advisor and educator in organizations ranging from early-stage companies, to government agencies and Fortune 100 organizations, to large multinational companies. Dr. Boudreau has published more than 60 books and articles, and his work has been featured in *Harvard Business Review*, *The Wall Street Journal*, and *Business Week*. He has won scholarly awards from the Academy of Management. Dr. Boudreau is a fellow of the National Academy of Human Resources and was formerly a professor at Cornell University.

Preface

The demand for accountability among all business functions has never been greater. Recent events show how vital decisions are about human resources in an increasingly uncertain and interconnected world. A key responsibility of organization leaders, human resource (HR) leaders, and consultants is to articulate the logical connections between progressive HR practices and firm performance, and they need to demonstrate those connections with data. This book provides logic and technology to look inside the "black box" between HR practices and financial/business performance.

Investing in people should be as systematic as investing in any other vital resource, based on logical frameworks and focused on optimization, not simply on reducing costs or mimicking best practices. This argues against the common "peanut-butter" approach to talent investments that spreads the same investments (for example, in training or staffing programs) over the entire organization, in an effort to be fair by being equal. Such approaches engender justifiable skepticism from leaders and employees who are asked to invest in programs or activities because HR—or even the CEO—says that "everyone must do it." That approach is in stark contrast to other resources, such as customers and technology, where investments are targeted where they have the greatest effect. Why not make greater talent investments where they matter most? This "decision science" approach provides the foundation for the techniques we present here. We emphasize that, ultimately, measurement is valuable when it improves important decisions about talent. That requires not simply more or better measures, but an integrated approach that combines those measures with logic, analytics, and knowledge processes (what we call the LAMP framework). Chapters are based on logic diagrams that show the links between particular HR programs, employee behaviors, and operational and financial outcomes. Each chapter also includes a discussion about process, describing opportunities and effective ways to communicate results to decision makers.

We draw extensively on our decades of experience assisting senior-level decision makers to better understand and measure the impact of talent decisions, and also on our research on the connections between talent and organizational outcomes. We have been fortunate to work with both practicing leaders and academic researchers. This combination is essential for talent measurement and decisions that achieve both practical relevance and logical rigor.

Investing in People draws upon research in psychology, economics, accounting, and finance to provide tools that leaders inside and outside the HR profession can use together to describe the financial results of their investments in people. We focus on HR investments with a rich history of data-based research, including staffing, training, workplace health, employee attitudes, and employee turnover, which also represent some of the most important strategic HR functions.

This book provides specific formulas and calculations that you can use to evaluate the impact of your own talent decisions. To make the formulas easier to use, we developed software to accompany the chapters on the following topics: absenteeism, turnover, health and welfare, attitudes and engagement, work-life issues, external employee sourcing, the economic value of job performance, payoffs from selection, and payoffs from training and development.

The Society for Human Resource Management (SHRM) provided generous support for the development of the software, and you can access this software at the SHRM website (http://hrcosting.com/hr/), regardless of whether you are a SHRM member. The software performs the calculations of measures so that readers can focus on the logic, analytics, and processes necessary to improve strategic decisions about talent.

Business leaders, inside and outside of the HR profession, need more rigorous, logical, and principles-based frameworks to understand the connections between human capital and organizational success. We hope that this book serves as a "go-to" resource for those frameworks.

Plan for the Book

Chapter 1, "Making HR Measurement Strategic," introduces the fundamental principle of this book, that HR measurement is valuable to the extent that it improves vital decisions about talent and how it is organized. This decision-based approach to HR measurement leads to different approaches from the traditional focus on HR services or resource expenditures. It emphasizes that effective HR measures must be embedded within a system that recognizes their role in enhancing decisions and organizational effectiveness. The elements of that framework are the guiding logic for each of the chapters that describe specific techniques and measures in selected HR areas.

Chapter 2, "Analytical Foundations of HR Measurement," describes four levels of sophistication in HR analytics, along with several analytical concepts that recur throughout this book. These are similar to foundational principles in finance or marketing, such as risk, return, and economies of scale. New to this edition is a discussion of conjoint analysis, a technique that researchers in a variety of fields use to identify the hidden rules that people use to make tradeoffs between different products or services and the values they place on different features. This chapter provides a primer on fundamental ideas that all organization leaders should understand about good measurement.

Beginning with Chapter 3, "The Hidden Costs of Absenteeism," we update the material from our first edition and also from Cascio's *Costing Human Resources* (4th ed., 2000) volume—revised, reconfigured, and presented in the context of the LAMP framework. Chapter 3 shows how to estimate, interpret, and manage absenteeism costs and other effects.

Chapter 4, "The High Cost of Employee Separations," describes how to calculate the fully loaded costs of employee turnover, and how to incorporate them into a complete framework of turnover effects. We show that turnover rates can easily be misinterpreted, and we show how to avoid that with better logic and measures. We also discuss the hidden costs of layoffs, a factor often ignored when organizations use layoffs to reduce labor costs.

Chapter 5, "Employee Health, Wellness, and Welfare," presents methods to assess the costs and benefits of employee assistance and worksite health-promotion programs. It also addresses the economics of employee smoking and obesity. In addition, the chapter discusses the value of disease-prevention investments and the role of health, wellness, and welfare programs in an age of rising health costs.

Chapter 6, "Employee Attitudes and Engagement," begins by distinguishing three important attitudes: job satisfaction, commitment, and engagement. It focuses on the economics of employee engagement, including research on how engagement and the feeling of working at a "best place to work" connect with customer service and financial results.

Chapter 7, "Financial Effects of Work-Life Programs," includes new findings on the economics of work-life programs and how to measure them. These techniques are useful as organizations increasingly struggle with fundamental questions about how to optimize their investments in talent to enhance employee work-life fit in an increasingly competitive work environment.

Chapter 8, "Staffing Utility: The Concept and Its Measurement," introduces utility analysis, an important research framework for understanding how investments in HR programs, such as staffing, training, and compensation, produce financial outcomes, and how to calculate them. New to Chapter 8 is a discussion of supply-chain analysis, an integrative framework whose objective is to optimize investments across the various elements of the staffing process, not simply to maximize payoffs within each element.

Chapter 9, "The Economic Value of Job Performance," addresses one of the most important financial issues related to talent: the financial value of improved job performance. It provides a framework for understanding where improving performance makes a big difference and where its effects are smaller. We also look at approaches to actually estimate the value of improving performance in particular jobs or roles.

Chapter 10, "The Payoff from Enhanced Selection," combines the utility analysis framework from Chapter 8 and the economics of job performance from Chapter 9 to calculate the economic value of staffing, including recruitment and selection. The formulas are based on decades of scholarly research and show how statistics such as correlations can be clues to significant organizational value. The software that accompanies the book simplifies the calculations so that readers can focus on the strategic implications of their findings (available at http://hrcosting.com/hr/).

Chapter 11, "Costs and Benefits of HR Development Programs," addresses one of the most significant organizational enterprises: employee development. Despite the massive investments in this area, across all developed countries, specific payoffs are often unknown; at a broader level, we cite research that shows that investments in training predict future stock prices. In this chapter, you learn how to use the utility analysis and performance value frameworks of Chapters 8 and 9 to estimate payoffs from learning and development within a logical and research-based framework that leaders can actually apply.

Chapter 12, "Talent Investment Analysis: Catalyst for Change," provides a capstone chapter that integrates the previous material. It's not enough to have solid logic, analysis, and measurements that show the economic effects of talent investments. Key decision makers must listen and act on them. This chapter describes strategies that we have used to communicate the financial implications of investing in people to employees and leaders outside the HR function. This chapter also describes opportunities to integrate the decision science approach to talent with ongoing organizational processes, such as strategy, budgeting, and performance management.

1

Making HR Measurement Strategic

This book will help you better understand how to analyze, measure, and account for investments in people. However, although data and analysis are important to investing in people, they are really just a means to an end. The ultimate purpose of an investment framework is to improve decisions about those investments. Decisions about talent, human capital, and organizational effectiveness are increasingly central to the strategic success of virtually all organizations.

According to 2010 research from the Hay Group, businesses listed in *Fortune* magazine as the world's most admired companies invest in people and see them as assets to be developed, not simply as costs to be cut. Consider how the three most admired companies in 64 industries—firms like UPS, Disney, McDonald's, and Marriott International—managed their people during the Great Recession, compared to their less-admired peers. Those companies were less likely to have laid off any employees (10 percent versus 23 percent, respectively). By even greater margins, they were less likely to have frozen hiring or pay, and by a giant margin (21 points), they were more likely to have invested the money and the effort to brand themselves as employers, not just as marketers to customers. They treat their people as assets, not expenses. Perhaps the most important lesson from the 2010 World's Most Admired companies is that they did not launch their enlightened human capital philosophies when the recession hit; they'd been following them for years. Once a recession starts, it's too late. "Champions know what their most valuable asset is, and they give it the investment it deserves—through good times and bad" (p. 82).[1]

It is surprising how often companies address vital decisions about talent and how it is organized with limited measures or faulty logic. How would your organization measure the return on investments that retain vital talent? Would the future returns be as clear as the tangible short-term costs to be saved by layoffs? Does your organization have a logical and numbers-based approach to understanding the payoff from improved employee health, improvements in how employees are recruited and selected, reductions in turnover and absenteeism, or improvements in how employees are trained and developed? In most organizations, leaders who encounter such questions approach them with far less rigor and analysis than questions about other resources such as money, customers, and technology. Yet measures have immense potential to improve the decisions of HR and non-HR leaders.

This book is based on a fundamental principle: HR measurement adds value by improving vital decisions about talent and how it is organized.

This perspective was articulated by John Boudreau and Peter Ramstad in their book, *Beyond HR*.[2] It means that HR measurements must do more than evaluate the performance of HR programs and practices, or prove that HR can be made tangible. Rather, it requires that HR measures reinforce and teach the logical frameworks that support sound strategic decisions about talent.

In this book, we provide logical frameworks and measurement techniques to enhance decisions in several vital talent domains where decisions often lag behind scientific knowledge, and where mistakes frequently reduce strategic success. Those domains are listed here:

- Absenteeism (Chapter 3)

- Employee turnover (Chapter 4)

- Employee health and welfare (Chapter 5)

- Employee attitudes and engagement (Chapter 6)

- Work-life issues (Chapter 7)

- External employee sourcing (recruitment and selection) (Chapter 8)

- The economic value of employee performance (Chapter 9)

- The value of improved employee selection (Chapter 10)

- The costs and benefits of employee development (Chapter 11)

Each chapter provides a logical framework that describes the vital key variables that affect cost and value, as well as specific measurement techniques and examples, often noting elements that frequently go unexamined or are overlooked in most HR and talent-measurement systems.

The importance of these topics is evident when you consider how well your organization would address the following questions if your CEO were to pose them:

Chapter 2: "I see that there is a high correlation between employee engagement scores and sales revenue across our different regions. Does that mean that if we raise engagement scores, our sales go up?"

Chapter 3: "I know that, on any given day, about 5 percent of our employees are absent. Yet everyone seems to be able to cover for the absent employees, and the work seems to get done. Should we try to reduce this absence rate, and if we did, what would be the benefit to our organization?"

Chapter 4: "Our total employment costs are higher than those of our competitors, so I need you to lay off 10 percent of our employees. It seems "fair" to reduce headcount by 10 percent in every unit, but we project different growth in different units. What's the right way to distribute the layoffs?"

Chapter 4: "Our turnover rate among engineers is 10 percent higher than that of our competitors. Why hasn't HR instituted programs to get it down to the industry levels? What are the costs or benefits of employee turnover?"

Chapter 5: "In a globally competitive environment, we can't afford to provide high levels of health care and health coverage for our employees. Every company is cutting health coverage, and so must we. There are cheaper health-care and insurance programs that can cut our costs by 15 percent. Why aren't we offering cheaper health benefits?"

Chapter 6: "I read that companies with high employee satisfaction have high financial returns, so I want you to develop an employee engagement measure and hold our unit managers accountable for raising the average employee engagement in each of their units."

Chapter 7: "I hear a lot about the increasing demand for work and life fit, but my generation found a way to work the long hours and have a family. Is this generation really that different? Are there really tangible relationships between work-life conflict and organizational productivity? If there are, how would we measure them and track the benefits of work-life programs?"

Chapter 8: "We expect to grow our sales 15 percent per year for the next 5 years. I need you to hire enough sales candidates to increase the size of our sales force by 15 percent a year, and do that without exceeding benchmark costs per hire in our industry. What are those costs?"

Chapter 9: "What is the value of good versus great performance? Is it necessary to have great performance in every job and on every job element? Where should

I push employees to improve their performance, and where is it enough that they meet the minimum standard?"

Chapter 10: "Is it worth it to invest in a comprehensive assessment program, to improve the quality of our new hires? If we invest more than our competition, can we expect to get higher returns? Where is the payoff to improved selection likely to be the highest?"

Chapter 11: "I know that we can deliver training much more cheaply if we just outsource our internal training group and rely on off-the-shelf training products to build the skills that we need. We could shut down our corporate university and save millions."

In every case, the question or request reflects assumptions about the relationship between decisions about human resource (HR) programs and the ultimate costs or benefits of those decisions. Too often, such decisions are made based on very naïve logical frameworks, such as the idea that a proportional increase in sales requires the same proportional increase in the number of employees, or that across-the-board layoffs are logical because they spread the pain[8] equally. In this book, we help you understand that these assumptions are often well meaning but wrong, and we show how better HR measurement can correct them.

Two issues are at work here. First, business leaders inside and outside of the HR profession need more rigorous, logical, and principles-based frameworks for understanding the connections between human capital and organization success. Those frameworks comprise a "decision science" for talent and organization, just as finance and marketing comprise decision sciences for money and customer resources. The second issue is that leaders inside and outside the HR profession are often unaware of existing scientifically supported ways to measure and evaluate the implications of decisions about human resources. An essential pillar of any decision science is a measurement system that improves decisions, through sound scientific principles and logical relationships.

The topics covered in this book represent areas where very important decisions are constantly made about talent and that ultimately drive significant shifts in strategic value. Also, they are areas where fundamental measurement principles have been developed, often through decades of scientific study, but where such principles are rarely used by decision makers. This is not meant to imply that HR and business leaders are not smart and effective executives. However, there are areas where the practice of decisions lags behind state-of-the-art knowledge.

The measurement and decision frameworks in these chapters are also grounded in general principles that support measurement systems in all areas of organizational decision making; such principles include data analysis and research design, the distinction between correlations and causes, the power of break-even analysis, and ways to account for economic effects that occur over time. Those principles are described in Chapter 2, "Analytical Foundations of HR Measurement," and then used throughout this book.

Next, we show how a decision-science approach to HR measurement leads to very different approaches from the traditional one, and we introduce the frameworks from this decision-based approach that will become the foundation of the rest of this book.

How a Decision Science Influences HR Measurement

When HR measures are carefully aligned with powerful, logical frameworks, human capital measurement systems not only track the effectiveness of HR policies and practices, but they actually teach the logical connections, because organization leaders use the measurement systems to make decisions. This is what occurs in other business disciplines. For example, the power of a consistent, rigorous logic, combined with measures, makes financial tools such as economic value added (EVA) and net present value (NPV) so useful. They elegantly combine both numbers and logic, and help business leaders improve in making decisions about financial resources.

Business leaders and employees routinely are expected to understand the logic that explains how decisions about money and customers connect to organization success. Even those outside the finance profession understand principles of cash flow and return on investment. Even those outside the marketing profession understand principles of market segmentation and product life cycle. In the same way, human capital measurement systems can enhance how well users understand the logic that connects organization success to decisions about their own talent, as well as the talent of those whom they lead or work with. To improve organizational effectiveness, HR processes, such as succession planning, performance management, staffing, and leadership development, must rely much more on improving the competency and engagement of non-HR leaders than on anything that HR typically controls directly.

Why use the term *science*? Because the most successful professions rely on decision systems that follow scientific principles and have a strong capacity to quickly incorporate new scientific knowledge into practical applications. Disciplines such as finance, marketing, and operations provide leaders with frameworks that show how those resources affect strategic success, and the frameworks themselves reflect findings from universities, research centers, and scholarly journals. Their decision models and their measurement systems are compatible with the scholarly science that supports them. Yet with talent and human resources, the frameworks that leaders in organizations use often bear distressingly little similarity to the scholarly research in human resources and human behavior at work[3] The idea of evidence-based HR management requires creating measurement systems that encourage and teach managers how to think more critically and logically about their decisions, and to make decisions that are informed and consistent with leading research.[4]

A vast array of research focuses on human behavior at work, labor markets, how organizations can better compete with and for talent, and how that talent is organized. Disciplines such as psychology, economics, sociology, organization theory, game theory, and even operations management and human physiology all contain potent research frameworks and findings based on the scientific method. A scientific approach reveals how decisions and decision-based measures can bring the insights of these fields to bear on the practical issues confronting organization leaders and employees. You will learn how to use these research findings as you master the HR measurement techniques described in this book.

Decision Frameworks

A decision framework provides the logical connections between decisions about a resource (for example, financial capital, customers, or talent) and the strategic success of the organization. This is true in HR, as we show in subsequent chapters that describe such connections in various domains of HR. It is also true in other, more familiar decision sciences such as finance and marketing. It is instructive to compare HR to these other disciplines. Figure 1-1 shows how a decision framework for talent and HR, which Boudreau and Ramstad called "talentship," has a parallel structure to decision frameworks for finance and marketing.

Finance is a decision science for the resource of money, marketing is the decision science for the resource of customers, and talentship is the decision science for the resource of talent. In all three decision sciences, the elements combine to show how one factor interacts with others to produce value. *Efficiency* refers to the relationship between what is spent and the programs and practices that are produced. *Effectiveness* refers to the relationship between the programs or practices and their effects on their target audience. *Impact* refers to the relationship between the effects of the practice on the target audience and the ultimate success of the organization.

To illustrate the logic of such a framework, consider marketing as an example. Investments in marketing produce a product, promotion, price, and placement mix. This is

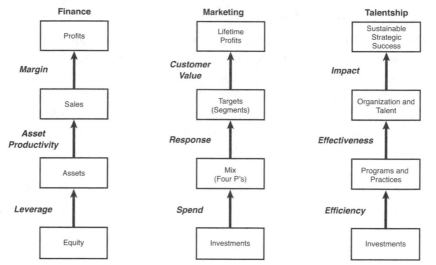

Finance	Marketing	Talentship
Profits	Lifetime Profits	Sustainable Strategic Success
Margin	*Customer Value*	*Impact*
Sales	Targets (Segments)	Organization and Talent
Asset Productivity	*Response*	*Effectiveness*
Assets	Mix (Four P's)	Programs and Practices
Leverage	*Spend*	*Efficiency*
Equity	Investments	Investments

Figure 1-1 Finance, marketing, and talentship decision frameworks.

efficiency. Those programs and practices produce responses in certain customer segments. This is effectiveness. Finally, the responses of customer segments create changes in the lifetime profits from those customers. This is impact.

Similarly, with regard to talent decisions, *efficiency* describes the connection between investments in people and the talent-related programs and practices they produce (such as cost per training hour). *Effectiveness* describes the connection between the programs/practices and the changes in the talent quality or organizational characteristics (such as whether trainees increase their skill). *Impact* describes the connection between the changes in talent/organization elements and the strategic success of the organization (such as whether increased skill actually enhances the organizational processes or initiatives that are most vital to strategic success).

The chapters in this book show how to measure not just HR efficiency, but also elements of effectiveness and impact. In addition, each chapter provides a logical framework for the measures, to enhance decision making and organizational change. Throughout the book, we attend to measures of efficiency, effectiveness, and impact. The current state of the art in HR management is heavily dominated by efficiency measures, so this book will help you see beyond the most obvious efficiency measures and put them in the context of effectiveness and impact.

Data, Measurement, and Analysis

In a well-developed decision science, the measures and data are deployed through management systems, used by leaders who understand the principles, and supported by professionals who add insight and expertise. In stark contrast, HR data, information, and measurement face a paradox today. There is increasing sophistication in technology, data availability, and the capacity to report and disseminate HR information, but investments in HR data systems, scorecards, and integrated enterprise resource systems fail to create the strategic insights needed to drive organizational effectiveness. HR measures exist mostly in areas where the accounting systems require information to control labor costs or to monitor functional activity. Efficiency gets a lot of attention, but effectiveness and impact are often unmeasured. In short, many organizations are "hitting a wall" in HR measurement.

Hitting the "Wall" in HR Measurement[5]

Type "HR measurement" into a search engine, and you will get more than 900,000 results. Scorecards, summits, dashboards, data mines, data warehouses, and audits abound. The array of HR measurement technologies is daunting. The paradox is that even when HR measurement systems are well implemented, organizations typically hit a "wall." Despite ever more comprehensive databases and ever more sophisticated HR data analysis and reporting, HR measures only rarely drive true strategic change.[6]

Figure 1-2 shows how, over time, the HR profession has become more elegant and sophisticated, yet the trend line doesn't seem to be leading to the desired result. Victory is typically declared when business leaders are induced or held accountable for HR measures. HR organizations often point proudly to the fact that bonuses for top leaders depend in part on the results of an HR "scorecard." For example, incentive systems might make bonuses for business-unit managers contingent on reducing turnover, raising average engagement scores, or placing their employees into the required distribution of 70 percent in the middle, 10 percent at the bottom, and 20 percent in the top.

Yet having business leader incentives based on HR measures is not the same as creating organization change. To have impact, HR measures must create a true strategic difference in the organization. Many organizations are frustrated because they seem to be doing all the measurement things "right," but there is a large gap between the expectations for the measurement systems and their true effects. HR measurement systems have much to learn from measurement systems in more mature professions such as finance and marketing. In these professions, measures are only one part of the system for creating organizational change through better decisions.

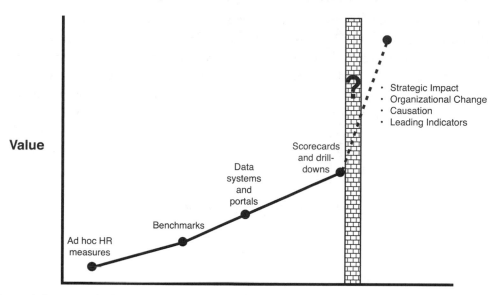

Figure 1-2 Hitting the "wall" in HR measurement.

Typically, HR develops measures to justify the investment in the HR function and its services and activities, or to prove a cause-effect connection between HR programs and organizational outcomes. Contrast this with financial measurement. Although it is certainly important to measure how the accounting or finance department operates, the majority of financial measures are not concerned with how finance and accounting programs and services are delivered. Financial measures typically focus on the outcomes—the quality of decisions about financial resources. Most HR measures today focus on how the HR function is using and deploying its resources and whether those resources are used efficiently. If the HR organization is ultimately to be accountable for improving talent decisions throughout the organization, HR professionals must take a broader and more complete perspective on how measurements can drive strategic change.

Correcting these limitations requires keeping in mind the basic principle expressed at the beginning of this chapter: Human capital metrics are valuable to the extent that they improve decisions about talent and how it is organized. That means that we must embed HR measures within a complete framework for creating organizational change through enhanced decisions. We describe that framework next.

The LAMP Framework

We believe that a paradigm extension toward a talent decision science is key to getting to the other side of the wall. Incremental improvements in the traditional measurement approaches will not address the challenges. HR measurement can move beyond the wall using what we call the LAMP model, shown in Figure 1-3. The letters in LAMP stand for logic, analytics, measures, and process, four critical components of a measurement system that drives strategic change and organizational effectiveness. Measures represent only one component of this system. Although they are essential, without the other three components, the measures and data are destined to remain isolated from the true purpose of HR measurement systems.

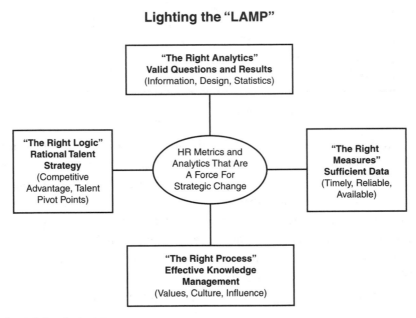

Figure 1-3 Lighting the LAMP.

The LAMP metaphor refers to a story that reflects today's HR measurement dilemma:

> One evening while strolling, a man encountered an inebriated person diligently searching the sidewalk below a street lamp.
>
> "Did you lose something?" he asked.
>
> "My car keys. I've been looking for them for an hour," the person replied.
>
> The man quickly scanned the area, spotting nothing. "Are you sure you lost them here?"

"No, I lost them in that dark alley over there."

"If you lost your keys in the dark alley, why don't you search over there?"

"Because this is where the light is."

In many ways, talent and organization measurement systems are like the person looking for the keys where the light is, not where they are most likely to be found. Advancements in information technology often provide technical capabilities that far surpass the ability of the decision science and processes to use them properly. So it is not uncommon to find organizations that have invested significant resources constructing elegant search and presentation technology around measures of efficiency, or measures that largely emanate from the accounting system.

The paradox is that genuine insights about human resources often exist in the areas where there are no standard accounting measures. The significant growth in HR out-sourcing, where efficiency is often the primary value proposition and IT technology is the primary tool, has exacerbated these issues.[7] Even imperfect measures aimed at the right areas may be more illuminating than very elegant measures aimed in the wrong places.

Returning to our story about the person looking for keys under the street lamp, it's been said, "Even a weak penlight in the alley where the keys are is better than a very bright streetlight where the keys are not."

Figure 1-3 shows that HR measurement systems are only as valuable as the decisions they improve and the organizational effectiveness to which they contribute. HR measurement systems create value as a catalyst for strategic change. Let's examine how the four compo-nents of the LAMP framework define a more complete measurement system. We present the elements in the following order: logic, measures, analytics, and, finally, process.

Logic: What Are the Vital Connections?

Without proper logic, it is impossible to know where to look for insights. The logic ele-ment of any measurement system provides the "story" behind the connections between the numbers and the effects and outcomes. In this book, we provide logical models that help to organize the measurements and show how they inform better decisions.

Most chapters provide "logic models" for this purpose. Examples include the connec-tions between health/wellness and employee turnover, performance, and absenteeism in Chapter 5, "Employee Health, Wellness, and Welfare." In Chapter 4, "The High Cost of Employee Separations," on employee turnover, we propose a logic model that shows how employee turnover is similar to inventory turnover. This simple analogy shows how to think beyond turnover costs, to consider performance and quality, and to optimize employee shortages and surpluses, not just eliminate them. In Chapter 8, "Staffing Utility: The Concept and Its Measurement," we propose a logic model that shows how selecting employees is similar to optimizing a supply chain for talent, to help leaders understand how to optimize all elements of employee acquisition, not simply maximize the validity of tests or the quality of recruitment sources. In Chapter 9, "The Economic Value of Job Performance," we propose a logic model that focuses on where differences in employee performance are most pivotal, borrowing from the common engineering idea that improving performance of every product component is not equally valuable.

Another prominent logic model is the "service-value-profit" framework for the customer-facing process. This framework depicts the connections between HR and management practices, which affect employee attitudes, engagement, and turnover, which then affect the experiences of customers, which affect customer-buying behavior, which affects sales, which affect profits. Perhaps the most well-known application of this framework was Sears, which showed quantitative relationships among these factors and used them to change the behavior of store managers.[8]

Missing or faulty logic is often the reason well-meaning HR professionals generate measurement systems that are technically sound but make little sense to those who must use them. With well-grounded logic, it is much easier to help leaders outside the HR profession understand and use the measurement systems to enhance their decisions. Moreover, that logic must be constructed so that it is understandable and credible not only to HR professionals, but to the leaders they seek to educate and influence. Connecting HR measures to traditional business models in this way was described as *Retooling HR*, by John Boudreau, in his book of that name.[9]

Measures: Getting the Numbers Right

The measures part of the LAMP model has received the greatest attention in HR. As discussed in subsequent chapters, virtually every area of HR has many different measures. Much time and attention is paid to enhancing the quality of HR measures, based on criteria such as timeliness, completeness, reliability, and consistency. These are certainly important standards, but lacking a context, they can be pursued well beyond their optimum levels, or they can be applied to areas where they have little consequence.

Consider the measurement of employee turnover. Much debate centers on the appropriate formulas to use in estimating turnover and its costs, or the precision and frequency with which employee turnover should be calculated. Today's turnover-reporting systems can calculate turnover rates for virtually any employee group and business unit. Armed with such systems, managers "slice and dice" the data in a wide variety of ways (ethnicity, skills, performance, and so on), with each manager pursuing his or her own pet theory about turnover and why it matters. Some might be concerned about losing long-tenure employees, others might focus on high-performing employees, and still others might focus on employee turnover where outside demand is greatest. These are all logical ideas, but they are not universally correct. Whether they are useful depends on the context and strategic objectives. Lacking such a context, better turnover measures won't help improve decisions. That's why the logic element of the LAMP model must support good measurement.

Precision is not a panacea. There are many ways to make HR measures more reliable and precise. Focusing only on measurement quality can produce a brighter light shining where the keys are not! Measures require investment, which should be directed where it has the greatest return, not just where improvement is most feasible. Taking another page from the idea of "retooling HR" to reflect traditional business models, organizations routinely pay greater attention to the elements of their materials inventory that have the greatest effect on costs or productivity. Indeed, a well-known principle is the "80-20 rule," which suggests that 80 percent of the important variation in inventory costs or quality is often driven by 20 percent of the inventory items. Thus, although organizations indeed track 100 percent of their inventory items, they measure the vital 20 percent with greater precision, more frequency, and greater accountability for key decision makers.

Why not approach HR measurement in the same way? Factors such as employee turnover, performance, engagement, learning, and absence are not equally important everywhere. That means measurements like these should focus precisely on what matters. If turnover is a risk due to the loss of key capabilities, turnover rates should be stratified to distinguish employees with such skills from others. If absence has the most effect in call centers with tight schedules, this should be very clear in how we measure absenteeism.

Lacking a common logic about how turnover affects business or strategic success, well-meaning managers draw conclusions that might be misguided or dangerous, such as the assumption that turnover or engagement have similar effects across all jobs. This is why every chapter of this book describes HR measures and how to make them more precise and valid. However, each chapter also embeds them in a logic model that explains how the measures work together.

Analytics: Finding Answers in the Data

Even a very rigorous logic with good measures can flounder if the analysis is incorrect. For example, some theories suggest that employees with positive attitudes convey those attitudes to customers, who, in turn, have more positive experiences and purchase more. Suppose an organization has data showing that customer attitudes and purchases are higher in locations with better employee attitudes. This is called a positive correlation between attitudes and purchases. Organizations have invested significant resources in improving frontline-employee attitudes based precisely on this sort of correlation. However, will a decision to improve employee attitudes lead to improved customer purchases?

The problem is that such investments may be misguided. A correlation between employee attitudes and customer purchases does not prove that the first one causes the second. Such a correlation also happens when customer attitudes and purchases actually cause employee attitudes. This can happen because stores with more loyal and committed customers are more pleasant places to work. The correlation can also result from a third, unmeasured factor. Perhaps stores in certain locations (such as near a major private university) attract college-student customers who buy more merchandise or services and are more enthusiastic and also happen to have access to college-age students that bring a positive attitude to their work. Store location turns out to cause both store performance and employee satisfaction. The point is that a high correlation between employee attitudes and customer purchases could be due to any or all of these effects. Sound analytics can reveal which way the causal arrow actually is pointing.

Analytics is about drawing the right conclusions from data. It includes statistics and research design, and it then goes beyond them to include skill in identifying and articulating key issues, gathering and using appropriate data within and outside the HR function, setting the appropriate balance between statistical rigor and practical relevance, and building analytical competencies throughout the organization. Analytics transforms HR logic and measures into rigorous, relevant insights.

Analytics often connect the logical framework to the "science" related to talent and organization, which is an important element of a mature decision science. Frequently, the most appropriate and advanced analytics are found in scientific studies that are published in professional journals. In this book, we draw upon that scientific knowledge to build the analytical frameworks in each chapter.

Analytical principles span virtually every area of HR measurement. In Chapter 2, we describe general analytical principles that form the foundation of good measurement. We also provide a set of economic concepts that form the analytical basis for asking the right questions to connect organizational phenomena such as employee turnover and employee quality to business outcomes. In addition to these general frameworks, each chapter contains analytics relevant specifically to the topic of that chapter.

Advanced analytics are often the domain of specialists in statistics, psychology, economics, and other disciplines. To augment their own analytical capability, HR organizations often draw upon experts in these fields, and upon internal analytical groups in areas such as marketing and consumer research. Although this can be very useful, it is our strong belief that familiarity with analytical principles is increasingly essential for all HR professionals and for those who aspire to use HR data well.

Process: Making Insights Motivating and Actionable

The final element of the LAMP framework is process. Measurement affects decisions and behaviors, and those occur within a complex web of social structures, knowledge frameworks, and organizational cultural norms. Therefore, effective measurement systems must fit within a change-management process that reflects principles of learning and knowledge transfer. HR measures and the logic that supports them are part of an influence process.

The initial step in effective measurement is to get managers to accept that HR analysis is possible and informative. The way to make that happen is not necessarily to present the most sophisticated analysis. The best approach may be to present relatively simple measures and analyses that match the mental models that managers already use. Calculating turnover costs can reveal millions of dollars that can be saved with turnover reductions, as discussed in Chapter 4. Several leaders outside of HR have told us that a turnover-cost analysis was the first time they realized that talent and organization decisions had tangible effects on the economic and accounting processes they were familiar with.

Of course, measuring only the cost of turnover is insufficient for good decision making. For example, overzealous attempts to cut turnover costs can compromise candidate quality in ways that far outweigh the cost savings. Managers can reduce the number of candidates who must be interviewed by lowering their selection standards. The lower the standards, the more candidates will "pass" the interview, so fewer interviews must be conducted to fill a certain number of vacancies. Lowering standards can create problems that far outweigh the cost savings from doing fewer interviews! Still, the process element of the LAMP framework reminds us that often best way to start a change process may be first to assess turnover costs, to create initial awareness that the same analytical logic used for financial, technological, and marketing investments can apply to human resources. Then the door is open to more sophisticated analyses beyond the costs. Once leaders buy into the idea that human capital decisions have tangible monetary effects, they may be more receptive to greater sophistication, such as considering employee turnover in the same framework as inventory turnover.

Education is also a core element of any change process. The return on investment (ROI) formula from finance is actually a potent tool for educating leaders in the key components of financial decisions. It helps leaders quickly incorporate risk, return, and cost in a simple logical model. In the same way, we believe that HR measurements increasingly will be used to educate constituents and will become embedded within the organization's learning and knowledge frameworks. For example, Valero Energy tracked the performance of both internal and external sources of applicants on factors such as cost, time, quality, efficiency, and dependability. It provided this information to hiring managers and used it to establish an agreement about what managers were willing to invest to receive a certain level of service from internal or external recruiters. Hiring managers learned about the tradeoffs between investments in recruiting and its performance.[10] We will return to this idea in Chapters 8, 9, and 10.

In the chapters that follow, we suggest where the HR measures we describe can connect to existing organizational frameworks and systems that offer the opportunity to get attention and to enhance decisions. For example, organizational budgeting systems reflect escalating health-care costs. The cost measures discussed in Chapter 5, offer added insight and precision for such discussions. By embedding these basic ideas and measures into the existing health-care cost discussion, HR leaders can gain the needed credibility to extend the discussion to include the logical connections between employee health and other outcomes, such as learning, performance, and profits. What began as a budget exercise becomes a more nuanced discussion about the optimal investments in employee health and how those investments pay off.

As another example, leaders routinely assess performance and set goals for their subordinates. Measuring the value of enhanced performance can make those decisions more precise, focusing investments on the pivot points where performance makes the biggest difference. Chapter 9 describes methods and logic for measuring the monetary impact of improved performance.

You will see the LAMP framework emerge in many of the chapters in this book, to help you organize not only the measures, but also your approach to making those measures matter.

Conclusion

HR measures must improve important decisions about talent and how it is organized. This chapter has shown how this simple premise leads to a very different approach to HR measurement than is typically followed today, and how it produces several decision-science-based frameworks to help guide HR measurement activities toward greater strategic impact. We have introduced not only the general principle that decision-based measurement is vital to strategic impact, but also the LAMP framework, as a useful logical system for understanding how measurements drive decisions, organization effectiveness, and strategic success. LAMP also provides a diagnostic framework that can be used to examine existing measurement systems for their potential to create these results. We return to the LAMP framework frequently in this book.

We also return frequently to the ideas of measuring efficiency, effectiveness, and impact, the three anchor points of the talentship decision framework of Boudreau and Ramstad. Throughout the book, you will see the power and effectiveness of measures in each of these areas, but also the importance of avoiding becoming fixated on any one of them. As in the well-developed disciplines of finance and marketing, it is important to focus on synergy between the different elements of the measurement and decision frameworks, not to fixate exclusively on any single component of them.

We show how to think of your HR measurement systems as teaching rather than telling. We also describe the opportunities you will have to take discussions that might normally be driven exclusively by accounting logic and HR cost cutting, and elevate them with more complete frameworks that are better grounded in the science behind human behavior at work. The challenge will be to embed those frameworks in the key decision processes that already exist in organizations.

Software to Accompany Chapters 3–11

To enhance the accuracy of calculations for the exercises that appear at the end of each chapter and make them easier to use, we have developed web-based software to accompany material in Chapters 3–11. The software covers the following topics:

- Employee absenteeism
- Turnover
- Health and welfare
- Attitudes and engagement
- Work-life issues
- External employee sourcing
- The economic value of job performance
- Payoffs from selection
- Payoffs from training (HR development)

Developed with support from the Society for Human Resource Management (SHRM), you can access this software from the SHRM website (http://hrcosting.com/hr/) anywhere in the world, regardless of whether you are a member of SHRM. Of particular note to multinational enterprises, the calculations can be performed using any currency, and currency conversions are accomplished easily. You can save, print, or download your calculations and carry forward all existing data to subsequent sessions. Our hope is that, by reducing the effort necessary to perform the actual calculation of measures, readers will spend more time focusing on the logic, analytics, and processes necessary to improve strategic decisions about talent.

References

1. Colvin, G., "How Are Most Admired Companies Different? They Invest in People and Keep Them Employed—Even in a Downturn," *Fortune* (22 March 2010): 82.

2. Boudreau, J. W., and P. R. Ramstad, *Beyond HR: The New Science of Human Capital* (Cambridge, Mass.: Harvard Business Press, 2007).

3. Rynes, S. L., A. E. Colbert, and K. G. Brown, "HR Professionals' Beliefs About Effective Human Resource Practices: Correspondence Between Research and Practice," *Human Resource Management* 41, no. 2 (2002): 149–174. See also Rynes, S. L., T. L. Giluk, and K. G. Brown, "The Very Separate Worlds of Academic and Practitioner Publications in Human Resource Management: Implications for Evidence-Based Management," *Academy of Management Journal* 50, no. 5 (2007): 987–1008.

4. Briner, R. B., D. Denyer, and D. M. Rousseau, "Evidence-Based Management: Concept Cleanup Time?" *Academy of Management Perspectives* 23, no. 4 (2009): 19–32.

5. This section draws material from Chapter 9 in Boudreau and Ramstad, *Beyond HR* (Boston: Harvard Business School Press, 2007).

6. Lawler, E. E. III, A. Levenson, and J. W. Boudreau, "HR Metrics and Analytics— Uses and Impacts," *Human Resource Planning Journal* 27, no. 4 (2004): 27–35.

7. Cook, M. F., and S. B. Gildner, *Outsourcing Human Resources Functions*, 2nd ed. (Alexandria, Va.: Society for Human Resource Management, 2006). See also Lawler, E. E. III, D. Ulrich, J. Fitz-enz, and J. Madden, *Human Resources Business Process Outsourcing* (Hoboken, N.J.: Jossey-Bass, 2000).

8. Rucci, A. J., S. P. Kirn, and R. T. Quinn, "The Employee-Customer-Profit Chain at Sears," *Harvard Business Review* (January–February 1998): 83–97.

9. Boudreau, John W., *Retooling HR: Using Proven Business Models to Improve Decisions About Talent* (Cambridge, Mass.: Harvard Business Publishing, 2010).

10. Boudreau, *Retooling HR*, Chapter 5.

2

Analytical Foundations of HR Measurement

The preceding chapter noted the importance of analytics within a broader frame work for a decision-based approach to human capital measurement. As you will see in the chapters that follow, each type of HR measurement has its own particular elements of analytics, those features of data analysis and design that ensure that the findings are legitimate and generalizable. However, it's also true that nearly every element of human resource management (HRM) relies on one or more supporting analytical concepts. These concepts are often the elements that scientists have identified as essential to drawing strong conclusions, or they reflect the tenets of economic analysis that ensure that the inferences that we draw from measures properly account for important economic factors such as inflation and risk.

As you read through the various chapters of this book, each of which focuses on a different aspect of HR measurement, you will repeatedly encounter many of these analytical concepts. In the interests of efficiency, we present some of the most common ones here so that you can refer back to this chapter as often as necessary to find a single location for their description and definition. They have in common general guidelines for interpreting data-based information. We present them in two broad groups: concepts in statistics and research design, and concepts in economics and finance. Within each category, we address issues in rough order from general to specific. Let's begin by considering why measures expressed in economic terms tend to get the attention of business leaders.

Traditional Versus Contemporary HR Measures

HRM activities—those associated with the attraction, selection, retention, development, and utilization of people in organizations—commonly are evaluated by using measures of individual behaviors, traits, or reactions, or by using statistical summaries of those measures. The former include measures of the reactions of various groups (top management, customers, applicants, or trainees), what individuals have learned, or how their behavior has changed on the job. Statistical summaries of individual measures include various ratios (for example, accident frequency or severity), percentages (for example, labor turnover), measures of central tendency and variability (for example, mean and standard deviation of performance measures, such as bank-teller shortages and surpluses), and measures of correlation (for example, validity coefficients for staffing programs, or measures of association between employee satisfaction and turnover).

Measuring individual behaviors, traits, or reactions and summarizing them statistically is the hallmark of most HR measurements, which are often largely drawn from psychology. More and more, however, the need to evaluate HRM activities in economic terms is becoming apparent. In the current climate of intense competition to attract and retain talent domestically and globally, operating executives justifiably demand estimates of the expected costs and benefits of HR programs, expressed in economic terms. They demand measures that are strategically relevant to their organizations and that rely on a defined logic to enhance decisions that affect important organizational outcomes. Reporting employee turnover levels for every position in an organization may seem to business leaders to be an administrative exercise for the HR department. However, they can often readily see the importance of analyzing and understanding the business and economic consequences of turnover among high performers ("A" players) who are difficult to replace, in a business unit that is pivotal to strategic success (for example, R&D in a pharmaceutical organization). Developing such measures certainly requires attention to calculating turnover appropriately and to the statistical formulas that summarize it. However, it also requires an interdisciplinary approach that includes information from accounting, finance, economics, and behavioral science. Measures developed in this way can help senior executives assess the extent to which HR programs are consistent with and contribute to the strategic direction of an organization.

Four Levels of Sophistication in HR Analytics

HR analytics is fact-based decision making. In the sections that follow, we describe four levels of sophistication used by Google's People Analytics Group: counting, clever counting, insight, and influence.[1] Each higher level requires mastery of the lower levels.

1.   **Counting:** All relevant data about the workforce are tracked, organized, and accessible. Getting this basic step right can be difficult. HR technology solutions—both off the shelf and internally built—can be clunky. The challenges of continually updating the database and ensuring that all end users, from line managers to HR generalists, are getting the data they need are unceasing. Google's current solution is a hybrid external vendor/internal customization model. It allows users to display headcount, attrition, promotion, and other data through customizable dashboards that have the ability to filter the data and display it according to hierarchy, employee location, and cost center, for example.

2.   **Clever counting:** Extrapolating from descriptive data yields new insights. For example, consider workforce planning. Using basic data on promotions, attrition, headcount by level, and anticipated organizational growth rate makes it possible to project the "shape" of your organization (the percentage of employees at each level) at the end of a year, at the end of two years, or after three-plus years. With the proper formulas in place, users can input anticipated future attrition/promotion and organizational growth rates to model different scenarios. By assigning salaries to employees at each level, one can see the financial impact of having an organizational shape that looks like a typical pyramid (with fewer employees at each level as one moves up the organization) or a more uniform distribution across levels, which would occur if the organization is not hiring but employees continue to receive promotions.

3. **Insight:** What drivers of the trends do you find through clever counting? The preceding example of modeling organizational shape is most useful if we can understand what's driving each component of the model. For example, we may find that the organization's projected shape in five years is top heavy. Why? Close investigation might show that promotion rates are too high, combined with attrition that is higher at lower levels than it is at higher levels. This process of inquiry provides the insight needed to understand the results of more sophisticated analyses.

4. **Influence:** The results of counting, clever counting, and insight can help make a difference. At this level, the relevant question is, how can we shape outcomes rather than just measure them? Insight from the organizational shape models described can lead to change if you partner with the right people in your organization. The overall objective is to ensure that managers have a shared understanding of the goals (for example, sustaining a pyramidal organizational structure) and the levers they can pull to achieve those goals. For example, if analysis shows that the current or projected future shape of the organization is top heavy, the levers include these:

   - Decrease yearly promotion rates

   - Launch attrition-prevention programs if insight has revealed that highest-performing employees are most likely to terminate

   - Backfill vacant positions at lower levels

The four steps to analytical sophistication do not apply only to workforce planning. Instead, they apply to any data collection and analysis activity, such as employee opinion surveys, employee selection research, or employee diversity analyses. Your goal should always be to get to the last step: influence.

Next, we describe some fundamental concepts from statistics and research design that help ensure that the kind of data gathered, and the calculations used to summarize the data, are best suited to the questions the data should answer. They are general interpretive concepts.

Fundamental Analytical Concepts from Statistics and Research Design

We make no attempt here to present basic statistical or research methods. Many excellent textbooks do that much more effectively than we can in the space available. Instead, we assume that the reader is generally familiar with these issues; our purpose here is to offer guidelines for interpretation and to point out some important cautions in those interpretations. In the following sections, we address three key concepts: generalizations from sample data, correlation and causality, and experimental controls for extraneous factors.

Generalizing from Sample Data

As a general rule, organizational research is based on samples rather than on populations of observations. A population consists of all the people (or, more broadly, units) about whom or which a study is meant to generalize, such as employees with fewer than two years of experience, customers who patronize a particular store, or trucks in a company's fleet. A sample represents a subset of people (or units) who actually participate in a study. In almost all cases, it is not practical or feasible to study an entire population. Instead, researchers draw samples.

If we are to draw reliable (that is, stable and consistent) and valid (that is, accurate) conclusions concerning the population, it is imperative that the sample be "like" the population—a representative sample. When the sample is like the population, we can be fairly confident that the results we find based on the sample also hold for the population. In other words, we can generalize from the sample to the population.[2]

One way to generate a representative sample is to use random sampling. A random sample is achieved when, through random selection, each member of a population is equally likely to be chosen as part of the sample. A table of random numbers, found in many statistics textbooks, can be used to generate a random sample. Here is how to use such a table. Choose any starting place arbitrarily. Look at the number—say, 004. Assuming that you have a list of names, such as applicants, count down the list to the fourth name. Choose it. Then look at the next number in the table, count down through the population, and choose that person, until you have obtained the total number of observations you need.

Sometimes a population is made up of members of different groups or categories, such as males and females, or purchasers of a product and nonpurchasers. Assume that, among 500 new hires in a given year, 60 percent are female. If we want to draw conclusions about the population of all new hires in a given year, based on our sample, the sample itself must be representative of these important subgroups (or strata) within the population. If the population is composed of 60 percent females and 40 percent males, we need to ensure that the sample is similar on this dimension.

One way to obtain such a sample is to use stratified random sampling. Doing so allows us to take into account the different subgroups of people in the population and helps guarantee that the sample represents the population on specific characteristics. Begin by dividing the population into subsamples or strata. In our example, the strata are based on gender. Then randomly select 60 percent of the sample observations from this stratum (for example, using the procedure described earlier) and the remaining 40 percent from the other stratum (males). Doing so ensures that the characteristic of gender in the sample represents the population.[3]

Many other types of sampling procedures might be used,[4] but the important point is that it is not possible to generalize reliably and validly from a sample to a population unless the sample itself is representative. Unfortunately, much research that is done in HR and management is based on case studies, samples of convenience, and even anecdotal evidence. Under those circumstances, it is not possible to generalize to a broader population of interest, and it is important to be skeptical of studies that try to do so.

Drawing Conclusions about Correlation and Causality

Perhaps one of the most pervasive human tendencies is to assume incorrectly that just because two things increase and decrease together, one must cause the other. The degree of relationship between any two variables (in the employment context, predictor and criterion) is simply the extent to which they vary together (covary) in a systematic fashion. The magnitude or degree to which they are related linearly is indicated by some measure of correlation, the most popular of which is the Pearson product-moment correlation coefficient, *r*. As a measure of relationship, *r* varies between −1.00 and +1.00. When *r* is 1.00, the two sets of scores (*x* and *y*) are related perfectly and systematically to each other. Knowing a person's status on variable *x* allows us to predict without error his or her standing on variable *y*.

In the case of an *r* of +1.00, high (low) predictor scores are matched perfectly by high (low) criterion scores. For example, performance review scores may relate perfectly to recommendations for salary increases. When *r* is −1.00, however, the relationship is inverse, and high (low) predictor scores are accompanied by low (high) criterion scores. For example, consider that as driving speed increases, fuel efficiency decreases. In both cases, positive and negative relationships, *r* indicates the extent to which the two sets of scores are ordered similarly. Given the complexity of variables operating in business settings, correlations of 1.00 exist only in theory. If no relationship exists between the two variables, *r* is 0.0, and knowing a person's standing on *x* tells us nothing about his or her standing on *y*. If *r* is moderate (positive or negative), we can predict y from *x* with a certain degree of accuracy.

Although correlation is a useful procedure for assessing the degree of relationship between two variables, by itself it does not allow us to predict one set of scores (criterion scores) from another set of scores (predictor scores). The statistical technique by which this is accomplished is known as regression analysis, and correlation is fundamental to its implementation.[5]

Sometimes people interpret a correlation coefficient as the percentage of variability in *y* that can be explained by *x*. This is not correct. Actually, the square of *r* indicates the percentage of variance in *y* (the criterion) that can be explained, or accounted for, given knowledge of *x* (the predictor). Assuming a correlation of $r = .40$, then $r^2 = .16$. This indicates that 16 percent of the variance in the criterion may be determined (or explained), given knowledge of the predictor. The statistic r^2 is known as the coefficient of determination.

A special problem with correlational research is that it is often misinterpreted. People often assume that because two variables are correlated, some sort of causal relationship must exist between the two variables. This is false. *Correlation does not imply causation!*

A correlation simply means that the two variables are related in some way. For example, consider the following scenario. An HR researcher observes a correlation between voluntary employee turnover and the financial performance of a firm (for example, as measured by return on assets) of –.20. Does this mean that high voluntary turnover causes poor financial performance of a firm? Perhaps. However, it is equally likely that the poor financial performance of a firm causes voluntary turnover, as some employees scramble to desert a sinking ship. In fact, such a reciprocal relationship between employee turnover and firm performance has now been demonstrated empirically.[6]

At a broader level, it is equally plausible that some other variable (for example, low unemployment) is causing employees to quit, or that a combination of variables (low unemployment in country A at the same time as a global economic recession) is causing high voluntary turnover in that country and low overall financial performance in a firm that derives much of its income from other countries. The point is that observing a correlation between two variables just means they are related to each other; it does not mean that one causes the other.

In fact, there are three necessary conditions to support a conclusion that x causes y.[7] The first is that y did not occur until after x. The second requirement is that x and y are actually shown to be related. The third (and most difficult) requirement is that other explanations of the relationship between x and y can be eliminated as plausible rival hypotheses.

Statistical methods alone generally cannot establish that one variable caused another. One technique that comes close, however, is structural equation modeling (SEM), sometimes referred to as LISREL (the name of one of the more popular software packages). SEM is a family of statistical models that seeks to explain the relationships among multiple variables. It examines the structure of interrelationships, expressed in a series of equations, similar to a series of multiple regression equations. These equations depict all of the relationships among constructs (the dependent and independent variables) involved in the analysis.

Although different methods can be used to test SEM models, all such models share three characteristics:

1. Estimation of multiple and interrelated dependence relationships

2. An ability to represent unobserved concepts in these relationships and to correct for measurement error in the estimation process

3. Defining a model to explain the entire set of relationships[8]

SEM alone cannot establish causality. What it does provide are statistical results of the hypothesized relationships in the researcher's model. The researcher can then infer from the results what alternative models are most consistent with theory. The most convincing claims of causal relationships, however, usually are based on experimental research.

Eliminating Alternative Explanations Through Experiments and Quasi-Experiments

The experimental method is a research method that allows a researcher to establish a cause-and-effect relationship through manipulation of one or more variables and to control the situation. An experimental design is a plan, an outline for conceptualizing the relations among the variables of a research study. It also implies how to control the research situation and how to analyze the data.[9]

For example, researchers can collect "before" measures on a job—before employees attend training—and collect "after" measures at the conclusion of training (and when employees are back on the job at some time after training). Researchers use experimental designs so that they can make causal inferences. That is, by ruling out alternative plausible explanations for observed changes in the outcome of interest, we want to be able to say that training caused the changes. Many preconditions must be met for a study to be experimental in nature. Here we merely outline the minimum requirements needed for an experiment.

The basic assumption is that a researcher controls as many factors as possible to establish a cause-and-effect relationship among the variables being studied. Suppose, for example, that a firm wants to know whether online training is superior to classroom training. To conduct an experiment, researchers manipulate one variable (known as the independent variable—in this case, type of training) and observe its effect on an outcome of interest (a dependent variable—for example, test scores at the conclusion of training). One group will receive classroom training, one group online training, and a third group no training. The last group is known as a "control" group because its purpose is to serve as a baseline from which to compare the performance of the other two groups. The groups that receive training are known as "experimental" or "treatment" groups because they each receive some treatment or level of the independent variable. That is, they each receive the same number of hours of training, either online or classroom. At the conclusion of the training, we will give a standardized test to the members of the control and experimental groups and compare the results. Scores on the test are the dependent variable in this study.

Earlier we said that experimentation involves control. This means that we have to control who is in the study. We want to have a sample that is representative of the broader population of actual and potential trainees. We want to control who is in each group (for example, by assigning participants randomly to one of the three conditions: online, classroom, or no training). We also want to have some control over what participants do while in the study (design of the training to ensure that the online and classroom versions cover identical concepts and materials). If we observe changes in post-training test scores across conditions, and all other factors are held constant (to the extent it is possible to do this), we can conclude that the independent variable (type of training) caused changes in the dependent variable (test scores derived after training is concluded). If, after completing this study with the proper controls, we find that those in one group (online, classroom, or no training) clearly outperform the others, we have evidence to support a cause-and-effect relationship among the variables.

Many factors can serve as threats to valid inferences, such as outside events, experience on the job, or social desirability effects in the research situation.[10]

Is it appropriate to accept wholeheartedly a conclusion from only one study? In most cases, the answer is no. This is because researchers may think they have controlled everything that might affect observed outcomes, but perhaps they missed something that does affect the results. That something else may have been the actual cause of the observed changes! A more basic reason for not trusting completely the results of a single study is that a single study cannot tell us everything about a theory.[11] Science is not static, and theories generated through science change. For that reason, there are methods, called meta-analysis, that mathematically combine the findings from many studies to determine whether the patterns across studies support certain conclusions. The power of combining multiple studies provides more reliable conclusions, and this is occurring in many areas of behavioral science.[12]

Researchers approaching organizational issues often believe that conducting a carefully controlled experiment is the ultimate answer to discovering the important answers in data. In fact, there is an important limitation of experiments and the data they provide. Often they fail to focus on the real goals of an organization. For example, experimental results may indicate that job performance after treatment A is superior to performance after treatments B or C. The really important question, however, may not be whether treatment A is more effective, but rather what levels of performance we can expect from almost all trainees at an acceptable cost, and the extent to which improved performance through training "fits" the broader strategic thrust of an organization.[13] Therefore, even well-designed experiments must carefully consider the context and logic of the situation, to ask the right questions in the first place.

Quasi-Experimental Designs

In field settings, major obstacles often interfere with conducting true experiments. True experiments require the manipulation of at least one independent variable, the random assignment of participants to groups, and the random assignment of treatments to groups.[14] However, some less complete (that is, quasi-experimental) designs still can provide useful data even though a true experiment is not possible. Shadish, Cook, and Campbell offer a number of quasi-experimental designs with the following rationale:[15]

> The central purpose of an experiment is to eliminate alternative hypotheses that also might explain results. If a quasi-experimental design can help eliminate some of these rival hypotheses, it may be worth the effort.

Because full experimental control is lacking in quasi-experiments, it is important to know which specific variables are uncontrolled in a particular design. Investigators should, of course, design the very best experiment possible, given their circumstances; where "full" control is not possible, however, they should use the most rigorous design that is possible. For example, suppose you were interested in studying the relationship between layoffs and the subsequent financial performance of firms. Pfeffer recently commented on this very issue:

> It's difficult to study the causal effect of layoffs—you can't do double-blind, placebo-controlled studies as you can for drugs by randomly assigning some companies to shed workers and others not, with people unaware of what "treatment" they are receiving. Companies that downsize are undoubtedly different in many ways (the quality of their management, for one) from those that don't. But you can attempt to control for differences in industry, size, financial condition, and past performance, and then look at a large number of studies to see if they reach the same conclusion.[16]

As a detailed example, consider one type of quasi-experimental design.[17]

This design, which is particularly appropriate for cyclical training programs, is known as the recurrent institutional cycle design. For example, a large sales organization presented a management development program, known as the State Manager Program, every two months to small groups (12–15) of middle managers (state managers). The one-week program focused on all aspects of retail sales (new product development, production, distribution, marketing, merchandising, and so on). The program was scheduled so that all state managers (approximately 110) could be trained over an 18-month period.

This is precisely the type of situation for which the recurrent institutional cycle design is appropriate—a large number of persons will be trained, but not all at the same time. Different cohorts are involved. This design is actually a combination of two (or more) before-and-after studies that occur at different points in time. Group I receives a pretest at Time 1, then training, and then a post-test at Time 2. At the same chronological time (Time 2), Group II receives a pretest, training, and then a post-test at Time 3. At Time 2, therefore, an experimental and a control group have, in effect, been created. One can obtain even more information (and with quasi-experimental designs, it is always wise to collect as much data as possible or to demonstrate the effect of training in several different ways) if it is possible to measure Group I again at Time 3 and to give Group II a pretest at Time 1. This controls the effects of history. Moreover, Time 3 data for Groups I and II and the post-tests for all groups trained subsequently provide information on how the training program is interacting with other organizational events to produce changes in the criterion measure.

Several cross-sectional comparisons are possible with the "cycle" design:

Group I post-test scores at Time 2 can be compared with Group II post-test scores at Time 2.

Gains made in training for Group I (Time 2 post-test scores) can be compared with gains in training for Group II (Time 3 post-test scores).

Group II post-test scores at Time 3 can be compared with Group I post-test scores at Time 3 (that is, gains in training versus gains [or no gains] during the no-training period).

To interpret this pattern of outcomes, all three contrasts should have adequate statistical power (that is, at least an 80 percent chance of finding an effect significant, if, in fact, the effect exists).[18] A chance elevation of Group II, for example, might lead to gross misinterpretations. Hence, use the design only with reliable measures and large samples.[19]

This design controls history and test-retest effects, but not differences in selection. One way to control for possible differences in selection, however, is to split one of the groups (assuming it is large enough) into two equivalent samples, one measured both before and after training and the other measured only after training, as shown in Table 2-1.

Table 2-1 Example of an Institutional Cycle Design

	Time 2	Time 3	Time 4
Group II$_a$	Measure	Train	Measure
Group II$_b$		Train	Measure

Comparison of post-test scores in two carefully equated groups (Groups IIa and IIb) is more precise than a similar comparison of post-test scores from two unequated groups (Groups I and II).

A final deficiency in the "cycle" design is the lack of adequate control for the effects of maturation. This is not a serious limitation if the training program is teaching specialized skills or competencies, but it is a plausible rival hypothesis when the objective of the training program is to change attitudes. Changes in attitudes conceivably could be the result of maturational processes such as changes in job and life experiences or growing older. To control for this effect, give a comparable group of managers (whose age and job experience coincide with those of one of the trained groups at the time of testing) a "post-test-only" measure. To infer that training had a positive effect, post-test scores of the trained groups should be significantly greater than those of the untrained group receiving the "post-test-only" measure.

Campbell and Stanley aptly expressed the logic of all this patching and adding:[20]

> One starts out with an inadequate design and then adds specific features to control for one or another of the recurrent sources of invalidity. The result is often an inelegant accumulation of precautionary checks, which lacks the intrinsic symmetry of the "true" experimental designs, but nonetheless approaches experimentation.

Remember, a causal inference from any quasi-experiment must meet the basic requirements for all causal relationships: that cause must precede effect, that cause must covary with effect, and that alternative explanations for the causal relationship are implausible.[21] Patching and adding may help satisfy these requirements.

Fundamental Analytical Concepts from Economics and Finance

The analytical concepts previously discussed come largely from psychology and related individual-focused social sciences. However, the fields of economics and finance also provide useful general analytical concepts for measuring HRM programs and consequences. Here, the focus is often on properly acknowledging the implicit sacrifices implied in choices, the behavior of markets, and the nature of risk.

We consider concepts in the following seven areas:

- Fixed, variable, and opportunity costs/savings
- The time value of money
- The estimated value of employee time using total pay
- Cost-benefit and cost-effectiveness analyses
- Utility as a weighted sum of utility attributes
- Conjoint analysis
- Sensitivity and break-even analysis

Fixed, Variable, and Opportunity Costs/Savings

We can distinguish fixed, variable, and opportunity costs, as well as reductions in those costs, which we call "savings." Fixed costs or savings refer to those that remain constant, whose total does not change in proportion to the activity of interest. For example, if an organization is paying rent or mortgage interest on a training facility, the cost does not change with the volume of training activity. If all training is moved to online delivery and the training center is sold, the fixed savings equal the rent or interest that is now avoided.

Variable costs or savings are those that change in direct proportion to changes in some particular activity level.[22] The food and beverage cost of a training program is variable with regard to the number of training participants. If a less expensive food vendor replaces a more expensive one, the variable savings represent the difference between the costs of the more expensive and the less expensive vendors.

Finally, opportunity costs reflect the "opportunities foregone" that might have been realized had the resources allocated to the program been directed toward other organizational ends.[23] This is often conceived of as the sacrifice of the value of the next-best alternative use of the resources. For example, if we choose to have employees travel to a training program, the opportunity cost might be the value they would produce if they were back at their regular locations working on their regular jobs. Opportunity savings are the next-best uses of resources that we obtain if we alter the opportunity relationships. For example, if we provide employees with laptop computers or handheld devices that allow them to use e-mail to resolve issues at work while they are attending the offsite training program, the opportunity savings represent the difference between the value that would have been sacrificed without the devices and the reduced sacrifice with the devices.

The Time Value of Money: Compounding, Discounting, and Present Value[24]

In general, the time value of money refers to the fact that a dollar in hand today is worth more than a dollar promised sometime in the future. That is because a dollar in hand today can be invested to earn interest. If you were to invest that dollar today at a given interest rate, it would grow over time from its present value (PV) to some future value (FV). The amount you would have depends, therefore, on how long you hold your investment and on the interest rate you earn. Let us consider a simple example.

If you invest $100 and earn 10 percent on your money per year, you will have $110 at the end of the first year. It is composed of your original principal, $100, plus $10 in interest that you earn. Hence, $110 is the FV of $100 invested for one year at 10 percent. In general, if you invest for one period at an interest rate of r, your investment will grow to $(1 + r)$ per dollar invested.

Suppose you decide to leave your $100 investment alone for another year after the first? Assuming that the interest rate (10 percent) does not change, you will earn $110 \times .10 = $11 in interest during the second year, so you will have a total of $110 + $11 = $121. This $121 has four parts. The first is the $100 original principal. The second is the $10 in interest you earned after the first year, and the third is another $10 you earn in the second year, for a total of $120. The last dollar you earn (the fourth part) is interest you earn in the second year on the interest paid in the first year ($10 \times .10 = $1).

This process of leaving your money and any accumulated interest in an investment for more than one period, thereby reinvesting the interest, is called compounding, or earning interest on interest. We call the result compound interest. At a general level, the FV of $1 invested for t periods at a rate of r per period is as follows:

$$FV = \$1 \times (1 + r)^t \qquad (2\text{-}1)$$

FVs depend critically on the assumed interest rate, especially for long-lived investments. Equation 2-1 is actually quite general and allows us to answer some other questions related to growth. For example, suppose your company currently has 10,000 employees. Senior management estimates that the number of employees will grow by 3 percent per year. How many employees will work for your company in five years? In this example, we begin with 10,000 people rather than dollars, and we don't think of the growth rate as an interest rate, but the calculation is exactly the same:

$$10{,}000 \times (1.03)^5 = 10{,}000 \times 1.1593 = 11{,}593 \text{ employees}$$

There will be about 1,593 net new hires over the coming five years.

Present Value and Discounting

We just saw that the FV of $1 invested for one year at 10 percent is $1.10. Suppose we ask a slightly different question: How much do we have to invest today at 10 percent to get $1 in one year? We know the FV is $1, but what is its PV? Whatever we invest today will be 1.1 times bigger at the end of the year. Because we need $1 at the end of the year:

$$PV \times 1.1 = \$1$$

Solving for the PV yields $1/1.1 = $0.909. This PV is the answer to the question, "What amount invested today will grow to $1 in one year if the interest rate is 10 percent?" PV is therefore just the reverse of FV. Instead of compounding the money forward into the future, we discount it back to the present.

Now suppose that you set a goal to have $1,000 in two years. If you can earn 7 percent each year, how much do you have to invest to have $1,000 in two years? In other words, what is the PV of $1,000 in two years if the relevant rate is 7 percent? To answer this question, let us express the problem as this:

$$\$1{,}000 = PV \times 1.07 \times 1.07$$

$$\$1{,}000 = PV \times (1.07)^2$$

$$\$1{,}000 = PV \times 1.1449$$

Solving for PV:

$$PV = \$1{,}000/1.1449 = \$873.44$$

At a more general level, the PV of $1 to be received t periods into the future at a discount rate of r is as follows:

$$PV = \$1 \times [1 / (1 + r)^t] = \$1 / (1 + r)^t \qquad (2\text{-}2)$$

The quantity in brackets, $1/(1 + r)^t$, is used to discount a future cash flow. Hence, it is often called a discount factor. Likewise, the rate used in the calculation is often called the discount rate. Finally, calculating the PV of a future cash flow to determine its worth today is commonly called discounted cash flow (DCF) valuation. If we apply the DCF valuation to estimate the PV of future cash flows from an investment, it is possible to estimate the net present value (NPV) of that investment as the difference between the PV of the future cash flows and the cost of the investment. Indeed, the capital-budgeting process can be viewed as a search for investments with NPVs that are positive.[25]

When calculating the NPV of an investment project, we tend to assume not only that a company's cost of capital is known, but also that it remains constant over the life of a project. In practice, a company's cost of capital may be difficult to estimate, and the selection of an appropriate discount rate for use in investment appraisal is also far from straightforward. The cost of capital is also likely to change over the life of a project because it is influenced by the dynamic economic environment within which all business is conducted. If these changes can be forecast, however, the NPV method can accommodate them without difficulty.[26]

Now back to PV calculations. PVs decline as the length of time until payment grows. Look out far enough, and PVs will be close to zero. Also, for a given length of time, the higher the discount rate is, the lower the PV. In other words, PVs and discount rates are inversely related. Increasing the discount rate decreases the PV, and vice versa.

If we let FV_t stand for the FV after t periods, the relationship between FV and PV can be written simply as one of the following:

$$PV \times (1 + r)^t = FV_t$$
$$PV = FV_t / (1 + r)^t = FV_t \times [1 / (1 + r)^t] \qquad (2\text{-}3)$$

The last result is called the basic PV equation. There are a number of variations of it, but this simple equation underlies many of the most important ideas in corporate finance.[27]

Sometimes one needs to determine what discount rate is implicit in an investment. We can do this by looking at the basic PV equation:

$$PV = FV_t / (1 + r)^t$$

There are only four parts to this equation: the present value (PV), the future value (FV_t), the discount rate (r), and the life of the investment (t). Given any three of these, we can always find the fourth. Now let's shift gears and consider the value of employees' time.

Estimating the Value of Employee Time Using Total Pay

Many calculations in HR measurement involve an assessment of the value of employees' time (for example, those involving exit interviews, attendance at training classes, managing problems caused by absenteeism, or the time taken to screen job applications). One way to account for that time, in financial terms, is in terms of total pay to the employee. The idea is to use the value of what employees earn as a proxy for the value of their time. This is very common, so we provide some guidelines here. However, at the end, we also caution that the assumption that total pay equals the value of employee time is not generally valid.

Should "total pay" include only the average annual salary of employees in a job class? In other words, what should be the valuation base? If it includes only salary, the resulting cost estimates will underestimate the full cost of employees' time, because it fails to include the cost of employee benefits and overhead. Overhead costs include such items as rent, energy costs, and equipment. More generally, overhead costs are those general expenses incurred during the normal course of operating a business. At times, these costs may be called general and administrative or payroll burden. They may be calculated as a percentage of actual payroll costs (salaries plus benefits).[28]

To provide a more realistic estimate of the cost of employee time, therefore, many recommend calculating it as the mean salary of the employees in question (for example, technical, sales, managerial) times a full labor-cost multiplier.[29] The full labor-cost multiplier incorporates benefits and overhead costs.

To illustrate, suppose that in estimating the costs of staff time to conduct exit interviews, we assume that an HR specialist is paid $27 per hour, and that it takes 15 minutes to prepare and 45 minutes to conduct each interview, for a total of 1 hour of his or her time. If the HR specialist conducts 100 exit interviews in a year, the total cost of his or time is, therefore, $2,700. However, after checking with the accounting and payroll departments, suppose we learn that the firm pays an additional 40 percent of salary in the form of employee benefits and that overhead costs add an additional 35 percent. The full labor-cost multiplier is, therefore, 1.75, and the cost per exit interview is $27 × 1.75 = $47.25. Over a 1-year period and 100 exit interviews, the total cost of the HR specialist's time is, therefore, $4,725—a difference of $2,025 from the $2,700 that included only salary costs.

Note that total pay, using whatever calculation, is generally not synonymous with the fixed, variable, or opportunity costs of employee time. It is a convenient proxy but must be used with great caution. In most situations, the costs of employee time (wages, benefits, overhead costs to maintain the employees' employment or productivity) simply don't change as a result of their allocation of time. They are paid no matter what they do, as long as it is a legitimate part of their jobs. If we require employees to spend an hour interviewing candidates, their total pay for the hour is no different than if we had not required that time. Moreover, they would still be paid even if they weren't conducting interviews. The more correct concept is the opportunity cost of the lost value that employees would have been creating if they had not been using their time for interviewing. That is obviously not necessarily equal to the cost of their wages, benefits, and overhead. That said, it is so difficult to estimate the opportunity cost of employees' time that it is very common for accounting processes just to recommend multiplying the time by the value of total pay. The important thing to realize is the limits of such calculations, even if they provide a useful proxy.

Cost-Benefit and Cost-Effectiveness Analyses

Cost-benefit analysis expresses both the benefits and the costs of a decision in monetary terms. One of the most popular forms of cost-benefit analysis is return on investment (ROI) analysis.

Traditionally associated with hard assets, ROI relates program profits to invested capital. It does so in terms of a ratio in which the numerator expresses some measure of profit related to a project, and the denominator represents the initial investment in a program. More specifically, ROI includes the following:[30]

1. The inflow of returns produced by an investment

2. The offsetting outflows of resources required to make the investment

3. How the inflows and outflows occur in each future time period

4. How much what occurs in future time periods should be "discounted" to reflect greater risk and price inflation

ROI has both advantages and disadvantages. Its major advantage is that it is simple and widely accepted. It blends in one number all the major ingredients of profitability, and it can be compared with other investment opportunities. On the other hand, it suffers from two major disadvantages. First, although the logic of ROI analysis appears straightforward, there is much subjectivity in the previous items 1, 3, and 4. Second, typical ROI calculations focus on one HR investment at a time and fail to consider how those investments work together as a portfolio. Training may produce value beyond its cost, but would that value be even higher if it were combined with proper investments in individual incentives related to the training outcomes?[31]

Consider a simple example of the ROI calculation over a single time period. Suppose your company develops a battery of pre-employment assessments for customer service representatives that includes measures of aptitude, relevant personality characteristics, and emotional intelligence. Payments to outside consultants total $100,000 during the first year of operation. The measured savings, relative to baseline measures in prior years, total $30,000 in reduced absenteeism, $55,000 in reduced payments for stress-related medical conditions, and $70,000 in reduced turnover among customer service represen-tatives. The total expected benefits are, therefore, $155,000.

ROI = Total expected benefit/program investment

ROI = $155,000 / $100,000 = 55 percent

Cost-effectiveness analysis is similar to cost-benefit analysis, but whereas the costs are still measured in monetary terms, outcomes are measured in "natural" units other than money. Cost-effectiveness analysis identifies the cost of producing a unit of effect (for example, in a corporate-safety program, the cost per accident avoided). As an example, consider the results of a three-year study of the cost-effectiveness of three types of work-site health-promotion programs for reducing risk factors associated with cardiovascular disease (hypertension, obesity, cigarette smoking, and lack of regular physical exercise) at three manufacturing plants, compared to a fourth site that provided health-education classes only.[32]

The plants were similar in size and in the demographic characteristics of their employees. Plants were allocated randomly to one of four worksite health-promotion models. Site A provided health education only. Site B provided a fitness facility; site C provided health education plus follow-up that included a menu of different intervention strategies; and site D provided health education, follow-up, and social organization of health promotion within the plant.

Over the three-year period of the study, the annual, direct cost per employee was $17.68 for site A, $39.28 for site B, $30.96 for site C, and $38.57 for site D (in 1992 dollars). The reduction in risks ranged from 32% at site B to 45% at site D for high-level reduction or relapse prevention, and from 36% (site B) to 51% (site D) for moderate reduction. These differences were statistically significant.

At site B, the greater amount of money spent on the fitness facility produced less risk reduction (–3%) than the comparison program (site A). The additional cost per employee per year (beyond those incurred at site A) for each percent of risks reduced or relapses prevented was –$7.20 at site B (fitness facility), $1.48 for site C (health education plus follow-up), and $2.09 at site D (health education, follow-up, and social organization of health promotion at the plant). At sites C and D, the percent of effectiveness at reducing risks/preventing relapse was about 1.3% to 1.5% per dollar spent per employee per year, and the total cost for each percent of risk reduced or relapse prevented was less than $1 per employee per year (66¢ and 76¢ at sites C and D, respectively).

In summary, both cost-benefit and cost-effectiveness analyses can be useful tools for evaluating benefits, relative to the costs of programs or investments. Whereas cost-benefit analysis expresses benefits in monetary terms and can accommodate multiple time periods and discount rates, cost-effectiveness analysis expresses benefits in terms of the cost incurred to produce a given level of an effect. Cost-benefit analysis enables us to compare the absolute value of the returns from very different programs or decisions, because they are all calculated in the same units of money. Cost-effectiveness, on the other hand, makes such comparisons somewhat more difficult because the outcomes of the different decisions may be calculated in very different units. How do you decide between a program that promises a cost of $1,000 per avoided accident versus a program that promises $300 per unit increase of employee satisfaction? Cost-effectiveness can prove quite useful for comparing programs or decisions that all have the same outcome (for example, which accident-reduction program to choose).

It's a dilemma when one must decide among programs that produce very different outcomes (such as accident reduction versus employee satisfaction) and when all outcomes of programs cannot necessarily be expressed in monetary terms. However, many decisions require such comparisons. One answer is to calculate "utilities" (from the word *use*) that attempt to capture systematically the subjective value that decision makers place on different outcomes, when the outcomes are compared directly to each other.

Utility as a Weighted Sum of Utility Attributes

Utility analysis is a tool for making decisions. It is the determination of institutional gain or loss anticipated from various courses of action, after taking into account both costs and benefits. For example, in the context of HRM, the decision might be which type of training to offer or which selection procedure to implement. When faced with a choice among alternative options, management should choose the option that maximizes the expected utility for the organization across all possible outcomes.[33]

In general, there are two types of decisions: those for which the outcomes of available options are known for sure (decisions under certainty), and those for which the outcomes are uncertain and occur with known or uncertain probabilities (decisions under uncertainty). Most theories about judgment and decision-making processes have focused on decisions under uncertainty, because they are more common.[34]

One such theory is subjective expected utility theory, and it holds that choices are derived from only two parameters:

- The subjective value, or utility, of an option's outcomes
- The estimated probability of the outcomes

By multiplying the utilities with the associated probabilities and summing over all consequences, it is possible to calculate an expected utility. The option with the highest expected utility is then chosen.

A rational model of decision making that has been used as a guide to study actual decision behavior and as a prescription to help individuals make better decisions is known as multi-attribute utility theory (MAUT). MAUT is a type of subjective expected utility theory that has been particularly influential in attempts to improve individual and organizational decision making. Here is a brief conceptual overview of how it works.

Using MAUT, decision makers carefully analyze each decision option (alternative program or course of action under consideration) for its important attributes (things that matter to decision makers). For example, one might characterize a job in terms of attributes such as salary, chances for promotion, and location. Decision weights are assigned to attributes according to their importance to decision makers. Each available option is then assessed according to a utility scale for its expected value on all attributes. After multiplying the utility-scale values by the decision weights and summing the products, the option with the highest value is selected.[35] Total utility values for each option are therefore computed by means of a payoff function, which specifies how the attribute levels are to be combined into an overall utility value.

To illustrate, suppose that a new MBA receives two job offers. She decides that the three most important characteristics of these jobs that will influence her decision are salary, chances for promotion, and location. She assigns the following weights to each: salary (.35), chances for promotion (.40), and location (.25). Using a 1–5 utility scale of the expected value of each job offer on each attribute, where 1 = low expected value and 5 = high expected value, suppose she assigns ratings to the two job offers as shown in Table 2-2.

Table 2-2   Multi-Attribute Utility Table Showing Job Attributes and Their Weights, the Values Assigned to Each Attribute, and the Payoff Associated with Each Alternative Decision

	Salary	Promotion	Location	Payoff (Weight × Value)
Weight	.35	.40	.25	
Job A values	3	4	2	3.15
Job B values	4	3	4	3.60

Based on this calculation of multi-attribute utility, the new MBA should accept job B because it maximizes her expected utility across all possible outcomes. MAUT models can encompass a variety of decision options, numerous and diverse sets of attributes reflecting many different constituents, and very complex payoff functions, but they generally share the characteristics shown in the simple example in the preceding table.[36]

Conjoint Analysis

Conjoint analysis (CA) is another technique that researchers in a variety of fields use to study judgment and decision making.[37] Its purpose is to identify the hidden rules that people use to make tradeoffs between different products or services, and the values they place on different features. Consider choices among employee benefits, for example. If a company understands precisely how employees make decisions and what they value in the various benefits offered, then it becomes possible to identify the optimum level of benefits that balance value to employees against cost to the company.

CA researchers generally present decision tasks to respondents, who provide their preferences for products or concepts with different attributes (for example, expected product reliability or color) and different levels of those attributes (for example, high/medium/low or red/blue/green, respectively). Ratings or rankings then serve as the dependent variable and attribute levels serve as independent variables in the general equation:

$$Y = \beta_1 X_1 + \beta_2 X_2 + \dots \beta_n X_n + \varepsilon \qquad (2\text{-}4)$$

Here, β represents the relative importance of an attribute and n equals the number of attributes. Note how Equation 2-4 resembles an analysis of variance or standard regression equation. Indeed, in its simplest form, CA is similar to an ANOVA, where attribute levels are dummy or contrast coded.[38] Like other multivariate methods used to investigate dependence relationships, CA derives a linear function of attribute levels that minimizes error between actual and estimated values. Researchers can use several software packages (such as SAS or Sawtooth) to estimate this function.

Whereas many multivariate methods require all independent variables to have the same (for example, linear) relationship with the dependent variable, CA allows each one to have a different relationship (for example, linear, quadratic, or stepwise), thereby making it extremely flexible when investigating complex decision-making issues.[39]

We noted earlier that CA researchers specify levels for each attribute (that is, independent variable) and then present respondents with scenarios having attributes with different combinations of these levels. Because levels are known, researchers need only to collect respondent ratings to use as the dependent variable. In so doing, they can estimate or "decompose" the importance that respondents assign to each attribute. Hence, researchers can learn how important different attributes are to respondents by forcing them to make tradeoffs in real time.[40]

Sensitivity and Break-Even Analysis

Both of these techniques are attempts to deal with the fact that utility values are estimates made under uncertainty. Hence, actual utility values may vary from estimated values, and it is helpful to decision makers to be able to estimate the effects of such variability. One way to do that is through sensitivity analysis.

In sensitivity analysis, each of the utility parameters is varied from its low value to its high value while holding other parameter values constant. One then examines the utility estimates that result from each combination of parameter values to determine which parameter's variability has the greatest effect on the estimate of overall utility.

In the context of evaluating HR programs, sensitivity analyses almost always indicate that utility parameters that reflect changes in the quality of employees caused by improved selection, as well as increases in the number (quantity) of employees affected, have substantial effects on resulting utility values.[41] Utility parameters that reflect changes in the quality of employees include improvements in the validity of the selection procedure, the average score on the predictor, and dollar-based increases in the variability of performance.

Although sensitivity analyses are valuable in assessing the effects of changes in individual parameters, they provide no information about the effects of simultaneous changes in more than one utility parameter. Break-even analysis overcomes that difficulty.

Instead of estimating the level of expected utility, suppose that decision makers focus instead on the break-even value that is critical to making a decision. In other words, what is the smallest value of any given parameter that will generate a positive utility (payoff)? For example, suppose we know that a training program conducted for 500 participants raises technical knowledge by 10 percent or more for 90 percent of the participants. Everyone agrees that the value of the 10 percent increase is greater than $1,000 per trainee. The total gain is, therefore, at least (500 × .90 = 450 × $1,000) $450,000. Assuming that the cost of the training program is $600 per trainee, the total cost is therefore $300,000 (500 × $600). Researchers and managers could spend lots of time debating the actual economic value of the increase in knowledge, but, in fact, it does not matter because even the minimum agreed-upon value ($1,000) is enough to recoup the costs of the program. More precisely, when the costs of a program are matched exactly by equivalent benefits—no more, no less—the program "breaks even." This is the origin of the term *break-even analysis.*[42]

The major advantages of break-even analysis suggest a mechanism for concisely summarizing the potential impact of uncertainty in one or more utility parameters.[43] It shifts emphasis away from estimating a utility value toward making a decision using imperfect information. It pinpoints areas where controversy is important to decision making (that is, where there is doubt about whether the break-even value is exceeded), versus where controversy has little impact (because there is little risk of observing utility values below break-even). In summary, break-even analysis provides a simple expedient that allows utility models to assist in decision making even when some utility parameters are unknown or are uncertain.

Conclusion

As noted at the outset, the purpose of this chapter is to present some general analytical concepts that we will revisit throughout this book. The issues that we discussed comprised two broad areas:

- Some fundamental analytical concepts from statistics and research design
- Some fundamental analytical concepts from economics and finance

In the first category, we considered the following concepts: cautions in generalizing from sample data, correlation and causality, and experiments and quasi-experiments. In the second category, we considered some economic and financial concepts in seven broad areas: fixed, variable, and opportunity costs/savings; the time value of money; estimates of the value of employee time using total pay; cost-benefit and cost-effectiveness analyses; utility as a weighted sum of utility attributes; conjoint analysis; and sensitivity and break-even analysis. All of these concepts are important to HR measurement, and understanding them will help you to develop reliable, valid metrics. It will be up to you, of course, to determine whether those metrics fit the strategic direction of your organization.

References

1. Cascio, Wayne, and Brian Welle, "Using HR Data to Make Smarter Organizational Decisions," pre-conference workshop presented at the annual conference of the Society for Industrial and Organizational Psychology, Atlanta, Ga., April 2010.

2. Jackson, S. L., *Research Methods and Statistics: A Critical Thinking Approach* (Belmont, Calif.: Wadsworth/Thomson Learning, 2003).

3. *Ibid.*

4. See, for example, Cochran, W. G., *Sampling Techniques*, 3rd ed. (New York: Wiley, 1997); and Kerlinger, F. N., and H. B. Lee, *Foundations of Behavioral Research*, 4th ed. (Stamford, Conn.: Thomson Learning, 2000).

5. For more on this, see Cohen, J., and P. Cohen, *Applied Multiple Regression/ Correlation Analysis for the Behavioral Sciences*, 3rd cd. (Hillsdale, N.J.: Lawrence Erlbaum, 2002); and Dancey, C. P., and J. Reidy, *Statistics Without Maths for Psychology: Using SPSS for Windows*, 3rd ed. (Harlow, England: Prentice Hall, 2004). Draper, N. R., and H. Smith, *Applied Regression Analysis*, 3rd ed. (New York: Wiley, 1998).

6. Guilford, J. P., and B. Fruchter, *Fundamental Statistics in Psychology and Education*, 6th ed. (New York: McGraw-Hill, 1978).

7. Kelly, K., S. Ang, G. H. H. Yeo, and W. F. Cascio, "Employee Turnover and Firm Performance: Modeling Reciprocal Effects," paper presented at the annual conference of the Academy of Management, Philadelphia, Penn., August 2007.

8. Rosnow, R. L., and R. Rosenthal, *Understanding Behavioral Science: Research Methods for Consumers* (New York: McGraw-Hill, 1984).

9. Hair, J. F., Jr., W. C. Black, B. J. Babin, R. E. Anderson, and R. L. Tatham, *Multivariate Data Analysis*, 6th ed. (Upper Saddle River, N.J.: Prentice Hall, 2006).

10. Kerlinger & Lee, 2000.

11. For more on this, see Shadish, W. R., T. D. Cook, and D. Campbell, *Experimental and Quasi-Experimental Designs for Generalized Causal Inference* (Boston: Houghton Mifflin, 2002).

12. Jackson, 2003.

13. Schmidt, F. L., and J. Hunter, "History, Development, Evolution, and Impact of Validity Generalization and Meta-Analysis Methods, 1975–2001," in *Validity Generalization: A Critical Review*, ed. K. R. Murphy (Mahwah, N.J.: Lawrence Erlbaum (2003a). Schmidt, F. L., and J. E. Hunter, "Meta-Analysis," in *Handbook of Psychology: Research Methods in Psychology* 2, ed. J. A. Schinka and W. F. Velicer (New York: John Wiley & Sons, 2003b).

14. Cascio, W. F., and H. Aguinis, *Applied Psychology in Human Resource Management*, 7th ed. (Upper Saddle River, N.J.: Prentice-Hall, 2011).

15. Kerlinger and Lee, 2000.

16. Shadish et al., 2002.

17. Pfeffer, J., "Lay Off the Layoffs," Newsweek Vol. 155(7) (February 15, 2010), downloaded from www.newsweek.com on February 15, 2010.

18. As presented by Cascio and Aguinis, 2011.

19. Cohen, J., *Statistical Power Analysis for the Behavioral Sciences*, 2nd ed. (Hillsdale, N.J.: Lawrence Erlbaum, 1988).

20. Shadish et al., 2002.

21. Campbell, D. T., and J. C. Stanley, *Experimental and Quasi-Experimental Designs for Research* (Chicago: Rand McNally, 1963).

22. Shadish et al., 2002.

23. Swain, M. R., W. S. Albrecht, J. D. Stice, and E. K. Stice, *Management Accounting*, 3rd ed. (Mason, Ohio: Thomson/South-Western, 2005).

24. *Ibid.*; and Rothenberg, J., "Cost-Benefit Analysis: A Methodological Exposition," in *Handbook of Evaluation Research* 2, ed. M. Guttentag and E. Struening (Beverly Hills, Calif.: Sage, 1975).

25. Material in this section is drawn largely from Brealey, R. A., S. C. Myers, and F. Allen, *Principles of Corporate Finance*, 9th ed. (New York: McGraw-Hill/Irwin, 2007); Ross, S. A., R. W. Westerfield, and B. D. Jordan, *Fundamentals of Corporate Finance*, 9th ed. (Burr Ridge, Ill.: McGraw-Hill/Irwin, 2010); and Watson, D., and A. Head, *Corporate Finance: Principles and Practice*, 5th ed. (London: Pearson Education, 2009). This is just a brief introduction to these concepts at a conceptual level and includes only rudimentary calculations.

26. Ross et al., 2010.

27. Watson and Head, 2009.

28. Ross et al., 2010.

29. Audit guide for consultants (August 1999). Downloaded from www.wsdot.wa.gov/NR/rdonlyres/53951C28-068F-4505-835B-58B2C9C05C7C/0/Chapter6.pdf on May 17, 2010. Also www.wsdot.wa.gov/publications/manuals/fulltext/m0000/AuditGuide/C6.pdf. on May 17, 2010. Overhead and indirect costs. Downloaded from www.ucalgary.ca/evds/files/evds/overhead_indcosts.pdf on May 17, 2010.

30. Raju, N. S., M. J. Burke, J. Normand, and D. V. Lezotte, "What Would Be If What Is Wasn't? Rejoinder to Judiesch, Schmidt, and Hunter," *Journal of Applied Psychology* 78 (1993): 912–916.

31. Boudreau, J. W., and P. M. Ramstad, "Talentship and HR Measurement and Analysis: From ROI to Strategic Organizational Change," *Human Resource Planning* 29, no. 1 (2006): 25–33.

32. Boudreau, J. W., and P. M. Ramstad, *Beyond HR: The New Science of Human Capital* (Boston, Mass.: Harvard Business School Publishing, 2007).

33. Erfurt, J. C., A. Foote, and M. A. Heirich, "The Cost-Effectiveness of Worksite Wellness Programs for Hypertension Control, Weight Loss, Smoking Cessation, and Exercise," *Personnel Psychology* 45 (1992): 5–27.

34. Cascio, W. F., "Utility Analysis," in *Encyclopedia of Industrial and Organizational Psychology* 2, ed. S. Rogelberg (Thousand Oaks, Calif.: Sage, 2007).

35. Slaughter, J. E., and J. Reb, "Judgment and Decision-Making Process," in *Encyclopedia of Industrial and Organizational Psychology* 1, ed. S. Rogelberg (Thousand Oaks, Calif.: Sage, 2007).

36. *Ibid.*

37. Boudreau, J. W., "Utility Analysis for Decisions in Human Resource Management," in *Handbook of Industrial and Organizational Psychology* 2, ed. M. D. Dunnette and L. M. Hough (Palo Alto, Calif.: Consulting Psychologists Press, 1991).

38. For more on conjoint analysis, see Hair et al. (2006). See also Lohrke, F., B. B. Holloway, and T. W. Woolley, "Conjoint Analysis in Entrepreneurship Research: A Review and Research Agenda," *Organizational Research Methods* 13, no. 1 (2010): 16–30.

39. *Ibid.*

40. Hair et al., 2006.

41. *Ibid.* See also Lohrke et al., 2010.

42. Boudreau, 1991.

43. Cascio, 2007.

3

The Hidden Costs of Absenteeism

Call centers (whether in one physical location or a remote configuration of workers from home) are finely tuned operations whose economic outcomes often depend on very precise optimization of staff levels against anticipated call volume.[1] Other similar operations include retail stores and restaurants. When an employee is unexpectedly absent in a call center, it may mean that calls are missed, that other workers must adjust and will do their jobs less effectively, or that a buffer of extra workers must be employed or kept on call to offset the effects of absence. What is it worth to reduce such absences? What costs can be avoided, and what is the likely effect of organizational investments designed to reduce the need or the motivation of employees to be absent?

A first reaction might be, "We should cut absences to zero, because employees should be expected to show up when they are scheduled." However, as discussed in this chapter, the causes of absence are highly varied, so cutting absence requires a logical approach to understanding why it happens. In fact, an increasing number of jobs have no absenteeism, because they have no real work schedule! They are project based and thus are accountable only for the ultimate results of their work. In such jobs, employees can work whatever schedule they want, as long as they produce the needed results on time. For many jobs, however, adhering to the work schedule is an important contribution to successful operations.

Sometimes it is cost-effective just to tolerate the absence level and allow work to be missed or employees to adjust. In other situations, it is very cost-effective to invest in ways to reduce absence. It depends on the situation.

Particularly when employees are absent because they are taking unfair advantage of company policies (such as claiming more sick leave than is appropriate), it is tempting to conclude that such absence must be reduced even if it takes a significant investment. It seems "unfair" to tolerate it. Upon further reflection, however, it's clear that absence is like any other risk factor in business. How we address it should be based on a logical and rational decision about costs and benefits. We need a logical understanding of the consequences of absence to make those decisions. We provide that logic in this chapter.

What Is Employee Absenteeism?

Let us begin our treatment by defining the term *absenteeism. Absenteeism* is any failure to report for or remain at work as scheduled, regardless of reason. The use of the words *as scheduled* is significant, for this automatically excludes vacation, personal leave, jury-duty leave, and the like. A great deal of confusion can be avoided simply by recognizing that if an employee is not on the job as scheduled, he or she is absent, regardless of cause. We focus here on unscheduled absence because it tends to be the most disruptive and costly of the situations when an employee is not at work. The employee is not available to perform his or her job as expected. This often means that the work is done less efficiently by another employee or is not done at all. Scheduled or authorized absences (such as vacations and holidays) are more predictable. This chapter describes in detail the potentially costly consequences of absence.

Although the definition of *absenteeism* might leave little room for interpretation, the concept itself is undergoing a profound change, largely as a result of the time-flexible work that characterizes more and more jobs in our economy. A hallmark of such work is that workers are measured not by the time they spend, but by the results they achieve. Consider, for example, the job of a computer programmer whose sole job is to write or evaluate computer code. The programmer is judged by whether the program runs efficiently and whether it does what it is supposed to do reliably. It doesn't matter when the programmer works (9 to 5 or midnight to dawn) or where the programmer works (at the office or at home).

If the work schedule doesn't matter and workers operate virtually, does the concept of absenteeism still have meaning? In the U. S., the number of people who work from remote locations at least once a month rose 39 percent from 2006 to 2008, to an estimated 17.2 million.[2] If workers never "report" for work, and if they are allowed to vary their work time, and are accountable only in terms of results, the concept of absenteeism ceases to be relevant. Many teleworkers fit this category. Many others do not, however, for they are expected to be available during a core time to participate in activities such as chats with coworkers or the boss, conference calls, or webcasts.

In short, absenteeism may still be a relevant concept in a world of telework. Measurement must evolve from traditional absence, where people are colocated, to the concept of being present in a virtual world. If a teleworker is surfing the web during a conference call, is he or she "absent"?

In fact, many of the effects of traditional absenteeism are still relevant, even if traditional accounting systems would not capture them. Before attempting to assess the costs of employee absenteeism, therefore, it is important to identify where absenteeism is a relevant concept.

Of course, absenteeism remains relevant for the millions of workers who are scheduled to report to a central location, such as a factory, an office, a retail store, or a call center. In fact, as noted earlier, even those who can work from home in a call center, such as Jet Blue's airline reservations agents, have to be at home and on the phone at certain times to make the scheduling work. More broadly, the growing importance of location-specific or time-specific customer service operations, such as the millions of employees who are engaged in repairs (of cars, appliances, or plumbing systems) or delivery (of pizzas, newspapers, or mail), makes employee absence a very real and potent issue for many organizations.

At the outset, let us be clear about what this chapter is and is not. It is not a detailed literature review of the causes of absenteeism, such as local unemployment, the characteristics of jobs,[3] gender, age, depression, smoking, heavy drinking, drug abuse, or lack of exercise.[4] Nor is it a thorough treatment of the noneconomic consequences of absenteeism, such as the effects on the individual absentee, coworkers, managers, the organization, the union, or the family. Instead, the primary focus in this chapter is on the economic consequences of absenteeism and on methods for managing absenteeism and sick-leave abuse in work settings where those concepts remain relevant and meaningful.

The Logic of Absenteeism: How Absenteeism Creates Costs

The logic of absenteeism begins by identifying its causes and consequences. To provide some perspective on the issue, we begin our next section by citing some overall direct costs and data that show the incidence of employee absenteeism in the United States and Europe. Then we focus more specifically on causes and consequences, and we present a high-level logic diagram that may serve as a "mental map" for decision makers to help them understand the logic of employee absenteeism.

Direct Costs and the Incidence of Employee Absenteeism

How much does unscheduled employee absenteeism cost? According to a 2008 Mercer survey of 465 companies, if one excludes planned absences (vacations, holidays), the total direct and indirect costs consume 9 percent of payroll.[5] Direct costs include actual benefits paid to employees (such as sick leave and short- and long-term disability), while indirect costs reflect reduced productivity (delays, reduced morale of coworkers, and lower productivity of replacement employees).

Thus, a 1,000-employee company that averages $50,000 in salary per employee would have an annual payroll of $50 million. Nine percent of that is $4.5 million, or about $4,500 per employee when direct and indirect costs are both considered.

In the United Kingdom, 2008 absences were also costly, as the following figures demonstrate:[6]

- Across all companies, £13.2 billion ($19.8 billion) was paid out to staff who were absent and to other employees to cover for absent staff.

- The average cost of sickness was £517 per employee ($775).

- Each worker took an average of 6.7 days in sickness each year.

- Figures for average days off were higher in the public sector (9) than in the private sector (5.8).

- The total days lost due to absenteeism each year in the United Kingdom are 172 million, of which 21 million are thought to be nongenuine (used to extend weekends, holidays, or for special events such as birthdays and football games). These cost employers an additional £1.6 billion ($2.4 billion).

In 2009, the average employee in the United States missed 1.7 percent of scheduled work time, or an average of 3.3 unscheduled absences per year.[7]

Causes

In the United Kingdom, the reasons given for absence are widespread but generally fall into one of three categories: illness, time off to deal with home and family responsibilities, and medical appointments.[8] In the United States, the leading cause of absenteeism is personal illness (35 percent), while 65 percent of absences are due to other reasons.[9] In the private sector, however, fully 40 percent of employees do not receive sick pay.[10] Figure 3-1 details the five most common causes cited by employees for being absent.

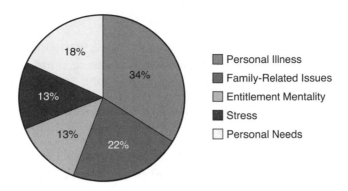

Source of data: "2007 CCH Unscheduled Absence Survey," *Human Resources Management Ideas & Trends* 664 (October 10, 2007).

Figure 3-1 Why are workers absent?

Consequences

The decision to invest in reducing absence requires that one consider the payoff. What consequences of absence will be avoided? We've noted that absence occurs only in jobs where employees are required to be at work, or available to be contacted remotely, at specified times. So the consequences of absence directly relate to the fact that an employee is unavailable to work as scheduled. Absence is more "pivotal" (changes in absence affect economic and strategic success more) when the situation has these characteristics:

- Others have to perform the work of the absent employee.

- A process must be stopped because of the absence of an employee.

- Activities must occur at a certain time and are delayed or missed because an employee is absent.

Categories of Costs

At a general level, four categories of costs are associated with employee absenteeism. We elaborate on each of these categories more fully in the sections that follow. For the moment, let us describe these categories as follows:

- Costs associated with absentees themselves (employee benefits and, if they are paid, wages)

- Costs associated with managing absenteeism problems (costs associated with supervisors' time spent dealing with operational issues caused by the failure of one or more employees to come to work)

- The costs of substitute employees (for example, costs of overtime to other employees or costs of temporary help)

- The costs of reduced quantity or quality of work outputs (for example, costs of machine downtime, reduced productivity of replacement workers, increased scrap and reworks, poor customer service)

In computing these costs, especially the costs of managing absenteeism problems and revenues foregone, researchers commonly use the fully loaded cost of wages and benefits as a proxy for the value of employees' time. However, as we cautioned in Chapter 2, "Analytical Foundations of HR Measurement," although this is very common, keep in mind that it is only an approximation; the assumption that total pay equals the value of employee time is not generally valid.

Figure 3-2 presents an illustration of the ideas we have examined thus far.

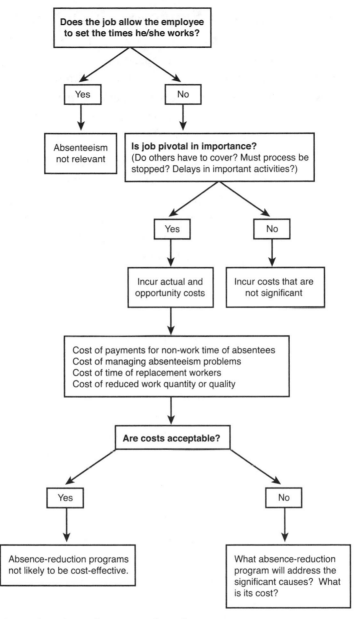

Figure 3-2 The logic of employee absenteeism: how absenteeism creates costs.

Analytics and Measures for Employee Absenteeism

In the context of absenteeism, *analytics* refers to formulas (for instance, those for absence rate, total pay, and supervisory time) and to comparisons to industry averages and adjustments for seasonality. Analytics also includes various methodologies used to identify the causes of absenteeism and to estimate variation in absenteeism across different segments of employees or situations. Such methodologies might comprise surveys, interviews with employees and supervisors, and regression analyses.

Measures, on the other hand, focus on specific numbers (for example, finding employee pay and benefit numbers, time sampling to determine the lost time associated with managing absenteeism problems, using the pay and benefits of supervisors as a proxy for the value of their time). Keep these important distinctions in mind as you work through the approach to costing employee absenteeism that is presented next, even though we offer both measures and analytics together here because they are so closely intertwined.

Estimating the Cost of Employee Absenteeism

At the outset, it is important to note an important irony: Even in organizations or business units where the concept of absence is relevant, the incidence and, therefore, cost of employee absenteeism is likely to vary considerably across departments or business units. It is considerably higher in organizations or units with low morale, as opposed to those with high morale.[11] It also varies across times of the year. With respect to seasonal variations in absenteeism rates, for example, surveys by the Bureau of National Affairs (BNA) in the United States have shown over many years that the incidence of employee absenteeism is generally higher in the winter months than it is in the summer months.[12] The costs of absenteeism are therefore likely to covary with seasonal trends, yet it is paradoxical that such costs are typically reported only as averages.

With respect to the cost of employee absenteeism, the following procedure estimates that cost for a one-year period, although the procedure can be used just as easily to estimate these costs over shorter or longer periods as necessary.[13]

Much of the information required should not be too time-consuming to gather if an organization regularly computes labor-cost data and traditional absence statistics. For example, absenteeism rate is generally based on workdays or work hours, as follows:

Absenteeism rate = [Absence days / Average work force size] × working days, or

Absenteeism rate = [Hours missed / Average work force size] × working hours

In either case, getting the right data involves discussions with both staff and management representatives. Figure 3-3 shows the overall approach.

---

1. Compute total employee hours lost to absenteeism for the period.
2. Compute weighted average wage or salary/hour/absent employee.
3. Compute cost of employee benefits/hour/employee.

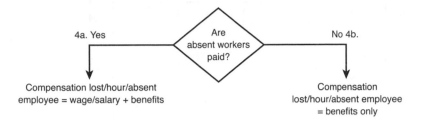

4a. Yes   Are absent workers paid?   No 4b.

Compensation lost/hour/absent employee = wage/salary + benefits

Compensation lost/hour/absent employee = benefits only

5. Compute total compensation lost to absent employees (1. X 4a. or 4b. as applicable).
6. Estimate total supervisory hours lost to employee absenteeism.
7. Compare average hourly supervisory salary + benefits.
8. Estimate total supervisory salaries lost to managing absenteeism problems (6. x 7.).
9. Compute the costs of substitute employees.
10. Estimate the costs of reduced quantity or quality of work outputs.
11. Estimate total costs of absenteeism (Σ items 5, 8, 9, and 10).
12. Estimate the total cost of absenteeism/employee (item 11 4 total number of employees).

Figure 3-3   Overall approach to computing employee absenteeism.

To illustrate this approach, we provide examples to accompany each step. The examples use the hypothetical firm Presto Electric, a medium-sized manufacturer of electrical components employing 3,000 people.

Step 1: Total Hours Lost to Absence

Determine the organization's total employee-hours lost to absenteeism for the period for all employees—blue collar, clerical, and management and professional—for whom the concept of absenteeism is relevant and for those whose jobs are pivotal to the overall success of the organization. Include both whole-day and part-day absences, and time lost for all reasons except organizationally sanctioned time off, such as vacations, holidays, or official "bad weather" days. For example, absences for the following reasons should be included: illness, accidents, funerals, emergencies, and doctor appointments (whether excused or unexcused).

As a basis for comparisons, Figure 3-4 illustrates monthly job absence rates as reported by the BNA. Note the higher absence rates in the fourth quarter, as opposed to the previous three, at least for 2009. Keep in mind also that these data reflect absence patterns during the Great Recession and may not be typical of other time periods.

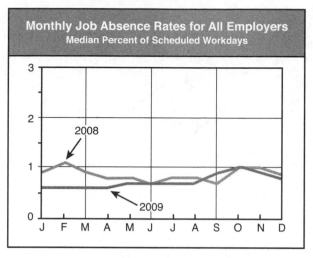

Source: BNA's job absence and turnover report, 4th quarter 2009. Reproduced with permission from the Bureau of National Affairs, *Human Resources Surveys and Reports* 40, no. 839 (March 10, 2010). www.bna.com/pdf/jat4q09.pdf.

Figure 3-4 Typical monthly job absence rates.

In our example, assume that Presto Electric's employee records show 88,200 total employee-hours lost to absenteeism for all reasons except vacations and holidays during the last year. This figure represents an absence rate of 1.5 percent of scheduled work time, about average in nonrecessionary times. Begin by distinguishing hours scheduled from hours paid. Most firms pay for 2,080 hours per year per employee (40 hours per week × 52 weeks). However, employees generally receive paid vacations and holidays, too, time for which they are not scheduled to be at work. If we assume two weeks vacation time per employee (40 hours × 2), plus 5 holidays (40 hours), annual hours of scheduled work time per employee are 2,080 − 80 − 40 = 1,960.

The total scheduled work time for Presto Electric's 3,000 employees is therefore 3,000 × 1,960 = 5,880,000. Given a 1.5 percent rate of annual absenteeism, total scheduled work hours lost annually to employee absenteeism are 88,200.

Step 2: Compensation for Absent Employees' Time

If your organization uses computerized absence reporting, then simply compute the average hourly wage/salary paid to absent employees. If not, compute the weighted average hourly wage/salary for the various occupational groups that claimed absenteeism during the period. If absent workers are not paid, skip this step and go directly to step 3.

For Presto Electric, assume that about 60 percent of all absentees are blue collar, 30 percent are clerical, and 10 percent are management and professional. For purposes of illustration, we will also assume that all employees are paid for sick days taken under the organization's employee-benefits program. Estimate the average hourly wage rate per absentee by applying the appropriate percentages to the average hourly wage rate for each major occupational group. Table 3-1 does just that.

Table 3-1   Determining the Average Hourly Wage Rate per Absentee

Occupational Group	Average Percent of Total Absenteeism	Average Hourly Wage	Weighted Average Hourly Wage
Blue collar	0.60	$26.20	$15.72
Clerical	0.30	18.90	5.67
Management and professional	0.10	42.30	4.24
Total			$25.63

Step 3: Benefits for Absent Employees' Time

Estimate the cost of employee benefits per hour per employee. The cost of employee benefits (profit sharing, pensions, health and life insurance, paid vacations and holidays, and so on) currently accounts for about 39 percent of total compensation.[14] One procedure for computing the cost of employee benefits per hour per employee is to divide the total cost of benefits per employee per week by the number of hours worked per week.

First, compute Presto's weekly cost of benefits per employee. Assume that the average annual salary per employee is $25.63 per hour × 2,080 (hours paid for per year), or $53,310.40. Let us further assume the following:

Average annual salary × 39 percent = Average cost of benefits per employee per year

$53,310.40 × 0.39 = $20,791.06

Average cost of benefits per year per employee / 52 weeks per year = Average weekly cost of benefits per employee

$20,791.06 / 52 = $399.83

Average weekly cost of benefits per employee / hours worked per week = Cost of benefits per hour per employee

$399.83 / 40 = $10.00 (rounded)

Step 4: Total Compensation for Absent Employees' Time

Compute the total compensation lost per hour per absent employee. This figure is determined simply by adding the weighted average hourly wage / salary per employee (item 2 in Figure 3-3) to the cost of employee benefits per hour per employee (item 3 in Figure 3-3). Thus:

$$\$25.63 + \$10.00 = \$35.63$$

Of course, if absent workers are not paid, item 4 in Figure 3-3 is the same as item 3.

Step 5: Total Compensation Cost for All Absent Employees

Compute the total compensation lost to absent employees. Total compensation lost, aggregated over all employee-hours lost, is determined simply by multiplying item 1 by item 4.a or 4.b, whichever is applicable. In our example:

$$88,200 \times \$35.63 = \$3,142,566.00$$

Step 6: Supervisory Time Spent on Absence Management

Estimate the total number of supervisory hours lost to employee absenteeism for the period. Survey data indicates that supervisors who deal with absenteeism problems spend an average of 3.4 hours a week managing absences.[15] That is approximately 41 minutes per day (3.4 / 5 days per week = 0.68 hours per day; 0.68 × 60 minutes = 40.8 minutes per day). Management issues include addressing production problems, locating and instructing replacement employees, checking on the performance of replacements, and counseling and disciplining absentees.

Organizations that want to develop their own in-house estimates might begin by interviewing a representative sample of supervisors using a semi-structured interview format to help them refine their estimates. Areas to probe include the effects of typically high-absence days (Mondays, Fridays, days before and after holidays, days after payday). Although interviews are quite common, diary keeping may actually be more effective. Time sampling for diary-keeping purposes is particularly important, for, as we noted earlier, absenteeism may vary over time. These are by no means the only methods available, and others might also prove useful. Keep in mind that it is true of estimates in general that the more experience companies accumulate in making the estimates, the more accurate the estimates become.[16]

Methodologically, it is difficult to develop an accurate estimate of the amount of time per day that supervisors spend, on average, dealing with problems of absenteeism. That time is most likely not constant from day to day or from one month to the next. In fact, the time per day, on average, that supervisors spend managing absenteeism problems is likely to vary considerably across departments or business units. Careful consideration of these issues when costing employee absenteeism will yield measurably more accurate results.

After you have estimated the average number of supervisory hours spent per day dealing with employee absenteeism problems, compute the total number of supervisory hours lost to the organization by multiplying three figures:

1. Estimated average number of hours lost per supervisor per day

2. Total number of supervisors who deal with problems of absenteeism

3. The number of working days for the period (including all shifts and weekend work)

In our example, assume that Presto Electric's data in these three areas is as follows:

1. Estimated number of supervisory hours lost per day: 0.68 hours

2. Total number of supervisors who deal with absence problems: 100

3. Total number of working days for the year: 245

Based on these data, the total number of supervisory hours lost to employee absenteeism is as follows:

$$0.68 \times 100 \times 245 = 16,660$$

Step 7: Pay Level for Supervisors

Compute the average hourly wage rate for supervisors, including benefits. Be sure to include only the salaries of supervisors who normally deal with problems of employee absenteeism. Typically, first-line supervisors in the production and clerical areas bear the brunt of absenteeism problems. Estimate Presto Electric's cost for this figure as follows:

Average hourly supervisory salary	$31.79
Cost of benefits per hour (39 percent of hourly salary)	+ 12.40
Total compensation per hour per supervisor	$44.19

Step 8: Total Supervisor Paid Time Spent on Absence

Compute total supervisory salaries lost to problems of managing absenteeism. This figure is derived simply by multiplying total supervisory hours lost on employee absenteeism (step 6) by the average hourly supervisory wage (step 7), as follows:

$$16,660 \times 44.19 = \$736,205.40$$

Step 9: Costs of Substitute Employees

If an organization chooses to replace workers who are absent, the key considerations are how many substitute employees it will hire and at what cost. Sometimes the total cost is a combination of these two elements, as when some additional workers are hired to replace absentees (say, from an agency that supplies temporary workers) and other, regular workers are asked to work overtime to fill in for the absentees. Alternatively, a very large organization, such as an automobile-assembly plant, might actually retain a regular labor pool that it can draw on to fill in for absent workers. At Presto Electric, let's assume that the firm incurs total costs of $385,000 per year for substitute employees.

Step 10: Costs of Reduced Quantity or Quality of Work Outputs

When fully productive, regularly scheduled employees are absent, chances are good either that their work is not done or, if it is, that there is a reduction in the quantity or quality of the work. The key considerations in this case are how much of a reduction there is in the quantity or quality of work and how much it costs. In terms of a reduction in productivity, survey data indicate that replacement workers are less productive and require the equivalent of 1.25 people to achieve the same amount of work as the absent employee.[17]

With respect to costs, they might include items such as the following:

- Machine downtime

- Increases in defects, scrap, and reworks

- Production losses

Consider an example. Suppose a small organization that is operating at full capacity has 100 salespeople in the field calling on accounts and soliciting orders every day. If the typical salesperson generates, on average, $1,000 worth of orders per day, and 10 salespeople are absent on a given day, the business lost to the organization (revenue foregone) due to employee absenteeism on that single day is $10,000.

The standard level of quality or quantity of work might also be compromised through the reduced productivity and performance of less experienced replacement workers, as when customers are served poorly by employees who are stretched trying to "cover" for their absent coworkers, and potential new business is lost as a result of operating "under capacity."[18]

As in step 6, some of these estimates will be difficult because many of the components are not reported routinely in accounting or HR information systems. Initially, therefore, determination of the cost elements to be included in this category, plus estimates of their magnitude, should be based on discussions with a number of supervisors and managers.

Over time, as the organization accumulates experience in costing absenteeism, it can make a more precise identification and computation of the costs to be included in this category. At Presto Electric, assume that productivity losses and inefficient materials usage as a result of absenteeism caused an estimated financial loss of $400,000 for the year.

Step 11: Total Absenteeism Costs

Compute the total estimated cost of employee absenteeism. Having computed or estimated all the necessary cost items, we now can determine the total annual cost of employee absenteeism to Presto Electric. Just add the individual costs pertaining to wages and salaries, benefits, supervisory salaries, substitute employees, and the costs of reduced quantity and quality (items 5, 8, 9, and 10). As Table 3-2 demonstrates, this cost is more than $4.5 million per year.

Step 12: Total Costs per Employee per Year

Compute the total estimated cost of absenteeism per employee per year. In some cases, this figure (derived by dividing the total estimated cost by the total number of employees) may be more meaningful than the total cost estimate because it is easier to grasp. In the case of our hypothetical firm, Presto Electric, this figure was $1,554.59 per year for each of the 3,000 employees on the payroll.

Table 3-2 Total Estimated Cost of Employee Absenteeism (Presto Electric)

1. Total employee-hours lost to absenteeism for the period	88,200
2. Weighted average wage/salary per hour per absent employee	$25.63
3. Cost of employee benefits per hour per absent employee	$10.00

4. Total compensation lost per hour per absent employee
  a. If absent workers are paid (wage/salary plus benefits)
  b. If absent workers are not paid (benefits only)
	$35.63

5. Total compensation lost to absent employees (Total employee-hours lost × 4.a or 4.b, whichever applies)	$3,142,566.00
6. Total supervisory hours lost on employee absenteeism	16,660
7. Average hourly supervisory wage, including benefits	$44.19
8. Total supervisory salaries lost to managing problems of absenteeism (Hours lost × Average hourly supervisory wage; Item 6 × Item 7)	$736,205.40
9. Costs of substitute employees	$385,000.00
10. Costs of reduced quantity and quality of work	$400,000.00
11. Total estimated cost of absenteeism (items 5, 8, 9, 10)	$4,663,771.40
12. Total estimated cost of absenteeism per employee (Total estimated costs / Total number of employees)	$1,554.59

Process: Interpreting Absenteeism Costs

As noted in Chapter 2, the purpose of the process component of the logic, analytics, measurements, and process (LAMP) model is to make the insights gained as a result of costing employee absenteeism actionable. The first step in doing that is to interpret absenteeism costs in a meaningful manner. To do so, begin by evaluating them—at least initially—against some predetermined cost standard or financial measure of performance, such as an industry-wide average. This is basically the same rationale organizations use when conducting pay surveys to determine whether their salaries and benefits are competitive.

While the Bureau of National Affairs and the U. S. Bureau of Labor Statistics publish absence rates and lost worktime rates (hours absent as a percent of hours worked) by industry, information on the cost of absenteeism is not published as regularly as are pay surveys. Very little information is available to help determine whether the economic cost of employee absenteeism is a significant problem. The costs of absenteeism to individual organizations occasionally do appear in the literature, but these estimates are typically case studies of individual firms or survey data from a broad cross-section of firms and industries rather than survey data from specific industries.

Is it worth the effort to analyze the costs of absenteeism to the overall organization and, more specifically, to strategically critical business units or departments where the concept of absenteeism is relevant? The answer is yes, for at least two compelling reasons. First, such an analysis calls management's attention to the severity of the problem. Translating behavior into economic terms enables managers to grasp the burdens employee absenteeism imposes, particularly in strategically critical business units that are suffering from severe absence problems. A six- or seven-figure cost is often the spark needed for management to make a concerted effort to combat the problem. Second, an analysis of the problem creates a baseline for evaluating the effectiveness of absence-control programs. Comparing the quarterly, semiannual, and annual costs of absenteeism across strategically critical business units or departments provides a measure of the success, or lack of success, of attempts to reduce the problem.

If we return to the logical elements of absence cost, we can consider the process you can use to relate those costs to ongoing budget and strategy issues in an organization:

- **Cost of payments for nonwork time of absentees:** At the outset, recognize that all lost time is connected. This includes absences due to injuries, accidents, short-term disabilities, and absences that are just a few days in duration. To connect absence to tangible process issues for business leaders, look for evidence that levels of paid time off are higher than standard, or benchmarks. Managers and other leaders often signal their interest in reducing the costs paid for nonwork time by noting that sick leave or unscheduled vacation days are higher than they expect. This is an opportunity to take the logic noted earlier and suggest how much sick leave or unscheduled vacation days might change if absence changed.

- **Cost of payments for time of those who manage absence:** The process signals here will be when supervisors note that they are spending a great deal of time on "nonproductive workforce-management" issues. Are statements like these common when supervisors are setting goals with their managers or during their own performance reviews? Do supervisors and managers often suggest that they could be more effective if they spent less time managing around absent employees? What would they be doing if they did not have to manage employee absence? Answers to these questions allow you to connect absence reductions to tangible changes in supervisor behavior.

- **Cost of time of replacement workers:** Signals that this is an important cost element emerge when business units see their total labor costs or headcount levels higher than other similar units or benchmarks. Leaders may complain that they often don't have enough work for all of their employees, but that they must keep the extra employees around to fill in. From a process standpoint, you can use the logic we have described to engage in a discussion about just how much pay for lost time would be reduced if some of the extra employees could be deployed elsewhere or even removed from the workforce.

- **Cost of reduced work quantity or quality:** The signals here will likely not be found in headcount numbers or labor-cost numbers. Instead, the process for unearthing this evidence will require looking at the performance numbers for operations themselves. Managers and executives might note very specific connections between the fact that when a particular worker fails to be at work, specific things don't get done, customers don't get served, or teams have to operate with less than full contributions. When exempt employees have unplanned absences, the 2008 Mercer study on the costs of absenteeism revealed that they make up just 44 percent of their work.[19] You can consider these examples and use the logic presented earlier to determine how much of the problem is due to absence and how much investing in absence reduction might change them.

In the next section, we present a case study that moves beyond the calculation of absenteeism costs to illustrate how awareness of those costs led a health-care clinic to address a critical operations issue.

Case Study: From High Absenteeism Costs to an Actionable Strategy

A large, multispecialty health-care clinic was experiencing high absence rates among employees with direct patient-care responsibilities. In terms of costs, the absenteeism problem was impacting the satisfaction of patients with the care they received (and influencing their perceptions of quality). No wonder: Fully 25 percent of patient-care work went undone, and 67 percent of non-patient-care work went undone. Remaining workers suffered from burnout and strained relationships with their supervisors. Of course, employee absenteeism was only one of several possible causes of these problems. Focusing only on reducing absenteeism, per se, might not address important, underlying employee-relations issues.

With the help of a consultant, the clinic sought to identify the root causes of employee absenteeism for the segment of the workforce that had direct patient-care responsibilities. It found that a majority of the absentees were parents who had young children. In many cases, those parents were unable to find emergency or sick-child care, and this caused last-minute staffing shortages due to unscheduled absences. Moreover, the Family Medical and Leave Act permits employees to use their own sick time to care for ill children (and requires employers to grant employees up to 12 weeks of unpaid annual leave).[20]

Based on this information, management of the clinic made the decision to provide sick-child care and backup child-care facilities both for patients when using the clinic and for employees to use in emergencies. Doing so yielded payoffs in attraction and in retention of members of this critical segment of the clinic's workforce. One year later, the unscheduled absence rate for employees using the backup child-care facility was 70 percent less than that of employees who were eligible but did not use the facility.[21]

This finding was certainly good news in terms of the overall employee absence rate, but it suggests the need for further diagnostic information to uncover reasons why employees who were eligible to use the sick-child and backup child-care facilities chose not to do so. That is the nature of HR research: Addressing one problem (in this case, excessive employee absenteeism) helps to identify additional ones that require management attention.

Other Ways to Reduce Absence

In the final part of this chapter, we present two other approaches to managing absenteeism and sick-leave abuse that may prove useful, depending on the diagnosis of root causes. These include positive incentives and paid time-off policies. We hasten to add, however, that organization-wide absenteeism-control methods (for example, rewards for good attendance, progressive discipline for absenteeism, daily attendance records) may be somewhat successful, but they might not be effective in dealing with specific individuals or work groups that have excessively high absenteeism rates. Special methods (such as flexible work schedules, job redesign, and improved safety measures) may be necessary for them. Careful analysis of detailed absenteeism-research data can facilitate the identification of these problems and suggest possible remedies.[22]

Controlling Absenteeism Through Positive Incentives

This approach focuses exclusively on rewards—that is, it provides incentives for employees to come to work. This "positive-incentive absence-control program" was evaluated over a five-year period: one year before and one year after a three-year incentive program.[23]

A 3,000-employee nonprofit hospital provided the setting for the study. The experimental group contained 164 employees who received the positive-incentive program, and the control group contained 136 employees who did not receive the program. According to the terms of the hospital's sick leave program, employees could take up to 96 hours—12 days per year—with pay. Under the positive-incentive program, employees could convert up to 24 hours of unused sick leave into additional pay or vacation. To determine the amount of incentive, the number of hours absent was subtracted from 24. For example, 24 minus 8 hours absent equals 16 hours of additional pay or vacation. The hospital informed eligible employees both verbally and in writing.

During the year before the installation of the positive-incentive program, absence levels for the experimental and control groups did not differ significantly. During the three years in which the program was operative, the experimental group consistently was absent less frequently, and this difference persisted during the year following the termination of the incentives. The following variables were not related to absence: age, marital status, education, job grade, tenure, and number of hours absent two or three years previously. Two variables were related to absence, although not as strongly as the incentive program itself: gender (women were absent more than men, a trend that appears even in the most recent data on absenteeism by gender[24]) and number of hours absent during the previous year.

Had the incentive program been expanded to include all 3,000 hospital employees, net savings were estimated at $112,000 (in 2010 dollars). This is an underestimate, however, because indirect costs were not included. Indirect costs include such things as the following:

- Overtime pay

- Increased supervisory time for managing absenteeism problems

- Costs of replacement workers

- Intentional overstaffing to compensate for anticipated absences

Cautions: A positive-incentive program may have no effect on employees who view sick leave as an earned "right" that should be used whether one is sick or not. Moreover, encouraging attendance when a person has a legitimate reason for being absent—for example, hospital employees with contagious illnesses—may be dysfunctional.

In and of itself, absence may simply represent one of many possible symptoms of job dissatisfaction. Attendance incentives may result in "symptom substitution," whereby declining absence is accompanied by increased tardiness and idling, decreased productivity, and even turnover. If this is the case, an organization needs to consider more comprehensive interventions that are based, for example, on the results of multiple research methods such as employee focus groups, targeted attitude surveys, and thorough analysis and discussion of the implications of the findings from these methods.

Despite the potential limitations, the study warranted the following conclusions (all monetary figures are expressed in 2010 dollars):

- Absenteeism declined an average of 11.5 hours per employee (32 percent) during the incentive period.

- Net costs to the organization (direct costs only) are based on wage costs of $29.35 per hour (composed of $22.58 in direct wages plus 30 percent more in benefits).

- Savings were $55,362 per year (11.5 hours × Average hourly wage [$29.35] × 164 employees).

- Direct costs to the hospital included 2,194 bonus hours, at an average hourly wage of $22.58 per hour = $49,540.

- Net savings were therefore $5,822 per year, for an 11.75 percent return on investment ($5,822 / $49,540).

Paid Time Off (PTO)

This approach to controlling absenteeism and the abuse of sick leave is based on the concept of consolidated annual leave. Sick days, vacation time, and holidays are consolidated into one "bank" to be drawn out at the employee's discretion. The number of paid time off (PTO) days that employees receive varies across employers. For example, at Pinnacol

Assurance, employees receive 20 days of PTO at the start of employment, 25 after five years, and 30 after nine years.[25]

Employees manage their own sick and vacation time and are free to take a day off without having to offer an explanation. If an employee uses up all of this time before the end of the year and needs a day off, that time is unpaid. What about unused sick time? "Buy-back programs" allow employees to convert unused time to vacation or to accrue time and be paid for a portion of it.

Employers that have instituted this kind of policy feel that it is a "win-win" situation for employees and managers. It eliminates the need for employees to lie (that is, abuse sick leave), and it takes managers out of the role of enforcers. Employees typically view sick leave days as a right—that is, "use them or lose them." PTO policies provide an incentive to employees not to take off unnecessary time, because excessive absence is still cause for dismissal. PTO is certainly a popular benefit. According to the Society for Human Resource Management's 2009 employee benefits report, 42 percent of respondents said their employers had such a plan. Employers rate them as the most effective of all absence-control programs.[26]

Summary Comments on Absence-Control Policies

A comprehensive review of research findings in this area revealed that absence-control systems can neutralize some forms of absence behavior and catalyze others.[27] Although the positive-incentive program described earlier was effective in reducing absenteeism over a three-year period, one study showed that absence-control policies could actually encourage absence.[28] In the firm studied, employees had to accumulate 90 days of unused sick leave before they could take advantage of paid sick leave (for one- to two-day absences). The policy suppressed absences only until employees reached the paid threshold, at which time they took sick leave ferociously.

Other studies have shown that punishments, or stricter enforcement of penalties for one type of absence, tend to instigate other forms of missing work.[29] This is not to suggest, however, that absence-control policies should be lenient. Unionized settings, where sick-leave policies are typically more generous, are clearly prone to higher absenteeism.[30] Such policies convey a relaxed norm about absenteeism, and research evidence clearly indicates that those norms can promote absence taking.[31]

Applying the Tools to Low Productivity Due to Illness: "Presenteeism"

Slack productivity from ailing workers is sometimes called presenteeism.[32] Like absenteeism, presenteeism is a form of withdrawal behavior. It often results from employees showing up but working at subpar levels due to chronic ailments,[33] and it is more sensitive to working-time arrangements than absenteeism is. Permanent full-time work, mismatches between desired and actual working hours, shift work, and overlong working weeks increase presenteeism, holding other worker characteristics constant.[34] Major reasons for presenteeism include a sense of obligation to coworkers, too much work, and impending deadlines.[35]

This is not a new category of costs, but rather an illustration of our fourth cost category: the costs of reduced quantity or quality of work. In a recent study, for example, researchers analyzed more than 1.1 million medical and pharmacy claims along with detailed responses from the Health and Work Performance Questionnaire in a multiyear study. It included ten corporations that employed more than 150,000 workers.[36] The study found that, on average, every $1 of medical and pharmacy costs is matched to $2.30 of health-related productivity costs—and that figure is much greater for some conditions. When health-related productivity costs are measured along with medical and pharmacy costs, the top chronic health conditions driving these overall health costs are depression, obesity, arthritis, back or neck pain, and anxiety.

Surprisingly, presenteeism may actually be a much costlier problem than its productivity-reducing counterpart, absenteeism. Unlike absenteeism, however, presenteeism isn't always apparent. Absenteeism is obvious when someone does not show up for work, but presenteeism is far less obvious when illness or a medical condition is hindering someone's work. Researchers are just beginning to address presenteeism and to estimate its economic effects.

- **Logic:** Research on presenteeism focuses on chronic or episodic ailments such as seasonal allergies, asthma, migraines, back pain, arthritis, gastrointestinal disorders, and depression.[37] Progressive diseases, such as heart disease and cancer, tend to occur later and life and generate the majority of direct health-related costs for companies. In contrast, the illnesses people take with them to work account for far lower direct costs, but they imply a greater loss in productivity because they are so prevalent, so often go untreated, and typically occur during peak working years. Those indirect costs have largely been invisible to employers.[38]

- **Analytics:** To be sure, methodological problems plague current research in this area. Different research methods have yielded quite different estimates of the on-the-job productivity loss—from less than 20 percent of a company's total health-related costs to more than 60 percent.[39] Beyond that, how does one quantify the relative effects of individual ailments on productivity for workers who suffer from more than one problem? The effects of such interactions have not been addressed. Nor has the effect on team performance been studied in cases when one member has a chronic health condition that precludes him or her from contributing fully to the team's mission.

- **Measures:** A key question to address is the link between self-reported presentee-ism and actual productivity loss. Some of the strongest evidence of such a link comes from several studies involving credit card call center employees at Bank One, which is now part of J. P. Morgan Chase.[40]

There are a number of objective measures of a service representative's productivity, including the amount of time spent on each call, the amount of time between calls (when the employee is doing paperwork), and the amount of time the person is logged off the system. The study focused on employees with known illnesses (identified from earlier disability claims) and lower productivity scores. One such study, a good example of analytics in action, involved 630 service representatives at a Bank One call center in Illinois. Allergy-related presenteeism was measured with such objective data as the amount of time workers spent on each call. During the peak ragweed pollen season, the allergy sufferers' productivity fell 7 percent below that of coworkers without allergies. Outside of allergy season, the productivity of the two groups was approximately equal.

- **Process:** The next step, of course, is to use this information to work with decision makers to identify where investments to reduce the costs of presenteeism offer the greatest opportunities to advance organizational objectives. One way to improve productivity is by educating workers about the nature of the conditions that afflict them and about appropriate medications to treat those conditions. Companies such as Comerica Bank, Dow Chemical, and J. P. Morgan Chase are among those that have put programs in place to help employees avoid or treat some seemingly smaller health conditions, or at least to keep productive in spite of them.[41] To ensure employee privacy, for example, Comerica Bank used a third party to survey its employees and found that about 40 percent of them suffered from irritable bowel syndrome (IBS), which can involve abdominal discomfort, bloating, or diarrhea. Extrapolating from that, the company estimated its annual cost of lost productivity to be at least $9 million a year (in 2010 dollars). Comerica now provides written materials for its employees about IBS and has sponsored physician seminars to educate workers on how to recognize and deal with it through their living habits, diet, and possible medications.

Education is one thing, but getting workers to take the drugs that their doctors prescribe or recommend is another. The Bank One study found that nearly one quarter of allergy sufferers did not take any kind of allergy medication. The same study also concluded that covering the cost of nonsedating antihistamines for allergy sufferers (roughly $21 a week for prescription medications, less for generics) was more than offset by the resulting gains in productivity (roughly $42 a week, based on call center employees' wages and benefits, which averaged $603 a week in 2010 dollars).[42]

These results raise a tantalizing question: Might a company's pharmacy costs actually be an investment in workforce productivity? Certainly, companies should monitor and control corporate health-care expenditures. It is possible, however, that by increasing company payments for medications to treat chronic diseases, companies might actually realize a net gain in workforce productivity and eliminate the opportunity costs of failing to address the presenteeism issue directly. One obvious example of this is the flu shot. Numerous studies have shown that the cost of offering free flu shots is far outweighed by the savings realized through reductions in both absenteeism and presenteeism.[43] Another simple approach to reducing presenteeism is to offer paid time off, as discussed earlier. Implementing even a modest program of sick leave may well offset the reduced productivity associated with chronic presenteeism.

Exercises

Software that calculates answers to one or more of the following exercises can be found at http://hrcosting.com/hr/.

1. Consolidated Industries, an 1,800-employee firm, is faced with a serious—and growing—absenteeism problem. Last year, total employee-hours lost to absenteeism came to 119,808. Of the total employees absent, 65 percent were blue collar (average wage of $25.15 per hour), 25 percent were clerical (average wage of $19.80 per hour), and the remainder were management and professional (average salary $37.60 per hour). On average, the firm spends 38 percent more of each employee's salary on benefits and, as company policy, pays workers even if they are absent.

The 45 supervisors (average salary of $29.35 per hour) involved in employee absenteeism problems estimate that they lose 40 minutes per day for each of the 245 days per work year just dealing with the extra problems imposed by those who fail to show up for work. Finally, the company estimates that it loses $729,500 in additional overtime premiums, in extra help that must be hired, and in lost productivity from the more highly skilled absentees. As HR director for Consolidated Industries, your job is to estimate the cost of employee absenteeism so that management can better understand the dimensions of the problem.

2. Inter-Capital Limited is a 500-employee firm faced with a 3.7 percent annual absenteeism rate over the 1,960 hours that each employee is scheduled to work. About 15 percent of absentees are blue collar (average wage $26.96 per hour), 55 percent are clerical employees (average wage $20.25 per hour), and the remainder are management and professional workers (average salary $44.50 per hour). About 40 percent more of each employee's salary is spent on benefits, but employees are not paid if they are absent from work. In the last six months, supervisors (average salary of $29.75 per hour) estimate that managing absenteeism problems costs them about an hour a day for each of the 245 days per work year. It's a serious problem that must be dealt with, since about 20 supervisors are directly involved with absenteeism. On top of that, the firm spends approximately $590,000 more on costs incidental to absenteeism. Temporary help and lost productivity can really cut into profits. Just how much is absenteeism costing Inter-Capital Limited per year per employee? (Use the software available at http://hrcosting.com/hr/.)

3. As a management consultant, you have been retained to develop two alternative programs for reducing employee absenteeism at Consolidated Industries (see question 1). Write a proposal that addresses the issue in specific terms. Exactly what should the firm do? (To do this, make whatever assumptions seem reasonable.)

References

1. Fox, A., "The Ins and Outs of Customer-Contact Centers," *HR Magazine* 55 (March 2010): 28–31. See also Fraser-Blunt, M., "Call Centers Come Home," *HR Magazine* 52, no. 1 (January 2007): 85–89.

2. Worldatwork, *Telework Trendlines 2009* (Scottsdale, Ariz.: Worldatwork, 2009). See also Fox, A., "At Work in 2020," *HR Magazine* (January 2010): 18–23.

3. Hausknecht, J. P., N. J. Hiller, and R. J. Vance, "Work-Unit Absenteeism: Effects of Satisfaction, Commitment, Labor-Market Conditions, and Time," *Academy of Management Journal* 51 (2008): 1,223–1,245. See also Rentsch, J. R., and R. P. Steel, "Testing the Durability of Job Characteristics as Predictors of Absenteeism over a Six-Year Period," *Personnel Psychology* 51 (1998): 165–190.

4. Harrison, D. A., and J. J. Martocchio, "Time for Absenteeism: A 20-Year Review of Origins, Offshoots, and Outcomes," *Journal of Management* 24, no. 3 (1998): 305–350. See also Johns, G., "Contemporary Research on Absence from Work: Correlates, Causes, and Consequences," in *International Review of Industrial and Organizational Psychology* 12, ed. C. L. Cooper and L. T. Robertson (New York: Wiley, 1997).

5. "Managing Employee Attendance," June 15, 2009. Downloaded May 11, 2010 from www.shrm.org/Research/Articles/Articles/Pages/ManagingEmployee Attendance.aspx. See also Klachefsky, M., "Take Control of Employee Absenteeism and the Associated Costs," October 9, 2008. Downloaded May 11, 2010 from www.mercer.com.

6. "Sickies and Long-Term Absence Give Employers a Headache—CBI/AXA Survey," May 14, 2008. Downloaded from www.cbi.org.uk on May 11, 2010.

7. Current Population Survey, U.S. Bureau of Labor Statistics, April 9, 2010. Downloaded from /www.bls.gov/cps/cpsaat46.pdf on May 12, 2010.

8. "Sickies and Long-Term Absence," 2008.

9. "Managing Employee Attendance," 2009.

10. Warren, J., "Cough If You Need Sick Leave," *Bloomberg Businessweek* (June 13, 2010): 33.

11. "Managing Employee Attendance," 2009.

12. BNA, "Job Absence and Turnover," 4th Quarter, 2009. Downloaded from www.bna.com/pdf/jat4q09.pdf on May 12, 2010.

13. This method is based upon that described by F. E. Kuzmits in "How Much Is Absenteeism Costing Your Organization?" *Personnel Administrator* 24 (June 1979): 29–33.

14. Cascio, W. F., *Managing Human Resources: Productivity, Quality of Work Life, Profits*, 8th ed. (Burr Ridge, IL: Irwin/McGraw-Hill, 2010).

15. Managing employee attendance, 2009.

16. Cascio, W. F., and H. Aguinis, "Applied Psychology in Human Resource Management," 7th ed. (Upper Saddle River, N.J.: Prentice-Hall, 2011).

17. "Managing employee attendance," 2009.

18. Cyboran, S. F., "Absence Management: Costs, Causes, and Cures," workshop presented at Mountain States Employers Council, HR Best Practices Conference, Denver, Col. April 13, 2006.

19. Klachefsky, 2008.

20. Society for Human Resource Management, *FMLA: An Overview of the 2007 FMLA survey* (Alexandria, Va.: SHRM, 2007).

21. Cyboran, 2006.

22. Miners, I. A., M. L. Moore, J. E. Champoux, and J. J. Martocchio, "Time-Serial Substitution Effects of Absence Control on Employee Time Use," *Human Relations* 48, no. 3 (1995): 307–326.

23. Schlotzhauer, D. L., and J. G. Rosse, "A Five-Year Study of a Positive Incentive Absence Control Program," *Personnel Psychology*, 38 (1985): 575–585.

24. Current Population Survey, U.S. Bureau of Labor Statistics, 2010.

25. Frase, M., "Taking Time Off to the Bank," *HR Magazine* 55 (March 2010): 41–46.

26. *Ibid.*

27. Harrison and Martocchio, 1998.

28. Dalton, D. R., and D. J. Mesch, "On the Extent and Reduction of Avoidable Absenteeism: An Assessment of Absence Policy Provisions," *Journal of Applied Psychology* 76 (1991): 810–817.

29. Miners et al., 1995.

30. Drago, R., and M. Wooden, "The Determinants of Labor Absence: Economic Factors and Workgroup Norms Across Countries," *Industrial and Labor Relations Review* 45 (1992): 764–778.

31. Harrison and Martocchio, 1998.

32. Goetzel, R. Z., S. R. Long, R. J. Ozminkowski, K. Hawkins, S. Wang, and W. Lynch, "Health, Absence, Disability, and Presenteeism Cost Estimates of Certain Physical and Mental Health Conditions Affecting U.S. Employers," *Journal of Occupational and Environmental Medicine* 46, no. 4 (2004): 398–412.

33. Rubinstein, S., "Nursing Employees Back to Health," *The Wall Street Journal*, 18 January 2005, D5.

34. Böckerman, P., and E. Laukkanen, "What Makes You Work While You Are Sick? Evidence from a Survey of Workers," *European Journal of Public Health* 20, no. 1 (2010): 43–46.

35. Gurschiek, K., "Sense of Duty Beckons Sick Employees to Work," *HR News* (April 29, 2008). Available at www.shrm.org/Publications/HRNews/Pages/SenseofDutyBeckons.aspx.

36. Loeppke, R., M. Taitel, V. Haufle, T. Parry, R. Kessler, and K. Jinnett, "Health and Productivity as a Business Strategy: A Multiemployer Study," *Journal of Occupational and Environmental Medicine* 51, no. 4 (2009): 411–428.

37. Hemp, P. "Presenteeism: At Work—But Out of It," *Harvard Business Review* 82 (October 2004): 1–9.

38. *Ibid.*

39. Goetzel et al., 2004.

40. Hemp, 2004.

41. Rubinstein, 2005.

42. Hemp, 2004.

43. *Ibid.*

4

The High Cost of
Employee Separations

Employee separations (often called turnover) occur when an employee permanently leaves an organization. Google developed a formula that predicts the probability that each employee will leave. *The Wall Street Journal* reported that Google's formula helps the company "get inside people's heads even before they know they might leave," says Laszlo Bock, who runs human resources for the company.[1] If we know someone may leave, should we try to stop him or her? The U.S. Bureau of Labor Statistics reports monthly job opening and labor turnover rates. Figure 4-1 shows the monthly results from years 2000–2010. These monthly rates translate into annual rates that were as high as 31 percent in 2001 and as low as 19 percent in 2009, following the global economic downturn. This figure varies widely by industry, with manufacturing figures ranging from 15 percent in 2001 to only 9 percent in 2009, and accommodations and food services from 63 percent in 2001 to 39 percent in 2009.[2]

To appreciate what that means for an individual firm, consider that, in the fiscal year ending January 2010, Wal-Mart reported employing 2.1 million associates worldwide.[3] The average annual quit rate for the retail trade industry in 2009 was 25 percent (down from 40 percent in 2006).[4] Each year, therefore, Wal-Mart must recruit, hire, and train about 525,000 new employees just to replace those who left.

Is this level of turnover good or bad for Wal-Mart? It is a safe bet that just processing and managing this level of employee turnover costs millions of dollars per year, but then Wal-Mart's annual after-tax profits were $14 billion in 2009.[5] So the cost of turnover for Wal-Mart is a big number but not a large percentage of its profits. Although Wal-Mart could likely save millions of dollars a year by reducing turnover, what would be the investment necessary to do that? Also, if turnover was reduced by hiring employees who have fewer alternative employment options (and thus are less likely to leave), might that also mean getting employees who are less qualified or who have lower performance?

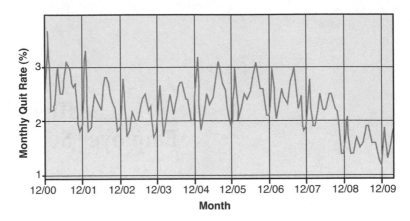

Figure 4-1 U.S. private sector quit rates for years 2000–2009.

Long-term employees also amass increased obligations in terms of pension and health-care coverage, so it is possible that Wal-Mart saves money in these areas if its workforce has shorter tenure.

On the other hand, perhaps the short tenure of the workforce reduces learning and customer service skills that would enhance Wal-Mart's performance. These are complex questions that are often overlooked when organizations adopt simple decision rules, such as "reduce all turnover to below the industry average." In this chapter, we provide frameworks to address such questions, and thus improve the ways organizations manage this important aspect of their talent resource.

The Logic of Employee Turnover: Separations, Acquisitions, Cost, and Inventory

Employee turnover is often measured by how many employees leave an organization. A more precise definition is that turnover includes replacing the departed employee (hence the idea of "turning over" one employee for another). We distinguish employee separations from the employee acquisitions that replace the separated employees. Employee separations and acquisitions are "external movements," meaning that they involve moving across the organization's external boundary. (We discuss movements inside the organization later.)

External movements define situations that include pure growth (acquisitions only), pure reduction (separations only), and all combinations of growth and reduction, including steady state, with the number of acquisitions equaling the number of separations.[6]

Employee turnover (where each separation is replaced by an acquisition) is one common and important combination, but the frameworks discussed here are helpful when managing any combination of external employee movements. We find it also very helpful to distinguish employee separations from employee acquisitions, although the term *turnover* usually refers to separations that are replaced.

Decisions affecting employee movement reflect three basic parameters:

- The quantity of movers

- The quality of movers (that is, the strategic value of their performance)

- The costs incurred to produce the movement (that is, the costs of acquisitions or separations)

Decisions affecting the acquisition of new employees (that is, selection decisions) require considering the quantity, quality, and cost of those acquisitions. Likewise, decisions affecting the separation of employees (that is, layoffs, retirements, and employee turnover) require considering the quantity, quality, and cost to produce the separations.

The important points to remember are that the results of decisions that affect acquisitions or separations are expressed through quantity, quality, and cost. Second, the consequences of these decisions often depend on the interaction between the effects of acquisitions and separations. Figure 4-2 shows these ideas graphically.

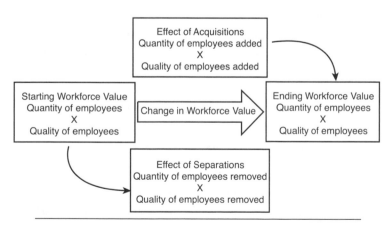

Figure 4-2 Logic of employee turnover.

In each period, two processes can change workforce value: Employees are added and employees separate. As time goes on, these same two processes continue, with the beginning workforce value in the new time period being the ending workforce value from the last time period. This diagram is useful to reframe how organization leaders approach employee separations, hiring, shortages, and surpluses. The diagram shows that if leaders consider only turnover rates and costs, they are focusing only on the two boxes shown at the bottom of Figure 4-2. When their only consideration is filling requisitions quickly, they are focusing on the quantity of employees added: only the top box.

The figure is intentionally similar to traditional raw materials or unfinished goods inventory diagrams that allow leaders easily to see that their decisions about workforce inventories are at least as important as their decisions about any other kind of inventory. They can also see the dangers of focusing only on one box, and they can see what additional factors they should consider if they want to optimize workforce quality, cost, shortages, and surpluses. This diagram makes it easier for leaders to see how things like turnover, time to fill, and hiring costs are integrated.

The word *turnover* actually originated with inventory management. In a retail store, inventory "turns over" when it is depleted (sold, stolen, spoiled, and so on) and replaced. The rate of inventory depletion is the turnover rate. Inventory management doesn't just focus solely on whether depletion rates are at benchmark levels or could be reduced. Indeed, if depletion is due to profitable sales, the organization may actually want to increase it.

Instead, inventory optimization integrates the depletion rate into broader questions concerning the optimum level of inventory, optimum costs of replenishing and depleting inventory, and how frequently shortages and surpluses occur. In the same way, employee turnover is best thought of as part of a system that includes the costs and patterns of employee acquisitions, the value and quality of the workforce, and the costs and investments that affect all of them. Boudreau and Berger developed mathematical formulas to express the overall payoff (utility) or net benefits of workforce acquisitions and separations.[7] In *Retooling HR,* Boudreau shows that the logic of Figure 4-2, combined with the use of inventory-optimization techniques, can retool turnover management beyond turnover reduction, to optimizing employee surpluses and shortages.[8] We return to this idea in Chapter 10, "The Payoff from Enhanced Selection."

This chapter focuses on identifying and quantifying the transaction costs associated with external employee separations and the transaction costs of the acquisitions to replace those who left (including the activities to acquire them and train them).

Two popular ways of classifying employee turnover are voluntary versus involuntary and functional versus dysfunctional. We discuss these distinctions next. Then, consistent with the LAMP framework that we introduced in Chapter 1, "Making HR Measurement Strategic," we discuss the analytics, measurement, and processes involved in computing, interpreting, and communicating the actual costs of employee turnover.

Voluntary Versus Involuntary Turnover

Turnover may be voluntary on the part of the employee (for example, resignation) or involuntary (for example, requested resignation, permanent layoff, retirement, or death). Voluntary reasons for leaving—such as another job that offers more responsibility, a return to school full time, or improved salary and benefits—are more controllable than involuntary reasons, such as employee death, chronic illness, or spouse transfer. Most organizations focus on the incidence of voluntary employee turnover precisely because it is more controllable than involuntary turnover. They are also interested in calculating the costs of voluntary turnover, because when these costs are known, an organization can begin to focus attention on reducing them, particularly where such costs have significant strategic effects.

Functional Versus Dysfunctional Turnover

A common logical distinction focuses on whether voluntary turnover is functional or dysfunctional for the organization. Employee turnover has been defined as functional if the employee's departure produces increased value for the organization. It is dysfunctional if the employee's departure produces reduced value for the organization. Often this is interpreted to mean that high performers who are difficult to replace represent dysfunctional turnovers, and low performers who are easy to replace represent functional turnovers.[9] Figure 4-2 provides a more precise definition. Turnover is functional when the resulting difference in workforce value is positive and high enough to offset the costs of transacting the turnover. Turnover is dysfunctional when the resulting difference in workforce value is negative or the positive change in workforce value doesn't offset the costs. The difficulty of replacement is not inconsistent with this idea, but it is a lot less precise. Does "difficult to replace" mean that replacements will be of lower value than the person who left, or that they will be of higher value but very costly?

Performance, of course, has many aspects associated with it. Some mistakes in selection are unavoidable, and to the extent that employee turnover is concentrated among those whose abilities and temperaments do not fit the organization's needs, that is functional for the organization and good for the long-term prospects of individuals, too. Other employees may have burned out, reached a plateau of substandard performance, or developed such negative attitudes toward the organization that their continued presence is likely to have harmful effects on the motivation and productivity of their coworkers. Here, again, turnover can be beneficial, assuming, of course, that replacements add more value than those they replaced.

On the flip side, the loss of hard-working, value-adding contributors is usually not good for the organization. Such high performers often have a deep reservoir of firm-specific knowledge and unique and valuable personal characteristics, such as technical and interpersonal skills. It is unlikely that a new employee would have all of these characteristics, and very likely that he or she would take a long time to develop them. Thus, voluntary turnover among these individuals, and the need to replace them with others, is likely to reduce the value of the workforce and produce costs associated with their separation and replacement. Voluntary turnover is even more dysfunctional, however, when it occurs in talent pools that are pivotal to an organization's strategic success.

Pivotal Talent Pools with High Rates of Voluntary Turnover

Just as companies divide customers into segments, they can divide talent pools into segments that are pivotal versus nonpivotal. Pivotal talent pools are those where a small change makes a big difference to strategy and value. Instead of asking "What talent is important?" the question becomes "Where do changes in the quantity or quality of talent make the biggest difference in strategically important outcomes?" For example, where salespeople have a lot of discretion in their dealings with customers, and those dealings have big effects on sales, the difference in performance between an average and a superior salesperson is large. Replacements also likely will be lower performers because the skills needed to execute sales are learned on the job; as a result, workforce value sees a substantial reduction when a high performer leaves and is replaced by a new recruit.

On the other hand, in some jobs, performance differences are smaller, such as in a retail food service job where there are pictures rather than numbers on the cash register and where meals are generally sold by numbers instead of by individualized orders. Here the value produced by high performers is much more similar to the value of average performers. The job is also designed so that replacement workers can learn it quickly and perform at an acceptable level. So in this job, voluntary turnover among high performers, who are replaced by average performers, does not produce such a large change in workforce value. If the costs of processing departures and acquisitions are low, it may be best not to invest in reducing such turnover.

Even in fast-food retail, deeply understanding the costs and benefits of employee turnover can be enlightening. David Fairhurst, vice president and Chief People Officer for McDonald's restaurants in Northern Europe, was voted in 2009 the most influential HR practitioner by *HR Magazine* in the United Kingdom. Fairhurst invited a university study examining the performance of 400 McDonald's restaurants in the United Kingdom. The study found that customer satisfaction levels were 20 percent higher in outlets that employed kitchen staff and managers over age 60 (the oldest was an 83-year-old woman employed in Southampton).[10]

Fairhurst later noted that "sixty percent of McDonald's 75,000-strong workforce are under 21, while just 1,000 are aged over 60 .... Some 140 people are recruited every day but only 1.0 to 1.5 percent of those are over 60."[11] So turnover among the older employees is much more significant than turnover among the younger ones.

We noted earlier that many analysts and companies refine an overall measure of employee turnover by classifying it as controllable or voluntary (employees leave by choice), or uncontrollable or involuntary (for example, retirement, death, dismissal, layoff). After pivotal pools of talent have been identified, it becomes important to measure their voluntary employee-turnover rates, to assess the cost of that voluntary turnover, to understand why employees are leaving, and to take steps to reduce voluntary and controllable turnover. Turnover rates in pivotal talent pools need not be high to be extremely costly. Ameriprise Financial provides its leaders with various "cuts" of turnover data by presenting them with a map that shows where the high performers are least engaged and, thus, most likely to leave.[12] Departures of high performers receive more attention than departures of middle or low performers, and those with low engagement get more attention because of their greater likelihood of leaving (see Chapter 6, "Employee Attitudes and Engagement").

Voluntary Turnover, Involuntary Turnover, For-Cause Dismissals, and Layoffs

This section shows how to compute the turnover cost elements. However, not all costs apply to all types of turnover. Let's first review which categories of costs apply to which type of employee separations. Table 4-1 provides a guide.

Table 4-1   How Turnover Cost Elements Apply to Different Types of Turnover

Cost Element	Voluntary Quits	For-Cause Dismissals	Involuntary Layoffs
Separation Costs			
Exit interview	X		
Administrative time	X	X	X
Separation pay		X	X
Unemployment tax	X	X	X

(Continues)

Table 4-1 (Continued)

Cost Element	Voluntary Quits	For-Cause Dismissals	Involuntary Layoffs
Pension and benefit payouts	X	X	X
Supplemental unemployment benefits			X
Severance pay in lieu of bonus			X
Accrued vacation and sick pay	X	X	X
Lawsuits by aggrieved employees		X	X
Replacement Costs			
Communicating job availability	X	X	
Pre-employment administrative time	X	X	
Entrance interview	X	X	
Testing	X	X	
Staff meeting	X	X	
Travel/moving expenses	X	X	
Post-employment information	X	X	
Medical exam	X	X	
Rehiring of former employees			X
Training Costs			
New employee orientation literature and activities	X	X	
Formal training	X	X	

Cost Element	Voluntary Quits	For-Cause Dismissals	Involuntary Layoffs
Instruction by experienced employee	X	X	
Lost Productivity			
Performance difference leavers vs. stayers	X		X
Lost business with departing employee	X		X
Lost institutional memory	X		X
Decreased survivor productivity	X	X	X
Lack of staff when business rebounds			X
Risk of labor actions and strikes		X	X
Damage to company reputation	X		X

In the sections that follow, we focus mostly on the costs associated with voluntary quits and for-cause dismissals. Such separations are by far the more prevalent in most companies. Moreover, most of the costs of layoffs are also associated with the other two types of turnover, so the analytic approaches described next can also be used for layoffs.

However, it is worth noting that the costs of layoffs are often much higher than most organizations realize, and some costs are unique to the layoff situation. In *Employment Downsizing and Its Alternatives,* Cascio notes that direct costs may be as much as $100,000 per layoff, and that, in 2008, IBM spent $700 million on employee restructuring.[13] Short-term or one-time costs of layoffs include most costs, and in the long run the costs of layoffs can include the rehiring of former employees, pension and severance payouts, and indirect costs of lost productivity. Longer-term concerns include additional lost time of survivors, who worry about losing their jobs, potential backlash from clients or customers if the layoffs are perceived as unfair, and increased voluntary separations.

How to Compute Turnover Rates

Conceptually, annual employee turnover is computed by adding up the monthly turnover for a 12-month period. Monthly turnover is calculated as the number of employee separations during the month divided by the average number of active employees during the same month. More generally, the rate of turnover in percent over any period can be calculated by the following formula:

$$\frac{Number\ of\ turnover\ incidents\ per\ period}{Average\ work\ force\ size} \times 100$$

In the United States, as shown in Figure 4-1, aggregate monthly turnover rates averaged about 1.5 percent, or 18 percent per year. The turnover rate in any given year can be misleading, however, because turnover rates are inversely related to unemployment rates (local, regional, and national). As Figure 4-1 shows, turnover rates were 1.5 to 2 times higher before 2008, when unemployment rates were lower, than after the 2009 economic downturn, when unemployment was higher. One study reported a correlation of −0.84 between unemployment and voluntary employee turnover in the years between 1945 and 1976.[14]

Typically, organizations compute turnover rates by business unit, division, diversity category, or tenure with the company. Then they attempt to benchmark those turnover rates against the rates of other organizations to gauge whether their rates are higher, lower, or roughly the same as those of competitors or their own industries. Many HR information systems allow managers to "drill down" on turnover rates in a vast number of ways. Indeed, probably hundreds of different turnover rates can be calculated, tracked, and put into various scorecards.

Logical Costs to Include When Considering Turnover Implications

Turnover can represent a substantial cost of doing business. Indeed, the fully loaded cost of turnover—not just separation and replacement costs, but also the exiting employee's lost leads and contacts, the new employee's depressed productivity while he or she is learning, and the time coworkers spend guiding the new employee—can easily cost 150 percent or more of the departing person's salary.[15] Pharmaceutical giant Merck & Company found that, depending on the job, turnover costs 1.5 to 2.5 times annual salary.[16] At Ernst & Young, the cost to fill a position vacated by a young auditor averaged 150 percent of the departing employee's annual salary.[17] These results compare quite closely to those reported in the *Journal of Accountancy*—namely, that the cost of turnover per person ranges from 93 percent to 200 percent of an exiting employee's salary, depending on the employee's skill and level of responsibility.[18]

Unfortunately, many organizations are unaware of the actual cost of turnover. Unless this cost is known, management may be unaware of the financial implications of turnover rates, especially among pivotal talent pools. Management also may be unaware of the need for action to prevent controllable turnover and may not develop a basis for choosing among alternative programs designed to reduce turnover.

Organizations need a practical procedure for measuring and analyzing the costs of employee turnover, because the costs of hiring, training, and developing employees are investments that must be evaluated just like other corporate resources. The objective in costing human resources is not only to measure the relevant costs, but also to develop methods and programs to reduce the more controllable aspects of these costs. Analytics and measurement strategies can work together to address these important issues.

Analytics

Analytics focuses on creating a design and analyses that will answer the relevant questions. Although computing turnover rates for various subcategories of employees or business units is instructive, our main focus in this chapter is on the financial implications associated with turnover. We use the term *analytics* to refer to formulas (for example, for turnover rates and costs), as well as the research designs and analyses that analyze the results of those formulas. Turnover measures are the techniques for actually gathering information—that is, for populating the formulas with relevant numbers. In the following sections, therefore, we describe how to identify and then measure turnover costs. You will see both formulas and examples that include numbers in those formulas. As you work through this information, keep in mind the distinction between analytics and measures.

The general procedure for identifying and measuring turnover costs is founded on three major separate cost categories: separation costs, replacement costs, and training costs.[19] In addition, it considers the difference in dollar-valued performance between leavers and their replacements. Finally, the fully loaded cost of turnover should include the economic value of lost business, if possible.[20] Notice how these elements precisely mirror the categories in Figure 4-2. There are costs of the transactions required to complete the separation of the former employee, and also of acquiring and training the replacement. The difference in performance between stayers and leavers is part of the change in workforce value, as is the business that is lost with the leaver.

For each of these categories, we first present the relevant cost elements and formulas (analytics); then we provide numeric examples to illustrate how the formulas are used (measures). The "pay rates" referred to in each category of costs refer to "fully loaded" compensation costs (that is, direct pay plus the cost of benefits).

Separation Costs

Figure 4-3 presents the key cost elements, together with appropriate formulas for each, that apply to separation costs. These include exit interviews (S_1); administrative functions related to termination, such as deletion of the exiting employee from payroll, employment, and benefits files (S_2); separation pay, if any (S_3); and unemployment tax, if applicable (S_4).

Thus:

Total separation costs (S_T) = $S_1 + S_2 + S_3 + S_4$

Cost Element	Formula				
Exit interview (S_1)	= cost of interviewer's time cost of terminating employee's time	= (time required prior to interview = time required for the interview	+ time required for the interview) x weighted average pay for terminated employees	x interviewer's pay rate during period x number of turnovers during period	x number of turnovers during period
Administrative functions related to termination (S_2)	= time required by HR dept. for administrative functions related to termination	x average HR dept. employee's pay rate	x number of turnovers during period		
Separation pay (S_3)	= amount of separation pay per employee terminated	x number of turnovers during period			
Unemployment tax (S_4)	= (unemployment tax rate - base rate)	x [($7,000 x number of employees earning at least $7,000) + (weighted average earnings if < $7,000 x (number of employees earning <$7,000)]	+ unemployment tax rate	x ($7,000 or weighted average earnings if <$7,000	x number of turnovers during period)

Source: Cascio, W.F., *Managing Human Resources: Productivity, Quality of Work Life, Profits,* 2nd ed., (New York: McGraw-Hill, 1989). Copyright © 1989 McGraw-Hill. Used with permission.

Figure 4-3 Measuring separation costs.

The cost of exit interviews is composed of two factors, the cost of the interviewer's time (preparation plus actual interview time) and the cost of the terminating employee's time (time required for the interview × weighted average pay rate for all terminated employees). This latter figure may be calculated as follows:

Times for exit interviews may be estimated in one of two ways:

- Time a random sample of exit interviews and calculate the average time.

- Interview a representative sample of managers who conduct exit interviews regularly and average their estimated times.

Each organization should specify exactly what administrative functions relate to terminations and the time required for them. Each of those activities costs money, and the costs should be documented and included when measuring separation costs.

Separation pay, for those organizations that offer it, can usually be determined from the existing accounting information system. Length of service, organization level, and the cause of termination are key factors that affect the amount of severance pay. Termination for poor performance generally does not include a severance package. Most lower-level employees receive one or two weeks of pay for each year they worked, up to a maximum of about 12 weeks. Midlevel managers typically receive anywhere from three to six months of pay; higher-level executives, six months to one year of pay; and chief executive officers with employment contracts two to three years of salary.[21] Fully 88 percent of organizations now require a signed release in exchange for payment, whether in a lump sum or through salary continuation. Medical benefits typically continue throughout the severance period.

Among organizations that do business in the United States, unemployment tax is relevant. For those doing business elsewhere, this item should not be included in separation costs. United States employers' unemployment tax rates include federal and state taxes, of which the federal tax equals 6.2 percent of the first $7,000 of each employee's earnings, and states impose a tax above that figure.[22] For example, in Colorado, the 2010 state tax is 2.48 percent of the first $10,000 in wages.[23] Due to rising jobless claims during the great recession, at least 35 states hiked their tax rates or wages subject to unemployment taxes in 2010.[24] Employers' actual tax rates are based on their history of claims. Those with fewer claims for unemployment benefits are subject to a lower unemployment tax than those with more unemployment claims. This increase in unemployment tax due to an increased incidence of claims is an element of separation costs.

In practice, high turnover rates that lead to high claims for unemployment compensation by former employees increase the cost of unemployment tax in two ways. First, the state increases the employer's tax rate (called the "penalty" in this instance). Second, the employer must pay additional, regular unemployment tax because of the turnovers. For example, consider a 100-employee firm with a 20 percent annual turnover rate (that is, 20 people) and a history of relatively few claims. The total increase in unemployment tax is computed as follows:

The penalty:

(New tax rate minus base rate) × [$10,000 × (100 + 20)]

= (5.4% − 5.0%) × [$1,200,000] = $4,800

Additional unemployment tax due to turnover:

(New tax rate) × ($10,000 × Number of turnovers during period)

= (5.4%) × ($10,000 x 20) = $10,800

Total additional unemployment tax due to turnover:

$4,800 + $10,800 = $15,600

What about the incremental costs associated with taxes to fund public retirement programs (such as the Social Security program in the U.S.)? These costs should be included only if the earnings of those who leave exceed the taxable wage base for the year. Thus, in the U.S. in 2010, the taxable wage base was $106,800, and the employer's share of those taxes was 7.65 percent. If an employee earning $80,000 per year leaves after six months, for example, the employer pays tax on only $40,000. If it takes one month to replace the departing employee, the replacement earns five months' wages, or $33,333. Thus, the employer incurs no additional social security tax because the total paid for the position for the year is less than $106,800. However, if the employee who left after six months was a senior manager earning $250,000 per year, the employer would already have paid the maximum tax due for the year for that employee. If a replacement works five months (earning $104,167), the employer then incurs additional social security tax for the replacement.

A final element of separation costs that should be included, if possible, is the cost of decreased productivity due to employee terminations. This may include the decline in the productivity of an employee prior to termination or the decrease in productivity of a the work group that lost the employee. The evidence regarding the effect on productivity as a result of downsizing is mixed. The American Management Association surveyed 700 companies that had downsized in the 1990s. In 34 percent of the cases, productivity rose, but it fell in 30 percent of them.[25] Firms that increased training budgets after a downsizing were more likely to realize improved productivity.[26]

Example: Separation Costs for Wee Care Children's Hospital

Let's now consider the computation of separation costs over one year for Wee Care Children's Hospital, a 200-bed facility that employs 1,200 people. Let's assume that Wee Care's monthly turnover rate is 2 percent. This represents 24 percent of the 1,200-person workforce per year, or about 288 employees. From Figure 4-3, we apply the following formulas (all costs are hypothetical):

Exit Interview (S_1)

Interviewer's time = (15 min. preparation + 45 min. interview) × $30/hour interviewer's pay + Benefits × 288 turnovers during the year

= $8,640

Weighted average pay + benefits per terminated employee per hour = sum of the products of the hourly pay plus benefits for each employee group times the number of separating employees in that group, all divided by the total number of separations, or in this case

= (19.96 × 75) + (23.44 × 87) + (26.97 × 65) + (29.13 × 37) + (34.46 × 14) + (47.17 × 10) divided by 288

= $25.42/hour

Terminating employee's time = 45 min. interview time × $25.42/hour weighted average pay + Benefits × 288 turnovers during the year

= $7,320.96

Total cost of exit interviews = $8,640 + $7,320.96

= $15,960.96

Administrative Functions (S_2)

S2 = Time to delete each employee × HR specialist's pay + Benefits/hour × Number of turnovers during the year

= 1 hour × $30 × 288

= $8,640

Separation Pay (S_3)

Suppose that Wee Care Children's Hospital has a policy of paying one week's separation pay to each terminating employee. Using the weighted average pay rate of the 288 terminating employees as an example, $25.42/hour × 40 hours/week = $1,016.80 average amount of separation pay per employee terminated.

Total Separation Pay = $1,016.80 × 288

= $292,838.40

Unemployment Tax (S_4)

Let's assume that because of Wee Care's poor experience factor with respect to terminated employees' subsequent claims for unemployment benefits, the state unemployment tax rate is 5.4 percent, as compared with a base rate of 5.0 percent. Let us further assume that turnovers occur, on the average, after four and a half months (18 weeks). If the weighted average pay + benefits of terminating employees is $25.42 per hour, and Wee Care pays an average of 35 percent of base pay in benefits, the weighted average pay alone is $16.52 per hour ($25.42 minus 35 percent). Over 18 weeks, the direct pay per terminating employee exceeds $10,000.

The dollar increase in unemployment tax incurred because of Wee Care's poor experience factor is therefore as follows:

$$(5.4\% - 5.0\%) \times [\$10,000 \times (1,200 + 288)]$$
$$= (0.004) \times [\$10,000 \times 1,488]$$
$$= \$59,520 \text{ [Penalty]}$$

$$+ (5.4\%) \times (\$10,000 \times 288)$$
$$= \$155,520 \text{ [Additional Tax]}$$

Total increase $= \$59,520 + \$155,520$
$$= \$215,040$$

Now that we have computed all four cost elements in the separation cost category, total separation costs ($\Sigma\, S_1, S_2, S_3, S_4$) can be estimated. This figure is as follows:

$$S_T = S_1 + S_2 + S_3 + S_4$$
$$= \$15,960.96 + \$8,640 + \$292,838.40 + \$215,040$$
$$= \$532,479.36$$

Replacement Costs

As shown in Figure 4-2, employees who replace those who leave are acquisitions. The overall value, or payoff, of those acquisitions depends on three factors: their quantity, quality, and cost. Replacement costs, as described in the following paragraphs, reflect only the quantity and cost of acquisitions, not their quality. We address the issue of staffing quality beginning in Chapter 8, "Staffing Utility: The Concept and Its Measurement."

Replacement costs are incurred by an organization when it replaces a terminated employee. Figure 4-4 shows the cost elements and the formulas for estimating them. As the figure indicates, there are eight categories of replacement costs:

1. Communication of job availability

2. Pre-employment administrative functions

3. Entrance interviews

4. Testing

5. Staff meetings

6. Travel/moving expenses

7. Post-employment acquisition and dissemination of information

8. Employment medical exams

The costs of communicating job availability vary by type of job and targeted labor market. Depending on the methods used in recruitment, these costs may range from the cost of an advertisement on the web, to employment agency fees paid by the employer.[27] Typically, these costs can be obtained from existing accounting records. If this communication process requires time from HR department employees, the cost of their time should also be included in replacement costs.

Administratively, several tasks are frequently undertaken in selecting and placing each new employee—for example, accepting applications, screening candidates, and checking references. These procedures can be expensive. For example, a simple background investigation that includes verification of last educational degree, a check with the last two employers, a five-year criminal check, and verification of the social security number costs only about $100. However, an extensive check that includes the previous items plus interviews with previous employers, teachers, neighbors, and acquaintances can run $15,000 or more. Unfortunately, organizational information systems do not routinely document the time required to perform these activities. However, the methods described earlier for estimating exit interview time requirements can be used to estimate the time needed for pre-employment administrative functions.

Virtually all organizations use entrance interviews to describe jobs, to communicate employee responsibilities and benefits, and to make some general assessments of candidates. The costs incurred when completing entrance interviews are a function of the length of the interview, pay rates of interviewers involved, and the number of interviews conducted. Valid staffing procedures can reduce future turnover and improve future employee performance. Decision makers should consider both costs and benefits. This chapter focuses on costs; Chapter 10 shows how to calculate the benefits from valid staffing procedures.

Many firms use pre-employment testing of some sort—for example, aptitude, achievement, drug, and honesty testing. To account properly for the costs of these activities, consider the costs of materials and supplies and the cost of scoring the tests. The costs of materials and scoring for aptitude, achievement, and honesty tests are often less than $25 per candidate. Drug testing costs roughly $45 to $65 for a simple screening test,[28] but confirming a positive test with more accurate equipment—a step recommended by most specialists—costs an additional $50 to $75.

For some classes of employees, especially top-level managers or other professionals, meetings or conferences may be held between the HR department and the department holding the vacant position. The estimated time for this meeting, multiplied by the sum of the pay and benefits rates for all attendees, provides a measure of this element of replacement costs. Travel and moving expenses can be extremely costly to organizations that pay these costs. Travel costs for candidates from a local labor market are minimal (carfare, parking, tolls), but travel costs for candidates who must fly in and stay in a hotel can average more than $1,500. Moving expenses can cover a range of elements, including mortgage differentials, lease-breaking expenses, company purchase of the old house, costs of moving personal effects from the old to the new location, closing costs, hook-up fees for utilities, and more. "Fully loaded" moving costs for middle managers average about $45,000 to $50,000, whereas a complete relocation package for executives averages about $70,000 per move.[29]

The seventh category of replacement costs is post-employment acquisition and dissemination of information. Pertinent information for each new employee must be gathered, recorded, and entered into various subsystems of an HR information system (for example, employee records, payroll files, benefits records). If flexible, cafeteria-style benefits are offered by an organization, an HR specialist could spend considerable time in counseling each new employee. The costs of this process can be estimated by calculating the time required for this counseling and multiplying it by the wage rates of employees involved. To compute the total cost of acquiring and disseminating information to new employees, multiply this cost by the number of acquisitions.

Pre-employment medical examinations are the final element of replacement costs. The extent and thoroughness—and, therefore, the cost—of such examinations varies greatly. Some organizations do not require them at all, some contract with private physicians or clinics to provide this service, and others use in-house medical staff. If medical examinations are contracted out, the cost can be determined from existing accounting data. If the exams are done in-house, their cost can be determined based on the supplies used (for example, x-ray film and laboratory supplies) and the staff time required to perform each examination. If the new employee is paid while receiving the medical examination, his or her rate of pay should be added to the examiner's pay rate in determining total cost. The following example estimates replacement costs for a one-year period based on Figure 4-4 for Wee Care Children's Hospital.

Cost Element	Formula			
Communicating job availability (R_1)	= [advertising and employment agency fees per termination	+ (time required for communicating job availability	x HR dept. employee's pay rate)]	x number of turnovers replaced during period
Pre-employment administrative functions (R_2)	= time required by HR dept. for pre-employment administrative functions	x average HR dept. employee's pay rate	x number of applicants during period	
Entrance interview (R_3)	= time required for interview	x interviewer's pay rate	x number of interviews during period	
Testing (R_4)	= (cost of materials per person	+ cost of scoring per person)	x number of tests given during period	
Staff meeting (R_5)	[= time required for meeting	x (HR dept. employee's pay rate	+ dept. representative's pay rate)]	x number of meetings during period
Travel/moving expenses (R_6)	= (average travel cost per applicant	x number of applicants)	+ average moving cost per new hire	x number of new hires
Post-employment acquisition and dissemination of information (R_7)	= time required for acquiring and disseminating information	x average HR dept. employee's pay rate	x number of turnovers replaced during period	
In-house medical examinations (R_8)	[= (time required for examination	x examiner's pay rate)	+ cost of supplies used]	x number of turnovers replaced during period
OR				
Contracted medical examinations (R_9)	= rate per examination	x number of turnovers replaced during period		

Source: Cascio, W. F., *Managing Human Resources: Productivity, Quality of Work Life, Profits,* 2nd ed. (New York: McGraw-Hill, 1989). Copyright © 1989 McGraw-Hill. Used with permission.

Figure 4-4 Measuring replacement costs.

Job Availability (R_1)

Assume that fees and advertisements average $350 per turnover, that three more hours are required to communicate job availability, that the HR specialist's pay and benefits total $30 per hour, and that 288 turnovers are replaced during the period. Therefore:

$$R_1 = [\$350 + (3 \times \$30)] \times 288$$

$$= \$126,720$$

Pre-Employment Administrative Functions (R_2)

Assume that pre-employment administrative functions to fill the job of each employee who left comprise five hours. Therefore:

$$R_2 = 5 \times \$30 \times 288$$

$$= \$43,200$$

Entrance Interview (R_3)

Assume that, on the average, three candidates are interviewed for every one hired. Thus, over the one-year period of this study, 864 (288 × 3) interviews were conducted, each lasting one hour. Therefore:

$$R_3 = 1 \times \$30 \times 864$$

$$= \$25,920$$

Testing (R_4)

Assume that aptitude tests cost $12 per applicant for materials and another $12 per applicant to score, and that, as a matter of HR policy, Wee Care uses drug tests ($45 per applicant) as part of the pre-employment process. The cost of testing is therefore as follows:

$$R_4 = (\$24 + \$45) \times (288 \times 3)$$

$$= \$59,616$$

Staff Meeting (R_5)

Assume that each staff meeting lasts one hour; that the average pay plus benefits of the new employee's department representative is $42; and that, for administrative convenience, such meetings are held, on average, only once for each three new hires (288 / 3 = 96). Therefore:

$$R_5 = (\$30 + \$42) \times 96$$

$$= \$6,912$$

Travel/Moving Expenses (R_6)

Assume that Wee Care pays moving expenses of $50,000, on average, for only one of every eight new hires. Therefore:

$$R_6 = [\$95 \times (288 \times 3)] + (\$50,000 \times 36)$$

$$= \$56,160 + \$1,620,000$$

$$= \$1,882,080$$

Post-Employment Acquisition and Dissemination of Information (R_7)

Assume that two hours are spent on these activities for each new employee. Therefore:

$$R_7 = 2 \times \$30 \times 288$$

$$= \$17,280$$

Pre-Employment Medical Examination (R_8 and R_9)

Assume that if the medical examinations are done at the hospital (in-house), each exam will take one hour; the examiner is paid $55 per hour; x-rays, laboratory analyses, and supplies cost $135; and 288 exams are conducted. Therefore:

$$R_8 = [(1 \times \$55) + \$135] \times 288$$

$$= \$54,720$$

If the exams are contracted out, let's assume that Wee Care will pay a flat rate of $250 per examination. Therefore:

$$R_9 = \$250 \times 288$$

$$= \$72,000$$

Wee Care therefore decides to provide in-house medical examinations for all new employees, so R_9 does not apply in this case. Total costs (R_T) can now be computed as the sum of R_1 through R_8:

$$R_T = \$126,720 + \$43,200 + \$25,920 + \$59,616 + \$6,912 + \$1,882,080 + \$17,280 + \$54,720$$

$$R_T = \$2,216,448$$

Training Costs

In virtually all instances, replacement employees must be oriented and trained to a standard level of competence before assuming their regular duties. As discussed in Chapter 11, "Costs and Benefits of HR Development Programs," this often involves considerable expense to an organization. For the present, however, assume that all replacement employees receive a total of 2 full days (16 hours) of new employee orientation from an HR department representative. After that, they are either placed in a formal training program, assigned to an experienced employee for some period of on-the-job training, or both. Figure 4-5 shows the cost elements and computational formulas for this category of turnover costs. The three major elements of training costs are informational literature plus new employee orientation, instruction in a formal training program, and instruction by employee assignment.

The cost of any informational literature provided to replacement employees must be considered a part of orientation and training costs. Unit costs for those items may be obtained from existing accounting records. Multiplying the unit costs by the number of replacement employees hired during the period yields the first element of training costs.

The cost of orientation includes the pay and benefits of the new employees who attend, as well as the pay and benefits of the HR representative who provides the orientation training times the number of hours of training.

New employees may also be involved in a formal training program. The overall cost of the training program depends on the cost of two major components: costs associated with trainers and costs associated with trainees. Whereas an organization incurs 100 percent of the costs associated with training replacements for employees who leave, the cost associated with trainers depends on the extent to which formal training is attributable to turnover. It is important, therefore, to distinguish the proportion of trainees who are replacements for employees who left, from the reminder who are in training due to other factors, such as planned expansion of the workforce. For the sake of simplicity, the costs of facilities, food, and other overhead expenses have not been included in these calculations.

Instead of, or in addition to, instruction in a formal training program, new employees may also be assigned to work with more experienced employees for a period of time or until they reach a standard level of competence. The overall cost of this on-the-job training must be determined for all replacement employees hired during the period, for it is an important element of training costs.

Notice that, in Figure 4-5, the cost of reduced productivity of new employees while they are learning is not included as an element of overall training costs. This is not because such a cost is unimportant. On the contrary, even if an organization staffs more employees to provide for a specified level of productivity while new employees are training, the cost of a decrease in the quantity and quality of goods or services produced is still very real. Less experienced employees may also cause an increase in operating expenses because of inefficient use of supplies and equipment. Other elements of lost productivity and lost business include factors such as additional overtime to cover one or more vacancies, cost of temporary help, the offsetting effects of wages and benefits saved due to the vacancy, and the cost of low morale among remaining employees.

Cost Element	Formula					
Informational literature (T_1)	= cost of informational package	x number of replacements during period				
Instruction in a formal training program (T_2)	= [length of training program	x average pay rate of trainer(s)	x number of programs conducted	x proportion of training costs attributed to replacements]		
	+ [average pay rate per trainee	x total number of replacements trained during period	x length of training program]			
Instruction by employee assignment (T_3)	= number of hours required for instruction	x [(average pay rate of experienced employee	x proportional reduction in productivity due to training	x number of experienced employees assigned to on-the-job training)	+ (new employee's pay rate	x number of instructions during period)]

Source: Cascio, W. F., *Managing Human Resources: Productivity, Quality of Work Life, Profits*, 2nd ed. (New York: McGraw-Hill, 1989). Copyright © 1989 McGraw-Hill. Used with permission.

Figure 4-5 Measuring training costs.

At high levels in organizations, and in other jobs where relationships with customers, leads, and contacts are critically important, the economic cost of business lost (that is, "opportunities foregone") may be substantial. On top of that, there may also be "ripple effects" associated with an employee's departure so that other employees follow him or her out the door. Situations such as these are especially prevalent when employee "stars" or "A-level" players depart and convince others to follow them. Executive recruiters call these situations "lift-outs." As *BusinessWeek* noted, "In a way, lift-outs are the iTunes of the merger world: Why buy the whole CD when all you really want are its greatest hits?[30] They can be especially costly, not to mention that they create huge gaps in staffing. They tend to occur when tightly knit groups or networks of employees (coworkers, former colleagues, classmates, or friends) decide to leave en masse.[31]

All of these costs are important. In the aggregate, they easily could double or triple the costs tallied thus far. When they can be measured reliably and accurately, they certainly should be included as additional elements of training costs. The same is true for potential productivity gains associated with new employees. Such gains serve to offset the costs of training. However, in many organizations, especially those providing services (for example, credit counseling, customer services, and patient care in hospitals), the measurement of these costs or gains is simply too complex for practical application. At the same time, these costs are seldom zero, and it is probably better to include a consensus estimate of their magnitude from a knowledgeable group of individuals than to assume either that they do not exist or that the cost is zero.

Now let us estimate the total cost of training employee replacements at Wee Care. Using the formulas shown in Figure 4-5, Wee Care estimates the following costs over a one-year period.

Informational Literature and New-Employee Orientation (T_1)

Assume that the unit cost of informational literature is $20 and that 288 employees are replaced. Each of the 288 replacements, at an average pay rate plus benefits of $25.42 per hour (see the earlier computation of S_1), attends 16 hours (two days) of general orientation to the hospital. This is provided in a two-day meeting that is held ten times per year, conducted by an HR representative, who receives $30 per hour in pay and benefits. The total cost of informational literature and new-employee orientation is, therefore, as follows:

$$T_1 = (\$20 \times 288) + (16 \times \$25.42 \times 288) + (10 \times 16 \times \$30)$$

$$= \$127,695.36$$

Instruction in a Formal Training Program (T_2)

New-employee training at Wee Care is conducted 10 times per year, and each training program lasts 40 hours (1 full week). The average pay plus benefits for instructors is $48 per hour, the average pay and benefits rate for trainees is $25.42 per hour, and of the 576 employees trained on the average each year, half are replacements for employees who left voluntarily or involuntarily. The total cost of formal training attributed to employee turnover is, therefore, as follows:

$$T_2 = (40 \times \$48 \times 10 \times 0.50) + (\$25.42 \times 288 \times 40)$$

$$= \$9,600 + \$292,838.40$$

$$= \$302,438.40$$

Instruction by Employee Assignment (T_3)

To ensure positive transfer between training program content and job content, Wee Care requires each new employee to be assigned to a more experienced employee for an additional week (40 hours). Experienced employees average $35 per hour in wages and benefits, and their own productivity is cut by 50 percent while they are training others. Each experienced employee supervises two trainees. The total cost of on-the-job training for replacement employees is, therefore, as follows:

$$T_3 = 40 \times [(\$35 \times 0.50 \times 144) + (\$25.42 \times 288)]$$

$$= 40 \times (\$2{,}520 + \$7{,}320.96)$$

$$= 40 \times \$9{,}840.96$$

$$= \$393{,}638.40$$

Total training costs can now be computed as the sum of T_1, T_2, and T_3:

$$T_T = \$127{,}695.36 + \$302{,}438.40 + \$393{,}638.40$$

$$= \$823{,}772.16$$

Performance Differences Between Leavers and Their Replacements

A final factor to consider in the tally of net turnover costs is the uncompensated performance differential between employees who leave and their replacements. We call this difference in performance (DP). DP needs to be included in determining the net cost of turnover because replacements whose performance exceeds that of leavers reduce turnover costs, and replacements whose performance is worse than that of leavers add to turnover costs.

To begin measuring DP in conservative, practical terms, compute the difference by position in the salary range between each leaver and his or her replacement. Assume that performance differentials are reflected in terms of deviations from the midpoint of the pay grade of the job class in question. Each employee's position in the salary range is computed as a "compa-ratio"; that is, salary is expressed as a percentage of the midpoint of that employee's pay grade. If the midpoint of a pay grade is $50,000 (annual pay), for example, an employee earning $40,000 is at 80 percent of the midpoint. Therefore, his or her compa-ratio is 0.80. An employee paid $50,000 has a compa-ratio of 1.0 (100 percent of the midpoint rate of pay), and an employee paid $60,000 has a compa-ratio of 1.2 because he or she is paid 120 percent of the midpoint rate of pay. Compa-ratios generally vary from 0.80 to 1.20 in most pay systems.[32]

To compute DP, use the following formula:

$$DP = \sum_{i=1}^{n} (CR_l - CR_r)MP_i$$

Here, DP is difference in performance between leaver and replacement, $\sum_{i=1}^{n}$ is summation over all leavers and their replacements, CR_l is the compa-ratio of the leaver, CR_r is the compa-ratio of the replacement, and MP_i is the annual rate of pay at the midpoint of the pay grade in question. Consider the following example:

$$CR_l = 0.80 \ CR_r = 1.0 \ MP_i = \$50,000$$

$$DP = (0.80 - 1.0) \times \$50,000$$

$$DP = (-0.20) \times \$50,000$$

$$DP = -\$10,000$$

DP is therefore subtracted from total turnover costs because the firm is gaining an employee whose performance is superior to that of the employee who was replaced.

If the compa-ratio of the leaver is 1.0, that of the replacement is 0.80, and the pay-grade midpoint is $50,000, then DP = $10,000. These costs are added to total turnover costs because the leaver was replaced by a lesser performer.

Why are differences in performance assumed to covary with differences in pay? Actually, this assumption is true only in a perfectly competitive labor market.[33] In a perfectly competitive labor market, every worker earns the marginal revenue product accrued to the firm from his or her labor. Thus, the firm is indifferent to workers whose compa-ratios are 0.80, 1.0, or 1.20 because each worker is paid exactly what he or she is "worth."

Many entry-level jobs (for example, management analysts) approximate conditions in which it is reasonable to assume that compa-ratio differences reflect performance differences. Above the entry level, however, labor markets are often imperfect because workers develop what economists call "firm-specific human capital."[34] Workers who have specific job knowledge that their firms value (for example, in banking, automobiles, or computers) tend to command higher wages. However, their value is reflected only partly in their higher wages. Wages reflect what economists call "opportunity costs," or the value of a worker's second-best employment opportunity. Competitors are able to offer only a wage that reflects the economic value of a worker to them. Therefore, opportunity costs and the wage rates paid to valued employees tend to reflect only the portion of a worker's economic value that is easily transferable from one employer to another (that is, "generic"). The portion of an employee's value that is not easily transferable, the firm-specific component, typically is reflected only partially in employee wages, if at all. Thus, the economic value of workers with firm-specific human capital is above their wage (opportunity cost) level but can be assumed to be proportionate to these wages.

If an employee with substantial amounts of firm-specific human capital leaves the firm and is replaced by a worker who lacks such firm-specific human capital, the replacement will receive a lesser wage. However, if a poor performer leaves and is replaced by a worker with more human capital, albeit non-firm-specific, the replacement will receive a higher wage than the leaver.[35] The difference in pay between leavers and their replacements thus represents an indicator, although an imperfect one, of the "uncompensated performance differential" due to firm-specific human capital, and it should be considered when determining the net costs of turnover.

The assumption that excess value to the firm is a function of wages paid and that excess value and wages covary in a linear (straight-line) fashion is conservative. In practice, the relationship can be curvilinear (positive or negative). For our purposes, however, the conservative assumption of a linear relationship between excess value and wages is appropriate. At the same time, higher (lower) wages paid to a replacement employee represent an additional, ongoing cost (or saving) to an organization. It is appropriate to calculate such a pay differential, for it is part of the differential value of the replacement, relative to the employee who left. Although an offsetting strategic value may justify paying a replacement more, that is often a subjective estimate by decision makers.

For Wee Care, assume that the net DP = $200,000. On average, therefore, the firm hired slightly poorer performers than it lost. The following equation, which uses the four major components of employee turnover, represents the total cost of employee turnover:

$$\text{Total cost of turnover} = S_T + R_T + T_T + D_P$$

Here, S_T is total separation costs, R_T is total replacement costs, T_T is total training costs, and DP is net differential performance between leavers and their replacements. For Wee Care, the total cost of 288 employee turnovers during a one-year period was as follows:

$467,967.36 + $2,216,448 + $823,772.16 + $200,000

= $3,508,387.50

This represents a cost of $12,166.90 for each employee who left the hospital.

The Costs of Lost Productivity and Lost Business

In several places earlier in this chapter, we mentioned that it is useful to include the costs of lost productivity and lost business in the fully loaded cost of employee turnover, if it is possible to tally such costs accurately. Seven additional cost elements might be included, as follows:[36]

- The cost of additional overtime to cover the vacancy (wages + benefits × number of hours of overtime)

- The cost of additional temporary help (wages + benefits × hours paid)

- Wages and benefits saved due to the vacancy (these are subtracted from the overall tally of turnover costs)

- The cost of reduced productivity while the new employee is learning the job (wages + benefits × length of the learning period × percentage reduction in productivity)

- The cost of lost productive time due to low morale of remaining employees (estimated as aggregate time lost per day of the work group × wages + benefits of a single employee × number of days)

- The cost of lost customers, sales, and profits due to the departure (estimated number of customers × gross profit lost per customer × profit margin in percent)

- Cost of additional (related) employee departures (if one additional employee leaves, the cost equals the total per-person cost of turnover)

In terms of analytics, one final caution is in order: Don't be misled by variability across departments or business units that are based on small numbers. After all, if a six-person department loses two employees, that's a 33 percent turnover rate. We noted in Chapter 2, "Analytical Foundations of HR Measurement," the dangers associated with generalizing from small samples that are not representative of the larger population they are designed to represent. In the case of small-sample turnover statistics, to make the sample more representative, it might make sense to segment employee turnover into broader categories that include larger numbers of employees.

Remember, the purpose of measuring turnover costs and using analytical strategies to reveal their implications is to improve managerial decision-making. Consider a brief example of one such an analysis.[37] Based on the model shown in Figure 4-2, the researchers developed an analytical model that captured the value associated with employee separations (turnover) and acquisitions (hires) over a four-year period. Their model estimated three components in each time period:

- **Movement costs:** The costs associated with employee separations and acquisitions

- **Service costs:** The pay, benefits, and associated expenses required to support the workforce

- **Service value:** The value of the goods and service produced by the workforce

Then they estimated the dollar-valued implications of three different pay plans (equal pay increases plus two types of pay-for-performance plans) and of the subsequent separation and acquisition patterns over the four years. They did so by subtracting the movement costs and service costs from the service value. In short, they subtracted each pay plan's costs from its benefits.

Traditional compensation-cost analysis suggested that a strong link between pay and performance would be unwise, given its extreme cost. When the potential benefits of workforce value were accounted for, however, a different conclusion emerged. By fully incorporating both costs and benefits into their model, the researchers showed that even under the most conservative assumptions, pay-for-performance was a valuable investment, with potentially very high payoffs for the firm, in part because it caused poor performers to leave more often and good performers to leave less often. This reinforces a point we made at the beginning of the chapter: Turnover is only one part of a family of external moves. Adopting a broader perspective is a wise strategy indeed.

Process

Organizational budgeting practices sometimes provide a natural opportunity to use the costs of employee turnover as part of a broader framework to demonstrate tangible economic payoffs from effective management practices. When line managers complain that they cannot keep positions filled or that they cannot get enough people to join as new hires, it is a prime opportunity to elevate the conversation.

Revenue at Superior Energy Services in New Orleans is based on billable hours. That fact gave Ray Lieber, the HR vice president, an opportunity to portray every separation as lost revenue. Nearly half of the separations were skilled operators or supervisors with high impact on revenue. Then he made the case for an investment in statistical modeling to predict how to reduce turnover. He discovered that the most significant factor was not higher pay or benefits, but one-on-one coaching from supervisors. Superior Energy invested in supervisor coaching training and saw turnover drop from 34 percent to about 27 percent.[38]

Thrivent Financial for Lutherans in Minneapolis had always assumed that the more experience a new hire had in the job he or she was hired into, the less likely that new hire was to leave, but it found just the opposite when it analyzed turnover data. That gave HR leaders at Thrivent the chance to get the attention of line management and to invest in studies to discover why those with more experience were more likely to leave. Similarly, at Wawa, Inc., a Pennsylvania food service and convenience company, leaders had suspected that hourly wage was the biggest factor in turnover among clerks, but careful analysis found that the most significant turnover predictor was hours worked. Those working more than 30 hours per week were classified as full-time and separated less. This discovery opened the door to moving from 30 percent part-time to 50 percent full-time, reducing turnover rates by 60 percent.[39]

As a final example, consider the SAS Institute of Cary, North Carolina. SAS is renowned for its low voluntary turnover rate among computer programmers. In an industry that routinely experiences 20 percent voluntary turnover per year among programmers, at

SAS, turnover runs about 3 percent per year. It does that largely through its enlightened management practices. Those practices are founded on the idea that in an intellectual capital business, attracting and retaining talent is paramount, and the way to attract and retain good people is to give them interesting work and interesting people to do it with, and treat them like the responsible adults they are.

SAS is justifiably famous for its pleasant physical work environment and generous, family-friendly benefits. Those benefits include an on-site 7,500-square-foot medical facility and a full-indemnity health plan that includes vision, hearing, and dental care; free physical exams; and free mammography. It also provides on-site Montessori day care, a fitness center, soccer, and softball fields. All this is free to employees and their families. The company even provides towels and launders exercise clothes—also for free. Finally, it provides elder care, domestic-partner benefits, and cafeterias with subsidized meals.[40]

Suppose that a line leader addresses the following question to HR leaders: "I'm happy that our turnover among programmers is 3 percent, but are we spending too much to keep them, and is it worth it?" In answering that very reasonable question, an HR leader might begin by reviewing the company's business model. In brief, it is as follows.[41]

SAS relies on annual product renewals from its clients, who use its software for deep analysis of their organizational databases. SAS also relies on employees for innovations and services that are tailored to those clients' particular industry requirements and their unique competitive positions in their industries. This means that client relationships with SAS advisers need to be based on a thorough, shared understanding about industry-specific competition and on long-term trust. This may be more important for SAS than for its competitors, whose business models are based more on software purchases than renewable licenses and whose value proposition is not so deeply dependent on close and well-informed relationships with clients.

One way that SAS creates the capability, opportunity, and motivation to achieve this kind of deep, common, client-focused synergy is by creating an employment model that attracts and motivates programmers, designers, and client advisers to join and stay for the long run. This is a distinctive value proposition because a long-term employment deal is unusual in professions where the norm is to move from project to project, often changing employers many times in a few years to find the most interesting work or a higher paycheck.

The HR leader might then present the cost implications of that 17 percent difference in employee turnover between SAS and the software industry. Table 4-2 includes some hypothetical calculations.

Table 4-2 Annual Opportunity Savings from Lower Employee Turnover among Programmers: SAS Versus the Software Industry

Annual turnover	3%	20%
Annual salary	$60,000	$60,000
Number per 1,000 programmers who leave	30	200
Cost of turnover per programmer (1.5 × salary)	$90,000	$90,000
Total cost	$2,700,000	$18,000,000
Annual opportunity savings at SAS	$15,300,000	

Of course, the annual opportunity savings does not include the incremental, yearly cost to SAS of providing such generous benefits to its employees. Assume, however, that the annual cost of benefits per SAS employee is as high as 50 percent of salary (compared to a 2008 U.S. average of 39 percent).[42] Its incremental, yearly cost, relative to its competitors', is thus roughly 11 percent higher. The total annual opportunity savings to SAS as a result of lower employee turnover may be viewed as an annuity that helps to pay for the benefits that keep employee turnover low. Because it takes a long time for a new employee to develop the kind of shared understanding and high level of trust with clients that is central to the SAS business model, retaining talent truly is critical to achieving the company's strategic objectives. The answer to the line leader's original question is that SAS's investments in generous employee benefits are likely to be worth it.

Exercise

Software that calculates answers to one or more of the following exercises can be found at http://hrcosting.com/hr/.

1. Ups and Downs, Inc., a 4,000-employee organization, has a serious turnover problem, and management has decided to estimate its annual cost to the company. Following the formulas presented in Figures 4-3, 4-4, and 4-5, an HR specialist collected the following information. Exit interviews take about 45 minutes (plus 15 minutes preparation); the interviewer, an HR specialist, is paid an average of $31 per hour in wages and benefits; and, over the past year, Ups and Downs, Inc., experienced a 27 percent turnover rate. Three groups of employees were primarily responsible for this: blue-collar workers (40 percent), who make an average of

$33.20 per hour in wages and benefits; clerical employees (36 percent), who make an average of $18.50 per hour; and managers and professionals (24 percent), who make an average of $44.75 per hour. The HR department takes about 90 minutes per terminating employee to perform the administrative functions related to terminations; on top of that, each terminating employee gets two weeks' severance pay. All this turnover also contributes to increased unemployment tax (old rate = 5.0 percent; new rate = 5.4 percent); because the average taxable wage per employee is $22.90, this is likely to be a considerable (avoidable) penalty for having a high turnover problem.

It also costs money to replace those terminating. All pre-employment physicals are done by Biometrics, Inc., an outside organization that charges $250 per physical. Advertising and employment-agency fees run an additional $550, on average, per termination, and HR specialists spend an average of four more hours communicating job availability every time another employee quits. Pre-employment administrative functions take another two and a half hours per terminating employee, and this excludes pre-employment interview time (one hour, on average). Over the past year, Ups and Downs, Inc., records also show that, for every candidate hired, three others had to be interviewed. Testing costs per applicant are $14 for materials and another $14 for scoring. Travel expenses average $85 per applicant, and one in every ten new hires is reimbursed an average of $55,000 in moving expenses. For those management jobs being filled, a 90-minute staff meeting is also required, with a department representative (average pay and benefits of $37.75 per hour) present. In the past year, 17 meetings were held. Finally, post-employment acquisition and dissemination of information takes 75 minutes, on average, for each new employee.

And of course, all these replacements have to be oriented and trained. Informational literature alone costs $19 per package, and a formal orientation program run by an HR specialist takes 2.5 days (20 hours) spread over the first two months of employment. New employees make an average of $22.50 per hour in wages and benefits. After that, a formal training program (run 12 times last year) takes four 8-hour days, and trainers make an average of $46 per hour in wages and benefits. About 65 percent of all training costs can be attributed to replacements for those who left. Finally, on-the-job training lasts three 8-hour days per new employee, with two new employees assigned to each experienced employee (average pay and benefits = $36.25 per hour). During training, each experienced employee's productivity dropped by 50 percent. Net DP was + $210,000. What did employee turnover cost Ups and Downs, Inc., last year? How much per employee who left? (Use the software available from http://hrcosting.com/hr/ for all computations.)

References

1. Morrison, Scott, "Google Searches for Staffing Answers," *The Wall Street Journal,* May 19, 2009, B1.

2. United States Department of Labor, Bureau of Labor Statistics, *Data Bases and Tables,* www.bls.gov/jlt/. Reports can be generated at http://data.bls.gov:8080/PDQ/outside.jsp?survey=jt.

3. Wal-Mart Corporation, Form 10-K, January 2010. www.sec.gov/Archives/edgar/data/104169/ 000119312510071652/d10k.htm.

4. Bureau of Labor Statistics.

5. McCarthy, Ryan, "Walmart Tops the Fortune 500 List Again," *Huffington Post,* June 8, 2010, www.huffingtonpost.com/2010/04/15/walmart-tops-fortune-500_n_538600.html.

6. Boudreau, J. W., and C. J. Berger, "Decision-Theoretic Utility Analysis Applied to Employee Separations and Acquisitions," *Journal of Applied Psychology Monograph* 70, no. 3 (1985): 581–612.

7. *Ibid.*

8. Boudreau, John W., *Retooling HR: How Proven Business Models Can Improve Human Capital Decisions* (Cambridge, Mass.: Harvard Business Press, 2010).

9. Martin, D. C., and K. M. Bartol, "Managing Turnover Strategically," *Personnel Administrator* 30, no. 11 (1985): 63–73.

10. Tyler, Richard, "Workers Over 60 Are Surprise Key to McDonald's Sales," *Telegraph,* August 13, 2009, www.telegraph.co.uk/finance/newsbysector/retailandconsumer/6017391/Workers-over-60-are-surprise-key-to-McDonalds-sales.html.

11. *Ibid.*

12. Boudreau, 2010.

13. Cascio, Wayne F., *Employment Downszing and Its Alternatives* (Washington, D.C.: SHRM Foundation, 2009).

14. Hulin, C. L., "Integration of Economics and Attitude/Behavior Models to Predict and Explain Turnover," paper presented at Annual Meeting of the Academy of Management, Atlanta, Ga., 1979.

15. Branch, S., "You Hired [']em, but Can You Keep [']em?" *Fortune* (November 9, 1998): 247–250.

16. Solomon, J., "Companies Try Measuring Cost Savings from New Types of Corporate Benefits," *The Wall Street Journal,* December 29, 1988, B1.

17. Hewlett, S. A., and C. B. Luce, "Off-Ramps and On-Ramps: Keeping Talented Women on the Road to Success," *Harvard Business Review* 83 (March 2005): 43–54.

18. Johnson, A. A., "The Business Case for Work-Family Programs," *Journal of Accountancy* 180, no. 2 (1995): 53–58.

19. Smith, H. L., and W. E. Watkins, "Managing Manpower Turnover Costs," *Personnel Administrator* 23, no. 4 (1978): 46–50.

20. Dooney, J., "Cost of Turnover," November 2005, retrieved from www.shrm.org/research on February 6, 2006.

21. Allbusiness.com, "Severance Pay," retrieved from www.Allbusiness.com on August 8, 2006.

22. Milkovich, G. T., J. M. Newman, and B. Gerhart, *Compensation,* 10th ed. (New York: McGraw-Hill, 2011).

23. Needleman, S. E., "Feeling Blue about Pink-Slip Taxes," *The Wall Street Journal,* April 6, 2010, B11.

24. Svaldi, A., "Bosses Will Pay for Layoffs," *The Denver Post,* April 18, 2010, 1K and 10K.

25. This data was reported in Cravotta, R., and B. H. Kleiner, "New Developments Concerning Reductions in Force," *Management Research News* 24, no. 3–4 (2001): 90–93.

26. Appelbaum, S. H., S. Lavigne-Schmidt, M. Peytchev, and B. Shapiro, "Downsizing: Measuring the Costs of Failure," *Journal of Management Development* 18, no. 5 (1999): 436–463.

27. Cascio, W. F. (2006). Managing Human Resources: Productivity, Quality of Work Life, Profits (6th ed, Ch. 6). Burr Ridge, IL: McGraw-Hill/Irwin.

28. Expomed.com (2006). Drug Testing. Retrieved from www.Expomed.com on August 10, 2006.

29. Hansen, F. (Nov. 2002). Reigning in relocation costs. Work force. Downloaded from www.work force.com on August 24, 2004.

30. McGregor, J. (Dec. 18, 2006). I can't believe they took the whole team. Business Week, p. 120, 122.

31. Wysocki, B., Jr. (March 30, 2000). Yet another hazard of the new economy: The Pied Piper effect. The Wall Street Journal, p. A1; A16.

32. Milkovich, G. T., & Newman, J. M. (2008). Compensation (9th ed.). Burr Ridge, IL: McGraw-Hill/Irwin.

33. Hirschey, M. (2006). Fundamentals of Managerial Economics (8th ed.) Mason, OH: South-Western Thompson Learning.

34. Becker, G. S. (1964). Human Capital. New York: National Bureau of Economic Research.

35. Lazear, E. P. (1998). Personnel Economics for Managers. NY: Wiley.

36. Dooney, 2005, op. cit.

37. Sturman, M. C., Trevor, C. O., Boudreau, J. W., & Gerhart, B. (2003). Is it worth it to win the talent war? Evaluating the utility of performance-based pay. Personnel Psychology, 56, 997-1035.

38. Bill Roberts. "Analyze This." HR Magazine. October, 2009. 35-41.

39. Ibid.

40. O'Reilly, C. A. III, & Pfeffer, J. (2000). Hidden Value. Boston: Harvard Business School Press.

41. Boudreau, J. W., & Ramstad, P. (2007). Beyond HR: The New Science of Human Capital. Boston, MA: Harvard Business School Press.

42. Society for Human Resource Management. (2008). 2008 employee benefits. Alexandria, VA: Society for Human Resource Management.

5

Employee Health, Wellness, and Welfare

W e often think of vital human capital decisions being made by business leaders and their HR colleagues, but some of the most important talent decisions in every organization are made by employees themselves. Employee decisions that affect their health and wellness have profound effects that are often overlooked. This chapter shows how to capture and evaluate these effects.

In 2009, Steve Burd, CEO of the U.S. supermarket chain Safeway, took eight trips to speak to U.S. politicians about reforming the health-care system. Safeway's health-care costs had been rising 10 percent per year for several years prior to 2004, but since then the company had kept health-care costs flat, compared to a 40 percent average increase in U.S. companies. How did Safeway do it? The company fully pays for an array of preventative visits and tests, but employees pay in full the next $1,000 in expenses and 20% of costs after that, up to a $4,000 maximum. Noting that 75 percent of health-care costs result from four conditions (cardiovascular disease, cancer, diabetes, and obesity), Safeway has a voluntary program that tests employees for smoking, weight, blood pressure, and cholesterol. Every area they pass results in a reduction in their insurance premiums of up to $1,560 per family per year.[1]

According to the Centers for Disease Control (CDC), "chronic diseases account for more than 75 percent of the nation's $2 trillion medical care costs."[2] Behavior determines approximately 50 percent of health status, and genetics and environment determine another 20 percent each. Access to care accounts for the remaining 10 percent.[3]

This chapter deals with the economic impacts of employee lifestyle choices on health-care costs, the return on investment of worksite health-promotion programs, and the costs and benefits of employee assistance programs. Our objective is not to describe the structure, content, or operational features of such programs, but rather to present methods for estimating their economic impact on an organization. To provide some background on this issue, let's begin by considering the relationship of unhealthy lifestyles to health-care costs. Following that, to provide some perspective on firm-level decisions about health-care expenditures, we present a logical framework that illustrates how changes in employee health affect financial outcomes.

Health, Wellness, and Worksite Health Promotion

It is important to note that the concept of health includes more than just the absence of illness. Wellness represents the balance of physical, emotional, social, spiritual, and intellectual health.[4] A 2009 Towers-Watson study found that companies that perform best in controlling health-care costs more often take these actions:[5]

- **Clearly articulate their strategies:** Fully 84 percent of high performers use results measures to build action plans for performance improvement, versus 43 percent of low performers.

- **Engage leaders:** The vast majority of high performers (86 percent) have secured senior management involvement, which is a critical performance factor (compared to 57 percent of low performers).

- **Understand their employee populations:** Three-quarters of high performers measure employee health status and risks by population segment (compared to 46 percent of low performers).

- **Engage employees:** Most high performers (65 percent) provide health-care communications, employee education, and access to health information year-round (compared to only 34 percent of low performers).

- **Optimize investments:** Fully 80 percent of high performers take steps to align subsidies and resources with employees' most significant needs (compared to only 29 percent of low performers).

- **Support employee health:** Seventy-four percent of high performers actively help employees understand and manage their health and health risks (compared to only 22 percent of low performers).

- **Measure for success:** The majority of high performers measure such critical success factors as employees' understanding and use of resources and tools (81 percent of high performers versus 47 percent of low performers), as well as employee attitudes and understanding of their benefit programs (82 percent of high performers versus 53 percent of low performers).

Skyrocketing Health-Care Costs Brought Attention to Employee Health

The potential relationships between employee health and organizational productivity are obvious, but the issue is particularly significant in the United States, where health care is largely paid for by corporations and individuals instead of being provided more universally by the government. Even in the United States, organizations did not begin to seriously address the issue of health-care cost containment until a substantial increase in health-care costs forced them to look for savings. How large of a run-up? From 2000 through 2005, U.S. employers hiked workers' annual contributions for family health coverage by 68 percent, from an average of $1,600 to $2,700.[6] A 2009 Kaiser Family Foundation study found that 22 percent of workers now pay deductibles of more than $1,000, up from 10 percent in 2006. Premiums for employer-sponsored health insurance rose 5 percent in 2009 to $13,375 for a family, more than doubling from $5,791 ten years ago.[7]

Rising health-care costs often translate into less disposable income for employees because wage increases have not kept pace with rising employee health-care contributions. Higher insurance premiums can also cut into disposable income. In 2010, the U.S. Department of Health and Human Services chided health insurance companies for "massive increases" such as the 39 percent premium increase for individual plans from one company in California.[8] To illustrate, average out-of-pocket medical costs for employees more than doubled between 2000 and 2005, with wages growing only 18 percent.[9] Employers may offset increased health-care costs by holding down wages.[10] Even with such cost shifting, health-related employer costs have risen dramatically. Moreover, no matter who bears the cost, opportunities to reduce such costs can benefit both employers and employees.

Two Broad Strategies to Control Health-Care Costs

To help control spiraling medical costs, organizations can pursue one or both of two broad tactics:

- Improve workers' health habits
- Reduce employer payments for employee health insurance or health care

Unfortunately, evidence indicates that employees who are most at risk often find it most difficult to change to healthier lifestyles, so the first strategy can be difficult. Employers can use economic incentives to motivate employees. A combination of the two approaches links employee lifestyle choices to their personal health insurance or medical-care costs. Rockford Products Corp., which makes metal parts used in items from Caterpillar earthmovers to yo-yos, combed through 15 years of records and found that

31 of 32 workers who had heart attacks or required major heart surgery—including 2 who keeled over in the factory—were smokers.[11] Pitney Bowes, Inc., used statistical modeling to identify future high-cost health claims caused by failure to adhere to prescribed medication. The company modified its pharmacy benefit structure to make such medications affordable. For example, the company moved statins used to treat high cholesterol and angiotensin-converting enzyme (ACE) inhibitors for treating high blood pressure to a zero-copay tier, making these drugs free of charge. "We see fewer emergency room visits, and we also see people being able to come to work and be more productive," says Andrew Gold, executive director of global benefits planning. "That creates an overall benefit to the company and to employees."[12]

Wellness programs therefore hold considerable promise as a strategy to reduce those costs. Support for such programs is growing, as a *Wall Street Journal*/Harris poll found.[13] More than half of all adults surveyed (53 percent) said it would be fair to ask people with unhealthy lifestyles to pay higher insurance premiums than people with healthy lifestyles, whereas 32 percent said it would be unfair. When asked the same question in 2003, 37 percent said it would be fair, whereas 45 percent said it would be unfair. The American Institute for Preventive Medicine estimates that 62 percent of employers have some type of health-improvement program in place.[14]

Of course, health and wellness investments can also translate into savings for companies. The 2010 Towers-Watson survey found that the high-performing companies had a health-care cost of $9,240 per employee per year, compared to $11,244 for low-performing companies. Although 35 percent of low performers reported double-digit cost increases in the prior year, 33 percent of high performers kept their cost increases below 4 percent. Even more interesting is that the cost reductions were not simply achieved by passing along costs to employees. The annual employee contribution in high-performing companies was $2,028, compared to $2,496 in low-performing companies.[15] As noted in Chapter 3, "The Hidden Costs of Absenteeism," research suggests that for every $1 spent on direct pharmacy costs, an organization incurs $2.30 in health-related productivity costs.

As lucrative as these returns can be, not all investments in employee health are appropriate for all companies, and they don't work equally well in all situations or for all employee groups. How can organizations analyze their options and make choices?

We now turn to the logic that connects investments in employee health and welfare to strategic organizational outcomes.

Logic: How Changes in Employee Health Affect Financial Outcomes

Simply put, the logic of the costs and benefits of employee health and wellness can be traced through the following logical connections:

- Organizations invest in programs that attract, select, develop, or encourage employees to improve their health at the worksite and in their lifestyles.

- Organizations invest in employee assistance programs to address specific employee health issues.

- Employees respond by adopting healthier lifestyle behaviors both at work and away from work.

- Healthier employees require less treatment for health problems, reducing employer-paid health-care services or group health insurance premiums.

- Healthier employees are available at work more often because they are absent less (due to both personal health and family health issues), and they separate less frequently.

- Healthier employees perform better at work due to greater physical and mental capacity.

Figure 5-1 shows logical connections between changes in employee health and financial outcomes. The process begins with organizational policies and practices that encourage employees to make healthy lifestyle choices, or with assistance with specific issues such as alcoholism or drug abuse. These might include staffing policies, changes in insurance programs (as those at Pitney Bowes, described previously), programs to educate employees about health-risk factors, health screenings, and opportunities to improve personal fitness. You're probably wondering, "Okay, but how much can my company expect to gain from these efforts?" One estimate attributes fully 15–25 percent of corporate health-care costs to employees' unhealthy lifestyles.[16]

In light of these potential savings, some companies have adopted policies to preempt higher health-care costs by not hiring those with unhealthy lifestyles in the first place. For example, Rockford Products imposes a $50 per month fee on employees who smoke, are obese, or suffer from hypertension.[17] Turner Broadcasting won't hire smokers. Multi-Developers won't hire anyone who engages in what the company views as high-risk activities: skydiving, piloting a private aircraft, mountain climbing, or motorcycling.

Weyco, Inc., an insurance-consulting firm, gave smokers 15 months to quit and offered smoking-cessation programs to help them do so. After that, it tested employees for evidence of nicotine in their bodies. If they failed the test, they were fired.[18]

Continuing on with the logic of Figure 5-1, if organizational policies and practices are effective, this should lead to changes in the behavior of employees, and, eventually, in the health of employees over time. Improved health may be reflected in outcomes such as higher levels of cardiovascular fitness, weight loss, and lower levels of stress. Those changes, in turn, should lead to changes in behaviors, such as reduced absences, accidents, and employee turnover, accompanied by higher levels of employee productivity. Changes in behavior should be reflected eventually in improved financial outcomes: fewer insurance claims; lower overall medical costs; reductions in the costs of employee absence, accidents, and turnover; and higher sales value of products and services.

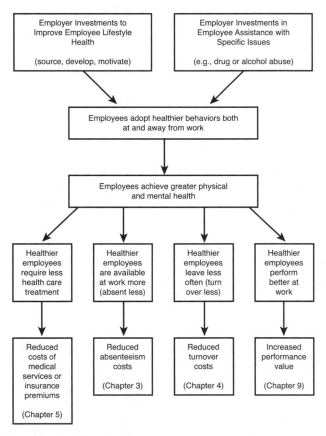

Figure 5-1 Logic of employee health and wellness.

The Typical Logic of Workplace Health Programs

As Figure 5-1 suggests, a useful first step in estimating the savings that accrue from a workplace health promotion (WHP) program is to choose which health-related costs are actually reduced. Some firms establish WHP programs with very specific objectives, such as to reduce the rising costs associated with premature births or to realize cost savings through early cancer detection and treatment. Programs with specific objectives make evaluation more straightforward. Unfortunately, however, the great majority of WHP programs are implemented without such specific objectives.

A survey of wellness program objectives for selected Fortune 500 companies showed these top five objectives:

1. To promote better health

2. To improve cardiovascular fitness

3. To reduce coronary risk factors

4. To decrease health-care costs

5. To improve employee relations[19]

How might we evaluate objectives 1 and 5? Improvements in objectives 2 and 3 are important, to be sure, but how do they relate specifically to a firm's health-care costs? Finally, with respect to objective 4, how might we demonstrate the extent to which a reduction in health-care costs was due to a WHP program and how much to other factors?

The 2010 Towers-Watson health-care cost survey revealed measurement practices and intentions shown in Figure 5-2. The measures tend to be closely focused on immediate program usage patterns and employee attitudes toward health management and benefits. Yet the ultimate outcomes of these attitudes and behaviors are not among the most commonly listed measures.

This is not to diminish the good intentions or employment commitment of firms that instituted wellness programs. However, comparing this list of objectives with the logical approach of Figure 5-1 suggests that setting more specific objectives and carefully analyzing the connections can significantly enhance the ability to measure the effects of such programs (and even the effects themselves).

Source: Towers-Watson. 2010 Health Care Cost Survey (Stamford, Conn.: Towers Watson, 2010), p. 17, Exhibit 20.

Figure 5-2 Health cost measurement in U.S. companies.

Legal Considerations and Incentives to Modify Lifestyles

At first glance, it might appear that changing employees' unhealthy lifestyles is a win-win for employer and employees. However, some practices would reject applicants with certain lifestyles or even dismiss employees for certain behaviors (for example, smoking, skydiving). If an employer wants to institute such policies, can employees contest them? U.S. civil rights laws generally don't protect individuals against such "lifestyle discrimination" because smokers and skydivers aren't named as protected classes. In addition, more than half of all states prohibit termination for various types of off-duty conduct (for instance, use of tobacco products). U.S. employers also need to beware of violating the Americans with Disabilities Act (ADA). Obesity, for example, is generally not considered to be a disability under the ADA.[20] However, in 2009, the U.S. government implemented the Genetic Information Nondiscrimination Act, which restricts employers' and health insurers' ability to collect and disclose genetic information, including family medical history. Some employers say the law stymies wellness-promotion efforts by barring them from offering financial incentives to complete health surveys that ask about family history.[21]

Analytics for Decisions about WHP Programs

Companies that market their WHP programs provide statistics to support their claims of savings in health-care costs, but calculating how much any given employer can expect to save is difficult because program sponsors use different methods to measure and report cost-benefit data. When a program's effects are measured and for how long they are measured are crucial considerations. For example, DuPont found that the greatest drop in absenteeism due to illness occurred in the first two or three years; then it leveled off. Other effects, which might not appear for three years or longer, are so-called lagged effects. The greatest savings should accrue over time because of the chronic nature of many illnesses that WHP programs seek to prevent. However, employers should actually expect to see an increase in health-care claims after initial health assessments are done, as employees remedy newly identified problems.[22]

In Chapter 1, "Making HR Measurement Strategic," we noted that analytics relies on rigorous research designs and statistical analyses to draw proper conclusions from data. In Chapter 2, "Analytical Foundations of HR Measurement," we emphasized the need to use control groups that did not participate in a treatment (for example, education about healthy lifestyles) in the context of an experimental or quasi-experimental research design to rule out alternative explanations for results.

Unfortunately, many companies use no control groups when evaluating their WHP programs. Without a control group of nonparticipating employees, it is difficult to tell how much of the improved health is due to the WHP program and how much is due to popular trends (for example, the general fitness craze), changes in state or local health policies and regulations, and changes in medical insurance. Other potential methodological problems include biases due to self-selection (those at high risk are less likely to participate) and employees who drop out of a program. The resulting evaluations have little internal or external validity because they report results only for employees who voluntarily participate in and complete the program.

Researchers also need to address unit-of-analysis issues. Thus, if data is evaluated across worksites at the level of the individual employee, the effect of a WHP program tends to be overstated because the design ignores within-worksite variation. In practice, substantial differences have been found across different worksites receiving the same intervention.[23] Conversely, if the unit of analysis is the plant or worksite, a very large number of sites per intervention is necessary to achieve adequate statistical power to detect effects, if they exist (see Chapter 2 for more on statistical power).

It is advisable to commit to health promotion with a corresponding commitment to data collection. Without data, evaluation is impossible. In the accompanying sidebar, General

Motors provides a good example of harnessing analytics and the power of existing data to gain insights into the potential value of workplace health programs.

Analytics and WHP to Deal with Obesity at General Motors

In analyzing the records of its 1.1 million beneficiaries, GM found that 26 percent were obese under federal guidelines (a body weight that exceeds standard height and weight by 20 percent or more). "Morbid" obesity refers to a body weight more than 100 percent above the norm or more than 100 pounds over the optimal weight.[24] GM also discovered that obese employees cost the company between $1,000 and $3,000 more in health services per year, on average, than beneficiaries who are not obese. That suggests that obesity is costing GM at least $286 million per year.[25] At the level of the individual employee, a longitudinal study of the impact of obesity on worker health and productivity found that obesity was equivalent to adding 20 years of age. Workers in their mid-20s and 30s had work limitations and cardiovascular risk factors similar to those of normal-weight workers in their 40s and 50s.[26]

As a result of collective bargaining with the United Auto Workers in late 2007, GM changed the way it pays for health care among employees and retirees.[27] At the same time, it also is encouraging improved employees' health, such as by installing gymnasiums at manufacturing plants. Installing gymnasiums is supported by some analytical evidence. The World Health Organization reported that workplace physical-activity programs in the United States can reduce the use of short-term sick leave by 6 percent to 32 percent, reduce health-care costs by 20 percent to 55 percent, and increase productivity by 2 percent to 52 percent.[28]

Measures: Cost Effectiveness, Cost-Benefit, and Return-on-Investment Analysis

Typically, the evaluation of a WHP program relies on some form of cost-effectiveness, cost-benefit, or return-on-investment (ROI) analysis. We discussed these concepts in some detail in Chapter 2, and we apply them here.

Cost-Effectiveness Analysis

Cost-effectiveness (C/E) analysis identifies the cost of producing a unit of effect within a given program. To illustrate, suppose a worksite hypertension-control program incurs an annual cost of $50,000 for a 100-employee population. The average reduction in diastolic blood pressure per treated individual is 8 millimeters of mercury (mm/Hg). The C/E ratio is as follows:

$$\$50,000 / 100 \div 8 \text{ mm/Hg} = \$62.50 \text{ per mm/Hg reduction}$$

C/E analysis permits comparisons of alternative interventions designed to achieve the same goal. For example, the cost of $62.50 to reduce each mm/Hg achieved by the program could be compared to alternative programs to reduce diastolic blood pressure that are not offered at the worksite. Unfortunately, from a financial perspective, C/E analysis fails to address the issue of whether the program should have been offered in the first place. Cost-benefit analysis overcomes that problem.

Cost-Benefit and Return-on-Investment Analysis

Cost-benefit (C/B) analysis expresses benefits in monetary terms. One of the most popular forms of C/B analysis is ROI analysis (noted in Chapter 2).

Suppose that a WHP program costs a firm $250,000 during its first year of operation. The measured savings are $65,000 from reduced absenteeism, $110,000 from reduced employer health-care payments (assuming a self-funded plan), and $90,000 from reduced employee turnover. The ROI before interest and taxes is calculated as shown in Table 5-1.

Table 5-1   ROI of WHP Program

Benefit Type	Benefit Amount
Reduced absenteeism	$65,000
Reduced health-care payments	$110,000
Reduced employee turnover	$90,000
Total expected benefits	$265,000
ROI = Total expected benefit ÷ Program investment	
ROI = $265,000 ÷ $250,000 = 106%	

The preceding analysis is for a single time period. Data for future time periods (costs and benefits) should be discounted to the present. The numbers provided here are abstract, and firms need to pay careful attention to how they derive them. With respect to absenteeism, for example, savings need to be attributed directly to the WHP program. Employees might take fewer sick days in a given year, and the cost savings from those days not used may be attributed to decreases in employee absenteeism, but how does one know that the savings are due to the WHP program? The same is true for savings attributed to reduced health-care payments or reduced employee turnover. Measures are blind to the logic and rationale behind the numbers. This is where sound analytics and research design play an important role. To attribute changes in any of the outcomes of interest to a WHP program, a combination of methods may be necessary, such as employee survey data combined with focus groups and structured individual interviews.

Conclusions Regarding Cost-Effectiveness, Cost-Benefit, and ROI Analyses

Although the logic and techniques of C/E and C/B analysis (including ROI) appear straightforward, there are several unresolved issues, as noted in Chapter 2. Much subjectivity is involved in the choice of variables to include in these models, in attributing savings directly to a WHP program, in estimating the timing and duration of program effects, and in discounting the dollar value of costs and benefits that occur in future time periods. Because of this subjectivity, it is important to conduct sensitivity analyses (to examine the impact of variations in assumptions on C/E and C/B ratios) and break-even analysis (see Chapter 2) to identify the minimum levels of dependent variables (such as early cancer detection or savings in absenteeism) that will allow recovery of investments in the WHP program.

Solving the Analysis and Measurement Dilemmas to Improve Decisions about WHP Programs

To summarize, these analytical issues can affect decisions about WHP programs:

1. Managers have difficulty identifying the health-related costs that actually decreased.

2. Program sponsors use different methods to measure and report costs and benefits.

3. Program effects may vary depending on when they are measured (immediate versus lagged effects).

4. Program effects may vary depending on how long they are measured.

5. Few studies use control groups.

6. Potential biases exist as a result of self-selection and exclusion of dropouts.

7. Analysis at the level of the individual employee ignores within-site variation. However, analysis at the level of the worksite may produce low statistical power to detect effects.

8. Data on effectiveness is limited in the choice of variables, estimation of the economic value of indirect costs and benefits, estimation of the timing and duration of program effects, and estimation of the present values of future benefits.

A sound experimental design is one that allows cause-and-effect relationships to emerge. In this section, we present an evaluation strategy that includes a mix of features that are rarely gathered in actual evaluations but should serve as an ideal toward which organizations should aim. The strategy begins with a determination of the demographics of an organization (age, gender, race, and ethnicity), identification of high-risk employees, expected participation rates, and start-up and maintenance costs required to reach an organization's goals (such as reducing the incidence and costs of undetected cancerous conditions).

The next step is to develop a testing and tracking system to quantify the outcomes of the WHP program for both participants and nonparticipants. Individuals in these two groups should be matched as closely as possible in terms of characteristics such as gender, age, weight category, and lifestyle variables. Pre- and post-comparisons can be made for both groups in terms of behavioral changes, health-care costs, fitness level, absenteeism, turnover, injury rate and severity, productivity, and job satisfaction. Quantifiable variables (such as health-care costs and absenteeism) must be analyzed separately by demographic or socioeconomic cohort, for both participants and nonparticipants. Regression, path analysis, or meta-analysis can rule out alternative explanations for observed results. Finally, cost-benefit analyses must include present and future benefits, expressed in current dollar values.

Although a growing number of studies report favorable C/E or C/B results, it is difficult to evaluate and compare the studies because no widely accepted approach currently exists for estimating costs and benefits. Different authors use different assumptions in their estimates of WHP intervention costs and dollar benefits, and small changes in assumptions can have large effects on the interpretation of results. Meta-analyses (that is, quantitative cumulations of research results across studies) and single studies that are based on very large sample sizes can deal with many of these methodological difficulties.[29] Several such analyses have now been done for WHP programs, as the next section demonstrates.

Process: Communicating Effects to Decision Makers

In communicating the results of WHP programs, it may be helpful to begin by presenting some national-level statistics to serve as benchmarks against which to measure a firm's employees. Consider four broad categories of such data: chronic conditions, smoking, regular exercise, and lifestyle choices.

Chronic Conditions

A 2007 Milken Institute report, *An Unhealthy America*,[30] analyzed 2003 data (the most recent available) from the Medical Expenditure Panel Survey by the Agency for Healthcare Research and Quality. Their findings included the statement that more than half of all Americans suffer from one or more chronic diseases. Each year millions of people are diagnosed with chronic disease, and millions more die from their condition. Despite dramatic improvements in therapies and treatment, disease rates have risen dramatically. Diabetes has become a new national epidemic, and rapidly rising rates of obesity and cardiovascular disease threaten to cancel the gains we have made over the past decades. The study estimated that the total impact of these diseases on the U.S. economy is $1.3 trillion annually, including productivity losses of $1.1 trillion per year and $277 billion per year spent on treatment.

A 2007 study in the *Journal of Occupational and Environmental Medicine* found that costs of productivity loss were four times the cost of direct medical costs for a chronic condition.[31] This includes the cost of "presenteeism" (see Chapter 3), in which employees are present at work but are producing much less due to poor health or distractions.[32]

Figure 5-3 shows the estimated cost projections for several chronic conditions through the year 2023.

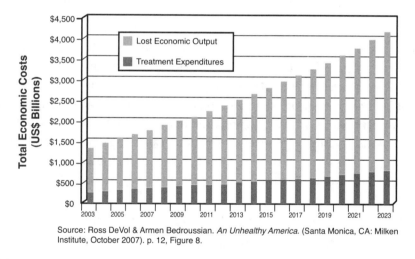

Source: Ross DeVol & Armen Bedroussian. *An Unhealthy America.* (Santa Monica, CA: Milken Institute, October 2007). p. 12, Figure 8.

Figure 5-3 Estimated treatment costs and lost economic output due to chronic conditions (2003–2023).

Milken Institute estimated that, with modest reductions in obesity and smoking, 27 percent of these costs might be avoided, amounting to trillions of dollars. Although these percentages may not apply to individual firms, this suggests that opportunities abound for reducing firms' health-care costs. Employees with chronic diseases such as asthma, diabetes, and congestive heart failure, all of which can be managed, account for 60 percent of the typical employer's total medical costs.[33] One report estimated that 4 percent of employees with serious health conditions account for almost half of their employers' annual healthcare spending.[34]

When you have presented this broad information as background, consider presenting a second, more focused set of information that relates more directly to ROI analyses of WHP programs in your own organization.

ROI Analyses of WHP Programs

The return for such programs has been reported at anywhere from $1.81 (Unum Life) to $6.15 (Coors) per dollar invested. Peer-reviewed evaluations and meta-analyses show that ROI is achieved through improved worker health, reduced benefit expense, and enhanced productivity.[35] A review of 72 articles concluded that health-promotion programs achieve an average ROI of $3.48 per $1 invested when considering health-care costs alone, $5.82 when considering absenteeism, and $4.30 when both health-care costs and absenteeism are considered.[36] In a separate investigation, researchers conducted a 38-month case study of 23,000 participants in Citibank N.A.'s health-management program. They reported that, within a two-year period, Citibank enjoyed an ROI of between $4.56 and $4.73.[37] A follow-up study found improvements in the risk profiles of participants, with the high-risk group improving more than the "usual-care" group as a result of more intensive programs.

Worksite health-promotion programs attempt to reduce the health risks of employees at high risk, while maintaining the health status of those at low risk. Using an 18-year data set comprised of 2 million current and former employees, University of Michigan researchers found that increases in costs when groups of employees moved from low risk to high risk were much greater than the decreases in cost when groups moved from high risk to low risk.[38] Programs designed to keep healthy people healthy will likely provide the greatest ROI.

In conclusion, when communicating results to decision makers in your firm, we recommend that you begin with some broad statistics on health care, move on to more focused results that relate to WHP, and finish with results from your own firm, rooted in strong inferences based on a research design such as the one shown in the preceding list. Chief financial officers (CFOs) may be a more receptive audience than one might think. Figure 5-4 shows the perceived percentage returns for each dollar spent improving workplace safety, among a sample of 231 corporate financial decision makers. Only 13 percent estimated returns at less than 100 percent, and 68.7 percent estimated returns between 100 percent and 300 percent. These results apply to investments in workplace safety, but they suggest that financial decision makers may be comfortable with estimated returns that are quite high compared to typical investments.

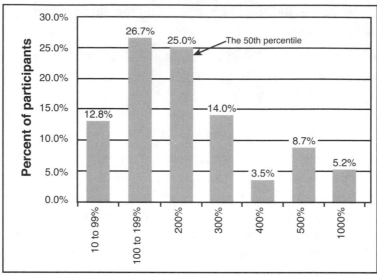

Adapted from Yueng-Hsiang Huang, Tom B. Leamon, Theodore K. Courtney, Sarah DeArmond, Peter Y. Chen, and Michael F. Blair, "Financial Decision Makers' Views on Safety," Professional Safety (April, 2009). www.asse.org.

Figure 5-4 Corporate financial officers' estimated returns to workplace safety investments.

Improving Employee Welfare at Work: Employee Assistance Programs (EAPs)

Whereas WHP programs focus on prevention, employee assistance programs (EAPs) focus on rehabilitation. An EAP is a system that provides confidential, professional care to employees whose job performance is or may become adversely affected by a variety of personal problems. Supervisors are taught to look for symptoms of declining work performance such as the following and then to refer employees to the EAP for professional help: predictable absenteeism patterns (for example, Mondays, Fridays, or days before or after holidays), unexcused or frequent absences, tardiness, and early departures; arguments with fellow employees; injuries caused to other employees through negligence, poor judgments and bad decisions; unusual on-the-job accidents; increased spoilage or broken equipment through negligence; involvement with the law; or a deteriorating personal appearance.[39]

The Logic of EAPs

Today 87 percent of employers with more than 1,000 employees and 51 percent of those with 50–99 employees offer EAPs.[40] Modern EAPs are comprehensive management tools that address behavioral risks in the workplace by extending professional counseling and medical services to all "troubled" employees. A troubled employee is an individual who is confronted by unresolved personal or work-related problems. Such problems run the gamut from alcoholism, drug abuse, and high stress to marital, family, and financial problems. Although some of these may originate "outside" the work context, they most certainly will have spillover effects to the work context.

An emerging application of EAPs for critical incident stress response (CISR) is for unexpected, life-threatening, and time-limited events that cause symptoms of post-traumatic stress syndrome. These might include the death of a child, attempted or actual physical assault, break-ins, or a suicide attempt or completed suicide of a patient or prisoner. A 2009 paper by Mark Attridge describes that a CISR program following bank robberies in Australia showed worker absence reduced by 60 percent, and medical benefits and workers' compensation costs reduced by 66 percent. CISR after raids at post office businesses reduced sickness and absence by 50 percent. CISR after traumatic incidents at an Australian prison reduced the costs of assisting stressed employees by 90 percent.[41] Indeed, the economic downturn produced a new sort of "critical incident," the experience of a job loss or impending financial hardship by the employee or a member of the family. Aetna Behavioral Health, part of Aetna Inc., a health insurer, saw a 60 percent increase in EAP program members seeking help in the third quarter of 2008 versus the same period in 2007, with financial stress the main source of the increase.[42]

Statistics such as these lead to one inescapable logical conclusion: The personal problems of troubled employees can have substantial negative economic impacts on employers. To help resolve those problems, many employers have adopted employee assistance programs.

Costs and Reported Benefits of EAPs

EAPs are either internal or external. An internal EAP is an in-house service staffed by company employees. An external EAP is a specialty-service provider hired by the employer; it may have multiple locations, to make it easy for clients to access. Such arrangements are especially convenient to small employers who do not have the resources to provide internal services. On the other hand, a comparison of the two models found that internal EAPs received 500 percent more referrals from supervisors and 300 percent more employee cases. Perhaps this is because most employees do not seek assistance on their own—they get help only when referred by their supervisors.[43] Costs of the two types of programs are similar: $21.83 per employee per year for internal programs and $18.09 for external programs.[44]

A large-scale review of the cost-effectiveness of EAPs concluded, "There is no published evidence that EAPs are harmful to corporate economies or to individual employees .... All of the published studies indicate that EAPs are cost-effective."[45] By offering assistance to troubled employees, the companies promote positive employee-relations climates, contribute to their employees' well-being, and enhance their ability to function productively at work, at home, and in the community.[46]

From a business perspective, well-run programs such as those at GM or ChevronTexaco seem to pay off, with benefit-cost ratios of 3:1, 5:1, or more. On the other hand, not all programs are equally effective, and anecdotal evidence of the effectiveness of EAPs abounds. Findings do not generalize across studies, however, unless the EAP is implemented in the same way. For example, as noted earlier, in some companies, counselors are available on-site. In other companies, it is possible to access an EAP counselor only through a toll-free telephone number. Evidence indicates that when counselors are available on-site instead of solely through a toll-free number, the programs are more effective.[47] Results of the programs will be more interpretable, to the extent that proper research designs and methods for collecting data are followed. This is the purpose of analytics in the LAMP model, and we consider it further in the next section.

Enhanced Analytical Considerations in EAPs

Actual results may not be quite as rosy as have been reported in the literature or the media. Evaluation may be ex-ante (estimates computed before implementation of an EAP) or ex-post (measurement of the costs and benefits of actual program operations and impacts after the fact). Evaluation may be expressed in qualitative terms or in quantitative terms.

If evaluation is expressed in quantitative terms, as many operating executives demand, two major issues must be considered. One is how to establish all program costs and benefits. To establish its costs, an EAP must incorporate an information system that can track factors such as insurance use, absenteeism, performance analysis, accidents, and attendance data. A second issue is how to express and translate the costs and benefits into monetary values. Benefits derived from an EAP may be very difficult to translate into economic terms. In addition, unless proper experimental controls are exercised, cause-effect relations between EAP involvement and one or more dependent variables may be difficult or impossible to identify. As a reminder, these ideas are summarized as follows:

- Identify all program costs and benefits.

- Express costs and benefits in economic terms.

- Demonstrate that implementation of the EAP has caused changes in outcomes of interest.

A Template for Measuring the Effects of EAPs

In the following sections, we present detailed methods for expressing the returns of EAPs in economic terms for four important outcomes: productivity, employee turnover, unemployment costs, and savings in supervisors' time. These are by no means exhaustive, but they illustrate high-quality analysis elements that are often feasible but overlooked in typical situations.

Productivity

The productivity losses associated with troubled employees can be staggering. Here is one method for determining the productivity cost (ex-ante) attributable to employees who abuse alcohol.[48] To use the method properly, compute the following formula separately for each age–gender cohort. Then sum the costs for all age–gender cohorts.

> Equation 1
>
> No. of workers in age–gender cohort in workforce
>
> × Proportion of workers in age–gender cohort with alcohol–abuse problems
>
> × Annual earnings
>
> × Productivity decrease attributable to alcohol
>
> = Cost of alcohol-related reduced productivity

Two key inputs to this formula might be difficult to acquire:

- The proportion of workers in each age–gender cohort with alcohol abuse problems

- The productivity decrease attributable to alcohol

Over all cohorts, however, national figures suggest that 5 percent to 10 percent of a typical workforce suffers from alcohol abuse,[49] and that the figure may be as high as 16 percent across all full-time employees.[50] In well-controlled studies, productivity losses attributable to alcohol abuse have ranged from 14 percent to 21 percent.[51] However, one researcher has estimated that personal problems overall affect 18 percent of the workforce, resulting in an overall productivity loss of 25 percent.[52] It is important to note that the latter figure is an estimate, not a precise number derived on the basis of controlled research. It is used in the calculations shown here simply for illustrative purposes. Keep this in mind in analyzing the example and in applying the formula to actual work situations.

For one age–gender cohort in any given workforce, inputs to Equation 1 might be as follows:

> 100 workers in age–gender cohort in workforce
>
> × 10 percent with alcohol abuse problems
>
> × Annual earnings of $45,000 per worker in cohort
>
> × 20 percent productivity decrease attributable to alcohol
>
> = Cost of alcohol-related reduced productivity of $90,000

At a more general level, the city of Phoenix developed the following formula through its Project Concern to determine the costs due to troubled employees, as well as (ex-ante) the amount of money that could be saved in terms of improved productivity through an EAP:[53]

> Equation 2
>
> Compute the average annual wage of employees by dividing the average total number of employees into the annual payroll for employees.
>
> Determine the proportion of the payroll for troubled employees. To do that, multiply the average annual wage by 18 percent of the total number of employees (average percentage of troubled employees identified across many studies).[54]
>
> Determine the present loss in productivity due to troubled employees. To do so, multiply the result of step 2 by 25 percent (average productivity loss across studies).[55]
>
> Identify the potential amount saved per year by an EAP. To do that, multiply the result of step 3 by 50 percent (actual success rate reported by Project Concern).

To illustrate, let us assume that a firm employs 100 workers, at an annual payroll cost of $4.5 million, or $45,000 per worker (step 1). To calculate the payroll for troubled employees, let us assume that 18 percent, or 18 workers, are troubled × $45,000 annual earnings/worker = $810,000 (step 2). To determine the present cost of reduced productivity for these troubled workers, multiply $810,000 × 25 percent = $202,500. Finally, to determine the potential amount of money that could be saved per year through an EAP, multiply $202,500 × 50 percent = $101,250.

Note that potential savings in this example reflect only the direct cost of labor (just one component of productivity). To the extent that such savings do not reflect the contribution of improved use of capital and equipment that can be realized by a fully productive employee, they will underestimate the actual level of savings the firm can realize.

Costs of Employee Turnover in EAPs

Turnover savings realized through the implementation of an EAP are "opportunity savings" (see Chapter 2) because they reflect costs that were not actually incurred.

In the hypothetical example that follows, let's assume that 10 percent of 2,500 employees (250) can be expected to quit each year. Assume further that of the 250 employees who are expected to quit, 20 percent of them (50 employees) use the firm's EAP. Of those 50, assume that 30 represent production employees, 10 are administrative/technical, and 10 are managerial. Based on the method for calculating the fully loaded cost of turnover that we described in Chapter 4, "The High Cost of Employee Separations," (that is, separation, replacement, and training costs), potential turnover costs may be stated as shown in Table 5-2.

Table 5-2 Potential Turnover Costs

	No. of People	No. Using EAP	Individual Cost	Total Cost
Production	150	30	$60,000	$1,800,000
Administrative/ technical	50	10	$82,500	$825,000
Managerial	50	10	$140,000	$1,400,000
Totals	**250**	**50**		**$4,025,000**

For those employees who use the company's EAP, assume that the actual number who terminate or quit after EAP involvement is as shown in Table 5-3, a 50 percent turnover reduction.

Table 5-3 Post-EAP Terminations

	No. of People	Individual Cost	Total Cost
Production	15	$60,000	$900,000
Administrative/ technical	5	$82,500	$412,500
Managerial	5	$140,000	$700,000
Totals	**25**		**$2,012,500**

Suppose as well that one result of EAP diagnosis is that some employees are hospitalized for their condition, at a cost of $295,600 per year. So, the overall cost of the EAP is the program budget of $400,000 plus the hospitalization of $295,600, or $695,600 per year.

To compute the ROI, use these numbers:

Turnover cost without EAP	$4,025,000
Turnover cost with EAP	$2,012,500
Net turnover cost benefit	$2,012,500
ROI ([benefit - cost]/cost)	$1,316,900 / $695,600
= 189 percent or $1.89 for every $1 invested	

Compiling this information year after year is particularly useful because numbers can be compared across years and trends can be identified.

Unemployment Compensation in EAPs

Assume in the preceding example that employees who quit draw unemployment compensation for an average of six weeks, at an average of 60 percent of full-time pay. If the firm's average hourly wage rate was $24 per hour in 2010, the savings in unemployment compensation would be $24 × 25 people × 40 hours/week × 6 weeks × .62 = $89,280. Obviously, this figure could be considerably larger if the hourly rate, the number of employees saved, or the duration of the unemployment compensation increased.

Savings in Supervisors' Time in EAPs

Continuing with our hypothetical example, if the EAP were not available, supervisors would be forced to deal with employee problems. The hours that supervisors save by not dealing with problems is equal to the total number of hours spent in counseling sessions for the 50 employees who took part in the firm's EAP. Assume that each employee received 20 hours of counseling, on average. Thus, the supervisors had at least 1,000 hours to carry out their duties more effectively. Assuming that the average cost of one hour of supervisory time (wages plus benefits and overhead costs) was $57.50 in 2010 dollars, the economic value of that time was $57.50 \times 1,000 = $57,500. Remember, as we cautioned in Chapter 2, the total pay of supervisors does not vary whether they are counseling troubled employees or not. The economic value of their time is simply a proxy, and an imperfect one at that, for the opportunity cost of the lost value that supervisors would have been creating if they had not been using their time to counsel troubled employees.

Future of Lifestyle Modification, WHP, and EAPs

Based on the research reviewed in this chapter, it is clear that WHP and EAP programs can yield significant payoffs to organizations that adopt them. However, it also is clear that the programs do not work under all circumstances and that the problems associated with assessing relative costs and benefits may be complex. At the very least, we need well-controlled, longitudinal studies to investigate program costs and benefits and the extent to which behavior changes are maintained over time. Moreover, the type and structure of programs should be evaluated for their success and impact on different populations of workers (older/younger; male/female; high, moderate, and low risk; racial or ethnic group), especially in light of the changes in the composition of the workforce that are taking place.[56] We need to understand the factors that affect employee participation or nonparticipation and the factors that promote long-term changes in behavior. If we then build these factors into lifestyle modification, WHP, and EAPs, and if we are successful in attracting troubled or at-risk employees into the programs, the programs will flourish, even in an era of limited resources.

Exercises

Software that calculates answers to one or more of the following exercises can be found at http://hrcosting.com/hr/.

1. Sobriety, Inc., a marketer of substance abuse programs, is concerned about the cost of alcohol abuse among its own employees. Based on the following data, what is the productivity cost associated with employees who abuse alcohol? Among all cohorts, the productivity decrease attributable to alcohol abuse is 20 percent.

Age–Gender Cohort	Number	Percentage with Alcohol Abuse Problems	Average Annual Earnings of Cohorts
Males, 25 and under	43	7%	$32,000
Males, 26–44	59	10%	$49,000
Males, 45 and over	38	5%	$64,000
Females, 25 and under	41	5%	$33,000
Females, 26–44	64	10%	$47,000
Females, 45 and over	34	7%	$61,000

2. The following data shows turnover costs for the 4,000 employees of Hulakon, Inc., for one year. In any given year, 12 percent of the employees can be expected to quit.

Employee Group	Number of Employees	Individual Cost of Employee Turnover
Production	250	$48,500
Clerical	175	$39,000
Management	55	$74,000

A total of 120 employees participate in the company's EAP (62 production employees, 44 clerical employees, and 14 managers). As a result of that involvement, the following numbers of employees actually quit.

Employee Group	Number of Employees
Production	31
Clerical	22
Management	7

Hospitalization costs comprise $189,000, or 56 percent of the total amount annually budgeted for the EAP. What is Hulakon's ROI for its employee assistance program for this one year?

3. Your firm is considering establishing an EAP, but it is unsure of which provider to select. Top management has asked you to assess the strengths and weaknesses of possible providers. Make a list of questions to ask each one.

References

1. Strassel, Kimberley A., "Mr. Burd Goes to Washington," *The Wall Street Journal*, June 19, 2009, A13.

2. Eric Kimbuende, Usha Ranji, Janet Lundy, & Alina Salganicoff (2010). *U.S. Healthcare Costs: Background Brief*. The Kaiser Family Foundation. March 2010. http://www.kaiseredu.org/topics_im.asp?imID=1&parentID=61&id=358#6b.

3. The Institute for the Future, "Health and Health Care 2010: The Forecast, The Challenge," (2nd ed.) 2003 page xxii. Princeton, NJ: Jossey-Bass. http://www.iftf.org/system/files/deliverables/SR-794_Health_%2526_Health_Care_2010.pdf.

4. M. P. O'Donnell, "Definition of health promotion: Part III: Expanding the definition," *American Journal of Health Promotion*, 1989, 3, 5.

5. Towers Watson press release, "Towers Perrin Health Care Cost Survey Shows Average Annual Per-Employee Cost of $9,660 in 2009—and the Health Care Affordability Gap Widens," September 24, 2008. www.towersperrin.com/tp/showdctmdoc.jsp?url=master_brand_2/usa/press_releases/2008/20080924/2008_09_24b.htm&country=global.

6. "Health Hazards," *BusinessWeek,* September 26, 2005, 13.

7. Johnson, Avery, "Firms Reducing Health Benefits, Surveys Find," *The Wall Street Journal,* September 26, 2009, A6

8. Yoest, Patrick, "Report Takes Aim at Rising Health-Insurance Premiums," *The Wall Street Journal Online,* February 18, 2010.

9. Weisser, C., and A. Gengler, "50 Ways to Cut Your Health Care Costs," *Money* (November 2006), 124–134.

10. Cascio, W. F., "The Costs—and Benefits—of Human Resources," in *International Review of Industrial and Organizational Psychology* 22, ed. G. P. Hodgkinson and J. K. Ford (Hoboken, NJ: John Wiley & Sons, 2007).

11. Aeppel, T., "Ill Will: Skyrocketing Health Costs Start to Pit Worker vs. Worker," *The Wall Street Journal* (June 17, 2003), A1, A6.

12. Sammer, Joanne, "Big Picture on Drug Benefits," *HR Magazine* 55, no. 3 (March 10, 2010), 33–36.

13. Miller, S., "More Favor Incentives to Change Employee Health Behavior," July 2006, at www.shrm.org/rewards/library_published/benefits/nonIC/CMS_017859.asp.

14. American Institute for Preventive Medicine, "The Health & Economic Implications of Worksite Wellness Programs," American Institute for Preventive Medicine. Farmington Hills, MI. 2008. Page 4. http://www.healthylife.com/template. asp?pageID=75.

15. Towers Watson, *2010 Health Care Cost Survey* (Stamford, Conn.: Towers-Watson, 2010). http://www.towerswatson.com/assets/pdf/1265/2010_HCCS.pdf.

16. C. Hirschman, "Off duty, out of work," *HRMagazine*, 48:2, February 2003, 50–56.

17. Aeppel, op. cit.

18. M. Safer, "Whose life is it anyway? Are employers' lifestyle policies discriminatory?," 60 Minutes, CBS Broadcasting, at www.cbsnews.com/ stories/2005/10/28/60minutes/main990617.shtml.

19. "Planning Wellness: Getting off to a Good Start," *Absolute Advantage*, 5:6, 2006, http://www.welcoa.org/freeresources/pdf/aa_v5.4.pdf.

20. Cascio, W. F., "Weight-Based Discrimination in Employment: Legal and Psychological Considerations," paper presented at the annual conference of the Society for Industrial and Organizational Psychology, Dallas, May 2006.

21. Tuna, Cari, "Wellness Efforts Face Hurdle," *The Wall Street Journal Online*, February 1, 2010.

22. Cascio, 2007.

23. R. E. Glasgow, J. R. Terborg, J. F. Hollis, H. H. Severson, and S. M. Boles, "Take heart: Results from the initial phase of a worksite wellness program," *American Journal of Public Health*, 85, 1995, 209–216. See also R. W. Jeffery, S. A. Forster, S. H. French, H. A. Kelder, H. A. Lando, D. R. McGovern, D. R. Jacobs, and J. E. Baxter, "The healthy worker project: A worksite intervention for weight control and smoking cessation," *American Journal of Public Health*, 83, 1993, 395–501.

24. Janus, P. A., "Weight Discrimination and the Law," 2002, at www.Lexis-Nexis. com.

25. Hawkins, L. Jr. "As GM Battles Surging Costs, Workers' Health Becomes an Issue," *The Wall Street Journal*, April 7, 2005, A1, A11.

26. Hertz, R. P., A. N. Unger, M. McDonald, M. B. Lustik, and J. Biddulph-Krentar, "The Impact of Obesity on Work Limitations and Cardiovascular Risk Factors in the U.S. Workforce," *Journal of Occupational and Environmental Medicine* 46, no. 12 (2004): 1,195–1,203.

27. The Automotive Lyceum, *2007 GM-UAW Labor Agreement*. Downloaded November 8, 2007 from www.christonium.com/automotive/ItemID=1193346768436.

28. World Health Organization, "Economic Benefits of Physical Activity," 2003, at www.who.int/hpr/physactiv/economic.benefits.shtml.

29. Schmidt, F. L., and N. S. Raju, "Updating Meta-analytic Research Findings: Bayesian Approaches Versus the Medical Model," *Journal of Applied Psychology* 92 (2007): 297–308. See also Hunter, J. S., and F. L. Schmidt, *Methods of Meta-Analysis: Correcting Error and Bias in Research Findings,* 2nd ed. (Thousand Oaks, Calif.: Sage, 2004).

30. DeVol, Ross, and Armen Bedroussian, *An Unhealthy America* (Santa Monica, Calif.: Milken Institute, October 2007).

31. Loeppke, R., et al., "Health and Productivity as a Business Strategy," *Journal of Occupational and Environmental Medicine* 49, no. 7 (2007): 712–721.

32. Sean Nicholson, Mark V. Pauly, Daniel Polsky, Claire Sharda, Helena Szrek, and Marc L. Berge "Measuring the Effects of Work Loss on Productivity with Team Production," *Health Economics* 15, no. 2 (2006): 111–123.

33. Britt, J., "Expert: Disease Management Programs Cut Health Care Costs," May 27, 2004, at www.shrm.org.

34. Lewis, Diane E., "Employers Focus on Chronic Ailments," *The Boston Globe* (May 4, 2006), B7. www.boston.com/business/healthcare/articles/2006/05/04/employers_focus_on_chronic_ailments/.

35. Britt, 2004.

36. Aldana, S. G., "Financial Impact of Health Promotion Programs: A Comprehensive Review of the Literature," *American Journal of Health Promotion* 15, no. 5 (2001): 295–320.

37. Ozminkowski, R. J., R. Z. Goetzel, M. W. Smith, R. I. Cantor, A. Shaughnessy, and M. Harrison, "The Impact of the Citibank N.A. Health Management Program on Changes in Employee Health Risks over Time," *Journal of Occupational and Environmental Medicine* 42, no. 5 (2000): 502–511.

38. Edington, D. W. "Emerging Research: A View from One Research Center," *American Journal of Health Promotion* 15, no. 5 (2001): 341–349.

39. N. R. Lockwood, "Employee assistance programs: An HR tool to address top issues in today's workplace," 2005, at www.shrm.org.

40. Galinsky, Ellen, James T. Bond, Kelly Sakai, Stacy S. Kim, and Nicole Guintoli, *2008 National Study of Employers* (New York: Families and Work Institute, 2008). See Table 13, p. 24. www.familiesandwork.org/site/research/reports/2008nse.pdf.

41. Attridge, Mark, *The Business Case for Workplace Critical Incident Stress Response: A Literature Review of Clinical and Cost-Effectiveness Research* (Crisis Care Network, June 30, 2009). www.crisiscare.com/news/news_wp_attridge.pdf.

42. Deaenlle, Conrad, "A Corporate Perk for a Stressful Time," *The New York Times,* January 18, 2009. www.nytimes.com/2009/01/18/jobs/.

43. S. Prochaska, "Employee assistance programs: What does HR need to know?" May 2003, at www.shrm.org.

44. U.S. Department of Health and Human Services, "Employee Assistance Programs: Fact Sheet," 2006, at http://workplace.samhsa.gov/WPResearch/EAP/FactsEAP final.html.

45. Blum, T., and P. Roman, *Cost-Effectiveness and Preventive Implications of Employee Assistance Programs* (Washington, D.C.: U. S. Department of Health and Human Services, 1995).

46. Stone, D. L., and D. A. Kotch, "Individuals' Attitudes Toward Organizational Drug Testing Policies and Practices," *Journal of Applied Psychology* 74 (1989): 518–521.

47. Collins, K. R., "Identifying and Treating Employee Substance Abuse Problems," January 2003, at www.shrm.org.

48. Parker, D. L., J. M. Shultz, L. Gertz, R. Berkelman, and P. L. Remington, "The Social and Economic Costs of Alcohol Abuse in Minnesota, 1983," *American Journal of Public Health* 77 (1987): 982–986.

49. N. R. Lockwood, "Employee assistance programs: An HR tool to address top issues in today's workplace," 2005, at www.shrm.org.

50. National Institute of Alcohol Abuse and Alcoholism, 2006, at www.niaaa.nih.gov/.

51. Parker et al., 1987.

52. Masi, D., *Designing Employee Assistance Programs* (New York: American Management Association, 1984).

53. Wagner, W. G., "Assisting Employees with Personal Problems," Alexandria, Va.: Personnel Administrator Reprint Collection Series, Employee Assistance Programs, 1984.

54. Masi, 1984.

55. Masi, 1984.

56. Lawler, E. E., and J. O'Toole, *The New American Workplace* (New York: Palgrave Macmillan, 2006).

6

Employee Attitudes and Engagement

Every year, *Fortune* magazine conducts an annual survey of the "100 Best Companies to Work For." Firms strive to be named to this list because they receive twice as many applications as firms that are not on the list, and they enjoy employee turnover levels that are less than half those of their competitors.[1] In short, people want to work at places where they are treated well. If satisfied employees really do fuel corporate profits, one would expect "100 Best" employers to outperform broad indexes of firms that are publicly traded—and they do.[2]

In one well-controlled study, for example, researchers compared the organizational performance of *Fortune's* "100 Best Companies to Work For" with two sets of other companies, a matched group and the broad market of publicly traded firms, over a six-year period.[3] They found that organization-level employee attitudes of the "100-Best" firms were both highly positive and stable over time. They also found that the return on assets and market-to-book value of the equity of publicly traded companies included on the "100 Best" list were generally better than those of a matched comparison group. That finding established an important link between employee attitudes and organization-level financial performance.

As for stock returns, the same study found that the "100 Best" companies outperformed the broad market when considering cumulative (longer-term) returns (82 percent versus 37 percent from 1998 to 2000), although not consistently for annual returns. The authors concluded: "At the very least, our study finds no evidence that positive employee relations comes at the expense of financial performance. Firms can have both."[4] Similar results have been reported in the accounting and finance literature.[5]

Of course, finding a correlation between financial performance and employee attitudes does not mean that enhancing employee attitudes *caused* the superior financial performance of the organizations in the study. Chapter 2, "Analytical Foundations of HR Measurement," showed that correlation is not the same as causation. For example, people like to work for companies that are financially successful. It is just as plausible that when companies become financially successful, their employees display positive attitudes. This is, in fact, the case for people whose jobs are a "central life interest."[6] For an investor, the link between employee attitudes and financial performance of the firm is a valuable signal, and the direction of causality is irrelevant. From a manager's perspective, however, "what causes what" is extremely important because it affects decisions about talent.

Given the positive financial results cited earlier for "100 Best" companies, it is perhaps not very surprising that measuring attitudes such as satisfaction, engagement, and commitment has become big business. There are many consulting products and internal organizational processes to define and track employee attitudes and to relate those attitudes to a variety of operational and financial results. Yet the working models of most business leaders are often no more sophisticated than a belief that "happy employees are productive employees" or that "becoming a great place to work will create superior financial results." Of course, a valuable logic and measurement system would do better, by articulating the connections between attitudes and organizational outcomes and directing measures to the areas that best articulate those connections.

Measures, often in the form of employee surveys, are valuable to the extent that they lead to actions or decisions designed to improve organizational effectiveness and to promote long-term, relevant change.[7] This chapter presents frameworks that HR and business leaders can use to collect and interpret relevant measures to make better decisions about programs to improve employee attitudes, even if the decision is not to invest in them. Such systems can certainly identify where attitude-assessment or employee-engagement programs are valuable. Our purpose, however, is not simply to provide tools to sell such investments, but to enhance decisions about employee attitudes.

Attitudes Include Satisfaction, Commitment, and Engagement

Attitudes are internal states that are focused on particular aspects of or objects in the environment. They include three elements: cognition, the knowledge an individual has about the focal object or employment aspect; the emotion an individual feels toward the object or aspect; and an action tendency, a readiness to respond in a predetermined manner to the object or aspect.

One reason that it is important to have a clear and logical framework for understanding how attitudes connect to organizational success is that attitudes are often multidimensional. Thus, job satisfaction is a multidimensional attitude. In its 2009 survey of employees from small, medium, and large companies in a wide range of industries, the Society for Human Resource Management found that the top five drivers of job satisfaction were job security, benefits, compensation/pay, opportunities to use skills and abilities, and a safe feeling in the work environment.[8]

Job satisfaction is related to, but not identical with, employee engagement. Job satisfaction connotes a state of satiation; it is an outcome. Engagement connotes activation—feelings of energy, enthusiasm, and a positive affective state.[9] Although conceptually distinct, the two are highly correlated.[10]

Likewise, organizational commitment is a bond or linking of an individual to the organization that makes it difficult to leave.[11] It is the emotional engagement that people feel toward a firm.[12] Commitment can be to the job or the organization and can take the form of a commitment to contribute, to stay, or both.

Commitment is closely related to the concept of employee engagement.[13] Engagement is a positive, fulfilling, work-related state of mind that is characterized by vigor, dedication, and absorption.[14] Vigor refers to high levels of energy and mental resilience while working, the willingness to invest effort in one's work, and persistence even in the face of difficulties. Dedication is characterized by a sense of significance, enthusiasm, inspiration, pride, and challenge at work. Absorption consists of being so fully concentrated, happy, and deeply engrossed in one's work that time passes quickly and one has difficulty detaching oneself from work.[15] Engagement fuels discretionary efforts and concern for quality. It is what prompts employees to identify with the success of their companies, to recommend them to others as good places to work, and to follow through to make sure problems get identified and solved.

Satisfaction, Commitment, and Engagement as Job Outcomes

The 2008 National Study of the Changing Workforce was based on survey responses from 2,769 wage and salaried employees.[16] That study identified six dimensions of effective workplaces that include both work and nonwork factors: job challenge and learning, autonomy, supervisor task support, climate of respect and trust, work-life fit, and economic security. The researchers found that greater overall workplace effectiveness, a summary index that includes all six criteria, was strongly related to three important work outcomes: greater engagement ($R^2 = .473$), job satisfaction ($R^2 = .466$), and desire to stay with the organization ($R^2 = .187$). At the same time, however, each outcome related somewhat differently to the six criteria, as shown in Table 6-1.

Table 6-1 Effective Workplace Dimensions That Significantly Predicted Work Outcomes, Rank-Ordered by Relative Importance

Greater Engagement	Greater Job Satisfaction	Greater Probability of Retention
1. Job challenge and learning	1. Economic security	1. Economic security
2. Climate of respect	2. Work-life fit	2. Work-life fit
3. Autonomy	3. Climate of respect	3. Job challenge and learning
4. Work-life fit	4. Autonomy	4. Supervisor task support
5. Economic security	5. Supervisor task support	5. Autonomy
6. Supervisor task support	6. Job challenge and learning	

Source: Aumann, K., and E. Galinsky, Families and Work Institute, 2008 National Study of the Changing Workforce. *The State of Health in the American Workforce: Does Having an Effective Workplace Matter?* (New York: Families and Work Institute, 2009).

Note, for example, that although job challenge and learning is the most important predictor of engagement, relative to the other effective workplace dimensions, it is the sixth-best predictor of job satisfaction and the third-best predictor of intent to stay. Whereas work-life fit and economic security rank fourth and fifth in the prediction of engagement, they are the two top predictors of job satisfaction and intent to stay, with economic security the best predictor of both.

The Logic Connecting Employee Attitudes, Behaviors, and Financial Outcomes

At a more general level, employee satisfaction, commitment, and engagement affect organizational performance through employee behaviors. Employees with lower attitudes may be absent, may be late for work, may quit more often, or may place less emphasis on customer satisfaction than those with more positive attitudes. Evidence indicates that this is often the case.[17] Figure 6-1 shows these ideas graphically.

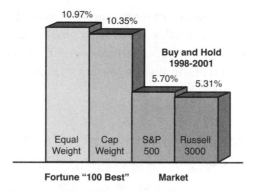

10.97% 10.35%

**Buy and Hold
1998-2001**

5.70% 5.31%

| Equal Weight | Cap Weight | S&P 500 | Russell 3000 |

Fortune "100 Best"   **Market**

Source: Frank Russell & Company, Fortune Magazine, 2002.

Figure 6-1 Logical relationships among employee attitudes, behaviors, and financial outcomes.

Figure 6-1 shows that enhancing employee attitudes can affect a firm's financial performance. Changing employee attitudes can have direct effects on employee turnover and absence, with the associated effects on the costs of absence and turnover (see Chapters 3, "The Hidden Costs of Absenteeism," and 4, "The High Cost of Employee Separations"). Having a reputation as a satisfying place to work may enhance the ability to recruit more or higher-quality applicants (see Chapters 8, "Staffing Utility: The Concept and Its Measurement," and 10, "The Payoff from Enhanced Selection"). In addition, some evidence suggests that employee attitudes directly affect employee performance, particularly the tendency for employees to do tasks that are beyond their formal job descriptions (often called "citizenship behaviors") and to convey positive emotions to customers. These latter connections show up in productivity or service costs and in sales and revenue levels (see Chapter 9, "The Economic Value of Job Performance").

It is also important to note that the relationships shown in Figure 6-1 vary depending on the nature of the talent pool and the work. For jobs whose contributions depend significantly on interacting with customers and conveying positive emotions, the effects of attitudes on service performance may be paramount. For jobs that seldom encounter a customer, but in which teamwork and cooperation are key, citizenship behaviors may be the vital connection. For jobs in which the costs of absence and turnover are very significant, the effects of attitudes on these behaviors may be the vital measurement question. Just as with all measurement, employee attitudes have different effects depending on what elements of employee behaviors are pivotal.

Of course, employee attitudes also relate to important outcomes that are less tangible or measurable by traditional financial systems, including individual growth and well-being, organizational adaptability, and goodwill. Many organizations measure employee attitudes not only because they provide leading indicators of tangible financial performance, but because they are a signal about more subtle nonfinancial results. In other words, they see improving employee attitudes as a worthy goal in and of itself. We recognize the nonfinancial outcomes of employee attitudes and their independent value as an organizational goal, but we focus in this chapter on the connections between financial outcomes and employee attitudes.

Employee Engagement and Competitive Advantage

It is important to note that engagement behaviors operate at the individual, team, and organizational levels.[18] From the perspective of competitive advantage, the aggregate level of employee engagement matters, for that affects work-unit performance as well as overall organizational performance. As Macey and Schneider (2008b) noted, "The unit manager responsible for a work group of 10 frontline employees thinks very differently about the meaning of 8 out of 10 people being engaged than does a division manager who thinks about 8,000 out of 10,000." These proportions have very different implications for the kinds of interventions the respective managers think about and the likely consequences of their change efforts.

At the level of the work unit, performance improves when highly engaged team members devote extra effort to innovation, cooperate with each other, and effectively adapt to change.[19] Having an engaged employee base can facilitate adaptation to change, which is essential to innovation, continuous improvement, and competitiveness.[20] If one aggregates these kinds of behaviors from highly engaged employees across work units of the organization, this should lead to the kinds of outcomes that speak directly to competitive advantage: improvements in customer satisfaction, profitability, and shareholder value.[21] These are the kinds of outcomes that managers and investors care about. Figure 6-2 shows graphically some relationships among individual, work-unit, and organizational levels of engagement and financial outcomes that produce competitive advantage.

Our next section describes a study that empirically linked high levels of employee engagement to improvements in service climate, customer loyalty, and financial outcomes.

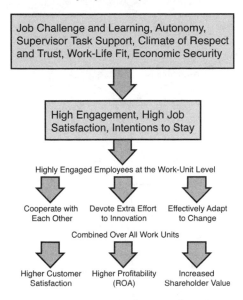

Figure 6-2 Logical relationships among behavioral indicators of employee engagement at the individual and work-unit levels, and, when aggregated at the organizational level, how engagement relates to competitive advantage.

Employee Engagement and Service Climate

A well-controlled field study suggests that employee engagement promotes a positive service climate (shared perceptions of practices and behaviors that are expected and rewarded with regard to customer service)[22] and customer loyalty.[23] The researchers selected a sample of three employees and ten customers from each of 120 hotel and restaurant work units. They demonstrated that organizational resources (for example, training, supervisor support, performance feedback) and employee engagement predict service climate, which, in turn, predicts employee performance and then customer loyalty.

Loyal customers, in turn, tend to do two things:

- Recommend the organization to others

- Generate repeat business

Both of these have been shown to lead to changes in revenue growth, lagged about one fiscal quarter.[24] Figure 6-3 illustrates graphically these logical connections.

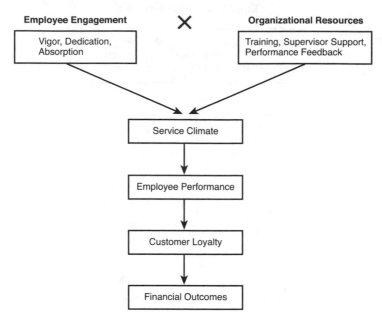

Figure 6-3 Logical connections among employee engagement, employee performance, customer loyalty, and financial outcomes.

Note in the figure that the relationship between employee engagement and organizational resources is multiplicative, not additive. That is, it is represented as employee engagement *times* organizational resources, not *plus* organizational resources, because if either of those is low or, in theory, zero, the other element cannot compensate enough to affect service climate and the remaining elements of the model in a positive manner.

At a broader level, the Corporate Leadership Council found that every 10 percent improvement in commitment can increase an employee's level of discretionary effort by 6 percent and performance by 2 percent, and that highly committed employees perform at a 20 percent higher level than noncommitted employees. Another study by Hewitt Associates reported that double-digit growth companies have 39 percent more highly engaged employees and 45 percent fewer highly disengaged employees than single-digit growth companies.[25] These studies provide very useful examples that connect employee attitude measures to intermediate processes, and ultimately to customer behaviors and financial results.

Still, these results do not allow us to say "what causes what." Although employee engagement may cause double-digit financial growth in companies, it is equally plausible that double-digit-growth companies are fun, exciting places to work, and, as a result, employees are highly engaged. Academic researchers, consulting firms, and the in-house research departments of large companies conduct studies like these regularly, and their findings are often extracted in media reports. To be better consumers of measures and correlations between attitudes and financial performance, it is important that readers be aware of key qualifications and limitations of study findings. The next sections of the chapter present a summary of common ways to measure attitudes and then introduce some analytical principles that help ensure that the conclusions from the data are valid.

Measures of Employee Attitudes

Measures of employee attitudes are fairly well developed.[26] Job satisfaction is a multidimensional attitude. We can assess how satisfied someone is with a job as a whole (the global feeling about the job) by asking, for example, "Overall, how much enjoyment do you find in your work?" Alternatively, we might assess and sum up satisfaction with facets of the job, such as satisfaction with pay, colleagues, the nature of the work, and supervision. If the purpose is to understand the overall effect of jobs, global ratings are the best choice. If the assessor wants to know how to improve job satisfaction in a particular situation, the facet approach is more diagnostic.[27]

Organizational commitment is also a multidimensional attitude with three distinct components. Affective commitment refers to an employee's emotional attachment to an organization and a desire to stay. Continuance commitment refers to the extent to which an employee believes that leaving would be costly. Normative commitment refers to an employee's feelings that staying with the current organization is the right thing to do.[28] There are well-developed measures of each of these components of commitment. For example, here is an item from the Organizational Commitment Questionnaire, a measure of affective commitment: "It would take a lot to get me to leave this organization."[29]

We noted earlier that employee engagement is closely related to job satisfaction and commitment, for it is a positive, fulfilling, work-related state of mind characterized by vigor, dedication, and absorption. Two well-known measures of engagement are the Gallup Organization's Q12 and the Utrecht Work Engagement Scale 9. The Q12 assesses 12 employee perceptions of work characteristics and people-related management practices (measures of employee satisfaction-engagement) that play a large role in triggering a profitable, productive workplace. Employees respond on a 1–5 Likert-type scale, where 5 is Extremely Satisfied and 1 is Extremely Dissatisfied. Consider three sample items:[30]

- I know what is expected of me at work.

- In the last six months, someone at work has talked to me about my progress.

- The mission/purpose of my company makes me feel that my job is important.

Each item is a causal contributor to engagement, and the composite or sum of the items is said to measure engagement through the measurement of its causes. Likewise, each item is actionable and generalizably related to important business outcomes,[31] as we describe in a later section.

The Utrecht Work Engagement Scale 9 (UWES-9)[32] is a nine-item measure of vigor, dedication, and absorption. Because the three factors are highly intercorrelated (above 0.8), it is probably best to use the total score from the UWES-9 as a measure of engagement at work. In responding to each item, employees indicate how often they feel this way about their jobs, from Never (0) to Always (6). Here are the nine items:

1. At my work, I feel bursting with energy.

2. At my job, I feel strong and vigorous.

3. When I get up in the morning, I feel like going to work.

4. I find the work that I do full of meaning and purpose.

5. I am enthusiastic about my job.

6. My job inspires me.

7. Time flies when I am working.

8. When I am working, I forget everything else around me.

9. I feel happy when I am working intensely.

Before adopting any particular measure, it is important to consider the logical relationships you want to examine. The descriptions in this section can help you make better choices. Broad, global measures of job satisfaction or commitment may be appropriate for examining general employee attitudes, but it may often be appropriate to choose measures that focus on particular work facets that more clearly distinguish the elements of satisfaction, commitment, or engagement. Too often organizations adopt the most popular or well-known measure, without realizing that decades of research have produced many alternatives.

Analytical Principles: Time Lags, Levels of Analysis, and Causal Ordering

The following sections address three important issues that can help illuminate attitude-behavior relationships: appropriate intervals of time to assess these relationships; individual and organizational levels of analysis; and causal relationships between attitudes and important organizational outcomes.

Time Lags

Unfortunately, the research literature produces no consensus about what the most appropriate time lag might be for collecting relevant information either on the same variable measured at two different times (for example, attitudes of employees about their supervisors) or when attempting to assess the relationship between two or more variables (for example, aggregated employee attitudes and organizational performance). Indeed, organizational performance may even drop a bit immediately following the implementation of a change in management practices, as the organization adapts.[33] At the very least, such relationships must be relatively stable. Stability is important because if a variable is not stable over time, it cannot be predicted reliably by another variable. Hence, if lagged analyses are the major focus of interest, the stability of those lags is important.

As an example of how different time lags can produce different results, consider the results of a longitudinal study.[34] The researchers analyzed employee attitude data from 35 companies over eight years at the organizational level of analysis relative to financial (return on assets) and market performance (earnings per share) using a variety of lagged analyses. They found consistent and significant positive relationships over various time lags between aggregated attitudes about satisfaction with security, pay, and overall job satisfaction (OJS) and financial and market performance.

The same researchers also examined one-year, two-year, three-year, and four-year lags. They found remarkable stability in employee attitudinal data at the organizational level of analysis. The one-year lags ranged from a low of 0.66 (satisfaction with work group) to a high of 0.89 (satisfaction with security). Even the four-year lags revealed substantial stability, ranging from a low of 0.40 (satisfaction with work facilitation) to a high of 0.78 (satisfaction with empowerment).

With respect to financial indicators, return on investment (ROI), return on equity (ROE), return on assets (ROA), and earnings per share (EPS) were significantly correlated across time. Median correlations were 0.57 (ROI-ROE), 0.73 (ROE-ROA), 0.94 (ROI-ROA), 0.38 (ROI-EPS), 0.48 (ROE-EPS), and 0.33 (ROA-EPS). However, they were differentially stable over time, with ROI being the least stable (median one-year lag $r = 0.47$) and ROA being the most stable (median one-year lag $r = 0.74$). Based on these results, the researchers used ROA as the most stable indicator of organizational financial performance. They used EPS as an indicator of market performance, although it was not as stable as ROA (median one-year lag $r = 0.49$).

These results show that both attitude measures and organizational performance measures may vary in their stability over different time spans. If possible, it is wise to collect data on attitudes and organizational outcomes (behavioral or financial) at multiple time periods and choose the interval that yields the most stable and representative relationships. It is also useful to consider the logical connections and strategic decision factors in choosing time lags. In organizations with stable and long-term employment relationships, the relationship between attitudes and financial outcomes spanning several years may be quite relevant and valuable, because such organizations would reap the rewards of attitude change over many years. In organizations where employee tenure or time in a job is less, the relevant strategic issue may be the effect of attitudes on outcomes that occur much sooner.

Levels of Analysis

Studies of the relationship between employee attitudes and customer satisfaction or turnover, using cross-lagged correlational analyses (that is, correlations between employee attitudes and customer satisfaction or turnover, computed at different times) have been inconclusive regarding the direction of causality, as noted previously.[35] Still, such studies provide tantalizing evidence that the collective employee attitudes of the organization or business unit may be correlated with overall performance of that organizational or business unit, even if, for particular individuals, the attitudes are only weakly correlated with individual-level performance. For example, we noted that the Gallup Organization identified 12 worker beliefs (measures of employee satisfaction-engagement) that relate most closely to workplace profits and productivity.[36] Its multiyear study was based on an analysis of data from more than 100,000 employees in 12 industries.

A subsequent meta-analysis (see Chapter 2) included data from almost 8,000 business units in 36 companies.[37] The results showed a consistent, reliable relationship between the level of the 12 beliefs among employees and unit-level outcomes such as profits, productivity, employee retention, and customer loyalty. At the level of the work group, groups that demonstrated positive attitudes were 50 percent more likely to achieve above-average customer loyalty and 44 percent more likely to have above-average profitability.

At the level of the business unit (division, plant, and so on), those in the top quartile on employee engagement had, on average, from $98,000 to $146,000 higher monthly revenues or sales (in 2010 dollars) than those in the bottom quartile. A $98,000 monthly difference translates into more than $1 million ($1,176,000) per year. Interestingly, researchers found significant variances among work groups or operating units within the same company, suggesting that even companies that do well overall may have significant opportunities to improve individual business units.

In a 2009 study of 50 multinational companies by the London office of Towers Watson, those with high levels of employee engagement outperformed those with low levels

---

on three important financial indicators: 12-month change in operating income (19.2 percent versus –32.7 percent), 12-month net income growth rate (13.7 percent versus –3.8 percent), and 12-month earnings per share growth rate (27.8 percent versus –11.2 percent).[38]

Understanding how the connections between attitudes and organizational outcomes vary depending on the unit of analysis is important. Again, one implication is that organizations should not presume that the whole story is in the relationships between individual employee attitudes and their behaviors. It appears that even when relationships at the individual level are weak, there may still be strong relationships when the aggregated attitudes of employees are related to aggregate performance at the work group or business unit level. Choosing the appropriate level of analysis is a matter both of the power of the statistical test and of the strategic question at hand. In most organizations, fundamental strategic issues involve business unit or work-group performance (for example, store sales, customer satisfaction, ROI), and interventions typically take place at the level of the unit, not at the level of the individual employee.[39] Thus, results suggesting that relationships may be more powerful or stable at this level of analysis are encouraging.

Causal Ordering

Based on meta-analysis, described earlier, the authors concluded that the causal order runs from employee attitudes to organizational performance, although they recognized that multidirectional (reciprocal) relationships might also be expected. In the earlier section on time lags, we cited a study that included longitudinal data from 35 companies on employee attitudes and longitudinal data from the same companies on organizational financial and market performance (eight years of data).[40] Using both of these sets of data, the researchers were able to explore questions involving causal ordering and time lags among the two sets of variables.

Their analyses revealed statistically significant and stable relationships across various time lags for three of seven attitude scales. Overall job satisfaction and satisfaction with security were predicted by ROA and EPS more strongly than the reverse, although some of the reverse relationships were also significant. Satisfaction with pay exhibited a more reciprocal relationship with ROA and EPS. Based on these results, it is clear that relationships among employee attitudinal variables and organizational performance are complex and may be multidirectional or reciprocal in nature. Researchers can therefore be misled if they simply assume, on the basis of cross-sectional data, that employee attitudes predict organizational financial or market performance, but not vice versa, and if they do not allow for the possibility of reciprocal relationships. To avoid this trap, researchers must collect employee attitude data and organizational performance data longitudinally, at multiple points in time. Doing so allows researchers to test forward and backward lags and to draw meaningful inferences about causal priorities.

The remainder of this chapter shows how financial and attitudinal measures can be synthesized to produce an estimate in dollars of the costs and benefits of human resource management programs designed to improve employee attitudes. We begin with the behavior-costing approach to attitude valuation and then illustrate its application at SYSCO Corporation.

Estimating the Financial Impact of Employee Attitudes: The Behavior-Costing Approach

The behavior-costing approach to employee attitude valuation is based on the assumption that measures of attitudes are indicators of subsequent employee behaviors.[41] These behaviors can be assessed using cost-accounting procedures, and they have economic implications for organizations. The conceptual framework underlying behavior costing stems from psychological theories that emphasize that employees' behavior at work is the result of choices about whether to appear at the workplace ("participation membership"),[42] and of choices about how to behave at work ("work strategies").[43] This framework assumes that employees will be more likely to come to work than be absent or quit if they are satisfied with their jobs. In addition, they are likely to exert more effort and to choose more effective job performance strategies if they expect to be rewarded, either intrinsically or extrinsically, for their efforts.[44]

These ideas suggest that attitudinal indexes of employee satisfaction and engagement should be the best predictors of participation membership, because they reflect perceptions of the rewards associated with being at work, They also suggest that attitudinal indexes of employee motivation should predict job performance, because they reflect some of the performance outcomes contingent on doing a good job: competence, achievement, and self-realization.

Behavior Costing at SYSCO: The Value-Profit Chain

SYSCO, the largest food marketer and distributor in North America, illustrates the behavior-costing approach nicely. It began with a logical framework that describes how SYSCO creates value from its human capital. The framework is based on a service-profit-chain model developed earlier.[45] That new model included a more descriptive explanation of the process of creating customer value, with a broader range than the service sector, per se. Figure 6-4 shows SYSCO's model.

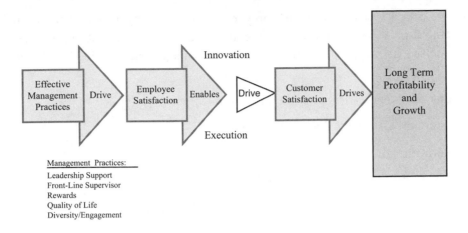

Source: *HR in Alignment: The Link to Business Results* (2004). Alexandria, VA: Society for Human Resource Management Foundation.

Figure 6-4 SYSCO's value-profit chain.

Logic: The Causal Model

As Figure 6-4 shows, effective management practices drive employee satisfaction (and engagement). A satisfied and engaged workforce, in turn, enables a company to pursue excellence in innovation and execution. The logical proposition is that higher employee satisfaction-engagement drives innovation and execution, which, in turn, enhances customer satisfaction, customer purchasing behavior, and, eventually, long-term profitability and growth. Certainly, management needs to put in place systems, people, technology, and processes that will initiate and sustain innovation and execution—the principal components of an effective value-profit chain. Technology and processes are easily copied by competitors, but a highly skilled, committed, and fully engaged workforce is difficult to imitate.

Analytics: Connecting the Model to Management Behaviors

SYSCO's basic management model—the set of practices that describe how the company seeks to engage the hearts and minds of employees with its employer brand—has been termed the 5-STAR management model.[46] That model is all about taking care of people, extending the same respect to employees as managers do to their external customers.

The framework is general enough to apply to any type of company structure or business model, and it gives businesses wide discretion in actual implementation. As Figure 6-4 shows, the five principles of the STAR model ("Management Practices" in Figure 6-4) are as follows:

- Ensuring that leaders offer direction and support
- Strengthening front-line supervisors
- Rewarding performance
- Addressing employees' quality of life
- Including employees by engaging them and leveraging diversity

Although specific leadership and management practices that address each of the 5-STAR principles are beyond the scope of this chapter, we want to emphasize that employee attitudes are integral components of the STAR model because, as a set, those attitudes reflect employee satisfaction-engagement, a key component of the value-profit chain. At a broader level, Figure 6-4 shows how SYSCO creates value from its human capital. It shows clearly the intermediate linkages between employee attitudes and financial performance. Indeed, the logic of the model is so compelling that it is taught to every manager and employee from the first day on the job.

Measures

To measure the attitudes of its employees, SYSCO developed a work climate/employee engagement survey built around each of the 5-STAR principles. All members of each SYSCO operating company participate in a comprehensive annual self-assessment and impromptu and informal assessments on an as-needed basis.[47] The total survey comprises 61 items, but SYSCO found that just 14 of them differentiated the top-performing 25 percent of its 147 operating companies from the bottom 25 percent. Table 6-2 shows these items.

Table 6-2 The 14 Most "Impactful" Items from SYSCO's Work Climate/Employee Engagement Survey

5-STAR Principle	Work Climate Survey Item
Leadership support	I know what is expected of me at work.
	Upper management spends time talking with employees about our business direction.
Front-line supervisor	My supervisor treats me with dignity and respect.
	My supervisor and I review my top goals and discuss how they contribute to the company's success.
	I have received constructive feedback on my performance within the last six months.
	My supervisor removes obstacles so I can do my job better.
Quality of life	I trust what the company tells me.
	Different departments of our company work together to get the job done.
Rewards	My pay is the same as or better than other companies in our market.
	Doing my job well leads to monetary rewards.
	Decisions made about promotions or job changes within this organization are fair.
Engagement/diversity	I am willing to work harder to make this company succeed.
	I am proud to work for SYSCO.

Source: Carrig, K., and P. M. Wright, *Building Profit Through Building People* (Alexandria, Va.: Society for Human Resource Management Foundation, 2006).

Consider just one of the items in Table 6-2, under "Front-line supervisor," item #4: "My supervisor removes obstacles so I can do my job better." A multiyear study of hundreds of knowledge workers in a variety of industries that tracked their day-to-day activities, emotions, and motivations through 120,000 journal entries strongly supports this driver of engagement. The study found that "workers reported feeling most engaged on days when they made headway or received support to overcome obstacles in their jobs."[48] They reported feeling least engaged when they hit brick walls. In short, small dents in work meant as much as large achievements.

Analytics Combined with Process: The SYSCO Web Portal for Managers

SYSCO has a decentralized organizational structure comprised of 147 autonomous operating companies. It employs an organization-wide rewards system to encourage managers of the autonomous operating companies to share information with each other and to transfer best practices within the organization. SYSCO built a "best business practices" web portal on its intranet to provide a platform for organization-wide improvement. The web architecture offered a framework for managers to do two things: share information on their own operating company's successful practices and learn from the best practices of other SYSCO operating companies.

SYSCO also assesses the performance of each operating company in terms of balanced-scorecard metrics in four areas: financial, operational, human capital, and customer performance. Scores on the work climate/employee engagement survey comprise one element of the human capital metrics, along with measures of productivity (employees per 100,000 cases shipped) and employee retention (among marketing associates, drivers, and night warehouse employees). Managers of operating companies can use the "best business practices" portal to identify and learn from operating companies in the top quartile of performance on one or more metrics in the balanced scorecard.

As an example, consider the area of safety (specifically, the costs of workers' compensation for work-related injuries). By leveraging best practices and shared, reciprocal visits among managers of its operating companies, SYSCO reduced the performance gap in workers' compensation costs between the top and bottom 25 percent of operating companies, and it increased company-wide safety results by nearly 50 percent over a five-year period. As a result, SYSCO cut by half its overall cost of workers' compensation as a percentage of sales. That represented a significant improvement in performance and an annual cost savings to the company of $36 million.[49] Note that operating managers worked with the *set* of key metrics—operations, financial, customers, and human capital—to leverage best practices to reduce the costs of workers' compensation. Work climate/employee engagement scores comprise only one element of human capital metrics, which, in turn, comprise only one component of the balanced scorecard. One cannot conclude that improvements in work climate/employee engagement scores alone contributed to reductions in the costs of workers' compensation.

SYSCO's in-house research also supports other links in the value-profit chain. Table 6-3 shows that SYSCO operating companies with the most satisfied employees consistently receive the highest scores from their customers and have higher retention of marketing associates and drivers.

The data in Table 6-3 are tantalizing, but some important questions are left unanswered. Clearly, retention is higher in operating companies with better associate satisfaction-engagement. Although results for customer loyalty and employee retention are in the right direction (high/low customer loyalty systematically tracks with high/low employee retention), it is not clear that those results are statistically significant and, thus, whether they generalize beyond the particular situation. Furthermore, causes and effects are not clear. Does making employees more satisfied and engaged cause customers to be more loyal? Or is it more rewarding to work in operating companies with loyal customers, and, as a result, that employees who work there tend to be more satisfied and engaged? The information in Table 6-3 simply does not provide answers to those important questions. This is not meant to deny the tangible and important contributions of the SYSCO analysis. It does, however, suggest that continued improvements in logic, analytics, measures, and process are vital, even in advanced systems like SYSCO's.

Table 6-3   Satisfied Employees Deliver Better Results

	High		Low		
Associate satisfaction	4.00–5.00	3.90–3.99	3.75–3.89	3.55–3.74	< 3.55
Customer loyalty score	4.55	4.40	4.25	4.15	4.05
Retention, marketing associates	88%	85%	81%	75%	76%
Retention, drivers	87%	81%	81%	75%	76%

Source: Carrig, K., and P. M. Wright, *Building Profit Through Building People* (Alexandria, Va.: Society for Human Resource Management Foundation, 2006).

Translating the Analysis into Dollar Values

Table 6-3 does not include cost savings associated with improvements in the retention of marketing associates and drivers, but those cost savings were significant. We can use those retention numbers, along with the costing principles discussed in Chapter 4, to provide an example of the economic effect of attitudes.

In 2000, retention rates for these groups were 75 percent and 65 percent, respectively. By 2005, those retention rates improved to 88 percent and 87 percent, respectively. SYSCO then estimated the replacement and training costs of these three groups of employees as $50,000 per marketing associate and $35,000 per driver. Assuming 100 employees per business unit, from 2000 to 2005, each business unit saved (in terms of costs that were not incurred) $650,000 among marketing associates and $770,000 among drivers, for a total savings of $1.42 million. Corporate-wide savings in retention over all categories of employees from 2000 to 2005, assuming 10,000 employees, totaled $156.5 million.[50] Such savings contributed to the firm's long-term profitability and growth.

Integrating the Attitude-Analysis System into Organizational Systems

Today top executives at SYSCO meet on a quarterly basis to review the metrics. Their purpose is to see whether those numbers are, in fact, consistent with the operating expenses and the pretax earnings of each operating company, as well as with those of the corporation as a whole. What led SYSCO executives to pay attention to the human capital indices? HR researchers found a high multiple correlation ($R^2 = 0.46$) between work climate/employee engagement scores, productivity, retention, and pretax earnings. This means that 46 percent of the variation in pretax earnings was associated with variation in the combination of these three employee-related variables.

In short, SYSCO leaders began to pay attention when they realized that the human capital indices served as indicators of financial results that the executives could see in their own operating companies. The relationship is lagged about six months, and although exact cause-effect relations have not been determined, the business model that the company uses assumes that employee satisfaction-engagement drives customer satisfaction, which drives long-term profitability and growth. In short, SYSCO has been able to determine not only what practices and processes are helping to drive the human capital indices, but also how those, in fact, influence the financial metrics over time. This led SYSCO to develop the business model shown earlier in Figure 6-4.

A Final Word

A number of challenges remain in relating attitudes to costs (see Table 6-4). Note that although the logic of the attitude-cost models shown in Table 6-4 is similar, the major differences lie in how much of the process chain each approach actually measures.

Certainly, refinements are needed in the methods described here, but the potential of cost-benefit comparisons of attitude-behavior relationships is enormous. If organizations can develop compelling, logical frameworks that relate employee attitudes and employee engagement to financial outcomes, and if they can use sound analytics and measures to draw meaningful conclusions from their data, they can engage in a more rational decision-making process regarding where they should and should not make investments. Most important, they will be able to identify critical decision pivot points where this kind of information will make the biggest difference.

Table 6-4 Assumptions, Advantages, and Challenges of Attitude-Cost Models

Model	Assumptions	Advantages	Challenges
Behavior costing	Attitudinal measures are indicators of subsequent employee behaviors/participation membership.	a. Relates attitudes to future costs.	a. Difficult to validate cost savings because analyses are based on correlational data.
		b. Yields the financial measure closely related to employee attitudes.	b. Best time lag for determining attitude-behavior relationships is unknown.
		c. Analysis is explicitly at individual, not at work group or organizational levels.	c. Instability in attitude-behavior relationships yields inaccurate financial changes.
Value-profit chain	Effective management actions drive employee satisfaction-engagement, which enables excellence in innovation and execution, which leads to customer satisfaction, which drives profitability and growth.	a. More complete specification of intermediate linkages between attitudes and outcomes.	a. Requires regular data collection, analysis, and reporting to leverage best practices.
		b. Analysis is explicitly at the work group or organizational levels.	b. "Best" time lag is unknown.
		c. More generally applicable than other models.	c. Longitudinal data required to test causal ordering of links in the model.

Exercises

1. Your boss has asked you for evidence that shows the link between employee attitudes such as job satisfaction, commitment, and engagement, and both individual and organizational outcomes. In other words, convince him that attitudes matter. What sort of evidence might you present?

2. Develop a logic diagram that shows the common and unique outcomes that employee satisfaction, commitment, and engagement might be related to.

3. What is SYSCO's value-profit chain? Explain each link in the model and why it is important in understanding how management practices affect employee satisfaction-engagement, customer satisfaction, and, ultimately, long-term profitability and growth.

4. You have read that SYSCO's value-profit chain serves as a business model for the company. As a senior manager, respond to the following questions:

   What implications might such a model have for recruitment, selection, orientation, training, performance management, and incentive compensation?

   What practical issues have to be considered in deploying the model throughout the company?

5. You are the CEO of a public relations company. You have just read about the 5-STAR management model in the value-profit chain and want to implement it in your company. Develop a detailed strategy for embedding the model into your organization's culture.

References

1. Cascio, W. F., and C. Young, "Work-Family Balance: Does the Market Reward Firms That Respect It?" in *From Work-Family Balance to Work-Family Interaction: Changing the Metaphor,* ed. D. F. Halpern and S. E. Murphy (Mahwah, N.J.: Lawrence Erlbaum Associates, 2005).

2. See, for example, Edmans, A., "Does the Stock Market Fully Value Intangibles? Employee Satisfaction and Equity Prices," (August 12, 2009), downloaded from http://ssrn.com/abstract=985735, May 28, 2010; Cappelli, P., "The Value of Being a Best Employer" (June 26, 2008), downloaded from www.hreonlne.com, June 26, 2008; and Watson, N. "Happy Companies Make Happy Investments," *Fortune* (May 27, 2002), 162.

3. Fulmer, I. S., B. Gerhart, and K. S. Scott, "Are the 100 Best Better? An Empirical Investigation of the Relationship between Being a 'Great Place to Work' and Firm Performance," *Personnel Psychology* 56 (2003): 965–993.

4. *Ibid.*

5. Filbeck, G., and D. Preece, "Fortune's Best 100 Companies to Work for in America: Do They Work for Shareholders?" *Journal of Business Finance & Accounting* 30, no. 5 (2003): 771–797.

6. Vosburgh, R. M., "State-Trait Returns! And One Practitioner's Request, *Industrial and Organizational Psychology* 1 (2008): 72–73.

7. Harter, J. K., and F. L. Schmidt, "Conceptual Versus Empirical Distinctions among Constructs: Implications for Discriminant Validity," *Industrial and Organizational Psychology* 1 (2008): 36–39. See also Macey, W. H., and B. Schneider, "Engaged in Engagement: We Are Delighted We Did It," *Industrial and Organizational Psychology* 1 (2008a): 76–83.

8. Society for Human Resource Management, *Employee Job Satisfaction: Understanding the Factors That Make Work Gratifying* (Alexandria, Va.: SHRM, 2009).

9. Macey, W. H., and B. Schneider, "The Meaning of Employee Engagement," *Industrial and Organizational Psychology* 1 (2008b): 3–30.

10. Newman, D. A., and D. A. Harrison, "Been There, Bottled That: Are State and Behavioral Work Engagement New and Useful Construct 'Wines'?," *Industrial and Organizational Psychology* 1 (2008): 31–35. See also Harter and Schmidt, 2008.

11. Klein, H. J., J. C. Molloy, and J. T. Cooper, "Conceptual Foundations: Construct Definitions and Theoretical Representations of Workplace Commitments," in *Commitment in Organizations,* ed. H. J. Klein, T. E. Becker, and J. P. Meyer (New York: Taylor & Francis, 2009). See also Mathieu, J. E., and D. M. Zajac, "A Review and Meta-analysis of the Antecedents, Correlates, and Consequences of Organizational Commitment," *Psychological Bulletin* 108, no. 2 (1990): 171–194.

12. Carrig, K., and P. M. Wright, *Building Profit through Building People: Making Your Workforce the Strongest Link in the Value-Profit Chain* (Alexandria, Va.: Society for Human Resource Management, 2006).

13. Macey and Schneider, 2008; Harter and Schmidt, 2008; and Newman and Harrison, 2008.

14. Schaufeli, W. B., A. B. Bakker, and M. Salanova, "The Measurement of Work Engagement with a Short Questionnaire: A Cross-National Study," *Educational and Psychological Measurement* 66 (2006): 701–716. See also Schaufeli, W. B., M. Salanova, V. González-Romá, and A. B. Bakker, "The Measurement of Engagement and Burnout: A Two-Sample Confirmatory Factor-Analytic Approach," *Journal of Happiness Studies* 3 (2002): 71–92.

15. Salanova, M., S. Agut, and J. M. Peiroá, "Linking Organizational Resources and Work Engagement to Employee Performance and Customer Loyalty: The Mediation of Service Climate," *Journal of Applied Psychology* 90 (2005): 1,216–1,227.

16. Aumann, K., and E. Galinsky, Families and Work Institute, 2008 National Study of the Changing Workforce. *The State of Health in the American Workforce: Does Having an Effective Workplace Matter?* New York: Families and Work Institute . Downloaded from www.familiesandwork.org/site/research/reports/HealthReport.pdf, June 1, 2010.

17. Brooks, S. M., J. W. Wiley, and E. L. Hause, "Using Employee and Customer Perspectives to Improve Organizational Performance," in *Customer Service Delivery*, ed. L. Fogli (San Francisco: Jossey-Bass, 2006); Cohen, A. "Organizational Commitment and Turnover: A Meta-analysis," *Academy of Management Journal* 36 (1993): 1,140–1,157; Ostroff, C., "The Relationship between Satisfaction, Attitudes, and Performance: An Organizational-Level Analysis," *Journal of Applied Psychology* 77 (1992): 963–974; Ryan, A. M., M. J. Schmit, and R. Johnson, "Attitudes and Effectiveness: Examining Relations at an Organizational Level," *Personnel Psychology* 49 (1996): 853–883; Rogg, K. L.,
D. B. Schmidt, C. Shull, and N. Schmitt, "Human Resource Practices, Organizational Climate, and Customer Satisfaction," *Journal of Management* 27 (2001): 431–449; and Schaufeli, W., and A. B. Bakker, "Job Demands, Job Resources, and Their Relationship with Burnout and Engagement: A Multi-sample Study," *Journal of Organizational Behavior* 25 (2004): 293–315.

18. Macey and Schneider, 2008a.

19. Griffin, M. A., S. K. Parker, and A. Neal, "Is Behavioral Engagement a Distinct and Useful Construct?," *Industrial and Organizational Psychology* 1 (2008): 48–51.

20. Graen, G., "Enriched Engagement through Assistance to Systems Change: A Proposal," *Industrial and Organizational Psychology* 1 (2008): 74–75.

21. Macey and Schneider, 2008b.

22. Schneider, B., S. S. White, and M. C. Paul, "Linking Service Climate and Customer Perceptions of Service Quality: Test of a Causal Model," *Journal of Applied Psychology* 83 (1998): 150–163.

23. Salanova et al., 2005.

24. Rucci, A. J., S. P. Kirn, and R. T. Quinn, "The Employee-Customer-Profit Chain at Sears," *Harvard Business Review* 76 (January/February 1998): 82–97.

25. Corporate Voices for Working Families, "Business Impacts of Flexibility: An Imperative for Expansion," November 2005, downloaded from www.cvworkingfamilies.org/system/files/Business%20Impacts%20of%20Flexibility.pdf, June 1, 2010.

26. Feldman, J. M., and J. G. Lynch, Jr. "Self-Generated Validity and Other Effects of Measurement on Belief, Attitude, Intention, and Behavior," *Journal of Applied Psychology* 73 (1988): 421–435; and Olson, J. M., and G. R. Maio, "Attitudes in Social Behavior," in *Handbook of Psychology, Volume. 5, Personality and Social Psychology,* ed. T. Millon and M. J. Lerner (Hoboken, N.J.: Wiley, 2003).

27. Parker, S. K. "Job Satisfaction," in *Encyclopedia of Industrial and Organizational Psychology, Volume 1,* S. ed. G. Rogelberg (Thousand Oaks, Calif.: Sage, 2007). See also Balzer, W. K., and J. Z. Gillespie, "Job Satisfaction Measurement," in *Encyclopedia of Industrial and Organizational Psychology, Volume 1,* ed. S. G. Rogelberg (Thousand Oaks, Calif.: Sage, 2007).

28. Allen, N. J., "Organizational Commitment," in *Encyclopedia of Industrial and Organizational Psychology, Volume 2,* ed. S. G. Rogelberg (Thousand Oaks, Calif.: Sage, 2007).

29. Mowday, R. T., R. M. Steers, and L. W. Porter, "The Measurement of Organizational Commitment," *Journal of Vocational Behavior* 14 (1979): 224–247.

30. *The Gallup Q12 Employee Engagement Questionnaire,* downloaded from www.shrm.org/Publications/hrmagazine/EditorialContent/2010/0510/Pages/0510fox3.aspx, May 19, 2010. See also Harter, J. K., F. L. Schmidt, and T. L. Hayes, "Business-Unit-Level Relationship between Employee Satisfaction, Employee Engagement, and Business Outcomes: A Meta-analysis," *Journal of Applied Psychology* 87 (2002): 268–279.

31. Harter and Schmidt, 2008.

32. Schaufeli, Bakker, and Salanova, 2006.

33. Pil, F. K., and J. P. MacDuffie, "The Adoption of High-Improvement Work Practices," *Industrial Relations* 35, no. 3 (1996): 423–455.

34. Schneider, B., P. J. Hanges, D. B. Smith, and A. N. Salvaggio, "Which Comes First: Employee Attitudes or Organizational Financial and Market Performance?," *Journal of Applied Psychology* 88, no. 5 (2003): 836–851.

35. Ryan, et al., 1996; Schneider, White, and Paul, 1998.

36. Micco, L., "Gallup Study Links Worker Beliefs, Increased Productivity," *HR News* (September 1998), 17.

37. Harter, Schmidt, and Hayes, 2002.

38. Fox, A., "Raising Engagement," *HR Magazine* (May 2010), 35–40.

39. Pugh, S. D., and J. Dietz, "Employee Engagement at the Organizational Level of Analysis," *Industrial and Organizational Psychology* 1 (2008): 44–47.

40. Schneider, Hanges, Smith, and Salvaggio, 2003.

41. Mirvis, P. H., and E. E. Lawler III, "Measuring the Financial Impact of Employee Attitudes," *Journal of Applied Psychology* 62 (1977): 1–8.

42. March, J. G., and H. A. Simon, *Organizations,* 2nd ed. (New York: Wiley, 1993).

43. Lawler, E. E., *Motivation in Work Organizations* (San Francisco, Calif.: Jossey-Bass, 1994).

44. Vroom, V. H., *Work and Motivation* (New York: Wiley, 1964).

45. Heskett, J. L., T. O. Jones, G. W. Loveman, W. E. Sasser, Jr., and L. A. Schlesinger, "Putting the Service-Profit Chain to Work," *Harvard Business Review* 72 (March/April 1994): 164–174.

46. Carrig and Wright, 2006.

47. *Ibid.*

48. Fox, 2010.

49. Carrig and Wright, 2006.

50. *Ibid.*

7

Financial Effects of Work-Life Programs

"Remixing" Rewards

onsider some of the ways that the workforce is changing, and how the attitudes, beliefs, and perceptions of employees are shaping today's workplaces.[1]

- The composition of the workforce now reflects the growing influence of Generation Y (about 70 million, born between 1979 and 1994), Generation X (about 35 million, born between 1965 and 1978), and Baby Boomers (about 77 million, born between 1946 and 1964).

- Especially among the members of Gen Y and Boomers, flexible work arrangements (89 and 87 percent, respectively) and the opportunity to give back to society (86 and 85 percent, respectively) trump the sheer size of the pay package. That's not as true for Gen Xers—people in their 30s and early 40s are 10 percent less likely to find this important.

- Fully 87 and 83 percent, respectively, of Gen Yers and Boomers say that work/life fit is important to them. That's also true of Gen Xers, but to a lesser degree.

- The majority of employees of all generations feel that they do not have enough time for the important aspects of their personal lives.

- Gender roles at home and at work have changed significantly. Women are now in the workforce in almost equal numbers as men, they are just as likely as men to want jobs with greater responsibility, and almost 80 percent of couples are dual earners.

- A climate of respect, a supportive supervisor, and better work-life fit have positive effects on the work, health, and well-being of both men and women of all generations.

- Being treated with respect by managers and supervisors has a stronger effect on the mental health of low-income employees than middle- or high-income employees.

Special Issues Parents Face

Working parents face a host of additional issues:[2]

- About 70 percent of mothers with school-age children work for pay outside the home, with 55 percent of mothers with infants younger than one year old employed outside the home.

- One in three children is born to a single mother; that group comprises seven million mothers in the United States who do not have a spouse to share the work of earning a livelihood and caring for children.

- More than 1.5 million single fathers are raising children without the financial or emotional support of a spouse. Considered another way, a father heads one in every five single-parent households.

- In 1997, women in dual-earner couples contributed an average of 39 percent of average family income. By 2008, that figure had increased significantly to an average of 44 percent. At the same time, 60 percent of men had annual earnings at least 10 percentage points higher than their spouses/partners, down from 72 percent of men in 1997.

- Men are taking more overall responsibility for care of their children (providing one-on-one care, as well as managing child-care arrangements) according to themselves *and* their wives/partners. This has led to increased work-life conflict, as 59 percent of fathers in dual-earner couples report experiencing some or a lot of conflict today, up from 35 percent in 1977. Not surprisingly, therefore, 70 percent of men say they would take a pay cut to spend more time with their families, and almost half would turn down a promotion if it meant less family time.[3]

- At the same time, there is pressure to maintain a two-income lifestyle. Few families can afford "luxuries" such as health insurance, mortgage payments, and grocery bills on one salary. Indeed, more American families file for bankruptcy every year than file for divorce.[4]

Can organizations enhance both employee productivity and the fit between their work and nonwork lives? When do investments in work and nonwork life fit become a recruitment and retention advantage? Is the advantage actually enough to offset the costs? In short, can investments to enhance the fit between work and nonwork actually pay off, and how much? As in other chapters, our purpose here is to follow the LAMP model presented in Chapter 1, "Making HR Measurement Strategic," to offer a logical, analytic, and measurement framework regarding work-life programs that might facilitate better decisions about investments in them. We conclude the chapter by providing some practical suggestions about the process of communicating results to decision makers. Let us begin by addressing a simple question: Just what is a work-life program?

Work-Life Programs: What Are They?

Although originally termed "work-family" programs, this book uses the term *work-life programs* to reflect a broader perspective of this issue. Work-life recognizes the fact that employees at every level in an organization, whether parents or nonparents, face personal or family issues that can affect their performance on the job. A work-life program includes any employer-sponsored benefit or working condition that helps an employee to enhance the fit between work and nonwork demands. At a general level, such programs span five broad areas:[5]

- **Child and dependent-care benefits** (for example, on-site or near-site child- or elder-care programs, and summer and weekend programs for dependents)

- **Flexible working conditions** (for example, flextime, job sharing, teleworking, part-time work, and compressed workweeks)

- **Leave options** (for example, maternity, paternity, and adoption leaves; sabbaticals; phased re-entry; and retirement schemes)

- **Information services and HR policies** (for example, cafeteria benefits, life-skill educational programs such as parenting skills, health issues, financial management and retirement, exercise facilities, and professional and personal counseling)

- **Organizational cultural issues** (for example, an organizational culture that is supportive with respect to the nonwork issues of employees, coworkers, and supervisors who are sensitive to family issues)

In Chapter 4, "The High Cost of Employee Separations," we described some of the financial payoffs from low employee turnover at SAS. We also described some of its wide array of employee benefits, including high-quality child care at $410 a month (versus $1,500 per month outside the company), 90% coverage of the health insurance premium, unlimited sick days, a medical center staffed by four physicians and 10 nurse practitioners (at no cost to employees), a free 66,000-square-foot fitness center and natatorium, a lending library, and a summer camp for children. This bounty of benefits stems from the company's core beliefs about minimizing distractions and that happy, healthy employees are more productive.

SAS has long been recognized as an innovator in encouraging employee work-life balance. Is it any surprise that SAS was named by *Fortune* magazine as the #1 best company to work for in America in 2010, or that it has made the "100 Best" list every year since it was created in 1998? The architect of this culture— based on "trust between our employees and the company"—is Jim Goodnight, its co-founder, and the only CEO that SAS has had in its 34-year history.

Some might think that, with all those perks, Goodnight was giving away the store. Not so. SAS has had an unbroken chain of profitability and growth every year in the 34 years since its founding. With 2009 revenues of $2.31 billion, it ranks as the world's largest privately owned software company. Voluntary turnover is the industry's lowest, at 2%. With more than 11,000 employees, 5,487 in the U.S., the company added 119 new jobs last year. A total of 26,432 people applied for those jobs.

Logical Framework

As the chapter-opening statistics make clear, pressures for work-life fit stem from a variety of sources. Whether an organization chooses to address those needs or not, each choice has consequences. Figure 7-1 is a logical framework to describe the conditions that affect the potential impact of work-life programs on behaviors and financial outcomes.

As Figure 7-1 shows, there are consequences, both behavioral and financial, to decisions to offer or not to offer one or more work-life programs. If an organization chooses not to offer such programs, there may be negative consequences with respect to job performance. Some of these potential impacts include heightened stress, more burnout, a higher likelihood of mistakes, and more refusals of promotions by employees already feeling the strain of pressures for better fit between their work and nonwork lives.

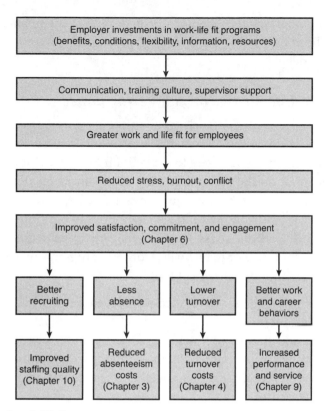

Figure 7-1 Logic of work-life fit.

Under these circumstances, job satisfaction, commitment to the organization, and engagement in one's job (vigor, absorption, dedication—see Chapter 6, "Employee Attitudes and Engagement") are likely to wane. When that happens, people begin to think about quitting, some actually do quit, and customer service may suffer. All of these consequences lead to significant financial outcomes, as Chapters 3–6 have demonstrated.

Assuming that an organization does offer one or more work-life programs, the financial and nonfinancial effects of those programs depend on several factors. These include the range, scope, cost, and quality of the programs; the extent and quality of communications about the programs to employees; training on how to manage work-life programs; and support for them from managers and supervisors. If those conditions are met, it is reasonable to expect that employees will achieve greater work and life fit. Such fit implies reduced stress, burnout, and conflict, along with increased engagement, satisfaction, and commitment. Those human-capital outcomes lead to improvements in talent management (reductions in withdrawal behaviors and voluntary turnover, and improvements in the ability to attract top talent); motivation to perform well; and financial, operational, and business outcomes. Chapters 3–6 documented some of the financial consequences associated with those outcomes. The following sections elaborate on the elements of Figure 7-1 in more detail.

Impact of Work-Life Strains on Job Performance

Companies can own tangible assets, such as patents, copyrights, and equipment, but they cannot own their own employees.[7] Conflicts between job demands and the demands of nonwork life may lead some employees to a condition known as "burnout." Employees suffering from burnout do the bare minimum, do not show up regularly, leave work early, and quit their jobs at higher rates than less-stressed employees.[8] To reduce such tensions, they may leave the workforce altogether or move to positions in other organizations that generate less work-life stress. For firms that are trying to build valuable human assets that are difficult to copy or to lure way, work-life programs may provide powerful retention and performance-enhancement tools.

Other employee-withdrawal behaviors, such as reduced effort while at work, lateness, and absenteeism, also diminish the value of human resources to an employer.[9] As shown in Chapter 3, "The Hidden Costs of Absenteeism," the number-one reason for unscheduled employee absenteeism is personal illness (34 percent). The number-two reason is family-related issues (22 percent). Taken together, these causes account for more than half of all absenteeism incidents. Work-life programs are designed to address precisely these underlying reasons for employee withdrawal. Work-life initiatives that incorporate flexibility into work scheduling, together with "family-friendly" features, can play a potentially important role in protecting a firm's investment in its human capital. This is especially true for professional employees.

Work-Life Programs and Professional Employees

The view of work-life programs as a strategy for protecting investments in human capital applies particularly well to professional employees. Professional employees are critical resources for organizations because of their expense, their relative scarcity, and the transferability of their skills.[10] In addition, professionals tend to be highly autonomous, substituting self-control for organizational control.

Attracting and retaining professionals is difficult because other employers value their skills. Work-life programs can be effective for attracting and retaining these employees.[11] Professionals in many countries are delaying the birth of their first child until they have achieved some measure of financial and career security. Given the relatively long years of education and training required of professionals, these people are especially likely to delay starting their families.[12] For this reason, work-family tensions tend to rise for many professionals as they reach their 30s and 40s. If organizations fail to provide assistance in handling this tension, they risk losing these valuable employees to employers that offer more flexibility.

From a competitive standpoint, because work-life programs are more highly developed in some organizations than in others, organizations with extensive work-life benefits may be better able to retain top-performing professionals despite efforts by competitors to bid them away. Consider how one public accounting firm does it.[13]

Crowe, Horwath, LLP

For accountants in tax and auditing practices in the United States, the busy season, January 2 to April 15, is recognized as a time when putting in extra hours and working on Saturdays is a given. To help ease that burden, Crowe, Horwath offers benefits targeted to help its people maintain work/life fit. In several offices, the firm offers complementary on-site babysitting on Saturdays during the busy season. Kids enjoy activities ranging from arts and crafts to group games, and special guests, like local firefighters. They also enjoy "going to work" with Mom or Dad.

The firm also offers a "road-warrior" program to those who travel overnight more than 30 percent of their scheduled workdays. Benefits include, among others, a weekend travel program to fly a significant other or a friend to their location, or the option to fly to a different destination instead of back home. As one senior staff member noted, "[The weekend-travel program] is great because it makes being out of town and away from family manageable. We get to have a little weekend getaway in places we might not normally have seen."

Offering programs like Crowe, Horwath's might lead some parents, mostly women, to decide that they don't have to opt out of the work force temporarily when they have children.

Opting Out

Today many companies recruit roughly equal numbers of female and male MBA graduates, but they find that a substantial percentage of their female recruits drop out within three to five years. The most vexing problem for businesses, therefore, is not finding female talent, but retaining it.[14]

How large is the opt-out phenomenon? A recent survey examined this phenomenon among 2,443 highly qualified women and a smaller comparison group of 653 highly qualified men (defined as those with a graduate degree, a professional degree, or a high-honors undergraduate degree).[15] Fully 37 percent of the women (43 percent of those with kids), as opposed to only 24 percent of the men (no statistical difference between those who are fathers and those who are not), took time off from their careers. Among women, the average break lasted 2.2 years (1.2 years for those in business), with 44 percent citing child- or elder-care responsibilities, compared with only 12 percent of men. Among men, who averaged one year off, the primary reason was career enhancement.

Although 93 percent of the women who took time off from work wanted to return, only 74 percent of them were able to do so. Even then, they paid a high price for their career interruptions, with the penalties becoming more severe the longer the break. Among women in business, the average loss in earnings was 28 percent, even though the average break among those women lasted little more than a year. When women spent three or more years out of the work force, they earned only 63 percent of the salaries of those who took no time out.

The same survey also found that many women cope with job-family tradeoffs by working part time, by reducing the number of hours they work in full-time jobs, and by declining to accept promotions. Women are less likely to opt out of work if their employers offer flexible career paths that allow them to ramp up and ramp down their professional responsibilities at different career points.[16] Flexibility is a key retention tool for women as well as for men.

The Toll on Those Who Don't Opt Out

Especially for those who do not or cannot opt out of working, family and personal concerns are a source of stress:[17]

- In professional-service firms, well over half the employees can expect to experience some kind of work-family stress in a three-month period.

- Staff members with work-family conflict are three times more likely to consider quitting (43 percent versus 14 percent).

- Staff members who believe that work is causing problems in their personal lives are much more likely to make mistakes at work (30 percent) than those who have few job-related personal problems (19 percent).

- On the other hand, employees with supportive workplaces and supportive supervisors report greater job satisfaction and more commitment to helping their companies succeed.

Organizations want their employees to be highly committed and fully engaged, but in many cases, that is just wishful thinking because of the spillover effect from issues at work to employees' personal lives off the job. Research has shown that the impact of work on employees' home lives is fairly well balanced among positive, negative, and neutral.[18] Regardless of the direction of the spillover, from work to personal life or from personal life to work, a meta-analytic review found that both types of conflict are negatively related to job and life satisfaction.[19]

Negative spillover effects are reflected in high stress, bad moods, poor coping, and insufficient quality and amount of time for family and friends. When employees are worried about personal issues outside of work, they become distracted, and their commitment wanes along with their productivity. Ultimately, both absenteeism and turnover (voluntary or involuntary) may increase. As we have noted, family/personal issues are widespread sources of stress, and conflicts between work and personal life affect productivity and general well-being.

The good news, however, is that the impact of employees' personal or family lives on work is generally positive. Fully half of employees in a large national study reported that their personal or family lives provide them with more energy for their jobs. Only 12 percent reported that their home lives undermined their energy for work, and 38 percent reported a balanced impact of their personal or family lives on their energy levels at work.[20] Organizational programs that support work-life fit reinforce these outcomes. Unfortunately, in many organizations, although the programs are available, formidable barriers may make it difficult for employees to use them.[21]

Enhancing Success Through Implementation

The mere presence of a work-life initiative is no guarantee of success. As shown in Figure 7-1, one must also consider the range, scope, quality, and cost of work-life initiatives, along with the quality and care with which they are deployed. Key factors to consider are the careful alignment of the programs with the strategic objectives of the organization, the extent and quality of communications about the programs, training for managers on how to make the programs work for them, and the extent of management and supervisory support for the programs. If implemented properly, work-life initiatives should reduce employee withdrawal behaviors, increase retention, and increase employees' motivation to perform well. Unfortunately, this is not always the case.

Both employers and employees have reasons for not using work-life programs. Many supervisors and higher-level managers, for example, think of "work-life" as "work-life equals work less." They see such programs benefiting employees only and not their organizations.[22] The challenge, then, is to help them view work-life initiatives as a new way of working that focuses on fitting work to the employee, not just fitting the employee to the organization's needs. Training can help them understand what research has shown: The single best predictor of health and well-being at work is work-life fit.[23]

Employees also have their reasons for not using work-life programs. Researchers in one study used focus groups to investigate why.[24] It revealed six major barriers to more widespread use of the programs:

- **Lack of communication** about the policies (vague or limited knowledge about them)

- **High workloads** (work builds up when employees take time off)

- **Management attitudes** (to some managers, employees who take advantage of the policies show lack of commitment; others are unwilling to accommodate differing needs of employees)

- **Career repercussions** (belief that if employees access work-life policies, their career progression will suffer)

- **The influence of peers** (fear that employee use of a work-life program will cause resentment or suggest that the employee is not a team player)

- **Administrative processes** (excessive paperwork and long approval processes)

In short, not just the policies, but also the environment in which they are implemented, make the biggest difference for employees.[25] Thus, a nationwide study by Canada's Department of Labor found that 70 percent of employees surveyed attributed problems with their respective companies' work-life programs to treatment by their immediate supervisors.[26] A follow-up study included a list of 26 items related to work-life fit. Seven of the nine items that were most strongly related to the success of these programs were related to the attitudes and behaviors of supervisors. Indeed, study after study has reinforced the critical role that immediate supervisors play in the overall success of work-life programs.[27]

An organization that truly is committed to work-life policies does more than simply provide them. It also takes tangible steps to create a workplace culture that supports and encourages the use of the policies,[28] and it offers streamlined processes to approve employee access to them. As Figure 7-1 illustrates, those steps include things such as a multichannel communication strategy to promote and publicize the organization's work-life policies (for example, company intranet, in-house newspaper, e-mail), coupled with training for managers on how to support employees who take advantage of them. For example, that training could be designed around the kinds of behaviors from supervisors that are reflected in just three items from the 2008 National Study of the Changing Workforce. Those items are strongly related to employee engagement, job satisfaction, and turnover intentions:[29]

- My supervisor is supportive when I have a work problem.

- My supervisor recognizes me when I do a good job.

- My supervisor keeps me informed of things I need to know to do my job well.

To break down barriers and to enhance decisions about where investments in work-life programs are likely to have the most significant strategic value, line managers need a logical framework (see Figure 7-1) and research results. Although work-life initiatives are only one determinant of employee behaviors, along with factors such as pay, working conditions, and the work itself, research indicates that they can have substantial effects on employee decisions to stay with an organization and to produce high-quality work. The next section focuses on analytics and measures that make those results meaningful.

Analytics and Measures: Connecting Work-Life Programs to Outcomes

As we pointed out in earlier chapters, the term *analytics* refers to the research designs and statistical models that allow us to draw meaningful conclusions from studies that purport to show linkages between programs and outcomes. The term *measures* refers to the actual data that populate those models and the formulas that accompany them. In the case of work-life programs, the measures include the investments in the programs, as well as measures of outcomes such as absence and turnover that are discussed in earlier chapters. The analytical challenges include ensuring that program effects are not confused with other factors (controlling for extraneous effects) and determining correlation and causation.

Child Care

U. S. employers lose an estimated $4 billion annually to absenteeism related to child care.[30] Several studies have examined the impact of child-care programs on absenteeism, retention, and return on investment. For example, Citigroup owns or participates in 12 child-care centers in the United States. Employees pay about half the cost to use Citigroup facilities managed by Bright Horizons Family Solutions or at non-Citigroup back-up centers. In two follow-up studies, Citigroup found the following:[31]

- A 51 percent reduction in turnover among center users compared to noncenter users

- An 18 percent reduction in absenteeism

- A 98 percent retention rate of top performers

Chase Manhattan Bank (now JPMorgan Chase) analyzed the return on investment (ROI) of its backup child-care program (that is, child care used in emergencies or when regular child care is unavailable). It found that child-care breakdowns were the cause of 6,900 days of missed work by parents. Because backup child care was available, these lost days were not incurred. When multiplied by the average daily salary of the employee in question (expressed in 2010 dollars), gross savings were $2,393,015. The annual cost of the backup child-care center was $1,131,170, for a net savings of $1,261,845 and an ROI of better than 110 percent.[32]

Finally, Canadian financial services giant CIBC recently bulked up its backup child-care program, rolling out the on-site service to 14 Canadian cities. Employees can take advantage of the program for up to 20 days a year at no cost to them. CIBC's Children's Care Center has saved more than 6,800 employee days since the first facility opened in 2002. The company estimates its cost savings over that period to be about $1.6 million (in 2010 dollars). Equally important, the program is a big winner with CIBC's workers.[33]

Simply offering child care is no guarantee of results like those we have described. Employers considering offering such a benefit should understand child-care service delivery, the cost of care and its availability, what is available in the local market, and any challenges it presents. In addition, employers need to consider the business case for offering child care.[34] Depending on the nature of the business, the goal may be to improve recruitment and retention, support the advancement of women, reduce absenteeism, retain high performers, or be an employer of choice. Then measure what matters, considering key drivers of the business and the goals established for the program.

Flexible Work Arrangements

When one stops to consider the effects of e-mail, smart phones, personal and family demands, and the 24/7 business environment, the inescapable conclusion for many employees is that 9 a.m. to 5 p.m. just isn't working anymore. Time is employees' most precious commodity. They want the flexibility to control their own time—where, when, and how they work. They want a better fit in their lives between work and leisure. Flexibility in schedules is important, as organizations strive to retain talented workers. Indeed, a recent survey of 182 organizations primarily in the U.S. and Canada revealed that 90 percent offer one or more flexible work arrangements to employees.[35] It is important to emphasize, however, that the concept of "flexibility" reflects a broad spectrum of possible work arrangements, as Figure 7-2 makes clear.

Accommodation-Based Flexibility
-Private deals based on individual's needs
-Inconsistent implementation, often secret
-Restricted access to flexibility

Business-Based Flexibility
-Decisions based on both businesses and individual needs
-Policy infrastructure that defines scheduling options and supports consistent implementation

Culture of Flexibility
-Incorporates options for formal arrangements as well as widespread, occasional flexibility
-Culture that rewards results achieved rather than time spent
-Flexibility viewed as a management strategy

Source: Corporate Voices for Working Families. (November 2005). Business Impacts of Flexibility: An Imperative for Expansion (p. 18). Retrieved from www.cvwf.org on May 18, 2006. Used with permission.

Figure 7-2 Implementing flexibility: A spectrum of practice.

In terms of specific initiatives, here are six broad categories of flexible work arrangements.[36]

1. **Choices in managing time**, which includes control over one's schedule and satisfaction with one's schedule

2. **Flex time and flex place**, which includes traditional flexibility, daily flexibility, and shift work, compressed workweeks, and working at home

3. **Reduced time**, which includes part-time and part-year work

4. **Time off** for small necessities, one's own or family members' illnesses, vacations and holidays, and volunteer work

5. **Caregiving leave**, which includes maternity and paternity leave

6. **Culture of flexibility**, which includes perceived jeopardy, supervisor support, and general obstacles for using flexibility

Research has revealed that 87 percent of employees at *all levels* say they want increased flexibility at work. These include employees from low-income families (median annual income of $15,600), middle-income families (median annual income of $62,400), and high-income families (median annual income of $140,400).[37] In terms of job levels (executives, managers, and professionals), the two most common flexible work arrangements are telework and flex time. Depending on the level of employee, 56–72 percent of companies offer these options. Among hourly and nonexempt employees, the following percentages of companies offer these options: flex time (49 percent), part-time work (42 percent), and telework (33 percent).[38]

Earlier we noted some key barriers to wider implementation of work-life programs. Flexible work schedules are no exception. "Flexibility is frequently viewed by managers and employees as an exception or employee accommodation, rather than as a new and effective way of working to achieve business results. A face-time culture, excessive workload, manager skepticism, customer demands, and fear of negative career consequences are among the barriers that prevent employees from taking advantage of policies they might otherwise use—and that prevent companies from realizing the full benefits that flexibility might bestow."[39]

To help inform the debate about flexible work arrangements, consider the financial and nonfinancial effects that have been reported for these key outcomes shown in Figure 7-1: *talent management* (specifically, better recruiting and lower turnover) and *human-capital outcomes* (increased satisfaction and commitment, decreased stress), which affect cost and performance, leading to *financial, operational, and business outcomes*. Here are some very brief findings in each of these areas, from a recent study of 29 American firms.[40]

Talent Management

IBM's global work-life survey demonstrated that, for IBM employees overall, flexibility is an important aspect of an employee's decision to stay with the company. Responses from almost 42,000 IBM employees in 79 countries revealed that work-life fit—of which flexibility is a significant component—is the second-leading reason for potentially leaving IBM, behind compensation and benefits. Conversely, employees with higher work-life fit scores (and, therefore, also higher flexibility scores) reported significantly greater job satisfaction and were much more likely to agree with the statement "I would not leave IBM."

In the corporate finance organization, 94 percent of all managers reported positive impacts of flexible work options on the company's "ability to retain talented professionals." In light of these findings showing the strong link between flexibility and retention, IBM actively promotes flexibility as a strategy for retaining key talent.

Human-Capital Outcomes: Employee Commitment

At Deloitte & Touche, one employee survey item asked whether employees agreed with the statement "My manager grants me enough flexibility to meet my personal/family responsibilities." Those who agreed that they have access to flexibility scored 32 percent higher in commitment than those who believed they did not have access to flexibility. Likewise, AstraZeneca found that commitment scores were 28 percent higher for employees who said they had the flexibility they needed, compared to employees who did not have the flexibility they needed.

Financial Performance, and Operational and Business Outcomes: Client Service

Concern for quality and continuity of client or customer service is often one of the concerns raised about whether flexibility can work in a customer-focused organization. To be sure that compressed workweeks did not erode traditionally high levels of customer service, the Consumer Healthcare division of GlaxoSmithKline surveyed customers as part of the evaluation of its flexibility pilot program. Fully 89 percent of customers said they had not seen any disruption in service, 98 percent said their inquiries had been answered in a timely manner, and 87 percent said they would not have any issues with the program becoming a permanent work schedule.

Studies such as these make it possible to reframe the discussion and to position flexibility not as a "perk," employee-friendly benefit, or advocacy cause, but as a powerful business tool that can enhance talent management, improve important human-capital outcomes, and boost financial and operational performance.[41]

Work-Life Policies and Firm Performance

A large-scale, empirical study of data from a series of surveys administered by the Ministry of Manpower, Singapore, from 1996 to 2003, investigated the indirect impact of work-life practices through employee turnover and the direct impact of work-life practices on firm performance.[42] The researchers defined firm performance in three ways: financial (return on assets [ROA]), employee productivity (logarithm of sales per employee), and investor return (one-year compounded stock-price return). What is unique about this study, relative to prior research, is that most prior research has examined the effects of work-life programs on employee turnover within a single firm. Data on employee turnover across a large sample of firms, in this study, 2,570 firms, is not easily available, and therefore has not been examined.

Work-Life Practices in Singapore

Employee benefits in Singaporean firms fall into two main categories: work-life benefits and resource benefits. Work-life benefits refer to benefits that allow employees to adjust their work hours or work location to accommodate their personal and family demands, such as various leave benefits and flexible working arrangements. Resource benefits refer to financial and other resources that firms give to employees, either as a form of welfare benefit or as performance incentives, such as transportation benefits and stock options.

The researchers analyzed data separately for management and nonmanagement employees. In addition, they examined four variables to indicate the extensiveness of work-life benefits in a firm:

- Number of work-life benefits (controlling for number of resource benefits)
- Annual leave entitlement
- Workweek pattern (compressed versus standard)
- Availability of part-time employment

Figure 7-3 presents the design of the study.

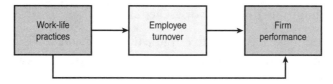

Source: Kelly, K., and S. Ang, *A Study on the Relationships between Work-Life Practices and Firm Performance in Singapore Firms*, technical report, Nanyang Business School. Nanyang Technological University, Singapore, October 2005.

Figure 7-3 Relationships between work-life variables, employee turnover, and firm performance.

As Figure 7-3 shows, the design of the study allowed the researchers to investigate the indirect impact of work-life practices through employee turnover and the direct impact of work-life practices on firm performance. They controlled for the size of the firm, ownership (publicly listed or private), industry (manufacturing or service), degree of industry concentration, and year (where multiple years of data were used). For stock return, they also controlled for the age of the firm and the systematic risk of the firm's stock (beta).

Figure 7-4 shows a typical result of the analysis.

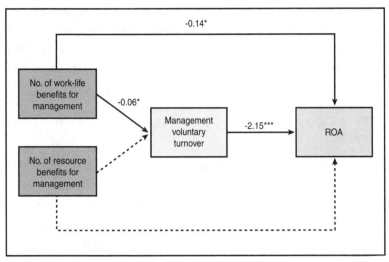

Note: *p < 0.05, **p < 0.01, *** p < 0.001

Source: Kelly, K., and S. Ang, *A Study on the Relationships between Work-Life Practices and Firm Performance in Singapore Firms*, technical report, Nanyang Business School. Nanyang Technological University, Singapore, October 2005.

Figure 7-4 Relationships between number of work-life benefits and number of resource benefits for management, management voluntary turnover, and ROA.

Based on 1,178 observations from the year 2003, and controlling for the number of resource benefits, firms that offer more work-life benefits for management employees have lower management voluntary turnover (standardized regression coefficient = −0.06). In turn, firms with lower management voluntary turnover generate higher ROA (standardized regression coefficient = −2.15). Hence, the indirect effect of the number of work-life benefits for management on ROA through turnover is positive (−0.06 × −2.15).

However, there is also a direct negative relationship between the number of work-life benefits for management and return on assets (standardized regression coefficient = −0.14), suggesting that implementing work-life benefits for management is financially costly for firms.

Overall Summary of Results

The results of this study indicate that voluntary turnover among managers as well as rank-and-file employees negatively affects firm financial performance, employee productivity, and investor return. Conversely, implementing work-life initiatives for both management and rank-and-file employees can be an effective business strategy for firms to reduce voluntary employee turnover. While the effects of reduced turnover do not quite offset the direct financial costs, reduced turnover is only one effect of work-life programs. The study found lower voluntary employee turnover in these firms:

- Firms that offer a larger number of work-life benefits to their employees

- Firms that have a higher proportion of employees with more generous annual leave entitlements

- Firms that have a higher proportion of employees on shorter workweeks

After reading these results, you may well be wondering what causes what. That is, do work-life programs drive reductions in employee turnover, or do firms with low turnover rates find it viable to invest in work-life programs? Fortunately, the results of a recent large-scale, longitudinal study have begun to shed light on this important issue.[43] Using data from 885 private-sector businesses in multiple industries over five years, researchers found multidirectional (reciprocal) relationships between firm performance (ROA) and both voluntary and involuntary turnover. That means that turnover was higher in poorer-performing firms, and that this was due both to poor firm performance causing employees to leave and to high employee turnover causing poorer firm performance. Furthermore, employee benefits moderated the negative relationships between firm performance and both voluntary and involuntary turnover. That means that employees in firms that offered a larger number of employee benefits were less likely to leave voluntarily when firm performance was poor. Correspondingly, firms that offered a larger number of employee benefits were less likely to respond to poor firm performance by terminating employees involuntarily.

What are the practical implications of these findings? Anticipate a possible spike in voluntary turnover when a firm performs poorly, but recognize that work-life benefits may offset that trend.

Stock Market Reactions to Work-Life Initiatives

A recent study examined stock market effects of 130 announcements among *Fortune 500* companies of work-life initiatives in *The Wall Street Journal*.[44] The study examined changes in share prices the day before, the day of, and the day after such announcements. The average share price reaction over the three-day window was 0.39 percent, and the average dollar value of such changes was approximately $60 million per firm.

Apparently, investors anticipate that firms will have access to more resources (such as higher-quality talent) following the adoption of a work-life initiative. There is a difference, however, between announcements and actual implementation. Only firms that do what they say they will do are likely to reap the benefits of work-life initiatives.

In another study, researchers used data from 1995 to 2002 to compare the financial and stock market performance of the "100 Best" companies for working mothers, as published each year by *Working Mother* magazine, to that of benchmark indexes of the performance of U.S. equities, the S&P 500, and the Russell 3000.[45] In terms of financial performance, expressed as revenue productivity (sales per employee) and asset productivity (ROA), the study found no evidence that *Working Mother* "100 Best" companies were consistently more profitable or consistently more productive than their counterparts in S&P 500 companies.

At the same time, however, the total returns on common stock among *Working Mother* "100 Best" companies consistently outperformed the broader market benchmarks in each of the eight years of the study. Although the researchers found no evidence to indicate that "100 Best" companies are handicapped in the marketplace by offering generous work-life benefits, companies with superior stock returns may have a lower cost of capital and, therefore, can afford to invest in such benefits. The results reflect associations, not causation, between firms that adopt family-friendly work practices and financial and stock market outcomes. Nonetheless, the results suggest the possibility that at least some of the association is due to the effects of family-friendly investments on market outcomes.

Process

In this chapter, you have read facts and interview results that describe work-life fit/misfit. You have also seen data that reflect both financial and nonfinancial effects of work-life programs. In this final section, we present some guidelines to help you inform decision makers in a systematic way about the costs and benefits of such programs. Let's begin with a general query: What does it all mean?

If the findings described at the beginning of this chapter generalize widely, it is clear that employees at all levels, both men and women, and the members of different generations, want a "new deal" at work. To advance this agenda, leaders need to take four actions:[46]

- Stop defining the desire for "doable" jobs as a women's issue. Men want this, too.

- Start viewing efforts to humanize jobs as a competitive advantage and business necessity, not as one-time accommodations for favored employees or executives.

- Realize that progress is actually possible and that many examples show that work at all levels can be retooled.

- Make it safe within your organization to talk about these issues. As former Xerox CEO Anne Mulcahy noted wryly, "Businesses need to be 24/7; individuals don't."[47]

Influencing Senior Leaders

Remember that the purpose of HR metrics is to influence decisions about talent and how it is organized. To do that, senior leaders have to buy in to the logic and analyses that underlie the adoption of work-life programs. At a general level, here is a three-pronged strategy to consider in securing that kind of buy-in:[48]

1. Make the business case for work-life initiatives through data, research, and anecdotal evidence.

2. Offer to train managers on how to use flexible management approaches—to understand that, for a variety of reasons, some people want to work long hours, way beyond the norm, but that's not for everybody. The objective is to train managers to understand that individual solutions will work better in the future than a one-size-fits-all approach.

3. Use surveys and focus groups to demonstrate the importance of work-life fit in retaining talent.

Recognize that no one set of facts and figures applies to all firms. It depends on the unique strategic priorities of each organization. Figure 7-1 provides a diagnostic logic for conversations about this. One might start by discussing whether such initiatives will be part of a recruitment strategy to help the organization become an employer of choice, a diversity strategy to promote the advancement of women and minorities, a total rewards strategy, a strategy to retain top talent, or a health and wellness strategy if the priority is stress reduction.[49] Find out what your organization and its employees care about right now, what the workforce will look like in three to five years, and therefore, what senior leaders will need to care about in the future.[50]

Second, don't rely on isolated facts. By itself, any single study or fact is only one piece of the total picture. Think in terms of a multipronged approach:

- External data that describe trends in your organization's own industry

- Internal data that outline what employees want and how they describe their needs.[51]

- Internal data, perhaps based on pilot studies, that examine the financial and non-financial effects of work-life programs. As one executive noted, "Nothing beats a within-firm story."[52]

Be sure to communicate the high costs of employee absenteeism and turnover to employers (see Chapters 3 and 4). For example, because most costs associated with employee turnover are hidden (separation, replacement, and training costs), many firms do not track them. With these costs identified, communicate the benefits of work-life initiatives in reducing them.

Include stories from your own workers that describe how work-life programs have helped them. Have quotes from people whom senior leaders know and care about. In other words, use a combination of quantitative and qualitative data to make your case.

Third, understand that decision makers may well be skeptical even after all the facts and costs have been presented to them. Perhaps more deeply rooted attitudes and beliefs may underlie the skepticism—such as a belief that allowing employees to attend to personal concerns through time off may erode service to clients or customers, or that people will take unfair advantage of the benefits, or that work-life issues are just women's issues. To inform that debate, HR leaders need to address attitudes and values, as well as data, on costs and benefits of work-life programs. As one set of authors noted:

> Every workplace, small or large, can undertake efforts to treat employees with respect, to give them some autonomy over how they do their jobs, to help supervisors support employees to succeed on their jobs, and to help supervisors and coworkers promote work-life fit.[53]

Ultimately, a system of work-life programs, coupled with an organizational culture that supports that system, will help an organization create and sustain competitive advantage through its people.

Exercises

1. Your boss is skeptical about claims that work-life fit is important to managers as well as employees. What evidence can you provide to offset this line of thinking?

2. What is a work-life program? What are some examples?

3. Describe the wage penalty associated with "opting out" of the workforce.

4. Why is work-life fit particularly important to professional employees?

5. Describe some of the key barriers to wider implementation of work-life programs.

6. Develop a strategy for informing the debate over whether to invest in work-life programs. What cautions would you build into your game plan?

7. Explain: The concept of "flexibility" reflects a broad spectrum of possible work arrangements.

8. What key features are critical to making decisions about whether to provide options for increased flexibility in work arrangements?

9. How do work-life programs relate to organizational performance?

10. You are given the following data regarding the costs and payoffs from employer-subsidized child-care arrangements in your 159-person professional services organization. Before offering childcare, employees missed 850 days of work each year. That has been cut by 170 days per year, at a cost savings of $315 per day in direct costs. Likewise, voluntary turnover among high performers has dropped by 22 percent, saving the company $1.1 million each year in costs that were not incurred. The full cost of the child-care program (design and delivery) is $650,000. What is the ROI of this investment?

References

1. Hewlett, S. A., L. Sherbin, and K. Sumberg, "How Gen Y and Boomers Will Reshape Your Agenda," *Harvard Business Review* 87 (July/August 2009): 3–9. See also Galinsky, E., K. Aumann, and
J. T. Bond, *The 2008 National Study of the Changing Workforce: Times Are Changing—Gender and Generation at Work and at Home* (New York: Families and Work Institute, 2009); Aumann, K., and E. Galinsky, *The 2008 National Study of the Changing Workforce: The State of Health of the American Workforce: Does Having an Effective Workplace Matter?* (New York: Families and Work Institute, 2009). See also Minton-Eversole, T., "Survey: In Hiring Game, Employers Attuned to Work/Life Balance Win," *HR News* (February 28, 2008). Downloaded from www.shrm.org on May 21, 2010.

2. Galinsky, E., et al., 2009. See also Halpern, D. F. (chair), *Public Policy, Work, and Families: Report of the APA Presidential Initiative on Work and Families* (Washington, D. C.: American Psychological Association, 2005); and Halpern, D. F., and S. E. Murphy, *From Work-Family Balance to Work-Family Interaction: Changing the Metaphor* (Mahwah, N.J.: Erlbaum, 2005).

3. Brady, D., "Hopping Aboard the Daddy Track," *BusinessWeek* (November 8, 2004), 100–101.

4. Warren, E., and A. W. Tyagi, *The Two-Income Trap: Why Middle-Class Mothers and Fathers Are Going Broke* (New York: Basic Books, 2003).

5. Sammer, J., "Generating Value through Work/Life Programs," June 2004, retrieved from www.shrm.org on June 1, 2010; and Bardoel, E. A., P. Tharenou, and S. A. Moss, "Organizational Predictors of Work-Family Practices," *Asia Pacific Journal of Human Resources* 36, no. 3 (1998): 31–49.

6. Sources: Moskowitz, M., R. Levering, and C. Tkaczyk, "100 Best Companies," *Fortune* (February 8, 2010), 75; "SAS Revenue Jumps 2.2% to Record $2.31 Billion" (January 21, 2010), downloaded from www.sas.com May 28, 2010; and "SAS Ranks No. 1 on *Fortune* 'Best Companies to Work For' List in America" (January 21, 2010), downloaded from www.sas.com on May 28, 2010.

7. *Fueling the Talent Engine: Finding and Keeping High Performers: A Case Study of Yahoo!* DVD (Alexandria, Va.: Society for Human Resource Management Foundation, 2005); and Coff, R. W., "Human Assets and Management Dilemmas: Coping with Hazards on the Road to Resource-Based Theory," *Academy of Management Review* 22 (1997): 374–403.

8. Maslach, C., and M. P. Leiter, "Early Predictors of Job Burnout and Engagement," *Journal of Applied Psychology* 93 (2008): 498–512; and Maslach, C., "Understanding Burnout: Work and Family Issues," in *From Work-Family Balance to Work-Family Interaction: Changing the Metaphor,* ed. D. F. Halpern and S. E. Murphy (Mahwah, N.J.: Erlbaum, 2005).

9. Konrad, A. M., and R. Mangel, "The Performance Effect of Work-Family Programs," paper presented at the annual convention of the Academy of Management, San Diego, August 1998.

10. *Ibid.*

11. Byrnes, N., "Treating Part-Timers Like Royalty," *BusinessWeek* (October 10, 2005), 78.

12. Konrad and Mangel, 1998.

13. "Taxing Time: Accounting Firm Maintains Work/Life Balance During Busy Season," March 10, 2010, downloaded from www.shrm.org on May 25, 2010.

14. Tyson, L. D., "What Larry Summers Got Right," *BusinessWeek* (March 28, 2005), 24.

15. Hewlett, S. A., and C. B. Luce, "Off-Ramps and On-Ramps: Keeping Talented Women on the Road to Success," *Harvard Business Review* 83 (March 2005): 43–54.

16. See also Brady, 2004.

17. Johnson, A. A., "Strategic Meal Planning: Work/Life Initiatives for Building Strong Organizations," paper presented at the conference on Integrated Health, Disability, and Work/Life Initiatives, New York, February 25, 1999.

18. Galinsky, Aumann, and Bond, 2009.

19. Kossek, E. E., and C. Ozeki, "Work-Family Conflict, Policies, and the Job-Life Satisfaction Relationship: A Review and Directions for Organizational Behavior–Human Resources Research," *Journal of Applied Psychology* 83 (1998): 139–149.

20. Galinsky, Aumann, and Bond, 2009.

21. De Cieri, H., B. Holmes, J. Abbott, and T. Pettit, "Achievements and Challenges for Work/Life Balance Strategies in Australian Organizations," *International Journal of Human /Resource Management* 16, no. 1 (2005): 90–103.

22. "Expert: Work-Life Initiatives Start at the Top," September 26, 2008), downloaded from www.shrm.org, May 25, 2010.

23. Aumann and Galinsky, 2009.

24. Waters, M. A., and E. A. Bardoel, "Work-Family Policies in the Context of Higher Education: Useful or Symbolic?" *Asia Pacific Journal of Human Resources* 44, no. 1 (2006): 67–82.

25. Blair-Loy, M., and A. S. Wharton, "Employees' Use of Work-Family Policies and the Workplace Social Context," *Social Forces* 80, no. 3 (2002): 813–845.

26. Canadian Department of Labor, "Voices of Canadians: Seeking Work-Life Balance," 2003, downloaded from http://dsp-psd.pwgsc.gc.ca/Collection/RH54-12-2003E.pdf, June 1, 2010.

27. Murphy and Zagorski, 2005. See also Zagorski, D. A., "Balancing the Scales: The Role of Justice and Organizational Culture in Employees' Search for Work-Life Equilibrium," unpublished doctoral dissertation, Claremont Graduate University, 2005.

28. Waters and Bardoel, 2006; Hewlett and Luce, 2005.

29. Aumann and Galinsky, 2009.

30. Gurschiek, K., "Child Care 'Investment' Creates Competitive Advantage," *HR News,* March 5, 2007, downloaded from www.shrm.org, May 25, 2010.

31. *Ibid.*

32. O'Connell, B., "No Baby Sitter? Emergency Child-Care to the Rescue," Compensation & Benefits Forum. Retrieved from www.shrm.org, May 25, 2010.

33. Shellenbarger, S., "If You'd Rather Work in Pajamas, Here Are Ways to Talk the Boss into Flex-Time," *The Wall Street Journal* (February 13, 2003), D1; and Conlin, M., J. Merritt, and L. Himelstein, "Mommy Is Really Home from Work," *BusinessWeek* (November 25, 2002), 101–104.

34. Gurschiek, 2007.

35. Culpepper and Associates, "Flexible Work Arrangements: Popular Alternatives to Enhance Benefits," June 26, 2009, downloaded from www.shrm.org, May 25, 2010; Corporate Voices for Working Families, "Business Impacts of Flexibility: An Imperative for Expansion," November 2005, downloaded from www. cvworkingfamilies.org/system/files/Business%20Impacts%20of%20Flexibility.pdf, June 1, 2010.

36. Galinsky, E., K. Aumann, and J. T. Bond, *The 2008 National Study of the Changing Workforce: Workplace Flexibility and Employees from Low-Income Households* (New York: Families and Work Institute, 2010).

37. *Ibid.*

38. Culpepper and Associates, 2009.

39. Corporate Voices for Working Families, 2005.

40. *Ibid.*

41. *Ibid.*

42. Kelly, K., and S. Ang, "A Study on the Relationships between Work-Life Practices and Firm Performance in Singapore Firms," technical report, Nanyang Business School, Nanyang Technological University, Singapore, October 2005.

43. Kelly, K., S. Ang, G. H. H. Yeo, and W. F. Cascio, "Employee Turnover and Firm Performance: Modeling Reciprocal Effects," manuscript currently under review.

44. Arthur, M., "Share Price Reactions to Work-Family Initiatives: An Institutional Perspective," *Academy of Management Journal* 46 (2003): 497–505.

45. Cascio, W. F., and C. Young, "Work-Family Balance: Does the Market Reward Firms That Respect It?" in *From Work-Family Balance to Work-Family Interaction: Changing the Metaphor,* ed. D. F. Halpern and S. E. Murphy (Mahwah, N.J.: Lawrence Erlbaum Associates, 2005).

46. Miller, J., and M. Miller, "Get a Life!" *Fortune* (November 28, 2005): 110.

47. *Ibid.*

48. "Expert: Work-Life Initiatives Start at the Top," 2008.

49. *Ibid.*

50. Pires, P. S., "Sitting at the Corporate Table: How Work-Family Policies Are Really Made," in *From Work-Family Balance to Work-Family Interaction: Changing the Metaphor* (Mahwah, N.J.: Erlbaum, 2005).

51. Caminiti, S., "Reinventing the Workplace," *Fortune* (September 20, 2004): S12–S15.

52. Roberts, B., "Analyze This!" *HR Magazine* (October 2009), 35–41.

53. Aumann and Galinsky, 2009.

8

Staffing Utility: The Concept and Its Measurement

Management ideas and programs often have been adopted and implemented because they were fashionable (for example, Total Quality Management, Quality Circles, reengineering) or commercially appealing, or because of the entertainment value they offered the target audience.[1] In an era of downsizing, deregulation, and fierce global competition, and as operating executives continue to examine the costs of HR programs, HR executives are under increasing pressure to demonstrate that new or continuing programs add value in more tangible ways. Indeed, an ongoing challenge is to educate managers about the business value of HR programs in areas such as staffing and training. While some of the business value of these programs may be expressed in qualitative terms (such as improvements in customer service, team dynamics, or innovation),[2] our focus in this chapter and the three that follow it is on methods to express the monetary value of HR programs.

This chapter and Chapter 10, "The Payoff from Enhanced Selection," address the payoffs from improved staffing. Chapter 11, "Costs and Benefits of HR Development Programs," illustrates how the logical frameworks for staffing can be adapted to calculate the monetary value of employee training and development. The monetary value estimation techniques have been particularly well developed when applied to staffing programs. The combination of analytics based on widely applicable statistical assumptions, plus a logical approach for combining information to connect to the quality of the workforce, and analytical frameworks and tools to understand how workforce quality affects pivotal organizational outcomes, has produced sophisticated frameworks.

We begin this chapter by describing the logic underlying the value of staffing decisions, in terms of the conditions that define that value and that, when satisfied, lead to high value. After that, we present a broad overview of utility analysis as a way to improve organizational decisions, especially decisions about human capital. Note that many of the examples in this chapter refer to "dollar-valued" outcomes because the research was conducted in the United States. However, the same concepts apply to any currency.

Recall from Chapter 2, "Analytical Foundations for HR Measurement," that utility analysis generally refers to frameworks that help decision makers analyze in a systematic manner the subjective value, or expected utility of alternative outcomes associated with a decision. The expected utility or usefulness of each outcome is obtained by summing a rating of the outcome's importance or value to the decision maker multiplied by the expectation or probability of achieving that outcome. After summing these values across all outcomes, the decision rule is to choose the option with the highest expected utility. The approach to staffing utility measurement is similar; instead of simple estimates and multiplication, however, the formulas incorporate more nuanced approaches to probabilities, value estimation, and combinations of the individual elements.

A Decision-Based Framework for Staffing Measurement

Measures exist to enhance decisions. With respect to staffing decisions, measures are important to the decisions of applicants, potential applicants, recruiters, hiring managers, and HR professionals. These decisions include how to invest scarce resources (money, time, materials, and so on) in staffing techniques and activities, such as alternative recruiting sources, different selection and screening technologies, recruiter training or incentives, and alternative mixes of pay and benefits to offer desirable candidates. Staffing decisions also include decisions by candidates about whether to entertain or accept offers, and by hiring managers about whether to devote time and effort to landing the best talent. Increasingly, such decisions are not made exclusively by HR or staffing professionals, but in conjunction with managers outside of HR and other key constituents.[3]

Effective staffing requires measurements that diagnose the *quality* of the decisions of managers and applicants. Typical staffing-measurement systems fail to reflect these key decisions, so they end up with significant limitations and decision risks. For example, selection tests may be chosen solely based on their cost and predictive relationships with turnover or performance ratings. Recruitment sources may be chosen solely based on their cost and volume of applicants. Recruiters may be chosen based solely on their availability and evaluated only on the volume of applicants they produce. Staffing is typically treated not as a process, but as a set of isolated activities (recruiting, selecting, offering/closing, and so forth).

Fixing these problems requires a systematic approach to staffing that treats it as a set of decisions and processes that begins with a set of outcomes, identifies key processes, and then integrates outcomes with processes. Consider outcomes, for example. We know that the ultimate value of a staffing system is reflected in the quality of talent that is hired or promoted and retained. In fact, a wide variety of measures exists to examine staffing quality, but generally these measures fall into seven categories:

- **Cost:** Cost per hire, cost of assessment activities (tests, interviews, background checks)

- **Time of activities:** Time to fill vacancies, time elapsed from interview to offer

- **Volume and yield:** Total number of applicants, yield of hires from applicants

- **Diversity and EEO compliance:** Demographic characteristics of applicants at each stage of the hiring process

- **Customer/constituent reactions:** Judgments about the quality of the process and impressions about its attractiveness

- **Quality attributes of the talent:** Pre-hire predictive measures of quality (selection tests, interviewer ratings), as well as post-hire measures of potential and competency

- **Value impact of the talent:** Measures of actual job performance and overall contribution to the goals of a unit or organization

This chapter focuses primarily on two of these measures: the quality and value impact of talent. At the same time, it is important not to lose sight of the broader staffing processes within which screening and selection of talent takes place. Figure 8-1 is a graphic illustration of the logic of the staffing process and talent flows.

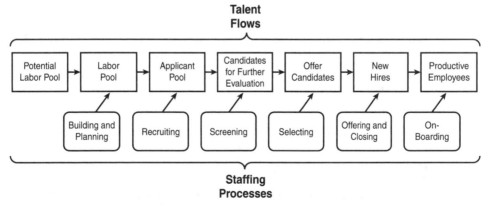

Figure 8-1 Logic of staffing processes and talent flows.

Groups of individuals (talent pools) flow through the various stages of the staffing process, with each stage serving as a filter that eliminates a subset of the original talent pool. The top row of Figure 8-1 shows the results of the filtering process, beginning with a potential labor pool that is winnowed through recruitment and selection to a group that receives offers and then is winnowed further as some accept offers and remain with the organization.

The "staffing processes" in the lower row show the activities that accomplish the filtering sequence, beginning with building and planning (forecasting trends in external and internal labor markets, inducing potential applicants to develop qualifications to satisfy future talent demands), and ending with on-boarding (orientation, mentoring, removing barriers to performance). Integrating measurement categories with the process steps shown in Figure 8-1 provides a decision-based framework for evaluating where staffing measures are sufficient and where they may be lacking.

Figure 8-1 might usefully be viewed as a supply-chain approach to staffing. To appreciate that analogy, consider that the pipeline of talent is very similar to the pipeline of any other resource. At each stage, the candidate pool can be thought of in terms of the quantity of candidates, the average and dispersion of the quality of the candidates, and the cost of processing and employing the candidates. Quantity, quality, and cost considerations determine the monetary value of staffing programs. We have more to say about these ideas in Chapter 10. Now that we have presented the "big picture" of the staffing process, let us focus more specifically on one component of that process: employee selection (specifically, on assessing the value of selection by means of utility analysis).

Framing Human Capital Decisions Through the Lens of Utility Analysis

Utility analysis is a framework to guide decisions about investments in human capital.[4] It is the determination of institutional gain or loss (outcomes) anticipated from various courses of action. When faced with a choice among strategies, management should choose the strategy that maximizes the expected utility for the organization.[5] To make the choice, managers must be able to estimate the utilities associated with various outcomes. Estimating utilities traditionally has been the Achilles heel of decision theory[6] but is a less acute problem in business settings, where gains and losses may be estimated by objective behavioral or cost accounting procedures, often in monetary terms.

Our objective in this chapter is to describe three different models of staffing utility analysis, focusing on the logic and analytics of each one. Chapter 9, "The Economic Value of Job Performance," Chapter 10, and Chapter 11 then build on these ideas, emphasizing measures and processes to communicate results to operating executives and to show how staffing, training, and other HR programs can be evaluated from a return on investment (ROI) perspective.

Overview: The Logic of Utility Analysis

As noted above, utility analysis considers three important parameters: quantity, quality, and cost. A careful look at Figure 8-1 shows that the top row refers to the characteristics of candidates for employment as they flow through the various stages of the staffing process. For example, the "applicant pool" might have a quantity of 100 candidates, with an average quality value of $100,000 per year and a variability in quality value that ranges from a low of $50,000 to a high of $170,000. This group of candidates might have an anticipated cost (salary, benefits, training, and so on) of 70 percent of its value. After screening and selection, the "offer candidates" might have a quantity of 50 who receive offers, with an average quality value of $150,000 per year, ranging from a low of $100,000 to a high of $160,000. Candidates who receive offers might require employment costs of 80 percent of their value, because we have identified highly qualified and sought-after individuals. Eventually, the organization ends up with a group of "new hires" (or promoted candidates, in the case of internal staffing) that can also be characterized by quantity, quality, and cost.

Similarly, the bottom row of Figure 8-1 reflects the staffing processes that create the sequential filtering of candidates. Each of these processes can be thought of in terms of the *quantity* of programs and practices used, the *quality* of the programs and practices as reflected in their ability to improve the value of the pool of individuals that survives, and the *cost* of the programs and practices in each process. For example, the quality of selection procedures is often expressed in terms of their validity, or accuracy in forecasting future job performance. Validity is typically expressed in terms of the correlation (see Chapter 2) between scores on a selection procedure and some measure of job performance, such as the dollar volume of sales. Validity may be increased by including a greater quantity of assessments (such as a battery of selection procedures), each of which focuses on an aspect of knowledge, skill, ability, or other characteristic that has been demonstrated to be important to successful performance on a job. Higher levels of validity imply higher levels of future job performance among those selected or promoted, thereby improving the overall payoff to the organization. As a result, those candidates who are predicted to perform poorly never get hired or promoted in the first place.

Decision makers naturally focus on the cost of selection procedures because they are so vividly depicted by standard accounting systems, but the cost of errors in selecting, hiring, or promoting the wrong person is often much more important. As explained in Chapter 9, the difference in value between an average performer versus a superior performer is often much higher than the difference in the cost of improving the staffing process. In the case of executives, a company often has to pay large fees to headhunters, and poor performance can have serious consequences in terms of projects, products, and customers. That cost can easily run $1 million to $3 million.[7]

In summary, the overall payoff to the organization (utility) from the use of staffing procedures depends on three broad parameters: quantity, quality, and cost. Each of the three staffing utility models that we examine in this chapter addresses two or more of these parameters. The models usually focus on the selection part of the processes of Figure 8-1, but they have implications for the other staffing stages, too. Each model defines the quality of candidates in a somewhat different way, so we start with the models that make relatively basic assumptions and move to those that are increasingly sophisticated.

Utility Models and Staffing Decisions

The utility of a selection device is the degree to which its use improves the quality of the individuals selected beyond what would have occurred had that device not been used.[8] In the context of staffing or employee selection, three of the best-known utility models are those of Taylor and Russell,[9] Naylor and Shine,[10] and Brogden, Cronbach, and Gleser.[11] Each of them defines the quality of selection in terms of one of the following:

- The proportion of individuals in the selected group who are considered successful

- The average standard score on a measure of job performance for the selected group

- The dollar payoff to the organization resulting from the use of a particular selection procedure

The remainder of this chapter considers each of these utility models and its associated measure of quality in greater detail.

The Taylor-Russell Model

Many decision makers might assume that if candidate ratings on a selection device (such as a test or interview) are highly associated with their later job performance, the selection device must be worth investing in. After all, how could better prediction of future performance not be worth the investment? However, if the pool of candidates contains very few unacceptable candidates, better testing may do little good. Or if the organization generates so few candidates that it must hire almost all of them, again, better testing will be of little use. Taylor and Russell translated these observations into a system for measuring the tradeoffs, suggesting that the overall utility or practical effectiveness of a selection device depends on more than just the validity coefficient (the correlation between a predictor of job performance and a criterion measure of actual job performance). Rather, it depends on three parameters: the validity coefficient (r), the selection ratio (SR, the proportion of applicants selected), and the base rate (BR, the proportion of applicants who would be successful without the selection procedure).

Taylor and Russell defined the value of the selection system as the "success ratio," which is the ratio of the number of hired candidates who are judged successful on the job divided by the total number of candidates that were hired. They published a series of tables illustrating the interactive effect of different validity coefficients, selection ratios, and base rates on the success ratio. The success ratio indicates the quality of those selected. The difference between the success ratio and the base rate (which reflects the success ratio without any added selection system) is a measure of the incremental value of the selection system over what would have happened if it had not been used. Let's develop this logic and its implications in more detail and show you how to use the tables Taylor and Russell developed.

Analytics

This model has three key, underlying assumptions:

1. It assumes fixed-treatment selection. (That is, individuals are chosen for one specified job, treatment, or course of action that cannot be modified.) For example, if a person is selected for Treatment A, a training program for slow learners, transfer to Treatment B, fast-track instruction, is not done, regardless of how well the person does in Treatment A.

2. The Taylor-Russell model does not account for the rejected individuals who would have been successful if hired (erroneous rejections). Because they are not hired, their potential value, or what they might contribute to other employers who now can hire them, is not considered.

3. The model classifies accepted individuals into successful and unsuccessful groups. All individuals within each group are regarded as making equal contributions. That means that being minimally successful is assumed to be equal in value to being highly successful, and being just below the acceptable standard is assumed to be equal in value to being extremely unsuccessful.

Of course, these assumptions may not hold in all situations; but even with these basic assumptions, Taylor and Russell were able to generate useful conclusions about the interplay between testing and recruitment. For example, the Taylor-Russell model demonstrates convincingly that even selection procedures with relatively low validities can increase substantially the percentage of those selected who are successful, when the selection ratio is low (lots of candidates to choose from) and when the base rate is near 50 percent (about half the candidates would succeed without further testing, so there are lots of middle-level candidates who can be sorted by better selection). Let us consider the concepts of selection ratio and base rate in greater detail.

The selection ratio is simply the number of candidates who must be hired divided by the number of available candidates to choose from. A selection ratio (SR) of 1.0 means the organization must hire everyone, so testing is of no value because there are no selection decisions to be made. The closer the actual SR is to 1.0, the harder it is for better selection to pay off. The opposite also holds true; as the SR gets smaller, the value of better selection gets higher. (For example, a selection ratio of .10 means the organization has ten times more applicants than it needs and must hire only 10 percent of the available applicants.) Figure 8-2 illustrates the wide-ranging effect that the SR may exert on a predictor with a given validity. In each case, Xc represents a cutoff score on the predictor. As you can see in Figure 8-2, even predictors with low validities can be useful if the SR is so low that the organization needs to choose only the cream of the crop. Conversely, with high selection ratios, a predictor must possess very high validity to increase the percentage successful among those selected.

It might appear that, because a predictor that demonstrates a particular validity is more valuable with a lower selection ratio, one should always opt to reduce the SR (become more selective). However, the optimal strategy is not this simple.[12] When the organization must achieve a certain quota of individuals, lowering the SR means the organization must increase the number of available applicants, which means expanding the recruiting and selection effort. In practice, that strategy may be too costly to implement, as later research demonstrated convincingly.[13]

Utility, according to Taylor and Russell, is affected by the base rate (the proportion of candidates who would be successful without the selection measure). To be of any use in selection, the measure must demonstrate incremental validity by improving on the BR. That is, the selection measure must result in more correct decisions than could be made without using it. As Figure 8-3 demonstrates, when the BR is either very high or very low, it is difficult it for a selection measure to improve upon it.

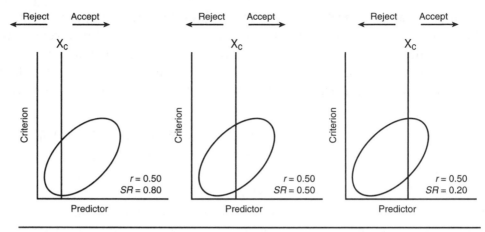

Note: The oval is the shape of a scatterplot corresponding to $r = 0.50$; $r =$ validity coefficient; $SR =$ selection ratio; $X_c =$ cutoff score.

Figure 8-2 Effect of varying selection ratios on a predictor with a given validity.

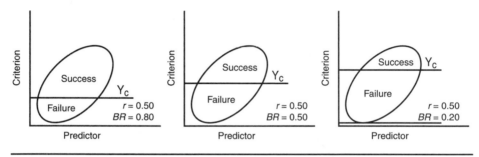

Note: The oval is the shape of a scatterplot corresponding to $r = 0.50$; $BR =$ base rate; $r =$ validity coefficient; $Y_c =$ minimum level of job performance.

Figure 8-3 Effect of varying base rates on a predictor with a given validity.

In each panel of the figure, Y_c represents the minimum level of job performance (criterion cutoff score) necessary for success. That value should not be altered arbitrarily. Instead, it should be based on careful consideration of the true level of minimally acceptable performance for the job.[14] Figure 8-3 illustrates that, with a BR of 0.80, it would be difficult for any selection measure to improve on the base rate. In fact, when the BR is 0.80 and half of the applicants are selected, a validity of 0.45 is required to produce an improvement of even 10 percent over base-rate prediction. This is also true at very low BRs (as would be the case, for example, in the psychiatric screening of job applicants). Given a BR of 0.20, an SR of 0.50, and a validity of 0.45, the percentage successful among those selected is 0.30 (once again representing only a 10 percent improvement in correct decisions). Selection measures are most useful when BRs are about 0.50.[15] Because the BR departs radically in either direction from this value, the benefit of an additional predictor becomes questionable. The lesson is obvious: Applications of selection measures to situations with markedly different SRs or BRs can result in quite different predictive outcomes. If it is not possible to demonstrate significant incremental utility by adding a predictor, the predictor should not be used, because it cannot improve on current selection procedures.

Figure 8-4 presents all of the elements of the Taylor-Russell model together. In this figure, the criterion cutoff (Y_c) separates the present employee group into satisfactory and unsatisfactory workers. The predictor cutoff (X_c) defines the relative proportion of workers who would be hired at a given level of selectivity. Areas A and C represent correct decisions—that is, if the selection measure were used to select applicants, those in area A would be hired and become satisfactory employees. Those in area C would be rejected correctly because they scored below the predictor cutoff and would have performed unsatisfactorily on the job. Areas B and D represent erroneous decisions; those in area B would be hired because they scored above the predictor cutoff, but they would perform unsatisfactorily on the job, and those in area D would be rejected because they scored below the predictor cutoff, but they would have been successful if hired.

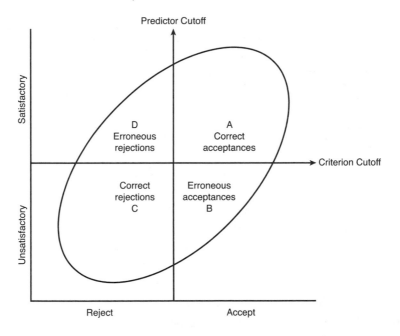

Note: The oval is the shape of the scatterplot that shows the overall relationship between predictor and criterion scores.

Figure 8-4 Effect of predictor and criterion cutoffs on selection decisions.

Taylor and Russell used the following ratios in developing their tables:

$$\text{Base rate} = \frac{A+D}{A+B+C+D} \tag{8-1}$$

$$\text{Selection ratio} = \frac{A+B}{A+B+C+D} \tag{8-2}$$

$$\text{Success ratio} = \frac{A}{A+B} \tag{8-3}$$

By specifying the validity coefficient, the base rate, and the selection ratio, and making use of Pearson's "Tables for Finding the Volumes of the Normal Bivariate Surface,"[16] Taylor and Russell developed their tables (see Appendix A). The usefulness of a selection measure thus can be assessed in terms of the success ratio that will be obtained if the selection measure is used. To determine the gain in utility to be expected from using the instrument (the expected increase in the percentage of successful workers), subtract the base rate from the success ratio (Equation 8-3 minus Equation 8-1). For example, given an SR of 0.10, a validity of 0.30, and a BR of 0.50, the success ratio jumps to 0.71 (a 21 percent gain in utility over the base rate—to verify this figure, see Appendix A).

The validity coefficient referred to by Taylor and Russell is, in theory, based on present employees who have already been screened using methods other than the new selection procedure. It is assumed that the new procedure will simply be added to a group of selection procedures used previously, and the incremental gain in validity from the use of the new procedure most relevant.

Perhaps the major shortcoming of this utility model is that it reflects the quality of the resulting hires only in terms of success or failure. It views the value of hired employees as a dichotomous classification—successful or unsuccessful—and as the tables in Appendix A demonstrate, when validity is fixed, the success ratio increases as the selection ratio decreases. (Turn to Appendix A, choose any particular validity value, and note what happens to the success ratio as the selection ratio changes from 0.95 to 0.05.) Under those circumstances, the success ratio tells us that more people are successful, but not *how much more* successful.

In practice, situations may arise in which one would not expect the average level of job performance to change as a function of higher selection standards, such as food servers at fast-food restaurants. Their activities have become so standardized that there is little opportunity for significant improvements in performance after they have been selected and trained. The relationship between the value of such jobs to the organization and variations in performance demonstrates essentially flat slopes. In such situations, it may make sense to think of the value of hired candidates as either being above the minimum standard or not.

For many jobs, however, one would expect to see improvements in the average level of employee value from increased selectivity. In most jobs, for example, a very high-quality employee is more valuable than one who just meets the minimum standard of acceptability. When it is reasonable to assume that the use of higher cutoff scores on a selection device will lead to higher levels of average job performance by those selected, the Taylor-Russell tables underestimate the actual amount of value from the selection system. That observation led to the development of the next framework for selection utility, the Naylor-Shine Model.

The Naylor-Shine Model

Unlike the Taylor-Russell model, the Naylor and Shine utility model does not require that employees be split into satisfactory and unsatisfactory groups by specifying an arbitrary cutoff on the criterion (job performance) dimension that represents minimally acceptable performance.[17] The Naylor-Shine model defines utility as the increase in the average criterion score (for example, the average level of job performance of those selected) expected from the use of a selection process with a given validity and SR. The quality of those selected is now defined as the difference in average level of quality of the group that is hired, versus the average quality in the original group of candidates.

Like Taylor and Russell, Naylor and Shine assume that the relationship between predictor and criterion is bivariate normal (both scores on the selection device and performance scores are normally distributed), linear, and homoscedastic. The validity coefficient is assumed to be based on the concurrent validity model.[18] That model reflects the gain in validity from using the new selection procedure *over and above* what is presently available using current information.

In contrast to the Taylor-Russell utility model, the Naylor-Shine approach assumes a linear relationship between validity and utility. That is, the higher the validity, the greater the increase in the average criterion score of the selected group compared to the average criterion score that the candidate group would have achieved. Equation 8-4 shows the basic equation underlying the Naylor-Shine model:

$$\overline{Z}_{yi} = r_{xy} \frac{\lambda_i}{\phi_i} \tag{8-4}$$

Here, $\overline{Z}_{yi}$ is the average criterion score (in standard-score units)[19] of those selected, r_{xy} is the validity coefficient, λ_i is the height of the normal curve at the predictor cutoff, Z_{xi}

(expressed in standard-score units), and ϕ_i is the selection ratio. Equation 8-4 applies whether r_{xy} represents a correlation between two variables or it is a multiple-regression coefficient.[20]

Using Equation 8-4 as a basic building block, Naylor and Shine present a series of tables (see Appendix B) that specify, for each SR, the standard (predictor) score that produces that SR, the ordinate of the normal curve at that point, and the quotient λ_i/ϕ_i. The quotient $\lambda_i/\phi_i = \bar{Z}_x$, the average predictor score of those selected. The tables can be used to answer several important HR questions:

- Given a specified SR, what will be the average criterion level (for example, performance level) of those selected?

- Given a certain minimum cutoff score on the selection device above which everyone will be hired, what will be the average criterion level ($\bar{Z}_{yi}$)?

- Given a desired improvement in the average criterion score (for example, performance) of those selected, and assuming a certain validity, what SR and/or predictor cutoff value (in standard score units) should be used?

Let's work through some examples, using the tables in Appendix B.

In each of the following examples, assume that r_{xy}, the validity of our predictor, is positive and equal to 0.40. Of course, it is also possible that the validity of a predictor could be negative (for example, higher levels of job satisfaction related systematically to lower intentions to quit). Under these circumstances, the general rule is to reverse the sign of r_{xy} and Z_{xi} everywhere in the calculations.

1. With a selection ratio of 50 percent ($\phi_i = 0.50$), what will be the average performance level of those selected?

   Solution: Enter the table at $\phi_i = 0.50$ and read $\lambda_i/\phi_i = 0.80$.

   $$\bar{Z}_{yi} = r_{xy}\, \lambda_i/\phi_i = (0.40)(0.80) = 0.32$$

   Thus, the average criterion score of those selected, using an SR of 0.50, is 0.32 Z-units (roughly one third of a standard deviation) better than the unselected sample.

2. With a desired cutoff score set at .96 standard deviations below the average of the applicant pool ($Z_{xi} = -0.96$), what will be the standardized value of the criterion ($\bar{Z}_{yi}$)?

   Solution: Enter the table at $Z_{xi} = -0.96$ and read $\lambda_i/\phi_i = 0.30$.

   $$\bar{Z}_{yi} = r_{xy}\, \lambda_i/\phi_i = (0.40)(0.30) = 0.12$$

Thus, using this cutoff score on our predictor results in an average criterion score of about one eighth of a standard deviation (0.12 Z-units) higher than the average of the unselected applicant pool.

3. If we want to achieve an average standardized level of performance on our criterion (such as job performance) among those selected that is half a standard deviation higher than the average of the applicant pool($\overline{Z}_{yi}$ = 0.50), and assuming a validity of .40, what SR do we need to achieve? What predictor cutoff value will achieve that SR?

Solution: Because $\overline{Z}_{yi} = r_{xy} \lambda_i / \phi_i$ then

$$\lambda_i / \phi_i = \overline{Z}_{yi} / r_{xy} = 0.50/0.40 = 1.25$$

Enter the table at $\lambda_i / \phi_i = 1.25$ and read $\phi_i = 0.2578$ and $Z_{xi} = 0.65$. Thus, to achieve an average improvement of 0.50 (one half) standard deviation in job performance, an SR of 0.2578 is necessary (we must select only the top 25.78 percent of applicants). To achieve that, we must set a cutoff score on the predictor of 0.65 standard deviations above the average among our applicants.

The Naylor-Shine utility approach is more generally applicable than Taylor-Russell because, in many, if not most, cases, an organization could expect an increase in average job performance as it becomes more selective, using valid selection procedures. However, "average job performance" is expressed in terms of standard (Z) scores, which are more difficult to interpret than are outcomes more closely related to the specific nature of a business, such as dollar volume of sales, units produced or sold, or costs reduced. With only a standardized criterion scale, one must ask questions such as "Is it worth spending $10,000 to select 50 people per year, to obtain a criterion level of 0.50 standard deviations (SDs) greater than what we would obtain without the predictor?"[21] Some HR managers may not even be familiar with the concept of a standard deviation and would find it difficult to attach a dollar value to a 0.50 SD increase in criterion performance.

Neither the Taylor-Russell nor the Naylor-Shine models formally integrates the concept of selection system cost, nor the monetary gain or loss, into the utility index. Both describe differences in the percentage of successful employees (Taylor-Russell) or increases in average criterion score (Naylor-Shine), but they tell us little about the benefits to the employer in monetary terms. The Brogden-Cronbach-Gleser model, discussed next, was designed to address these issues.

The Brogden-Cronbach-Gleser Model

Brogden showed that, under certain conditions, the validity coefficient is a direct index of "selective efficiency." That means that if the criterion and predictor are expressed in standard score units, r_{xy} represents the ratio of the average criterion score made by persons selected on the basis of their predictor scores ($\overline{Z}_y$) to the average score made if one had selected them based on their criterion scores ($\overline{Z}_{y'}$). Of course, it is usually not possible to select applicants based on their criterion scores (because one cannot observe their criterion scores before they are hired), but Brogden's insight means that the validity coefficient represents the ratio of how well an actual selection process does, compared to that best standard. Equation 8-5 shows this algebraically:

$$r_{xy} = \frac{\overline{Z}_y}{\overline{Z}_{y'}} \tag{8-5}$$

The validity coefficient has these properties when (1) both the predictor and criterion are continuous (that is, they can assume any value within a certain range and are not divided into two or more categories), (2) the predictor and criterion distributions are identical (not necessarily normal, but identical), (3) the regression of the criterion on the predictor is linear, and (4) the selection ratio (SR) is held constant.[22]

As an illustration, suppose that a firm wants to hire 20 people for a certain job and must choose the best 20 from 85 applicants. Ideally, the firm would hire all 85 for a period of time, collect job performance (criterion) data, and retain the best 20, those obtaining the highest criterion scores. The average criterion score of the 20 selected this way would obviously be the highest obtainable with any possible combination of 20 of the 85 applicants.

Such a procedure is usually out of the question, so organizations use a selection process and choose the 20 highest scorers. Equation 8-5 indicates that the validity coefficient may be interpreted as the ratio of the average criterion performance of the 20 people selected on the basis of their predictor scores compared to the average performance of the 20 who would have been selected had the criterion itself been used as the basis for selection. To put a monetary value on this, if selecting applicants based on their actual behavior on the job, would save an organization $300,000 per year over random selection, a selection device with a validity of 0.50 could be expected to save $150,000 per year. Utility is therefore a direct linear function of validity, when the conditions noted previously are met.

Equation 8-5 does not include the cost of selection, but Brogden later used the principles of linear regression to demonstrate the relationships of cost of selection, validity, and selection ratio to utility, expressed in terms of dollars.[23]

Recall that our ultimate goal is to identify the monetary payoff to the organization when it uses a selection system to hire employees. To do this, let's assume we could construct a criterion measure expressed in monetary terms. We'll symbolize it as $y_\$$. Examples of this might include the sales made during a week/month/quarter by each of the salespersons on a certain job, or the profit obtained from each retail operation managed by each of the store managers across a country, or the outstanding customer debts paid during a week/month/quarter for the customers handled by each of a group of call-center collection agents. If we call that criterion measure y, then here is a plain-English and mathematical description of Brogden's approach.[24]

Step 1: Express the Predictor-Criterion Relationship As a Formula for a Straight Line

Recall the formula for a straight line that most people learn in their first algebra class, shown here as Equation 8-6.

$$y = a + bx \qquad (8\text{-}6)$$

where:

> y = dependent variable, or criterion (such as a job performance measure)
>
> x = independent variable that we hope predicts our criterion (such as job performance)
>
> a = y-intercept, or where the line crosses the y-axis of a graph when $x = 0$
>
> b = slope, or "rise over the run" of the line—that is, the change in y (for example, change in sales) for every one-unit change in x (score on a sales-aptitude test).

First, let's change this equation slightly. Let's substitute the symbol b_0 for a, b_1 for b, and $y_\$$ for y. In this way, we go from Equation 8-6 above to Equation 8-7.

$$\hat{y}_\$ = b_0 + b_1 x \qquad (8\text{-}7)$$

Then let's add an e after the x, to reflect that there is some random fluctuation or "error" in any straight-line estimate, and we get Equation 8-8.

$$\hat{y}_\$ = b_0 + b_1 x + e \qquad (8\text{-}8)$$

Our original formulas (Equations 8-6 and 8-7) described the points that fall *exactly on* a straight line, but Equation 8-8 describes points that fall *around* a straight line. Figure 8-5 shows this idea as a straight line passing through an ellipse. The ellipse represents the cloud of score combinations that might occur in an actual group of people, and the line in the middle is the one that gets as close as possible to as many of the points in the cloud. Some people describe this picture as a hot dog on a stick.

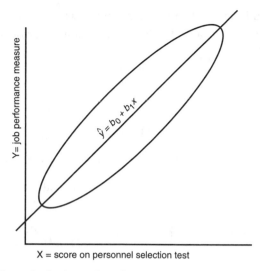

Figure 8-5 Dispersion of actual criterion and predictor scores.

In the context of staffing, x would be each employee's score on some selection process, and y would be the same employee's subsequent criterion score (such as performance on the job). If we don't know yet how someone is going to perform on the job (which we can't know before the person is hired), a best guess or estimate of how the employee might perform on the job would be the $\hat{y}_s$ value obtained from plugging the applicant's x score into Equation 8-7.

The letter e in Equation 8-8 is called "error," because although our estimate $\hat{y}_s$ from Equation 8-7 might be a good guess, it is not likely to be exactly the level of job performance obtained by that applicant later on the job. Note that because y is the actual performance attained by that applicant, then $y - \hat{y}_s = e$. The "error" by which our original predicted level of job performance, $\hat{y}_s$, differed from the applicant's actual job performance, y, is equal to e.

Ordinary least-squares regression analyses can be used to calculate the "best"-fitting straight line (that is, Equation 8-7), where *best* means the formula for the straight line $\hat{y}_s = b_0 + b_1 x$ (Equation 8-7) that minimizes the sum of all squared errors (e^2). This is where the "least-squares" portion of the "ordinary least-squares" label comes from.

Step 2: Standardize x

To get back to the validity coefficient, we need to convert the actual, or "raw," scores on our predictor and criterion to standardized form. Starting with Equation 8-7, reprinted here as Equation 8-9, let's see how this works.

$$\hat{y}_s = b_0 + b_1 x \qquad (8\text{-}9)$$

Let's first standardize all the applicants' selection process scores (that is, take their original scores, subtract the average, and divide by the standard deviation), as shown in Equation 8-10:

$$z_i = \frac{x_i - \bar{x}}{SD_x}$$

(8-10)

Where:

x_i = selection process score earned by applicant i

z_i = "standard" or Z score corresponding to the x_i score for applicant i

$\bar{x}$ = average or mean selection process score, typically of all applicants, obtained in some sample

SD_x = standard deviation of xi around $\bar{x}$, or $SD_x = \sqrt{\dfrac{\sum\limits_{i=1}^{n}(x_i - \bar{x})^2}{n-1}}$

When Equation 8-9 is modified to reflect the fact that x is now standardized, it becomes Equation 8-11.

$$\hat{y}_\$ = b_0 + b_1 z$$

(8-11)

Step 3: Express the Equations in Terms of the Validity Coefficient

Finally, let's modify Equation 8-11 to show the role of the validity coefficient using this selection process. We want to know the expected value (or the most likely average value) of $y_\$$ for the hired applicants. Modifying Equation 8-11 to express all the elements with a capital E for expected value, we have this:

$$E(y_\$) = E(b_0) + E(b_1)E(z_s)$$

(8-12)

Thus, $E(y_\$)$ means the "expected value of the criterion, y, in monetary terms." Also note that the letter s is now subscripted to the letter z, to show that the criterion scores are from the group of applicants who are actually selected (subscript s stands for "selected").

Remember that "expected value" typically means "average," so $E(y_\$) = \bar{y}_\$$ and $e(z_s) = \bar{z}_s$. Substituting these values into Equation 8-11 yields the following:

$$\bar{y}_\$ = E(b_0) + E(b_1)\bar{z}_s$$

(8-13)

We can calculate $\bar{z}_s$ simply by standardizing the selection test scores of all applicants, averaging just the scores of the individuals who were actually selected (hence the subscript s). When no selection system is used (that is, if applicants had been chosen at random), zs is expected to be the same as the average of z scores for all applicants. By definition, the average of all z scores in a sample is always 0. So when $\bar{z}_s = 0$. then $E(b_1)\bar{z}_s = 0$ also, and $E(b_0)$ will be the average monetary value of the criterion for individuals selected at random from the applicant pool. The symbol for the expected or average monetary criterion score for all applicants is $, so we can substitute $ for $E(b_0)$ in Equation 8-13.

Finally, the value of $E(b_1)$ is obtained using multiple-regression software (for example, the regression function in Excel). This is the regression coefficient or beta weight associated with x (as opposed to the "constant," which is the estimate of $E(b_0)$). By definition, the regression coefficient can also be defined as in Equation 8-14.

$$b_1 = r_{xy}\left(\frac{SD_y}{SD_x}\right) \qquad (8\text{-}14)$$

where:

r_{xy} = simple correlation between test scores on the personnel selection test x and the criterion measure y.

SD_y = standard deviation of the monetary value of the criterion (such as job performance).

SD_x = standard deviation of all applicants' selection-test scores.

Recall, however, that we standardized applicant test scores in using Equation 8-10 to create the z variable used in Equation 8-11. The standard deviation of z scores is always 1.0. So substituting 1 for SD_x, Equation 8-14 becomes $b_1 = r_{xy}SD_y$.

Substituting $\mu_{\$}$ for $E(b_0)$ and $r_{xy}SD_y$ for b_1 in Equation 8-13, we get this:

$$\bar{y}_{\$} = \mu_{\$} + r_{xy}SD_y\bar{z}_{\$} \qquad (8\text{-}15)$$

Equation 8-15 describes the total expected monetary value of each selected applicant. To calculate the expected average improvement in utility, or the improvement in the monetary value produced by using the staffing system, we can subtract the expected value without using the system, which is $\mu_{\$}$, from both sides of equation. Because $\mu_{\$}$ is the monetary value of criterion performance the organization expects when it chooses applicants at random, $\bar{y}_{\$} - \mu_{\$}$ is equal to the expected gain in monetary-valued performance from using the staffing process, as shown in Equation 8-16.

$$\bar{y}_{\$} - \mu_{\$} = \mu_{\$} + r_{xy}SD_y\bar{z}_{\$} \qquad (8\text{-}16)$$

Step 4: Subtract the Costs of the Selection Process

Selecting applicants requires resources. If we use the letter C to stand for the cost of applying the selection process to one applicant, and the term N_a to stand for the total number of applicants to whom the selection process is applied, then the total cost of the selection process is the product of N_a and C. If we divide that by the number of applicants actually selected, that gives us the average cost of the selection process per selected applicant. Finally, if we subtract the average selection process cost per selected applicant from the average value expressed in Equation 8-15, we get Equation 8-17.

$$\bar{y}_\$ - \mu_\$ = r_{xy}SD_y\bar{z}_s - \frac{N_aC}{N_s} \tag{8-17}$$

Finally, the left side of Equation 8-17 is often symbolized as ΔU, to stand for the "change in utility" per applicant selected, as shown in Equation 8-18.

$$\Delta U = r_{xy}SD_y\bar{z}_s - \frac{N_aC}{N_s} \tag{8-18}$$

Cronbach and Gleser elaborated and refined Brogden's derivations with respect to utility in fixed-treatment selection, and they arrived at the same conclusions regarding the effects of r, SDy, the cost of selection, and the selection ratio on utility in fixed-treatment selection. Utility properly is regarded as linearly related to validity and, if cost is zero, is proportional to validity.[25] They also adopted Taylor and Russell's interpretation of the validity coefficient for utility calculations (that is, concurrent validity). The validity coefficient based on present employees assumes a population that has been screened using information other than the new selection measure. The selection ratio is applied to this population.

Cronbach and Gleser argued, as did Taylor and Russell and Naylor and Shine, that selection procedures should be judged on the basis of their contribution over and above the best strategy available that makes use of prior, existing information. Thus, any new procedure must demonstrate incremental utility before it is used. Suppose, however, that an organization wants to replace its old selection procedures with new ones. Under such circumstances, the appropriate population for deriving a validity coefficient, SD_y, and SR, should be the *unscreened* population.[26] Figure 8-6 presents a summary of the three utility models that we have discussed.

Models	Utility Index	Data Requirements	Distinctive Assumptions
Taylor-Russell (1939)	Increase in percentage successful in selected group	Validity, base rate, selection ratio	All selectees classified as either successful or unsuccessful. Equal criterion performance by all members of each group; cost of selection = $0.
Naylor-Shine (1965)	Increase in mean criterion score of selected group	Validity, selection ratio	Validity linearly related to utility; cost of selection = $0.
Brogden-Cronbach-Gleser (1965)	Increase in dollar payoff of selected group	Validity, selection ratio, criterion standard deviation in dollars	Validity linearly related to utility; cost of selection ≠ $0, criterion performance evaluated in dollars.

Note: All three models assume a validity coefficient based on present employees (concurrent validity).

Source: W. F. (1980). Responding to the demand for accountability: A critical analysis of three utility models. Organizational Behavior and Human Performance, 25, p.42.

Figure 8-6 Summary of the utility indexes, data requirements, and assumptions of three utility models.

Process: Supply-Chain Analysis and Staffing Utility[27]

In this chapter, we have focused exclusively on the utility of staffing decisions, but look carefully again at Figure 8-1. In the conventional approach to staffing, activities like sourcing, recruitment, initial screening, selection, offers, on-boarding of new hires, performance management, and retention tend to be viewed as independent activities, each separate from the others. Such a micro-level, or "silo" orientation, has dominated the field of HR almost from its inception, and within it, the objective has been to maximize payoffs for each element of the overall staffing process. We believe that there is a rich opportunity for HR professionals to develop and apply an integrative framework whose objective is to optimize investments across the various elements of the staffing process, not simply to maximize payoffs within each element.

To do that, we believe there is much to learn from the field of supply-chain analysis. Supply-chain analysis pays careful attention to the ultimate quality of materials and components. Reframing utility analysis within that framework makes optimization opportunities more apparent. Perhaps more important, the supply-chain framework may help solve one of the thorniest issues in utility analysis: the disturbingly stubborn difficulty in getting key decision makers to embrace it. How? By relating utility analysis to a framework that is familiar to decision makers outside of HR, and one that they already use.

Essentially, the decision process involves optimizing costs against price and time, to achieve levels of expected quality/quantity and risks associated with variations in quality/quantity. If the quality or quantity of acquired resources falls below standard or exhibits excessive variation, decision makers can evaluate where investments in the process will make the biggest difference.

When a line leader complains that he or she is getting inferior talent, or not enough talent for a vital position, HR too often devises a solution without full insight into the broader supply chain. HR often responds by enhancing interviews or tests and presenting evidence about the improved validity of the selection process. Yet a more effective solution might be to retain the original selection process with the same validity, but to recruit from sources where the average quality of talent is higher.

Likewise, consider what happens when business leaders end up with too few candidates, and instruct HR to widen the recruitment search. HR is often too eager to respond with more recruiting activities, when, in fact, the number of candidates presented to business leaders is already sufficient. The problem is that some leaders are better at inducing candidates to accept offers. The more prudent response may be to improve the performance of the leaders who cause candidates to reject offers.

Leaders are accustomed to a logical approach that optimizes all stages of the supply chain when it comes to raw materials, unfinished goods, and technology. Why not adopt the same approach to talent? Consider an example of one company that did just that.

Valero Energy, the 20,000-employee, $70 billion energy-refining and marketing company, developed a new recruitment model out of human capital metrics based on applying supply-chain logic to labor. According to Dan Hilbert, Valero's manager of employment services, "Once you run talent acquisition as a supply chain, it allows you to use certain metrics that you couldn't use in a staffing function .... We measure every single source of labor by speed, cost, and efficiency."[28] Computer-screen "dashboards" show how components in the labor supply chain, such as ads placed on online job boards, are performing according to those criteria. If the dashboard shows "green," performance is fine. If it shows "yellow" or "red," Valero staffing managers can intervene quickly to fix the problem.[29] By doing that, the company can identify where it can recruit the best talent at the most affordable price. From a strategic perspective, it also can identify whether it is better to recruit full-time or part-time, to contract workers, or to outsource the work entirely.

We have more to say in later chapters about applying supply-chain logic to decisions about talent, but for now, the important point to emphasize is that talent flows and staffing processes are parts of a larger system. Our objective should be to optimize overall decisions regarding quantity, quality, and cost against price and time.

Conclusion

This chapter presents some complex but elegant statistical logic. It's sometimes hard to follow at first, but as Figure 8-1 shows, it is actually rather intuitive. The idea of each of the three "selection utility" models is to estimate how much higher the quality of the selected employees will be, compared to the quality of the candidates for selection. That change in quality depends on how selective the organization can be, how well it predicts future performance, and how much differences in performance quality translate into differences in value to the organization.

The utility models are best used with an understanding of their logic, assumptions, and data requirements. If you make that investment, you have a logical system for making wiser and more strategically relevant decisions about how to select talent both from the outside and within the organization.

These equations would be fine if we actually had a monetarily valued criterion to use in estimating SD_y. When a job produces very clear monetarily valued outcomes such as sales, waste, or profit, we might associate these values with each individual on the job and calculate the standard deviation of those values. Still, that would not reflect the standard deviation we might have seen in the pool of applicants, because the people on the job have already been screened in the course of the selection process. Also, even in jobs with obvious monetary outcomes, such as sales, other elements of the job may be quite important but are not reflected in individual monetary results (such as when salespeople actually sell less because they are training their colleagues). In short, the value and the process for estimating SD_y address a fundamental question in all of human resources and talent management: "How much are differences in performance worth?"

At this point, you might be wondering how organizations can actually estimate the dollar value of differences in performance quality. Indeed, SD_y has been the subject of much debate, and there are several methods for estimating it. We discuss those in the next chapter. You might also wonder whether this same kind of logic (estimating how much better quality our employees are after a certain HR program, compared to their quality without it) might apply to programs other than selection. We have much more to say about the strategic use of utility analysis in guiding investment decisions about human capital in Chapters 10 and 11.

Exercises

Software that calculates answers to one or more of the following exercises can be found at http://hrcosting.com/hr/.

---

1. Use the Taylor-Russell tables (see Appendix A) to solve these problems by filling in the following table:

Validity	SR	BR	Success Ratio
0.25	0.20	0.30	
0.55	0.70	0.80	
0.20	0.70	0.80	
0.10	0.50	0.50	
0.55	0.50	0.50	

2. Use the Naylor-Shine tables (see Appendix B) to solve these problems by filling in the following table:

r_{xy}	ϕ_i	z_{xi}	z-bar$_{yi}$
0.35	0.7019		
0.22		−0.30	
0.47			0.65
−0.47			0.65

3. Using the Brogden-Cronbach-Gleser continuous-variable utility model, what is the net gain over random selection (ΔU overall and per selectee), given the following information?

Quota for selection: 20

SR: 0.20

SD_y (standard deviation of job performance expressed in dollars): $30,000

r_{xy}: 0.25

C_y: $35

Hint: To find N, the number recruited, divide the quota for selection by the SR.

4. Given the following information on two selection procedures, and using the Brogden-Cronbach-Gleser model, what is the relative *difference* in payoff (overall and per selectee) between the two procedures? For both procedures, quota = 50, SR = 0.50, and SD_y = $45,000.

$r_y1: 0.20 \qquad C_1: \$200$

$r_y2: 0.40 \qquad C_2: \$700$

5. You are a management consultant whose task is to do a utility analysis using the following information regarding secretaries at Inko, Inc. The validity of the Secretarial Aptitude Test (SAT) is 0.40, applicants must score 70 or better to be hired, and only about half of those who apply actually are hired. Of those hired, about half are considered satisfactory by their bosses. How selective should Inko be to upgrade the average criterion score of those selected by $\bar{Z}_y = 0.5$? What utility model did you use to solve the problem? Why?

References

1. Crainer, S., and D. Dearlove, "Whatever Happened to Yesterday's Bright Ideas?" *Across the Board* (May/June 2006): 34–40.

2. Cascio, W. F., and L. Fogli, "The Business Value of Employee Selection," in *Handbook of Employee Selection,* ed. J. L. Farr and N. T. Tippins (pp. 235–252). (New York: Routledge, 2010).

3. *Ibid.* See also Boudreau, J. W., and P.M. Ramstad, "Beyond Cost-Per-Hire and Time to Fill: Supply-Chain Measurement for Staffing," Los Angeles, CA: Center for Effective Organizations, CEO publication G 04-16 (468).

4. Boudreau, J. W., and P.M. Ramstad, "Strategic Industrial and Organizational Psychology and the Role of Utility Analysis Models," in *Handbook of Psychology* 12, ed. W. C. Borman, D. R. Ilgen, and R. J. Klimoski, (pp. 193-221). (Hoboken, N.J.: Wiley, 2003).

5. Brealey, R. A., S. C. Myers, and F. Allen, *Principles of Corporate Finance,* 8th ed. (Burr Ridge, Ill.: Irwin/McGraw-Hill, 2006).

6. Cronbach, L. J., and G. C. Gleser, *Psychological Tests and Personnel Decisions,* 2nd ed. (Urbana, Ill.: University of Illinois Press, 1965).

7. Byrnes, N., and D. Kiley, "Hello, You Must Be Going," *BusinessWeek,* February 12, 2007, 30–32; and Berner, R., "My Year at Wal-Mart," *BusinessWeek,* February 12, 2007, 70–74.

8. Blum, M. L., and J. C. Naylor, *Industrial Psychology: Its Theoretical and Social Foundations,* revised ed. (New York: Harper & Row, 1968).

9. Taylor, H. C., and J. T. Russell, "The Relationship of Validity Coefficients to the Practical Effectiveness of Tests in Selection," *Journal of Applied Psychology* 23 (1939): 565–578.

10. Naylor, J. C., and L. C. Shine, "A Table for Determining the Increase in Mean Criterion Score Obtained by Using a Selection Device," *Journal of Industrial Psychology* 3 (1965): 33–42.

11. Brogden, H. E., "On the Interpretation of the Correlation Coefficient As a Measure of Predictive Efficiency," *Journal of Educational Psychology* 37 (1946): 64–76; Brogden, H. E., "When Testing Pays Off," *Personnel Psychology* 2 (1949): 171–185; and Cronbach and Gleser, 1965.

12. Sands, W. A., "A Method for Evaluating Alternative Recruiting-Selection Strategies: The CAPER Model," *Journal of Applied Psychology* 57 (1973): 222–227.

13. Boudreau, J. W., and S. L. Rynes, "Role of Recruitment in Staffing Utility Analyses," *Journal of Applied Psychology* 70 (1985): 354–366.

14. Boudreau, J. W., "Utility Analysis for Decisions in Human Resource Management," in *Handbook of Industrial and Organizational Psychology* 2 (2nd ed.), ed. M. D. Dunnette and L. M. Hough (Palo Alto, Calif.: CPP, 1991).

15. Taylor and Russell, 1939.

16. Pearson, K., *Tables for Statisticians and Biometricians,* vol. 2 (London: Biometric Laboratory, University College, 1931).

17. Naylor and Shine, 1965.

18. This means that the new selection procedure is administered to present employees who already have been screened using other methods. The correlation (validity coefficient) between scores on the new procedure and the employees' job performance scores is then computed.

19. To transform raw scores into standard scores, we used the following formula : $x - \bar{x} \div SD$, where x is the raw score, $\bar{x}$ is the mean of the distribution of raw scores, and SD is the standard deviation of that distribution. Assuming that the raw scores are distributed normally, about 99 percent of the standard scores will lie within the range −3 to + 3. Standard scores (Z-scores) are expressed in standard deviation units.

20. A multiple-regression coefficient represents the correlation between a criterion and two or more predictors.

21. Boudreau, 1991.

22. Brogden, 1946.

23. Brogden, 1949.

24. The authors would like to thank Professor Craig J. Russell for allowing us to adapt the framework that he developed.

25. Cronbach and Gleser, 1965.

26. Boudreau, 1991.

27. Material in this section comes from Cascio, W. F., and J. W. Boudreau, "Utility of Selection Systems: Supply-Chain Analysis Applied to Staffing Decisions," in *Handbook of I/O Psychology*, Vol. 2, ed. S. Zedeck (Washington, D.C.: American Psychological Association, 2011, pp. 421-444).

28. Hilbert, cited in Schneider, C., "The New Human-Capital Metrics," retrieved August 5, 2008 from www.cfo.com.

29. Valero Energy, "2006 Optimas Awards," *Workforce Management* (March 13, 2006).

9

The Economic Value of Job Performance

Consider this single question: Where would a change in the availability or quality of talent have the greatest impact on the success of your organization? Talent pools that have great impact are known as pivotal talent pools. Alan Eustace, Google's vice president of engineering, told *The Wall Street Journal* that one top-notch engineer is worth 300 times or more than the average and that he would rather lose an entire incoming class of engineering graduates than one exceptional technologist.[1]

This estimate was probably not based on precise numbers, but the insight it reveals regarding where Google puts its emphasis is significant. Recasting performance management to reflect where differences in performance have large impact allows leaders to engage the logic they use for other resources and make educated guesses that can be informative.[2] In defining pivotal talent, an important distinction is often overlooked. That distinction is between average value and variability in value. When strategy writers describe critical jobs or roles, they typically emphasize the average level of value (for example, the general importance, customer contact, uniqueness, or power of certain jobs). Yet a key question for managers is not which talent has the greatest average value, but rather, in which talent pools performance variation creates the biggest strategic impact.[3]

Impact (discussed in Chapter 1, "Making HR Measurement Strategic") identifies the relationship between improvements in organization and talent performance, and sustainable strategic success. The pivot point is where differences in performance most affect success. Identifying pivot points often requires digging deeply into organization- or unit-level strategies to unearth specific details about where and how the organization plans to compete, and about the supporting elements that will be most vital to achieving that competitive position. These insights identify the areas of organization and talent that make the biggest difference in the strategy's success.[4]

Pivotal Talent at Disney Theme Parks

Consider a Disney theme park. Suppose we ask the question the usual way: What is the important talent for theme park success? What would you say? There's always a variety of answers, and they always include the characters. Indeed, characters such as the talented people inside the Mickey Mouse costumes are very important. The question of talent impact, however, focuses on pivot points. Consider what happens when we frame the question differently, in terms of impact: Where would an improvement in the quality of talent and organization make the biggest difference in our strategic success? Answering that question requires looking further to find the strategy pivot points that illuminate the talent and organization pivot points.

One way to find the pivot points in processes is to look for constraints. These are like bottlenecks in a pipeline: If you relieve a constraint, the entire process works better. For a Disney theme park, a key constraint is the number of minutes a guest spends in the park. Disney must maximize the number of "delightful" minutes. Disneyland has 85 acres of public areas, many different "lands," and hundreds of small and large attractions. Helping guests navigate, even delighting them as they navigate, defines how Disney deals with this constraint. Notice how the focus on the constraint allows us to see beneath the customer delight strategy and identify a pivotal process that supports it.

Figure 9-1 applies this concept to two talent pools in the Disney theme park: Mickey Mouse and the park sweeper.

Mickey Mouse is important but not necessarily pivotal. The top line represents the performance of the talent in the Mickey Mouse role. The curve is very high in the diagram because performance by Mickey Mouse is very valuable. However, the variation in value between the best-performing Mickey Mouse and the worst-performing Mickey Mouse is not that large. In the extreme left side of the figure, if the person in the Mickey Mouse costume engaged in harmful customer interactions, the consequences would be strategically devastating. That is shown by the very steep downward slope at the left. That's why the Mickey Mouse role has been engineered to make such errors virtually impossible. The person in the Mickey Mouse costume is never seen, never talks, and is always accompanied by a supervisor who manages the guest encounters and ensures that Mickey doesn't fall down, get lost, or take an unauthorized break. What is often overlooked is that because the Mickey Mouse job is so well engineered, there is also little payoff to investing in *improving* the performance of Mickey Mouse once the person meets the high standards of performance. Mickey should not improvise or take too long with any one guest, because Mickey must follow a precise timetable so that everyone gets a chance to "meet" Mickey and so that guests never see two Mickeys at the same time.

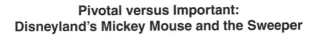

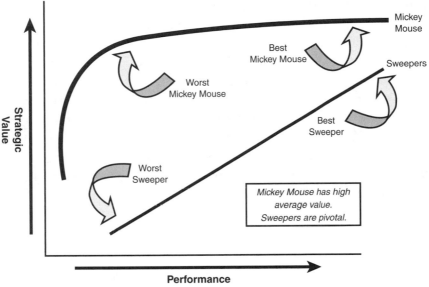

Source: John W. Boudreau and Peter M. Ramstad (2007). Beyond HR: The New Science of Human Capital. Boston: Harvard Business School Publishing.

Figure 9-1 Performance-yield curves for sweepers versus Mickey Mouse.

If performance differences that most affect the guest experience are not with Mickey Mouse, then where are they? When a guest has a problem, folks such as park sweepers and store clerks are most likely to be nearby in accessible roles, so guests approach them. People seldom ask Cinderella where to buy a disposable camera, but hundreds a day ask the street sweeper. The lower curve in Figure 9-1 represents sweepers. The sweeper curve has a much steeper slope than Mickey Mouse because variation in sweeper performance creates a greater change in value. Disney sweepers are expected to improvise and make adjustments to the customer service process on-the-fly, reacting to variations in customer demands, unforeseen circumstances, and changes in the customer experience. These make pivotal differences in Disney's theme park strategy to be the "Happiest Place on Earth." To be sure, these pivot points are embedded in architecture, creative settings, and the brand of Disney magic. Alignment is key. In fact, it is precisely because of this holistic alignment that interacting with guests in the park is a pivotal role and the sweeper plays a big part in that role. At Disney, sweepers are actually front-line customer representatives with brooms in their hands.[5]

Logic: Why Does Performance Vary Across Jobs?

Performance is more (or less) variable across jobs for two main reasons.[6] One of these is the nature of the job, or the extent to which it permits individual autonomy and discretion. For example, when job requirements are specified rigidly, as in some fast-food restaurants, important differences in ability or motivation have less noticeable effects on performance. If one's job is to cook French fries in a restaurant, and virtually all the variables that can affect the finished product are preprogrammed—the temperature of the oil in which the potatoes are fried, the length and width of the fries themselves, the size of a batch of fries, and the length of time that the potatoes are fried—there is little room for discretion. That is the objective, of course: to produce uniform end products. As a result, the variability in performance across human operators (what the utility analysis formulas in Chapter 8, "Staffing Utility: The Concept and Its Measurement," symbolized as SD_y) will be close to zero.

On the other hand, the project leader of an advertising campaign or a salesperson who manages all the accounts in a given territory has considerable discretion in deciding how to accomplish the work. Variation in individual abilities and motivation can lead to large values of SD_y in those jobs, and also relative to other jobs that vary in terms of the autonomy and discretion they permit. Empirical evidence shows that SD_y increases as a function of job complexity.[7] As jobs become more complex, it becomes more difficult to specify precisely the procedures that should be used to perform them. As a result, differences in ability and motivation become more important determinants of the variability of job performance.

A second factor the influences the size of SD_y is the relative value to the organization of variations in performance. In some jobs, performance differences are vital to the successful achievement of the strategic goals of an organization (for example, software engineers who design new products for leading-edge software companies) and others that are less so (for example, employees who send out bills in an advertising agency). Even though there is variability in performance of employees in the billing department, that variability is not as crucial to the success of the firm as is the variability in the performance of project leaders at the agency. In short, pivotalness—and, thus, SD_y—is affected by the relative position of a job in the value chain of an organization.[8]

In the Disney example shown in Figure 9-1, the sweeper role has a higher SD_y than Mickey Mouse because variations in sweeper performance (particularly when they respond to guests) cause a larger change in strategic value than variations in Mickey Mouse performance. Mickey Mouse is vital to the Disney value chain, however. So it is important to understand the difference between average value of performance and pivotalness, the latter being reflected in SD_y. High pivotalness and high average value often occur together, but not always.

The impact of performance variation in jobs requires considering the strategy of the organization (sustainability, strategic success, pivotal resources and processes, and organization and talent pools).[9] The same job can have very different implications for performance differences, depending on the strategy and work processes of the organization. Consider the role of front-line associates at two different fast-food organizations: McDonald's and Starbucks. Both roles involve preparing the product, interacting with customers, taking payments, working with the team, keeping up good attendance, and executing good job performance. The description for these roles might look similar at both Starbucks and McDonald's, yet McDonald's and Starbucks choose to compete differently.

McDonald's is known for consistency and speed. Its stores automate many of the key tasks of food preparation, customer interaction, and team roles. Each McDonald's product has an assigned number so that associates need only press the number on the register to record the customer order. Indeed, it is not unusual to hear customers themselves ordering by saying, "I'll take a number 3 with a Coke, and supersize it." Contrast that with Starbucks. Starbucks baristas are a highly diverse and often multitalented group. The allure of Starbucks as a "third place" (home, work, and Starbucks) is predicated, in part, on the possibility of interesting interactions with Starbucks baristas. Blogs, tweets, and Facebook pages are devoted to the Starbucks baristas. Some of them are opera singers and actually sing out the orders. Their personal styles are clearly on display and range from Gothic to country to hipster. Few online pages are devoted to McDonald's associates. Starbucks counts on that diversity as part of its image.[10] This means that it needs to give its baristas wide latitude to sing, joke, and chat with customers.

Figure 9-2 shows this relationship graphically, with McDonald's on the left and Starbucks on the right. McDonald's designs its systems to limit both the downside of performance mistakes and the upside of too-creative improvising. Starbucks encourages innovation and "style" to get the upside (at the extreme right side is a barista whose style goes "viral," drawing Internet attention to the brand), accepting the downside on the left (sometimes a barista may do something that offends a few customers).

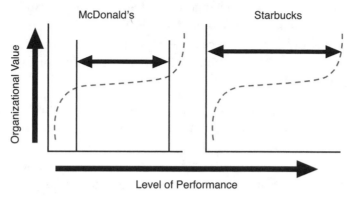

Figure 9-2 Value of job performance for front-line workers at McDonald's vs. Starbucks.

Graphic depictions of performance-yield curves, such as the ones in Figures 9-1 and 9-2, can help identify where decisions should focus on achieving a minimum standard level of performance (as with billers in an advertising agency or French fries cooks in a fast-food restaurant) versus improving performance (as with sweepers in a theme park or software designers). Such depictions also provide a way to think about the risks and returns to performance at different levels. This helps people avoid making decisions based on well-meaning but potentially simplistic rules, such as "Find the best candidate for every position."[11]

Indeed, the idea that performance variation in certain areas has greater impact than performance variation in others is a fundamental premise of engineering, where different components of a product, project, or software program are held to different tolerances, depending on the role they play. The upholstery in a commercial aircraft can vary from its ideal standard by quite a lot, but the hydraulics cannot. This is often called *Kano analysis,* named after Noriaki Kano, who coined the term in the 1980s. He showed how improved performance has widely differing effects.[12] Thus, approaching work performance in this way allows human resource leaders, I/O psychologists, and business leaders to communicate about work performance using proven business tools, which John Boudreau has termed "retooling HR."[13]

In terms of measurement, the value of variation in employee performance is an important variable that determines the likely payoff of investments in HR programs. Most HR programs are designed to improve performance. All things equal, such programs have a higher payoff when they are directed at organizational areas where performance variation has a large impact on processes, resources, and, ultimately, strategic success. A 15 percent improvement in performance is not equally valuable everywhere. Ideally, we would like to translate performance improvements into monetary values. If we can do that, we can measure whether the performance improvement we expect from a program, such as more accurate selection, improved training, or more effective recruitment, justifies the cost of the program.

As yet no perfect measure of the value of performance variation exists, but a great deal of research has addressed the issue. We provide a guide to the most important findings in the later sections. First, we show how the value of performance variation (in the form of SD_y) fits into the formulas for the utility, or monetary value, of staffing programs that we discussed in Chapter 8.

Analytics: The Role of SD_y in Utility Analysis

As Equations 8-14 through 8-18 showed in Chapter 8, SD_y (the monetary value of a difference of one standard deviation in job or criterion performance) translates the improvement in workforce quality from the use of a more valid selection procedure into economic terms.

Without SD_y, the effect of a change in criterion performance could be expressed only in terms of standard Z-score units. However, when the product, Z-score units are multiplied by the monetary-valued SD_y, the gain is expressed in monetary units, which are more familiar to decision makers. As you will see in Chapter 11, "Costs and Benefits of HR Development Programs," and in Equation 11-1, the same SD_y variable can also be used to translate the statistical effects of training and development programs into monetary terms.

Note again that we often refer to dollar-valued performance or use the dollar sign as a subscript, but the conclusions are valid for any other currency.

Most parameters of the general utility equation for staffing and for development can be obtained from records. For staffing, this includes such variables as the number of people tested, the cost of testing, and the selection ratio. For development, this includes the number of people trained, the cost of training, and the duration of the training effects. However, SD_y usually cannot be obtained from existing records. Traditionally, SD_y has been the parameter of the utility equation that is the most difficult to obtain.[14] Originally, SD_y was estimated using complicated cost-accounting methods that are both costly and time-consuming. Those procedures involve first costing out the dollar value of the job behaviors of each employee[15] and then computing the standard deviation of these values. The complexity of those approaches led to newer approaches that rely on estimates from knowledgeable persons. The next section describes alternative approaches for measuring SD_y.

Measures: Estimating the Monetary Value of Variations in Job Performance (SD_y)

In general, two types of methods are used for estimating the standard deviation of job performance in monetary terms. The first is cost accounting, which uses accounting procedures to estimate the economic value of the products or services produced by each employee in a job or class of jobs, and then calculates the variation in that value across individuals. The second method is sometimes called "behavioral" and combines the judgments from knowledgeable people about differences in the value of different performance levels. Several alternative judgment-based approaches are used. Table 9-1 lists the cost-accounting and judgment-based alternatives.

Table 9-1 Alternative Approaches for Estimating SD_y

Estimation Approach	Description
Cost accounting	
Cost accounting	Calculate the accounting value of each person's accounting outcomes, such as production or sales, and calculate the standard deviation of those values across individuals.
Judgment-Based Approaches	
40 percent rule	Multiply the average total remuneration of the group by 40 percent.
Global estimation	Ask experts to estimate the value of performance at the average, 85th percentile and 15th percentile, of the performance distribution, and calculate the differences between the pairs of percentile estimates.
CREPID	Identify the individual elements of performance, weight them by contribution to economic value, multiply average remuneration by the importance weight of each element, rate individual performance on each element, multiply performance by monetary value for each dimension for each individual, and sum to get a monetary value for each individual. Calculate the standard deviation of those values across individuals.

System effectiveness technique	Estimate the percentage difference in performance effectiveness between a superior and an average performer, and multiply that percentage by the cost of the system and capital used on the job.
Superior equivalents technique	Estimate how many fewer employees would be required to achieve a certain level of performance if the employees were one standard deviation better. Calculate the average cost of employees, and multiply that by the difference in the number of superior employees required, compared to the number of average employees, to determine the employment-cost savings of having superior versus average employees.

The remainder of the chapter discusses each of these approaches in more detail.

Cost-Accounting Approach

If you could determine the economic value of each employee's performance, you could calculate directly the standard deviation of performance value simply by taking the standard deviation of those values. That's the idea behind the cost-accounting approach. In a job that is purely sales, it may be reasonable to say that each person's sales level, minus the cost of the infrastructure and remuneration he or she uses and receives, would be a reasonable estimate of the economic value of his or her performance. Unfortunately, aside from sales positions, most cost-accounting systems are not designed to calculate the economic value of each employee's performance, so adapting cost accounting to that purpose proved complex for most jobs.

Cost-accounting estimates of performance value require considering elements such as the following:[16]

- Average value of production or service units.

- Quality of objects produced or services accomplished.

- Overhead, including rent, light, heat, cost depreciation, or rental of machines and equipment.

- Errors, accidents, spoilage, wastage, damage to machines or equipment due to unusual wear and tear, and so on.

- Such factors as appearance, friendliness, poise, and general social effectiveness in public relations. (Here, some approximate value would have to be assigned by an individual or individuals having the required responsibility and background.)

- The cost of spent time of other employees and managers. This includes not only the time of supervisors, but also that of other workers.

Researchers in one study attempted to apply these ideas to the job of route salesperson in a Midwestern soft-drink bottling company that manufactures, merchandises, and distributes nationally known products.[17] This job was selected for two reasons: There were many of individuals in the job, and variability in performance levels had a direct impact on output. Route salespersons were paid a small weekly base wage, plus a commission on each case of soft drink sold. The actual cost-accounting method to compute SD_y involved eight steps:

1. Output data on each of the route salespersons was collected from the records of the organization on the number of cases sold and the size and type of package, for a one-year period (to eliminate seasonality).

2. The weighted average sales price per case unit (SP_u) was calculated using data provided by the accounting department.

3. The variable cost per case unit (VC_u) was calculated and subtracted from the average price. Variable costs are costs that vary with the volume of sales, such as direct labor, direct materials (syrup cost, CO_2 gas, crowns, closures, and bottles), variable factory overhead (state inspection fees, variable indirect materials, variable indirect labor), and selling expenses (the route salesperson's commission).

4. Contribution margins per case unit (CM_u) were calculated as the sales price per unit minus the variable cost per unit.

5. The contribution margins calculated in step 4 were multiplied by the output figures (step 1), producing a total one-year dollar-valued contribution margin for each route salesperson. This figure represents the total amount (in dollars and cents) each salesperson contributed toward fixed costs and profit.

6. Not all differences in sales were assumed to be due to differences in route salespersons' performance. Other factors, such as the type of route, partially determined sales, so it was important to remove these influences. To accomplish this, the sales of each route were partitioned into two categories: home market and cold bottle. Home market represents sales in large supermarkets and chain stores, in which the product is purchased and taken home to consume. Cold bottle represents sales such as those from small convenience stores and vending operations, in which the product is consumed on location. Top management agreed that home market sales are influenced less by the efforts of the route salesperson, but the route salesperson exercises greater influence over the relative sales level in the

cold-bottle market because the route salesperson has a greater degree of flexibility in offering price incentives, seeking additional display space, and so forth. The critical question was, "How much influence does the route salesperson have in each of the respective sectors?" The percentage of sales or contributions attributable to the efforts of the route salesperson was determined by a consensus of six top managers, who estimated the portions of home-market sales and cold-bottle sales attributable to the efforts of the route salesperson at 20 percent and 30 percent, respectively.

7. The percentages calculated in step 6 were multiplied by the total contribution margins calculated in step 5, yielding a total contribution margin for each route salesperson. Figure 9-3 shows an example calculation. This served as the cost accounting-based estimate of each route salesperson's worth to the organization.

Product	SP_u	-	VC_u	=	CM_u	×	Sales Output[a]	=	GCM
1	$5.00	-	$2.75	=	$2.25	×	40,000	=	$90,000
2	$7.60	-	$4.85	=	$2.75	×	20,000	=	$55,000
3	$8.30	-	$5.65	=	$2.65	×	15,000	=	$39,750
					Gross Contribution Generated by RSA			=	$184,750

SP_u = sales price per unit of product; VC_u = variable cost per unit of product;

CM_u = contribution margin per unit of product; GCM = gross contribution margin.

[a] = Numbers of cases.

Figure 9-3 Sample of the total contribution attributable to route Salesperson A (RSA) using cost-accounting procedures.

8. The standard deviation of these values was the cost accounting-based estimate of SD_y. This approach, called contribution costing, is generally not used for external reporting purposes, but it is generally recommended for internal, managerial reporting purposes.[18]

The Estimate of SD_y

The cost accounting-based procedure produced an estimate of SD_y of $32,982 (all figures in 2010 dollars)[19], with an average value of job performance of $93,522. Estimates of average worth ranged from $27,107 to $240,163. These values were skewed positively (Q3 – Q2 = $29,370, greater than Q2 – Q1 = $12,742), meaning that the difference between high and average was greater than the difference between average and low. This makes sense, because the values were calculated for experienced job incumbents, among whom very low performers would have been eliminated.

Cost-accounting systems focus on determining the costs and benefits of units of product, not units of performance, and thus require a good deal of translation to estimate performance value. So although the accounting data on which the estimates are based is often trusted by decision makers, the array of additional estimates required often creates doubt about the objectivity and reliability of the cost-accounting estimates. Over the past few decades, several alternative approaches for estimating the economic value of job performance have been developed that require considerably less effort than the cost-accounting method. Comparative research has made possible some general conclusions about the relative merits of these methods.

The 40 Percent Rule

Some researchers have recommended estimating SD_y as 40 percent of average salary.[20] They noted that wages and salaries average 57 percent of the value of goods and services in the U.S. economy, implying that 40 percent of average salary is the same as 22.8 percent (0.40×0.57), or roughly 20 percent, of the average value of production. Thus, they suggested using 40 percent of salary to estimate SD_y[21] is about the same as using 20 percent of average output for SD_y. They symbolized this productivity-based estimate as SD_p. In other words, if you knew the average output, you could calculate the value of a one-standard-deviation performance difference as 20 percent of that average output.

To examine whether the standard deviation of output was about 20 percent of average output, a summary of the results of 68 studies that measured work output or work samples found that low-complexity jobs such as routine clerical or blue-collar work had SD_p values that averaged 15 percent of output. Medium-complexity jobs such as first-line supervisors, skilled crafts, and technicians had average SD_p values of 25 percent, and high-complexity jobs, such as managerial/professional, and complex technical jobs had average SD_p values of 46 percent. For life-insurance sales jobs, SD_p was very large (97 percent of average sales), and it was 39 percent for other sales jobs.[22] It appears that there are sizable differences in the amounts of performance variation in different jobs (recall how different the performance variation was among sweepers versus Mickey Mouse), and the 20 percent rule may underestimate or overestimate them.

Based on this evidence, some have suggested that SD_p might be directly estimated from the complexity of the job. In other words, use a value of 39 percent for sales jobs, 15 percent for clerical jobs, and so on. A drawback is that SD_p is expressed as the percentage of average output, not in monetary values.[23] Getting a monetary value thus would require multiplying the percentage by the money value of average output. You could try to estimate the monetary value of average output in a job, but that has many of the same difficulties as the cost-accounting approach described earlier in this chapter.

No estimate is perfect, but fortunately, utility estimates need not be perfectly accurate, just as with any estimate of business effects. For decisions about selection procedures, only errors large enough to lead to incorrect decisions are of any consequence. Moreover, the jobs with the largest SD_y values—often those involving leadership, management, or intellectual capital—often have many opportunities for individual autonomy and discretion, and are handled least well by cost-accounting methods. So to some degree, subjective estimates are virtually unavoidable. Next, we examine some of the most prominent methods to gather judgments that can provide SD_y estimates.

Global Estimation

The global estimation procedure for obtaining rational estimates of SD_y is based on the following reasoning: If the monetary value of job performance is distributed as a normal curve, the difference between the monetary value of an employee performing at the 85th percentile (one standard deviation above average) versus an employee performing at the 50th percentile (average) equals SD_y.[24]

In one study, the supervisors of budget analysts were asked to estimate both 85th and 50th percentile values.[25] They were asked to estimate the average value based on the costs of having an outside firm provide the services. SD_y was calculated as the average difference across the supervisors. Taking the average of the values provided by multiple raters may cancel out the idiosyncratic tendencies, biases, and random errors of each single individual.

In the budget analyst example, the standard error of the SD_y estimates across judges was $4,149, implying that the interval $35,126 to $48,817 should contain 90 percent of such estimates (all results expressed in 2010 dollars). Thus, to be extremely conservative, one could use $35,126, which is statistically 90 percent likely to be less than the actual value.

An Example of Global SD_y Estimates for Computer Programmers

The following is a detailed explanation of how the global estimation procedure has been used to estimate SD_y. The application to be described used supervisors of computer programmers in ten federal agencies.[26] The actual study was published in 1979, but the technique has been used in many studies since that time, across many different jobs, with similar results.[27] To test the hypothesis that dollar outcomes are normally distributed, the supervisors were asked to estimate values for the 15th percentile (low-performing programmers), the 50th percentile (average programmers), and the 85th percentile (superior programmers). The resulting data thus provides two estimates of SD_y. If the distribution is approximately normal, these two estimates will not differ substantially in value. Here is an excerpt of the instructions presented to the supervisors:[28]

> The dollar utility estimates we are asking you to make are critical in estimating the relative dollar value to the government of different selection methods. In answering these questions, you will have to make some very difficult judgments. We realize they are difficult and that they are judgments or estimates. You will have to ponder for some time before giving each estimate, and there is probably no way you can be absolutely certain your estimate is accurate when you do reach a decision. But keep in mind [that] your estimates will be averaged in with those of other supervisors of computer programmers. Thus, errors produced by too high and too low estimates will tend to be averaged out, providing more accurate final estimates.

> Based on your experience with agency programmers, we would like for you to estimate the yearly value to your agency of the products and services produced by the average GS 9-11 computer programmer. Consider the quality and quantity of output typical of the average programmer and the value of this output. In placing an overall dollar value on this output, it may help to consider what the cost would be of having an outside firm provide these products and services.

> Based on my experience, I estimate the value to my agency of the average GS 9-11 computer programmer at _____ dollars per year.

> We would now like for you to consider the "superior" programmer. Let us define a superior performer as a programmer who is at the 85th percentile. That is, his or her performance is better than that of 85% of his or her fellow GS 9-11 programmers, and only 15% turn in better performances. Consider the quality and quantity of the output typical of the superior programmer. Then estimate the value of these products and services. In placing an overall dollar value on this output, it may again help to consider what the cost would be of having an outside firm provide these products and services.

> Based on my experience, I estimate the value to my agency of a superior GS 9-11 computer programmer to be _____ dollars per year.

> Finally, we would like you to consider the "low-performing" computer programmer. Let us define a low-performing programmer as one who is at the 15th percentile. That is, 85% of all GS 9-11 computer programmers turn in performances

better than the low-performing programmer, and only 15% turn in worse performances. Consider the quality and quantity of the output typical of the low-performing programmer. Then estimate the value of these products and services. In placing an overall dollar value on this output, it may again help to consider what the cost would be of having an outside firm provide these products and services.

Based on my experience, I estimate the value to my agency of the low-performing GS 9-11 computer programmer at _____ dollars per year.

The wording of these questions was developed carefully and pretested on a small sample of programmer supervisors and personnel psychologists. None of the programmer supervisors who returned questionnaires in the study reported any difficulty in understanding the questionnaire or in making the estimates.

The two estimates of SD_y were similar. The mean estimated difference in value (in 2010 dollars) of yearly job performance between programmers at the 85th and 50th percentiles in job performance was $40,281 (SE = $6,199). The difference between the 50th and 15th percentiles was $36,886 (SE = $3,835). The difference of $3,395 was roughly 8 percent of each of the estimates and was not statistically significant. The distribution was at least approximately normal. The average of these two estimates, $38,583, was used as the final SD_y estimate.

Modifications to the Global Estimation Procedure

Later research showed that the global estimation procedure produces downwardly biased estimates of utility.[29] This appears to be so because most judges equate average value with average wages despite the fact that the value of the output as sold of the average employee is larger than average wages. However, estimates of the coefficient of variation of job performance ($SD_y/\overline{Y}$ or SD_p) calculated from supervisory estimates of the three percentiles (50th, 85th, and 15th) were quite accurate. This led the same authors to propose a modification of the original global estimation procedure.[30] The modified approach estimates SD_y as the product of estimates of the coefficient of variation ($SD_y/\overline{Y}$) and an objective estimate of the average value of employee output ($\overline{Y}$). In using this procedure, one first estimates $\overline{Y}$ and SD_p separately and then multiplies these values to estimate SD_y.

SD_p can be estimated in two ways: by using the average value found for jobs of similar complexity[31] or by dividing supervisory estimates of SD_y by supervisory estimates of the value of performance of the 50th-percentile worker. Researchers tested the accuracy of this method by calculating supervisory estimates of SD_p from 11 previous studies of SD_y estimation and then comparing these estimates with objective SD_p values.[32] Across the 11 studies, the mean of the supervisory estimates was 44.2 percent, which was very close to the actual output-based mean of 43.9 percent. The correlation between the two sets of values was .70. These results indicate that supervisors can estimate quite accurately the magnitude of relative (percent of average output) differences in employee performance.

With respect to calculating the average revenue value of employee output ($\overline{Y}$), the researchers began with the assumption that the average revenue value of employee output is equal to total sales revenue divided by the total number of employees.[33] However, total sales revenue is based on contributions from many jobs within an organization. Based on the assumption that the contribution of each job to the total revenue of the firm is proportional to its share of the firm's total annual payroll, they calculated an approximate average revenue value for a particular job (A) as follows:

$$\text{Job A value} = \text{Total revenue} \times (\text{Job A payroll} / \text{Total payroll}) \qquad (9\text{-}1)$$

$$\overline{Y} = \text{Job A value} / \text{Job A number of employees} \qquad (9\text{-}2)$$

SD_y then can be estimated as (SD_p), where SD_p is computed using one of the two methods described earlier. An additional advantage of estimating SD_y from estimates of SD_p is that it is not necessary that estimates of SD_y be obtained from dollar-value estimates. Although the global estimation procedure is easy to use and provides fairly reliable estimates across supervisors, we offer several cautions regarding the logic and analytics on which it rests.

Empirical findings support the assumption of linearity between supervisory performance ratings and annual worth ($r = .67$),[34] but dollar-valued job performance outcomes are often not normally distributed.[35] Hence, comparisons of estimates of SD_y at the 85th–50th and 50th–15th percentiles may not be meaningful.

We do not know the basis for each supervisor's estimates. Using general rules of thumb, such as job complexity, has merit, but this can be enhanced by using a more well-developed framework, such as the "actions and interactions" component of the HC BRidge model to identify and clarify underlying relationships.[36] This means describing those challenges and resulting actions that the best employees might do versus actions of the average employees. This can help leaders and employees visualize the actual work differences.

Supervisors often find estimating the dollar value of various percentiles in the job performance distribution rather difficult. Moreover, the variation among each rater's SD_y estimates is usually as large as or larger than the average SD_y estimate. In fact, one study found both the level of agreement among raters and the stability over time of their SD_y estimates to be low.[37]

To improve consensus among raters, two strategies have been used:

- Provide an anchor for the 50th percentile.[38]

- Have groups of raters provide consensus judgments of different percentiles

Despite these problems, several studies have reported close correspondence between estimated and actual standard deviations when output measured as the value of sales[39] or cost-accounting estimates were used. However, when medical claims cost data was used, the original global estimation procedure overestimated the actual value of SD_y by 26 percent.[40]

The methods discussed so far require that we assume that the monetary value of job performance is distributed normally, and they require experts to make an overall estimate of value across often widely varying job performance elements. An alternative procedure that makes no assumption regarding the underlying normality of the performance distribution and that identifies the components of each supervisor's estimate is described next.

The Cascio-Ramos Estimate of Performance in Dollars (CREPID)

The Cascio-Ramos estimate of performance in dollars (CREPID) was developed under the auspices of the American Telephone and Telegraph Company and was tested on 602 first-level managers in a Bell operating company.[41] The rationale underlying CREPID is as follows. Assuming that an organization's compensation program reflects current market rates for jobs, the economic value of each employee's labor is reflected best in his or her annual wage or salary. As we discussed earlier in this chapter, this is probably a low estimate, as the average value produced by an employee must be more than average wages to offset the costs of wages, overhead, and necessary profit. Later, we will see that this assumption indeed leads to conservatively low estimates of SD_y. CREPID breaks down each employee's job into its principal activities, assigns a proportional amount of the annual salary to each principal activity, and then requires supervisors to rate each employee's job performance on each principal activity. The resulting ratings then are translated into estimates of dollar value for each principal activity. The sum of the dollar values assigned to each principal activity equals the economic value of each employee's job performance to the company. Let us explain each of these steps in greater detail.

1. Identify principal activities. To assign a dollar value to each employee's job performance, first we must identify what tasks each employee performs. In many job analysis systems, principal activities (or critical work behaviors) are identified expressly. In others, they can be derived, under the assumption that to be considered "principal," an activity should comprise at least 10 percent of total work time. To illustrate, let us assume that the job description for an accounting supervisor involves eight principal activities.

2. Rate each principal activity in terms of time/frequency and importance. It has long been recognized that rating job activities simply in terms of the time or frequency with which each is performed is an incomplete indication of the overall weight to be assigned to each activity. For example, a nurse may spend most of the work-week performing the routine tasks of patient care. However, suppose the nurse must respond to one medical emergency per week that requires, on an average, one hour of his or her time. To be sure, the time/frequency of this activity is short, but its importance is critical. Research shows that simple 0–7 point Likert-type rating scales provide results that are almost identical to those derived from more complicated scales.[42]

3. Multiply the numerical ratings for time/frequency and importance for each principal activity. The purpose of this step is to develop an overall relative weight to assign each principal activity. The ratings are multiplied. Thus, if an activity never is done, or if it is totally unimportant, the relative weight for that activity should be zero. The following illustration presents hypothetical ratings of the eight principal activities identified for the accounting supervisor's job.

Principal Activity	Time/ Frequency	× Importance	= Total	Relative Weight
1	4.0	4	16.0	16.8
2	5.0	7	35.0	36.8
3	1.0	5	5.0	5.3
4	0.5	3	1.5	1.6
5	2.0	7	14.0	14.7
6	1.0	4	4.0	4.2
7	0.5	3	1.5	1.6
8	3.0	6	18.0	19
			95.0	100%

After doing all the multiplication, sum the total ratings assigned to each principal activity (95 in the preceding example). Then divide the total rating for each principal activity by sum, or all the ratings, to derive the relative weight for the activity (for example, $16 \div 95 = 0.168$, or 16.8 percent). Knowing each principal activity's relative weight allows us to allocate proportional shares of the employee's overall salary to each principal activity, as is done in step 4.

4. Assign dollar values to each principal activity. Take an average (or weighted average) annual rate of pay for all participants in the study (employees in a particular job class) and allocate it across principal activities according to the relative weights obtained in step 3.

To illustrate, suppose that the annual salary of each accounting supervisor is $50,000.

Principal Activity	Relative Weight (%)	Dollar Value ($)
1	16.8	8,400
2	36.8	18,400
3	5.3	2,650
4	1.6	800
5	14.7	7,350
6	4.2	2,100
7	1.6	800
8	19	9,500
		50,000

5. Rate performance on each principal activity on a 0–200 scale. Note that steps 1–4 apply to the job, regardless of who does that job. The next task is to determine how well each person in that job performs each principal activity. This is the performance appraisal phase. The higher the rating on each principal activity, the greater the economic value of that activity to the organization.

CREPID uses a modified magnitude-estimation scale to obtain information on performance.[43] To use this procedure, a value (say, 1.0) is assigned to a referent concept (for example, the average employee, one at the 50th percentile on job performance), and then all comparisons are made relative to this value. In the study of accounting supervisors, operating managers indicated that even the very best employee was generally not more than twice as effective as the average employee. Thus, a continuous 0–2.0 scale was used to rate each employee on each principal activity.

6. Multiply the point rating (expressed as a decimal number) assigned to each principal activity by the activity's dollar value. To illustrate, suppose that the following point totals are assigned to accounting supervisor C. P. Ayh:

Principal Activity	Performance (0 to 2 scale)	Dollar Value	Dollar-Weighted Performance
1	1.35	8,400	11,340.00
2	1.00	18,400	18,400.00
3	1.25	2,650	3,312.50
4	2.00	800	1,600.00
5	1.00	7,350	7,350.00
6	0.50	2,100	1,050.00
7	0.75	800	600.00
8	1.50	9,500	14,250.00

7. Compute the overall economic value of each employee's job performance by adding the last column of step 6. In our example, the overall economic value of Mr. Ayh's job performance is $57,902.50, or $7,902.50 more than he is being paid.

8. Over all employees in the study, compute the mean and standard deviation of dollar-valued job performance. When CREPID was tested on 602 first-level managers at a Bell operating company, the mean of dollar-valued job performance was only $2,340 (3.4 percent) more than the average actual salary of all employees in the study. However, the standard deviation (SD_y) was almost $23,791 (all figures in 2010 dollars), which was more than three and a half times larger than the standard deviation of the actual distribution of salaries. Such high variability suggests that supervisors recognized significant differences in performance throughout the rating process.

It is important to point out that CREPID requires only two sets of ratings from a supervisor:

- A rating of each principal activity in terms of time/frequency and importance (the job analysis phase)

- A rating of a specific subordinate's performance on each principal activity (the performance appraisal phase)

CREPID has the advantage of assigning each employee a specific value that can be analyzed explicitly for appropriateness and that may also provide a more understandable or credible estimate for decision makers. Focusing attention on elements of a job allows leaders to discuss the relative pivotalness of those elements. This idea has proven useful in considering how to apply engineering concepts such as Kano analysis to calculate the value of employee performance.[44] For example, consider the engineers at a Disney theme park. Unlike typical thrill-ride parks, the designers of Disney rides must be much more attuned to imagery, songs, and stories, because Disney uses the songs, characters, and stories of its rides across its full gamut of products. Consider that the hit film *Pirates of the Caribbean* began as a ride at Disneyland.

Hence, for a Disney ride designer (or "imagineer," as they are called at Disney), the difference between being good and great at songs may be much more pivotal than being good versus great at ride physiology. The ride *It's A Small World* has a song that is immediately recognizable all across the world, but its engineering sophistication is not that high. Thus, for Disney, ride engineers might be hired and rewarded more for great songs and stories than for the most advanced thrill-ride capability. CREPID would assign a much higher weight to the music than the physiology design elements of Disney engineers. At a more traditional thrill-ride park, such as Cedar Point in Ohio, the opposite might be true.[45]

However, as noted earlier, CREPID assumes that average wage equals the economic value of a worker's performance. This assumption is used in national income accounting to generate the GNP and labor-cost figures for jobs where output is not readily measurable (for example, government services). That is, the same value is assigned to both output and wages. Because this assumption does not hold in pay systems that are based on rank, tenure, or hourly pay rates, CREPID should not be used in these situations.[46]

System Effectiveness Technique

This method was developed specifically for situations in which individual salary is only a small percentage of the value of performance to the organization or of the equipment operated (for example, an army tank commander or a fighter pilot, or a petroleum engineer on an oil rig).[47]

Logic

In essence, it calculates the difference in system effectiveness between the average performer and someone who is one standard deviation better than average. It multiplies that value by the cost of the system, assuming that the superior performer achieves higher performance using the same cost, or that the superior performer achieves the same performance level at less cost. For example, suppose we estimate that a superior performer (one standard deviation better than average) is 20 percent better than an average performer and that it costs $100,000 to run the system for a month. We multiply the

20 percent by $100,000 to get $20,000 per month as the monetary difference between superior and average performers. The assumption is that the superior performer saves us $20,000 per month to achieve the same results, or that he or she achieves $20,000 more per month using the same cost of capital.

This approach distinguishes the standard deviation of performance in dollars, from the standard deviation of output units of performance (for example, number of hits per firing from an army tank commander). It is based on the following equation.

$$\text{SD of performance in monetary units} = C_u(\text{SD of performance in output units}/ Y_1) \tag{9-3}$$

Here, C_u is the cost of the unit in the system. (It includes equipment, support, and personnel rather than salary alone.) Y_1 is the mean performance in output units. Equation 9-3 indicates that the SD of performance in monetary units equals the cost per unit times the ratio of the SD of performance in output units to the average level of performance, Y_1. However, estimates from Equation 9-3 are appropriate only when the performance of the unit in the system is largely a function of the performance of the individual in the job.

Measures

To assess the standard deviation of performance in monetary units, using the system-effectiveness technique, researchers collected data on U.S. Army tank commanders.[48] They obtained these data from technical reports of previous research and from an approximation of tank costs. Previous research indicated that meaningful values for the ratio SD_y/Y_1 range from 0.2 to 0.5. Tank costs, consisting of purchase costs, maintenance, and personnel, were estimated to fall between $739,674 and $1.23 million per year (in 2010 dollars). For purposes of Equation 9-1, C_u was estimated at $739,674 per year, and the ratio of SD of performance in output units/Y_1 was estimated at 0.2. This yielded the following:

$$\text{SD of performance in dollars} = \$739,674 \times 0.2 = \$147,935$$

Superior Equivalents Technique

An alternative method, also developed by the same team of researchers for similar kinds of situations, is the superior equivalents technique. It is somewhat like the global estimation procedure, but with one important difference. Instead of using estimates of the percentage difference between performance levels, the technique uses estimates of how many superior (85th-percentile) performers would be needed to produce the output of a fixed number of average (50th-percentile) performers. This estimate, combined with an estimate of the dollar value of average performance, provides an estimate of SD_y.

Logic

The first step is to estimate the number (N85) of 85th-percentile employees required to equal the performance of some fixed number (N50) of average performers. Where the value of average performance (V50) is known or can be estimated, SD_y may be estimated by using the ratio N50 / N85 times V50 to obtain V85, and then subtracting V50. That reduces as follows:

$$SD_y = V85 - V50 \qquad\qquad (9\text{-}4)$$

But by definition, the total value of performance at a certain percentile is the product of the number of performers at that level times the average value of performance at that level, as follows:

$$V85 = (V50 \times N50) / N85 \qquad\qquad (9\text{-}5)$$

Combining Equations 9-4 and 9-5 yields this:

$$SD_y = V50 \left[(N50 / N85) - 1\right] \qquad\qquad (9\text{-}6)$$

Measures

The researchers developed a questionnaire to obtain an estimate of the number of tanks with superior tank commanders needed to equal the performance of a standard company of 17 tanks with average commanders.[49] A fill-in-the-blanks format was used, as shown in the following excerpt.

> For the purpose of this questionnaire an "average" tank commander is an NCO or commissioned officer whose performance is better than about half his fellow TCs. A "superior" tank commander is one whose performance is better than 85% of his fellow tank commanders.

The first question deals with relative value. For example, if a "superior" clerk types ten letters a day and an "average" clerk types five letters a day then, all else being equal, five "superior" clerks have the same value in an office as ten "average" clerks. In the same way, we want to know your estimate or opinion of the relative value of "average" vs. "superior" tank commanders in combat. I estimate that, all else being equal, _____ tanks with "superior" tank commanders would be about equal in combat to 17 tanks with "average" tank commanders.

Questionnaire data was gathered from 100 tank commanders enrolled in advanced training at a U.S. Army post. N50 was set at 17 as a fixed number of tanks with average commanders, because a tank company has 17 tanks. Assuming that organizations pay average employees their approximate worth, the equivalent civilian salary for a tank commander was set at $73,535 (in 2010 dollars).

The median response given for the number of superior TCs judged equivalent to 17 average TCs was 9, and the mode was 10. The response 9 was used as most representative of central tendency. Making use of Equation 9-3, V85 was calculated as follows:

$$(\$73,535 \times 17) / 9 = \$138,899$$

In terms of Equation 9-4:

$$SD_y = \$73,535 \left[(17 \div 9) - 1\right] = \$65,364$$

This is considerably less than the SD$ value ($136,800) that resulted from the system effectiveness technique. SD_y also was estimated using the global estimation procedure. However, there was minimal agreement either within or between groups for estimates of superior performance, and the distributions of the estimates for both superior performance and for average performance were skewed positively. Such extreme response variability illustrates the difficulty of making these kinds of judgments when the cost of contracting work is unknown, equipment is expensive, or other financially intangible factors exist. Such is frequently the case for public employees, particularly when private-industry counterparts do not exist. Under these circumstances, the system effectiveness technique or the superior equivalents technique may apply.

One possible problem with both of these techniques is that the quality of performance in some situations may not translate easily into a unidimensional, quantitative scale. For example, a police department may decide that the conviction of one murderer is equivalent to the conviction of five burglars. Whether managers do, in fact, develop informal algorithms to compare the performance of different individuals, perhaps on different factors, is an empirical question. Certainly, the performance dimensions that are most meaningful and useful will vary across jobs.

This completes our examination of five different methods for estimating the economic value of job performance. Researchers have proposed variations of these methods,[50] but at this point, the reader might naturally ask whether any one method is superior to the others. Our final section addresses that question.

Process: How Accurate Are SD_y Estimates, and How Much Does It Matter?

In terms of applying these ideas in actual organizations, the logical idea that there are systematic differences in the value of improving performance across different roles or jobs is much more important than the particular estimate of SD_y. When business leaders ask HR professionals how much a particular HR program costs, often they are actually wondering whether the improvement in worker quality it will produce is worth it. The distinction between the average value of performance versus the value of improving performance is often extremely helpful in reframing such discussions to uncover very useful decisions.

As discussed in Chapter 2, "Analytical Foundations of HR Measurement," if the question is reframed from "How much is this program worth?" to "How likely is it that this investment will reach at least a minimum acceptable level of return?," the process of making the correct decision is often much more logical, so better decisions are more likely. In terms of SD_y, this means that it is often the case that even a wide range of SD_y values will yield the same conclusion—namely, that what appeared to be very costly HR program investments are actually quite likely to pay off. In fact, the break-even level of SD_y (the level needed to meet the minimal acceptable level of return) is often lower than even the most conservative SD_y estimates produced by the techniques described here.

A review of 34 studies that included more than 100 estimates of SD_y concluded that differences among alternative methods for estimating SD_y are often less than 50 percent.[51] Even though differences among methods for estimating SD_y may be small, those differences can become magnified when multiplied by the number of persons selected, the validity, and the selection ratio. Without any meaningful external criterion against which to compare SD_y estimates, we are left with little basis for choosing one method over another. This is what led the authors of one review to state, "Rather than focusing so much attention on the estimation of SD_y, we suggest that utility researchers should focus on understanding exactly what Y represents."[52]

In terms of the perceived usefulness of the utility information, research has found that different SD_y techniques influence managers' reactions differently (the 40 percent rule was perceived as more credible than CREPID), but these differences accounted for less than 5 percent of the variance in the reactions.[53] At a broader level, another study found that managers preferred to receive information about the financial results of HR interventions rather than anecdotal information, regardless of the overall impact of such programs (low, medium, or high).[54]

Utility analyses should reflect the context in which decisions are made.[55] For example, is the task to choose among alternative selection procedures? Or is it to decide between funding selection program or buying new equipment? All utility analyses involve uncertainty and risk, just like any other organizational measurement. By taking uncertainty into account through sensitivity or break-even analysis (see Chapter 2), any of the SD_y estimation methods may be acceptable because none yields a result so discrepant as to change the decision in question. Instead of fixating on accuracy in estimating SD_y, HR and business leaders should use the logic of performance variability to understand where it matters. If a wide range of values yields the same decision, debating the values is not productive.

The broader issue requires answers to questions such as the following: Where would improvements in talent, or how it is organized, most enhance sustainable strategic success? We began this chapter by focusing on performance-yield curves and the notion of pivotal talent. We emphasized that it is important to distinguish average value from variability in value, and that a key question for managers is not which talent has the greatest average value, but rather, in which talent pools performance variation creates the biggest strategic impact. The estimation of SD_y provides an answer to one important piece of that puzzle.

It is important that HR and business leaders also attend to the larger question. Beyond simply the slope of the performance-value curve (reflected in SD_y), the shape of the curves can be informative. In what jobs or roles is performance at standard good enough? In what jobs or roles is the issue to reduce risk, not necessarily to improve performance levels (such as airline pilots, and nuclear plant operators)? Conversely, in what jobs or roles can downside risk be accepted, for the chance that innovation and creativity create great value (such as Starbucks baristas)? Traditional approaches to job analysis, goal setting and performance management tend to overlook these questions. Yet it is within these processes that HR and business leaders often have the greatest opportunity to understand deeply not only the dollar value of performance differences (SD_y), but the very nature of how work performance contributes to organizational value.[56]

Sometimes it is best to start at a less complex high level. For example, the IBM Institute for Business Value interpreted the idea of "pivotal roles" to recommend that organizations define and distinguish *focal jobs* defined as "positions that make a clear and positive difference in a company's ability to succeed in the marketplace." The Institute authors suggest developing "heat maps" that identify which parts of a business are *core* (necessary to stay in business but not differentiating in the marketplace), *competitive* (gets the organization considered by a potential customer), and *differentiating* (significantly influences the buying decisions of customers). The idea is that performance variation in the "competitive" and "differentiating" parts of the organization is likely to be more valuable than in the "core."[57] Figure 9-4 is an example of such a heat map.

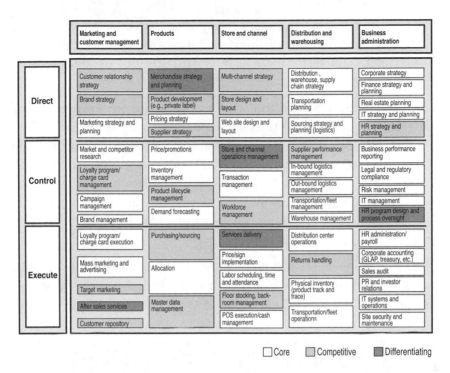

	Marketing and customer management	Products	Store and channel	Distribution and warehousing	Business administration
Direct	Customer relationship strategy	Merchandise strategy and planning	Multi-channel strategy	Distribution, warehouse, supply chain strategy	Corporate strategy
	Brand strategy	Product development (e.g., private label)	Store design and layout	Transportation planning	Finance strategy and planning
	Marketing strategy and planning	Pricing strategy	Web site design and layout	Sourcing strategy and planning (logistics)	Real estate planning
		Supplier strategy			IT strategy and planning
					HR strategy and planning
Control	Market and competitor research	Price/promotions	Store and channel operations management	Supplier performance management	Business performance reporting
	Loyalty program/ charge card management	Inventory management	Transaction management	In-bound logistics management	Legal and regulatory compliance
	Campaign management	Product lifecycle management		Out-bound logistics management	Risk management
	Brand management	Demand forecasting	Workforce management	Transportation/fleet management	IT management
				Warehouse management	HR program design and process oversight
Execute	Loyalty program/ charge card execution	Purchasing/sourcing	Services delivery	Distribution center operations	HR administration/ payroll
	Mass marketing and advertising	Allocation	Price/sign implementation	Returns handling	Corporate accounting (GLAP, treasury, etc.)
			Labor scheduling, time and attendance		Sales audit
	Target marketing		Floor stocking, back-room management	Physical inventory (product track and trace)	PR and investor relations
	After sales services	Master data management			IT systems and operations
	Customer repository		POS execution/cash management	Transportation/fleet operations	Site security and maintenance

☐ Core   ☐ Competitive   ■ Differentiating

Source: Lesser, Eric, Denis Brousseau, and Tim Ringo, *Focal Jobs: Viewing Talent Through a Different Lens.* (Somers, N.Y.: IBM Institute for Business Value, 2009).

Figure 9-4 Heat map showing what organization processes are most differentiating.

Even such a simple categorization can start a valuable conversation about performance variation and what it means. Then the tools described here can be used to get more specific, attaching consequences and perhaps even monetary values to such performance differences. The next chapter provides an example of embedding the value of performance within a specific decision framework, by applying utility analyses to employee selection. The chapter will also show the role of economic factors, employee flows, and break-even analysis in interpreting such results.

Exercises

Software that calculates answers to one or more of the following exercises can be found at http://hrcosting.com/hr/.

1. Divide into four- to six-person teams and do either A or B, depending on feasibility.

A. Choose a production job at a fast-food restaurant and, after making appropriate modifications of the standard-costing approach described in this chapter, estimate the mean and standard deviation of dollar-valued job performance.

B. The Tiny Company manufactures components for word processors. Most of the work is done at the 2,000-employee Tiny plant in the Midwest. Your task is to estimate the mean and standard deviation of dollar-valued job performance for Assemblers (about 200 employees). You are free to make any assumptions you like about the Tiny Assemblers, but be prepared to defend your assumptions. List and describe all the factors (along with how you would measure each one) that your team would consider in using standard costing to estimate SD_y.

2. Jim Hill is the manager of subscriber accounts for the Prosper Company. The results of a job analysis indicate that Jim's job includes four principal activities. A summary of Jim's superior's ratings of the activities and Jim's performance of each of them follows:

Principal Activity	Manager Importance Rating	Jim's Performance (0 to 2)
1	4.5	1.00
2	3.0	2.00
3	6.0	0.50
4	1.0	1.00

Assuming that Jim is paid $62,000 per year, use CREPID to estimate the overall economic value of his job performance.

3. Assume that an average SWAT team member is paid $55,000 per year. Complete the following questionnaire. Then use the results to estimate SD_y by means of the superior equivalents technique.

For purposes of this questionnaire, a "superior" SWAT team member is one whose performance is better than about 85 percent of his fellow SWAT team members. Please complete the following item:

I estimate that, all else being equal, _____ "superior" SWAT team members would be about equal to 20 "average" SWAT team members.

References

1. Tam, P. W., and K. J. Delaney, "Talent Search: Google's Growth Helps Ignite Silicon Valley Hiring Frenzy," *The Wall Street Journal* (November 23, 2005), A1.

2. Boudreau, John W., *Retooling HR: Using Proven Business Tools to Make Better Decisions About Talent* (Boston: Harvard Business Press, 2010).

3. Boudreau, 2010; Boudreau, J. W., and P. M. Ramstad, "Strategic Industrial and Organizational Psychology and the Role of Utility Analysis Models," in *Handbook of Psychology, Volume 12, Industrial and Organizational Psychology,* ed. W. C. Borman, D. R. Ilgen, and R. J. Klimoski (Hoboken, N.J.: Wiley, 2003).

4. Boudreau, J. W., and P. Ramstad, *Beyond HR: The New Science of Human Capital* (Boston: Harvard Business School Press, 2007).

5. A more complete treatment of the Disney example, as well as the concept of pivotalness and performance-yield curves, can be found in Boudreau and Ramstad, 2007.

6. Cabrera, E. F., and J. S. Raju, "Utility Analysis: Current Trends and Future Directions," *International Journal of Selection and Assessment* 9 (2001): 92–102.

7. Hunter, J. E., F. L. Schmidt, and M. K. Judiesch, "Individual Differences in Output Variability As a Function of Job Complexity," *Journal of Applied Psychology* 75 (1990): 28–42.

8. Boudreau and Ramstad, 2007.

9. *Ibid.*

10. *Ibid.*

11. Boudreau, 2010.

12. Kano, Noriaki, Nobuhiku Seraku, Fumio Takahashi, and Shinichi Tsuji, "Attractive Quality and Must-Be Quality," *Journal of the Japanese Society for Quality Control* 14, no. 2 (April 1984): 39–48. http://ci.nii.ac.jp/Detail/detail.do?LOCALID=ART0003570680&lang=en.

13. Boudreau, 2010.

14. Cronbach, L. J., and G. C. Gleser, *Psychological Tests and Personnel Decisions,* 2nd ed. (Urbana, Ill.: University of Illinois Press, 1965). See also Raju, N. S., M. J. Burke, and J. Normand, "A New Approach for Utility Analysis," *Journal of Applied Psychology* 75 (1990): 3–12; and Boudreau and Ramstad, 2003.

15. Brogden, H. E., and E. K. Taylor, "The Dollar Criterion—Applying the Cost Accounting Concept to Criterion Construction," *Personnel Psychology* 3 (1950): 133–154.

16. Brogden, H. E., and E. K. Taylor, "The Dollar Criterion—Applying the Cost Accounting Concept to Criterion Construction," *Personnel Psychology* 3 (1950): 133–154.

17. Greer, O. L., and W. F. Cascio, "Is Cost Accounting the Answer? Comparison of Two Behaviorally Based Methods for Estimating the Standard Deviation of Job Performance in Dollars with a Cost Accounting–Based Approach," *Journal of Applied Psychology* 72 (1987): 588–595.

18. Horngren, C. T., G. M. Foster, S. M. Datar, and Madhav V. Rajan, *Cost Accounting: A Managerial Emphasis,* 13th ed. (Upper Saddle River, N.J.: Prentice Hall, 2008). See also Cherrington, J. O., E. D. Hubbard, and D. Luthy, *Cost and Managerial Accounting* (Dubuque, Ia.: Wm. C. Brown, 1985).

19. Time-period dollar conversions were calculated using the U.S. Consumer Price Index approach and the calculator at the Bureau of Labor Statistics website (http://data.bls.gov/cgi-bin/cpicalc.pl).

20. Schmidt, F. L., and J. E. Hunter, "Individual Differences in Productivity: An Empirical Test of Estimates Derived from Studies of Selection Procedure Utility," *Journal of Applied Psychology* 68 (1983): 407–414.

21. Subsequent research indicates that this guideline is quite conservative. See Judiesch, M. K., F. L. Schmidt, and K. K. Mount, "An Improved Method for Estimating Utility," *Journal of Human Resource Costing and Accounting* 1, no. 2 (1996): 31–42.

22. Hunter, Schmidt, and Judiesch, 1990.

23. Boudreau, J. W., "Utility Analysis," in *Human Resource Management: Evolving Roles and Responsibilities,* ed. L. Dyer (Washington, D.C.: Bureau of National Affairs, 1988).

24. Schmidt, F. L., J. E. Hunter, R. C. McKenzie, and T. W. Muldrow, "Impact of Valid Selection Procedures on Workforce Productivity," *Journal of Applied Psychology* 64 (1979): 610–626.

25. In a normal distribution of scores, + 1SD corresponds approximately to the difference between the 50th and 85th percentiles, and −1SD corresponds approximately to the difference between the 50th and 15th percentiles.

26. Schmidt, Hunter, McKenzie, and Muldrow, 1979.

27. Boudreau and Ramstad, 2008.

28. Schmidt, Hunter, McKenzie, and Muldrow, 1979.

29. Judiesch, M. K., F. L. Schmidt, and M. K. Mount, "Estimates of the Dollar Value of Employee Output in Utility Analyses: An Empirical Test of Two Theories," *Journal of Applied Psychology* 77 (1992): 234–250.

30. *Ibid.* See also Judiesch, M. K., F. L. Schmidt, and M. K. Mount, "An Improved Method for Estimating Utility," *Journal of Human Resource Costing and Accounting* 1, no. 2 (1996): 31–42.

31. Hunter, Schmidt, and Judiesch, 1990.

32. Judiesch, Schmidt, and Mount, 1996.

33. Judiesch, Schmidt, and Mount, 1992.

34. Cesare, S. J., M. H. Blankenship, and P. W. Giannetto, "A Dual Focus of SD_y Estimations: A Test of the Linearity Assumption and Multivariate Application," *Human Performance* 7, no. 4 (1994): 235–255.

35. Burke, M. J., and J. T. Frederick, "Two Modified Procedures for Estimating Standard Deviations in Utility Analyses," *Journal of Applied Psychology* 69 (1984): 482–489; Lezotte, D. V., N. S. Raju, M. J. Burke, and J. Normand, "An Empirical Comparison of Two Utility Analysis Models," *Journal of Human Resource Costing and Accounting* 1, no. 2 (1996): 110–130; and Rich, J. R., and J. W. Boudreau, "The Effects of Variability and Risk on Selection Utility Analysis: An Empirical Simulation and Comparison," *Personnel Psychology* 40 (1987): 55–84.

36. Boudreau and Ramstad, 2007.

37. Desimone, R. L., R. A. Alexander, and S. F. Cronshaw, "Accuracy and Reliability of SD_y Estimates in Utility Analysis," *Journal of Occupational Psychology* 59 (1986): 93–102

38. Bobko, P., R. Karren, and J. J. Parkington, "The Estimation of Standard Deviations in Utility Analyses: An Empirical Test," *Journal of Applied Psychology* 68 (1983): 170–176; Burke and Frederick, 1984; and Burke, M. J., and J. T. Frederick, "A Comparison of Economic Utility Estimates for Alternative Rational SD_y Estimation Procedures," *Journal of Applied Psychology* 71 (1986): 334–339.

39. Greer and Cascio, 1987.

40. Lezotte et al., 1996.

41. Cascio, W. F., and R. A. Ramos, "Development and Application of a New Method for Assessing Job Performance in Behavioral/Economic Terms," *Journal of Applied Psychology* 71 (1986): 20–28.

42. Weekley, J. A., B. Frank, E. J. O'Connor, and L. H. Peters, "A Comparison of Three Methods of Estimating the Standard Deviation of Performance in Dollars," *Journal of Applied Psychology* 70 (1985): 122–126.

43. Stevens, S. S., "Issues in Psychophysical Measurement," *Psychological Review* 78 (1971): 426–450.

44. Boudreau and Ramstad, 2007; Boudreau, 2010.

45. *Ibid.*

46. Boudreau, J. W., "Utility Analysis for Decisions in Human Resource Management," in *Handbook of Industrial and Organizational Psychology,* Volume 2, 2nd ed., ed. M. D. Dunnette and L. M. Hough (Palo Alto, Calif.: Consulting Psychologists Press, 1991).

47. Eaton, N. K., H. Wing, and K. J. Mitchell, "Alternate Methods of Estimating the Dollar Value of Performance," *Personnel Psychology* 38 (1985): 27–40.

48. *Ibid.*

49. *Ibid.*

50. Raju, Burke, and Normand, 1990; Judiesch, M. K., F. L. Schmidt, and J. E. Hunter, "Has the Problem of Judgment in Utility Analysis Been Solved?" *Journal of Applied Psychology* 78 (1993): 903–911; and Law, K. S., and B. Myors, "A Modification of Raju, Burke, and Normand's (1990) New Model for Utility Analysis," *Asia Pacific Journal of Human Resources* 37, no. 1 (1999): 39–51.

51. Boudreau, 1991.

52. Arvey, R. D., and K. R. Murphy, "Performance Evaluation in Work Settings," *Annual Review of Psychology* 49 (1998): 141–168.

53. Hazer, J. T., and S. Highhouse, "Factors Influencing Managers' Reactions to Utility Analysis: Effects of SD_y Method, Information Frame, and Focal Intervention," *Journal of Applied Psychology* 82 (1997): 104–112.

54. Mattson, B. W., "The Effects of Alternative Reports of Human Resource Development Results on Managerial Support," *Human Resource Development Quarterly* 14, no. 2 (2003): 127–151.

55. Cascio, W. F., "The Role of Utility Analysis in the Strategic Management of Organizations," *Journal of Human Resource Costing and Accounting* 1, no. 2 (1996): 85–95; Cascio, W. F., "Assessing the Utility of Selection Decisions: Theoretical and Practical Considerations," in *Personnel Selection in Organizations,* ed. N. Schmitt and W. C. Borman (San Francisco: Jossey-Bass, 1993): 39–335; and Russell, C. J., A. Colella, and P. Bobko, "Expanding the Context of Utility: The Strategic Impact of Personnel Selection," *Personnel Psychology* 46 (1993): 781–801.

56. Boudreau, 2010.

57. Lesser, Eric, Denis Brousseau, and Tim Ringo, *Focal Jobs: Viewing Talent through a Different Lens* (Somers, N.Y.: IBM Institute for Business Value, 2009).

10

The Payoff from Enhanced Selection

Have you ever made a profit from a catering business or dog walking? Do you prefer to work alone or in groups? Have you ever set a world record in anything? The right answer might help you get a job at Google, Inc. Google received more than 100,000 job applications every month in 2007, and to deal with that volume of applications, Google created an algorithm that sifts through answers to an elaborate online survey. The answers are fed into a series of formulas created by Google's mathematics experts that calculate a score between 0 and 100 to "predict how well a person will fit into its chaotic and competitive culture." Lazlo Bock, Google's vice president for people operations, joined Google in spring 2006 and found the selection process rejecting candidates with engineering GPAs of less than 3.7 out of 4.0, and taking two months to consider candidates because each one was submitted to more than half a dozen interviews. After analyzing survey questions as diverse as pet ownership, magazine subscriptions, and introversion, and comparing them with work performance factors as diverse as job rating and organizational citizenship, Google found that "too much schooling can be a detriment" in some jobs. The company created different surveys for candidates in different areas, such as engineering, sales, finance, and human resources.[1]

Is it worth it to invest so much time and energy into this system? Are the cost savings from the online approach actually worth it, or does Google give up lots of value by fore-going the half-dozen interviews? Recall from Chapter 9, "The Economic Value of Job Performance," that Alan Eustace, Google's vice president of engineering, told *The Wall Street Journal* that one top-notch engineer is worth 300 times or more than the average and that he would rather lose an entire incoming class of engineering graduates than one exceptional technologist.[2] Should Google be selecting more carefully for its technologists than engineers? The tools in this chapter are designed to answer questions like these.

Chapter 8, "Staffing Utility: The Concept and Its Measurement," provided you with the logical and mathematical models for calculating the utility of staffing. Chapter 9 showed how to estimate an important element of staffing utility models: the monetary value of the standard deviation of performance. When you put the models of Chapter 8 together with the estimates of Chapter 9, you end up with powerful analytical frameworks that help predict when investments in enhanced selection will pay off. Lacking the frameworks provided here, organization leaders often see only the costs of such programs. Or, well-meaning psychologists present leaders with statistics such as validity coefficients out of context. Decision makers may ignore the difficult-to-understand value of improved selection and instead focus only on the costs, which often causes them to forego valuable opportunities.

By the same token, staffing professionals often become so focused on improving the elegance of staffing systems that they lose sight of the need to balance costs and benefits. Improved validity in employee selection is not always worth the cost, and it is certainly not equally valuable in every situation. The logic of Chapter 8 and the estimation methods of Chapter 9 combine to provide clues about where staffing investments have the greatest payoff.

Employee selection is quite similar to other business processes. In essence, investing in employee selection is an example of gathering information to improve our ability to predict the performance of a risky asset. In this case, the "asset" is a new hire, but the logic of the decision is the same logic that supports decisions to invest in research on financial investments, mineral exploration, consumer preferences, and any other uncertain resource.

In Chapter 8 (Figure 8-1), we introduced the idea of a supply chain approach to staffing, showing that the pipeline of talent is very similar to the pipeline of any other resource. At each stage, the candidate pool can be thought of in terms of the quantity of candidates, the average and dispersion of the quality of the candidates, and the cost of processing and employing the candidates. Quantity, quality, and cost considerations determine the monetary value of staffing programs, and the utility models of Chapter 8 showed how to calculate and combine these factors.

In this chapter, we tie these ideas together to show how to actually calculate the value of improved employee selection and other aspects of the talent supply chain.[3] We show how valid selection procedures (for external and internal candidates) can pay off handsomely for organizations. Moreover, we show how the basic utility formulas can incorporate important financial considerations, to make utility estimates more comparable with estimates of investment returns for other resources such as technology, advertising, and so on.

To date, utility analysis has not been used widely. Yet it has the potential to provide an answer to the increasing calls for greater rigor and economic justification for HR investments (see Chapter 1, "Making HR Measurement Strategic"). This chapter shows how to make utility analysis estimates compatible with other financial estimates, which we believe will make it easier for HR leaders to "retool" utility analysis within the logic of proven business tools.[4] Thus, business leaders will develop shared mental models and make better decisions about staffing and other HR programs.

We begin with an example of tangible results from improved staffing, estimated with the Brogden-Cronbach-Gleser model described in Chapter 8.[5] Then we consider the effects of five considerations that help make staffing payoffs more realistic and better connected to traditional financial logic:

- Economic factors (variable costs, taxes, and discounting)

- Employee flows

- Probationary periods

- The use of multiple selection devices

- Departures from top-down hiring

Then we address the issue of risk and uncertainty in utility analysis and offer several tools to aid in decision making. We conclude the chapter by focusing on processes used to communicate the results of utility analyses to decision makers.

The Logic of Investment Value Calculated Using Utility Analysis

Figure 10-1 presents the logic of utility analysis, along with some situational factors that may affect quantity, quality, and cost.

We discussed several of these factors in Chapters 8 and 9. In Chapter 8, Equation 8-17 showed how the Brogden-Cronbach-Gleser model combines several of these factors, namely the selection ratio (SR), the validity of the selection procedure (r), the variability or standard deviation of job performance expressed in monetary terms (SD_y), the average score of those hired on the predictor, and the average cost per selectee of applying the selection process to all applicants $[(N_a \times C)/N_s]$, to determine an unadjusted estimate of the utility of a selection process. The remaining factors shown in Figure 10-1 may increase or decrease the unadjusted utility estimate. We discuss each of them after we illustrate the computation of the unadjusted estimate in the following section.

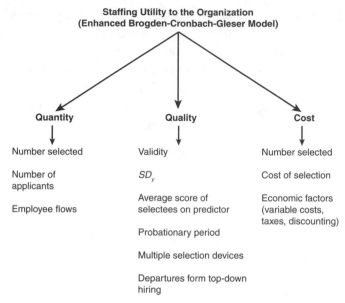

Staffing Utility to the Organization
(Enhanced Brogden-Cronbach-Gleser Model)

Quantity	Quality	Cost
Number selected	Validity	Number selected
Number of applicants	SD_y	Cost of selection
Employee flows	Average score of selectees on predictor	Economic factors (variable costs, taxes, discounting)
	Probationary period	
	Multiple selection devices	
	Departures form top-down hiring	

Figure 10-1 The logic of utility analysis and factors that can affect payoffs.

Example: A Selection Test for Computer Programmers

A 1979 study of computer programmers in the federal government examined the productivity implications of a more valid selection procedure, called the Programmer Aptitude Test (PAT).[6] The PAT demonstrated high validity for predicting the performance of computer programmers (the estimated true validity is 0.76), and that validity was essentially constant across many organizations. Thus, it was reasonable to use this validity estimate to examine the payoffs from using the PAT in the federal government and in the economy as a whole. The cost of administering the PAT per examinee was $36 (all figures are adjusted to 2010 dollars).[7]

The study focused on the selection of federal government computer programmers at the GS-5 through GS-9 levels, with GS-5 being the lowest level in this occupational series. Beyond GS-9, it was unlikely for an aptitude test such as the PAT to be used in selection. Applicants for higher-level programmer positions were required to have considerable expertise in programming and were selected on the basis of achievement and experience instead of directly based on programming aptitude.

Although this 1979 example is somewhat dated, it is the example with the most complete data needed to calculate the monetary value of selection. The logic used here applies to any selection decision.

Measuring the Utility Components

In terms of quantity, the average number of GS-5 through GS-9 programmers selected was 618 per year. Estimating on the basis of U.S. census data in 1979, 10,210 computer programmers could be hired each year in the U.S. economy using the PAT. The average tenure for government programmers was found to be 9.69 years; in the absence of other information, this tenure figure was assumed for the private sector as well. The average gain in utility per selectee per year was multiplied by 9.69 to yield a total employment period gain in utility per selectee.

It was not possible to determine the prevailing selection ratio (SR) for computer programmers either in the general economy or in the federal government, so the utility analysis formula was used to do sensitivity analysis using an SR of 0.05 and then substituting SRs in intervals of 0.10 from 0.10 to 0.80.

In terms of validity, it's possible for the PAT to replace a prior procedure with zero validity in some cases, but in other situations, the PAT replaced a procedure with lower but nonzero validity. Thus, utilities were calculated assuming previous-procedure true validities of 0.20, 0.30, 0.40, and 0.50, as well as zero.

SDy was calculated as the average of the two estimates obtained from experts, using the global estimation procedure described in Chapter 9. The estimate was $38,613 per person per year (in 2010 dollars).

When the previous procedure was assumed to have zero validity, its associated testing cost also was assumed to be zero. When the previous procedure was assumed to have a nonzero validity, its associated cost was assumed to be the same as that of the PAT (that is, $36 per applicant). Cost of testing was charged only to the first year, as if the procedure was used only once, to select the first group of programmers.

The Brogden-Cronbach-Gleser general utility equation was modified to obtain the equation actually used in computing the utilities.

$$\Delta U = tN_s(r_1 - r_2)SD_y\lambda/\varphi - N_s(c_1 - c_2)/\varphi \qquad (10\text{-}1)$$

Here, ΔU is the gain in productivity in dollars from using the new selection procedure for one year; t is the tenure in years of the average selectee (here 9.69); N_s is the number selected in a given year (this figure was 618 for the federal government and 10,210 for the U.S. economy); r_1 is the validity of the new procedure, here the PAT ($r_1 = 0.76$); r_2 is the validity of the previous procedure (r_2 ranges from 0 to 0.50); c_1 is the cost per applicant of the new procedure, here $36; and c_2 is the cost per applicant of the previous procedure, here zero or $36. The terms SD_y, λ, and φ are as defined previously in Chapter 8. This equation gives the productivity gain that results from one year's use of the new (more valid) selection procedure, but not all these gains are realized the first year; they are spread out over the 9.69-year tenure of the new employees.

Analytics: Results of the Utility Calculation

The estimated gains in productivity in (2010) dollars varied from $19.5 million to $334 million. Those gains would result from one year's use of the PAT to select computer programmers in the federal government for different combinations of selection ratios and previous-procedure validity. When the SR is 0.05 (the government is assumed to be very selective) and the previous procedure has no validity (the maximum relative value for the PAT), use of the PAT for one year produces an aggregate productivity gain of $334 million. At the other extreme, if the SR is 0.80 (relatively unselective) and the validity of the procedure the PAT replaces is 0.50, the estimated gain is only $19.5 million.

To illustrate how those figures were derived, assume that the SR = 0.20 and the previous procedure has a validity of 0.30. All other terms are as defined previously.

$$\Delta U = 9.69(618)(0.76 - 0.30)(\$38,613)(0.2789 \div 0.20) - 618(\$36 - \$36)/0.20$$

$$\Delta U = 9.69(618)(0.46)(\$38,613)(1.3945) - 0$$

$$\Delta U = \$148,327,660$$

The gain per selectee can be obtained by dividing the value of total utility by 618, the assumed yearly number of selectees. When this is done for our example ($148,327,660 / 618), the gain per selectee is $240,012. That figure is still quite high, but remember that not all of those gains are realized during the first year. They are spread out over the entire tenure of the new employees. Gains per year per selectee can be obtained by dividing the total utility first by 618 and then by 9.69, the average tenure of computer programmers. In our example, this produces a per-year gain of $24,769 per selectee—or, to carry it even further, a $12 gain per hour per year per selectee (assuming 2,080 hours per work year). Other research has often produced equally stunning estimates of the monetary value of improved selection.[8]

Process: Making Utility Analysis Estimates More Comparable to Financial Estimates

Evidence presented in the studies we have described leads to the inescapable conclusion that how people are selected makes an important, practical difference. The implications of valid selection procedures for workforce productivity are clearly much greater than most of us might have suspected, but are they as high as these studies suggest? Standard investment analysis would suggest that considerations such as the costs of improved performance, inflation and risk, and the tax implications of higher profits from better selection should all be accounted for, to make these estimates comparable to investment calculations for more traditional resources. This translation may be essential to the process of gaining support from business leaders outside of HR. The idea is that, by using proven business logic and applying it to the question of selection utility, the results will be more credible and more easily understood.

Figure 10-1 showed that the cost of a selection program depends not only on the number of individuals selected and the cost of selection, but also on several additional economic factors. These include variable costs, taxes, and discounting. Why are these important? By taking them into account, decision makers can evaluate the soundness of HR investments more comparably with other investments. Other financial investments routinely account for these factors, so failing to consider them in estimating the value of staffing produces utility estimates that are overstated compared to other investments. Decision makers will want to compare HR investments on compatible terms with other investments, so these adjustments help make HR utility estimates more comparable.

Logic: Three Financial Adjustments

Failing to adjust utility estimates creates overestimates under any or all of three conditions.[9] First, where variable costs (for example, incentive- or commission-based pay, benefits, variable raw materials costs, and variable production overhead) rise with productivity, a portion (V) of the gain in value calculated using Equation 10-1 will go to pay such costs. Second, organizations must pay a portion of the profit as tax liabilities (TAX). Third, where costs and benefits accrue over time, the values of future costs and benefits are worth less than present costs and benefits, so future values must be discounted to reflect the opportunity costs of returns foregone. Benefits received in the present or costs delayed into the future would be invested to earn returns. A dollar received today at a 10 percent annual return would be worth $1.21 in two years. A future benefit worth $1.21 in two years has a "present value" of $1.00.

Analytics: Calculating the Economic Adjustments

The following utility formula takes these three economic factors into account.[10]

$$\Delta U = (N)\left\{\sum_{t=1}^{T}\left[1/(1+i)^t\right]\right\}(SD_{sv})(1+V)(1-TAX)(r_{x,sv})(\overline{Z}_x)-C_T(1-TAX) \quad (10\text{-}2)$$

Here, ΔU is the change in overall worth or utility after variable costs, taxes, and discounting; N is the number of employees selected; t is the time period in which an increase in productivity occurs; T is the total number of periods (for example, years) that benefits continue to accrue to an organization; i is the discount rate; SD_{sv} is the standard deviation of the sales value of productivity among the applicant or employee population (this is similar to SD_y in previous utility models but is called sales value to reflect the idea of translating productivity into the sales revenue it would generate, and to distinguish it from profits); V is the proportion of sales value represented by variable costs; TAX is the organization's applicable tax rate; $r_{x,sv}$ is the validity coefficient between predictor (x) and sales value (similar to $r_{x,y}$ in previous utility models); and C_T is the total selection cost for all applicants (equal to the number selected divided by the selection ratio).

Those economic considerations suggest large potential reductions in unadjusted utility estimates. For example, researchers computed an SD_{sv} value of $38,613 (in 2010 dollars) in their utility analysis of the PAT.[11] Although this may have been appropriate for federal government jobs because the federal government is not taxed, it would not be appropriate for private-sector organizations that face variable costs and taxes.

Assuming that the net effect of variable costs is to reduce gains by 5 percent, $V = -0.05$. Assuming a marginal tax rate (the tax rate applicable to changes in reported profits generated by a decision) of 45 percent, the after-cost, after-tax, one-year SD_y value is as follows:

$(SD_{sv}) \times (1 + V) \times (1 - TAX)$

$(\$38,613) \times (1 - 0.05) \times (1 - 0.45) = \$20,175$

This is 52 percent of the original value.

Now, assuming a financial discount rate of 10 percent, if the average tenure of computer programmers in the federal government was just two years, the appropriate discount factor (DF) adjustment would be as shown in Equation 10-3.

$$DF = \sum_{t=1}^{T} 1/(1+i)^t = 1/(1 + 0.10)^1 + 1/(1 + 0.10)^2 = 1.74 \qquad (10\text{-}3)$$

Over 10 years, DF = 6.14, but the average tenure of computer programmers in the federal government (at the time of the study) was computed to be 9.69 years. Hence, the appropriate adjustment needed to discount the computed utility values 6.03. So, to reflect discounting, the per-year utility should be multiplied by 6.03, instead of 9.69.

When all three of those factors—variable costs, taxes, and discounting—are considered, the per-selectee utility values over 9.69 years that were reported in the study of computer programmers range from $10,210 (which is [$19.5 million / 618 = $31,553 per selectee × (6.03/9.69) × 0.52]) to $174,886 ($334 million / 618 = $540,453 per selectee × (6.03/9.69) × 0.52).

These values still are substantial, but they are 67 percent lower than the unadjusted values. Such significant effects argue strongly that HR leaders should be careful to make their monetary payoff estimates as compatible as possible with standard investment calculations. Note that the adjustments above multiplied the total to adjust for the discount factor (6.03/9.69) and the combination of variable costs and taxes (52 percent of the unadjusted value). This is because the cost difference was zero. If it was non-zero, the added value elements would be adjusted as shown here, but the cost should be adjusted by the tax rate.

How Talent Creates "Compound Interest:" Effects of Employee Flows on Utility Estimates

The idea of compound interest is one of the most important principles in investing. Compound interest refers to the fact that if you make an investment that earns interest in the first year, and you add that interest to your original investment, then in the second year, you earn interest on the original investment as well as the first-year interest, and so on. It turns out that when organizations select better employees, the benefits of their improved performance also "compound" over time. This significantly increases the value of improved employee quality over time, just as compound interest significantly increases the returns on investments over time.

Employee flows into, through, and out of an organization influence the value of a staffing program or any other HR intervention.[12] We showed earlier that failure to consider the effects of variable costs, taxes, and discounting tends to overstate utility estimates. Conversely, failure to consider the effect of employee flows may understate utility estimates. The utility analysis formulas originally introduced reflected a selection program used to hire a single group and often reflected only the first-year effect of those better-selected employees. They expressed the utility of adding one new, better-selected cohort to the existing workforce. Yet in any investment, the cumulative benefit over time is relevant. One would not evaluate an investment in improved quality control for raw materials merely on the first order received. In the same way, selection utility should reflect the cumulative effects on all employees selected over time.

Logic: Employee Flows

Earlier we multiplied the one-year selection benefit obtained by using the PAT by the average tenure (9.69 years) of the better-selected programmers.[13] Yet this still reflects the effects of hiring only one group whose members stay for several years.

In practice, valid selection programs are reapplied year after year, as employees flow into and out of the workforce. A program's effects on cohorts hired in later years will occur in addition to its lasting effects on previously hired cohorts. These are additive cohort effects.[14] By altering the terms N and T in Equation 10-2, we can account for the effect of employee flows.

Employee flows generally affect utility through the period-to-period changes in the number of *treated* employees in the workforce. Note that we use the term "treated employees" to mean employees that are affected by an improved HR program, such as the group hired with an improved test. Such employees are added to a workforce containing existing or untreated employees. The number of treated employees in the workforce k periods in the future (N_k) may be expressed as shown in Equation 10-4.

$$N_k = \sum_{t=1}^{k}(N_{a_t} - N_{s_t})$$
(10-4)

Here, N_{a_t} is the number of treated employees added to the workforce in period t, and N_{s_t} is the number of treated employees subtracted from the work force in period t. For example, consider the makeup of the workforce in the fourth year, after a new selection procedure was applied for four years ($k = 4$); that 100 persons were hired in each of the four years; and that 10 of them left in Year 2, 15 in Year 3, and 20 in Year 4. The following results are observed from the inception of the program ($t = 1$) to year 4 ($t = 4$):

$$N_4 = (100 - 0) + (100 - 10) + (100 - 15) + (100 - 20)$$

$$N_4 = 355$$

Thus, the term N_k reflects both the number of employees treated in previous periods and their expected separation pattern. The formula for the utility (ΔU_k) occurring in the kth future period that includes the economic considerations of Equation 10-2 may be written as shown in Equation 10-5.

$$\Delta U_k = \left[\sum_{t=1}^{k}(N_{a_t} - N_{s_t})\right]\left\{\left[1/(1+i)^k\right](r_{x,sv})(\bar{Z}_x)(SD_{sv})(1+V)(1-TAX)\right\} \\ -C_k(1-TAX)\left[1/(1+i)^{(k-1)}\right]$$
(10-5)

This formula modifies the quantity element by keeping track of how many treated employees are in the workforce in each year. Then, after multiplying that number by the increased productive value of the treated employees, the relevant discount rate, cost, tax, and other factors are applied for that particular year.

For simplicity, the utility parameters $r_{x, sv}$, V, SD_{sv}, and TAX are assumed to be constant over time. This assumption is not necessary, and sometimes the factors may vary. Note also that the cost of treating (for example, selecting) the N_{ak} employees added in period k (C_k) is now allowed to vary over time. However, C_k is not simply a constant multiplied by N_{ak}. Some programs (for example, assessment centers) have high initial startup costs of development, but these costs do not vary with the number treated in future periods. Also, the discount factor for costs $[1/(1 + i)^{(k - 1)}]$ reflects the exponent $k - 1$, assuming that such costs are incurred one period prior to receiving benefits. Where costs are incurred in the same period as benefits are received, k is the proper exponent.[15]

Analytics: Calculating How Employee Flows Affect Specific Situations

For illustration, let's use an SD_y value of $25,000 and calculate the Year 4 utility, assuming the flow pattern described previously. We calculated $N_4 = 355$. If the discount rate is 10 percent, then the discount factor is .683 for year-4 benefits and .751 for year-3 selection costs. The validity of the procedure is 0.40; the selection ratio is 0.50 (and, therefore, the average standardized test score of those selected is 0.3989 / 0.50 = 0.80, from earlier chapters); SD_{sv} per person-year is $25,000; variable costs = –0.05; taxes = 0.45; and C_k, the cost of treating the 100 employees added in Year 4, is $(100/.5) \times \$36 = \$7,200$.

$$\Delta U_4 = (355 \times .683 \times .40 \times .80 \times \$25,000 \times .95 \times .55) - (\$7,200 \times .751 \times .55)$$

$$\times 0.55)] - (\$7,200 \times .751 \times 0.55)$$

$$\Delta U_4 = \$1,013,504 - \$2,974 = \$1,010,530$$

$$\$1,013,504 - \$2,974 = \$1,010,530$$

This figure equals the total one-year value of the improved performance of all the better selected employees who are still with the organization in the fourth year.

To express the utility of a program's effects over F periods, the one-period utility estimates (ΔU_k) are summed. Thus, the complete utility model reflecting employee flows through the workforce for a program affecting productivity in F future periods may be written as shown in Equation 10-6.

$$\Delta U = \sum_{k=1}^{F}\left[\sum_{t=1}^{k}(N_{a_t} - N_{s_t})\right]\left\{\left[1/(1+i)^k\right](r_{x,sv})\times(\bar{Z}_x)(SD_{sv})(1+V)(1-TAX)\right\} - \sum_{k=1}^{F}\left\{C_k(1-TAX)\left[1/(1+i)^{(k-1)}\right]\right\} \quad (10\text{-}6)$$

The duration parameter F in Equation 10-6 is not employee tenure, but rather how long a program affects the workforce. Now, let's apply employee flows to the programmer example, where average tenure was 9.69 years, which we'll round up to 10 years. Assume that the PAT in the computer programmer study is applied for 15 years, and, for simplicity, assume that each hired group of programmers stays for 10 years. If 618 programmers are added each year, for the first 10 future periods N_k will increase by 618 in each period. For example, in Year 10, 6,180 programmers selected using the PAT have been added to the workforce, and none have left:

$$N_{10} = \sum_{t=1}^{10}(618-0) \qquad (10\text{-}7)$$

Beginning in future period 11, however, one PAT-selected cohort leaves in each period ($N_{s_t} = 618$). However, in Years 11 through 15, by continuing to apply the PAT to select 618 new replacements (that is, $N_{a_t} = 618$), the number of treated programmers in the workforce is maintained. Thus, in Years 11–15, N_{a_t} and N_{s_t} offset each other and N_k remains unchanged at 6,180. Assuming that the government stops using the test in Year 15, starting in future period 16, the cost and number added (C_k and N_{a_t}) become zero, assuming that the organization returns to random selection. However, the treated portion of the workforce does not disappear immediately. Earlier-selected cohorts continue to separate (that is, $N_{s_t} = 618$), and N_k falls by 618 each period until the last-treated cohort (selected in future period 15) separates in future period 25. Figure 10-2 shows N_k for each of the 25 periods. (In Figure 10-2, $F = 25$ periods.)

Period (k)	N_k
1	618
2	1,236
3	1,854
4	2,472
5	3,090
6	3,708
7	4,326
8	4,944
9	5,562
10	6,180
11	6,180
12	6,180
13	6,180
14	6,180
15	6,180
16	5,562
17	4,944
18	4,326
19	3,708
20	3,090
21	2,472
22	1,854
23	1,236
24	618
25	0

Note: N_k = number of employees receiving a given treatment who remain in the workforce:

Source: Adapted from Boudreau, J. W. (1983). Effects of employee flows on utility analysis of human resource productivity improvement programs. Journal of Applied Psychology 68, 400. Copyright © 1983 by the American Psychological Association. Reprinted with permission.

Figure 10-2 Example of employee flows over a 25-year period.

Now we can add the economic factors to the utility model that reflects employee flows. Assuming, as we did in our earlier example, that $V = -0.05$, $TAX = 0.45$, and the discount rate is 10 percent, the total expected utility of the 15-year application of PAT (the sum of the 25 one-period utility estimates, ΔU_k in Equation 10-5) was estimated to be $286.2 million (in 2010 dollars).[16] This is considerably higher than the estimate in the original study of $148.3 million (in 2010 dollars), even after reflecting variable costs, taxes, and discounting.

The most important lesson to learn from the principle of employee flows is that one-cohort utility models often understate actual utility because they reflect only the first part of a larger series of outcomes.

These numbers imply very high payoffs to improved employee selection, when we consider the impact on many employee cohorts over time. It is the same idea as the high cumulative impact of quality control in supply chains, when applied to many years of receiving raw materials orders. The reason the numbers are so high in this case is that the cost of the selection improvement is modest (a test costing less than $50 per applicant), and the difference in value between a good and a very good computer programmer is high ($38,613 per year).

Clearly, this can vary across situations. In the case of Google, at the beginning of this chapter, the cost of developing the algorithm, gathering the online data, analyzing the data, and so on would likely be much higher than $50 per applicant. That said, if the estimate of the value of performance variation among engineers is anywhere near Alan Eustace's estimate of 300 times, Google can justify even multimillion-dollar selection systems. The point is not so much the precision of the calculation, but the logic and analysis that motivate more productive conversations.

Logic: The Effects of a Probationary Period

At Whole Foods Market, new employees are selected by a process that looks a lot like the Survivor television show. A new employee is hired provisionally, works side by side with his or her future team members, and at the end of four weeks is offered a permanent job only if at least two thirds of the team votes to hire him or her. A powerful way to augment the accuracy of staffing systems is to allow new employees to actually do the job for a while—keep the employees who work out and dismiss those who don't.[17] This can be expensive, because Whole Foods has to pay probationary employees their salaries and benefits, and it involves the time and effort of the other employees who observe and rate the probationary workers. At the same time, the added accuracy and value of the better-screened work force may offset the increased costs. The utility formulas we have developed can diagnose the conditions that determine when such a probationary period will pay off.

The utility effect of a probationary period is reflected by modifying the utility equation to reflect the difference in performance between the pool of employees hired initially and those who survive the probationary period.[18] Whether a new hire is considered successful depends on his or her performance rating at the end of the probation period.

Because lower performers are dismissed, the average performance of a given selected cohort increases after the probationary period. The actual amount of the improvement depends on two things: the validity of the selection process used to weed out low performers, and the performance cutoff that determines success during probation. The costs of paying and training employees who are later dismissed, together with any separation costs, must also be taken into account among the overall costs of a probationary-hiring program.

Interestingly, a probationary period reduces the harmful effect of selection errors, because they are corrected very quickly. Poor-performing employees are weeded out consistently and early instead of being retained longer in "permanent" positions that require a longer process of formal dismissal. So the value of selection procedures used with a probationary period is less than would be the case if the same selection process were used without the probationary period. Improved selection has value when it reduces hiring errors, but when a probationary period catches those errors, the value of avoiding them is less. Overall, the combined value of improved selection and a probationary period can be higher or lower than using either one alone. It depends on their relative validity, the severity of selection errors, and the variability in the applicant population. All of this is elegantly reflected in the utility model, which can be used to examine these factors in combination to identify the optimum combination.

Another way to look at probationary periods is as a special case of the employee movement model that we described in Chapter 4, "The High Cost of Employee Separations," in Figure 4-1. In essence, the probationary period is a "controlled turnover" process, in which the validity of the dismissal decision determines the value of turnover to the organization. Finally, when seen this way, it is clear that the combination of selection and probation is much like the supply chain model of Chapter 8, with probation being similar to quality control after raw materials have been accepted and placed into the production process.

A combination of screening raw materials when they arrive and then monitoring their quality as they enter the production process may add great value if the cost of errors is quite high and if a lot of valuable information can be gathered after the materials are in the production process. That's the same logic Whole Foods is using. By selecting applicants carefully and then having the team observe them as they enter the workplace, Whole Foods is behaving as if the cost of an error is very high and assumes that the team members can see things that the selection process might miss.

Logic: Effects of Job Offer Rejections

Does it matter whether top-scoring applicants reject your offers and you must move on to lower-scoring applicants? In a tight labor market, organizations may be forced to lower their minimum hiring requirements to fill vacancies.[19] Should organizations work harder to land their best candidates? What are the monetary implications of offer rejections? The logical and analytical selection utility models described here can help answer such questions.

Rejecting job offers produces the same effect as reducing hiring standards. It increases SRs and lowers the gains from more valid selection. For example, if an organization needs to select 20 percent of its applicants to fill its positions, but half of its offers get rejected, that is the same as having a 40 percent selection ratio.

In general, offer rejections reduce the value of better selection more when:

- There is a higher correlation between the quality of the applicants and their probability of rejecting the offer.

- There is a larger proportion of rejected job offers.[20]

How large are the potential losses? One study found, that under realistic circumstances, unadjusted utility formulas could overestimate gains by 30 to 80 percent. To some extent, these utility losses caused by job offer rejection can be offset by additional recruiting efforts that increase the size of the applicant pool and, therefore, restore smaller SRs. Yet if the probability of accepting a job offer is negatively correlated with applicant quality (the better applicants are more likely to reject an offer), increasing the number of applicants may not be as effective as increasing the attractiveness of the organization to the better ones.

Again, the supply chain analogy applies. This is the same tradeoff that must be considered when bidding on scarce production inputs (such as oil field rights and rare components). The organization can increase the number of sellers, make itself more attractive to the sellers (perhaps through pricing or other perks), or a combination of both. As with a supply-chain, the right answer is found by better understanding the variables that determine the value of improved selection and recruitment.

Logic: The Effect of Multiple Selection Devices

Our example assumed that the organization implemented one new selection procedure, a test for computer programmers. Most organizations use multiple selection devices, such as application forms, interviews, background checks; aptitude, ability, personality, or work sample tests; medical exams; and assessment centers. Although the validity of some of these devices may be low, each has demonstrated validities greater than zero.[21] Essentially, when multiple selection devices are combined, the overall validity of the combination may be higher, assuming that each of them provides unique and valid information. If the costs of using multiple devices are relatively low and the value of performance variability is high, the higher costs are often offset by the increased predictive power of the combination of predictors.

Process: It Matters How Staffing Processes Are Used

Similar to the effect of rejected offers is the situation in which an organization decides to deviate from the practice of making job offers to the top-scoring candidates. To test this, researchers examined the impact on the productivity of forest rangers of three approaches:

1. Using top-down selection

2. Selecting those who meet a minimum required test score equal to the average

3. Selecting those who meet a minimum required score set at one SD below the average[22]

Top-down selection produced a productivity increase of about 13 percent (which translated into millions of dollars) compared to random selection. Under option 2, the value of output gains was only 45 percent as large as the dollar value for top-down selection. Under option 3, the value of output gains was only 16 percent of the top-down figure. Employers who deviate from top-down selection when performance variation is significant do so at substantial economic cost.

Cumulative Effects of Adjustments

At this point, you're probably asking yourself how adjustments for all five of these factors—economic variables, employee flows, probationary periods, multiple selection devices, and rejected job offers—affect estimates of utility. One study used computer simulation of 10,000 scenarios, each of which comprised various values of the five factors just noted. Utility estimates were then computed using the five adjustments applied independently.[23]

The study found that although the unadjusted utility values we've seen are quite substantial, the effects of economic factors, departures from top-down hiring, and probationary periods can reduce them substantially. Accounting for economic variables had the largest effect, followed, in rank order, by multiple selection devices, departures from top-down hiring, probationary period, and separations of high performers. The total set of adjustments reduced the utility values by a median level of 91 percent, with a minimum reduction of 71 percent. Thus, considering reasonable values of these adjustments, the remaining utility values might be between 9 percent and 29 percent as large as the unadjusted values. The simulation actually produced negative utility estimates (the costs of improved selection exceeded the benefits) in 16 percent of the cases.

These results suggest that although valid selection procedures may often lead to positive payoffs for the organization, actual payoffs depend significantly on organizational and situational factors that affect the quantity, quality, and cost of the selection effort. The message is that organizations should give careful consideration and analysis to such investments. There is significant potential payoff but also significant potential risk in a poor decision. The tools and formulas in this chapter, together with those in Chapters 8 and 9, provide a framework for improving those decisions.

Meta-analyses of multiple studies often show that the validity of such characteristics as intelligence or conscientiousness for predicting job performance is consistently positive. It is tempting to conclude that hiring based on these factors must invariably contribute to improvements in performance that are worth the investment. However, validity is only one consideration in determining the overall value of a selection system to an organization.

The hallmark of a decision science is its ability to apply consistent frameworks to diverse situations, obtaining different results depending on vital factors. The results of this chapter show that the payoff from improved selection is potentially, but not necessarily, very large. Wise organizations will use the frameworks to examine their particular situations and make sound decisions based on their unique opportunities and constraints.

Dealing with Risk and Uncertainty in Utility Analysis

As you have seen through this chapter and the two previous ones, many factors might increase or decrease expected payoffs from utility analysis.[24] Taking these factors into account often means making estimates or accepting that measures are imperfect. Sometimes decision makers react to imperfect measures by ignoring rejected offers or economic conditions. Yet as we have seen, such factors may be quite significant in the payoff to improved selection. Uncertainty need not preclude doing utility analysis, however. Just as with any area of business, the answer to uncertainty can be to isolate it and analyze its effects. Researchers have used three techniques to deal with such uncertainty in selection utility analysis: break-even analysis, Monte Carlo analysis, and confidence intervals.

Break-Even Analysis

We reviewed break-even analysis in Chapter 2, "Analytical Foundations of HR Measurement." We noted two of its advantages:

- It shifts emphasis away from estimating a precise utility value toward making a good decision even with imperfect information.

- It pinpoints areas where controversy is important to decision making (that is, where there is doubt about whether the break-even value is exceeded), versus where controversy has little impact (because there is little risk of observing utility values below break-even).

One comprehensive review of the utility-analysis literature reported break-even values for 42 studies that estimated the parameter SD_y.[25] Without exception, the break-even values fell at or below 60 percent of the estimated value of SD_y. In many cases, the break-even value was less than 1 percent of the estimated value of SD_y. This suggests that, in most studies, the precise value of SD_y was not a determining factor in whether better selection paid off. The break-even value is often very low for the choice of whether to implement a particular HR program. However, this simply shows that the HR program is better than nothing. In more realistic settings, when the HR program is compared to other organizational investments, differences in SD_y estimates could actually affect the ultimate decision.[26] Also, decision makers may consider uncertainty about other factors (such as validity or selection ratios) in addition to SD_y in making capital-budgeting decisions.[27] Nonetheless, break-even analysis can be used in all these situations, and it often helps to clarify what really matters, leading not only to better decisions, but to better logical analysis.

In summary, break-even analysis of the SD_y parameter (or any other single parameter in the utility model) seems to provide two additional advantages:

- It allows practicing managers to appreciate how little variability in job performance is necessary before valid selection procedures begin to pay positive dividends.

- Even if decision makers cannot agree on an exact point estimate of SD_y, they can probably agree that it is higher than the break-even value.

Monte Carlo Analysis

A second approach to dealing with risk and uncertainty is computer-based (Monte Carlo) simulation to assess the extent of variability of utility values, and thus to provide a sound basis for decision making.[28] This technique is often used in operations management for decisions about processes such as manufacturing and supply chain, or in consumer research on issues such as the likely response to new marketing initiatives. In essence, Monte Carlo analysis creates a distribution of values for one or more elements of a calculation. For example, you might want to explore SD_y values ranging from $1,000 per person to $10,000 per person. You might assume that the number of applicants and the number hired in a given year will vary within some range of values.

To implement a Monte Carlo analysis, you draw a value for each of the variables from its assumed distribution, input that value into the utility equation, and then calculate the utility value. Doing this repeatedly for many values of the parameters in combination produces an array of utility outcomes. Computer technology permits researchers to run tens of thousands such experimental values. In examining the pattern of resulting utility values, it is possible to estimate the average, range, and likelihood that various utility values will occur.

By modeling and analyzing uncertainty within the Monte Carlo analysis, we can better predict the likely outcomes and the risks of observing very low or very high utility values. To illustrate, the study described earlier was a Monte Carlo analysis that varied all the elements of the utility model with employee flows and economic factors, by analyzing 10,000 scenarios that combined different elements.[29]

Confidence Intervals

A third approach is to compute a standard error of the utility estimate and then to derive a 95 percent confidence interval around that estimate.[30] Because 2.5 percent of the normal distribution falls below a value that is 1.96 standard deviations below the average, and 2.5 percent of the distribution falls above a value that is 1.96 standard deviations above the average, we can calculate a 95 percent confidence interval surrounding a particular estimate of utility (U), as shown in Equation 10-8.

$$(U - 1.96 \times SE_u) \leq U \leq (U + 1.96 \times SE_u) \quad (10\text{-}8)$$

Although there are problems with the method used to compute the standard error of the utility estimate, especially the assumption that all components in the equation are independent and normally distributed, research suggests that it provides a serviceable approximation.[31] To illustrate this method, researchers applied it to the estimated utility of the PAT in predicting the performance of computer programmers in the federal government.[32] They found that the values of SE_u were very large, about half the size of the utility estimate itself. This means that the experts who estimated SD_y had less agreement than might have been predicted.

As one observer commented, "Ironically, the impressively large size of utility estimates per se have (sic) been almost overemphasized ... while the standard error of utility has been largely ignored. If we are to be impressed by the size of utility, we must similarly be impressed by the size of the uncertainty in these estimates."[33] To date, we have tended to view utility values as point estimates rather than as predictions under uncertainty. Given the uncertainty of many of the parameters of the utility model, confidence intervals are probably more appropriate and should be reported routinely.

Process: Communicating the Impact of Utility Analyses to Decision Makers

Research suggests that how utility results are presented makes a big difference. Presented in the wrong way, utility analysis results appear to actually *reduce* the support of managers for a valid selection procedure, even though the net benefits of the procedure are very large.[34] In one experiment, managers were presented with an unadjusted estimated payoff from a selection program of more than $105 million (in 2010 dollars), representing a return on investment of 14,000 percent. Results this large strain credulity, and thus it is no surprise that the managers did not accept them. Moreover, a fundamental principle of financial economics is that high returns carry high risks. Thus, presenting business leaders with such extraordinary estimated returns understandably would cause them to assume that the investment is highly speculative.[35] Yet some controversy arises here, because two subsequent studies failed to replicate these findings, and their conclusions and implications have been challenged.[36]

As we noted earlier, in the section on Monte Carlo analysis, another approach is to provide leaders with a range of possible values. Recall the study described earlier that used a computer-based simulation to generate 10,000 scenarios based on prior research and adjusted for different levels of economic factors and other considerations. The estimates showed an average payoff of $2,964,222 (in 2010 dollars), more than a 96 percent reduction from the unadjusted values. The median return was $2,313,275. The smallest outcome was an estimated loss of $3,428,601, and the largest predicted gain (after adjustment) was $22,831,890. Even this gain was still more than 71 percent smaller than the initial (unadjusted) estimate presented to the non-HR managers.[37]

Now, with ranges like this, it's little wonder that many HR leaders, I/O psychologists, and business leaders concluded that estimating the monetary value of enhanced employee selection is mostly guesswork. An investment with a range of values from negative $3 million to positive $23 million may seem like just rolling the dice. However, are business leaders prepared to forego an investment that may produce such a high payoff in fear of the downside?

These are precisely the sorts of decisions that leaders make about other resources. When such uncertainty exists in the face of potentially high payoffs, wise organizations often invest in studies that can make estimates more precise. Using Monte Carlo techniques can show leaders which variables in the utility framework contribute most to the variation in anticipated payoffs. Perhaps organizations could study those variables more deeply and reduce the uncertainty, just as they might do with an uncertain supply chain, customer response to a new product, or R&D pipeline.[38]

We actually know very little about how decision contexts or organizational characteristics affect the reactions of managers to the results of utility analyses. If we study the thought processes of leaders who make decisions about investments in improved selection or other HR programs, we can learn more about where their beliefs and impressions may be incorrect.[39]

Beyond those concerns is a genuine need for utility analysts to shift their focus. The fundamental question is not, "How do we construct the best HR measure?" Instead, it is, "How do we induce changes through HR measurement systems?" HR measurement is not an end in and of itself, but rather a decision-support system that can have powerful effects if users pay careful attention to the sender, the receivers, the strategy they use to transmit their message, and the organization of their message.[40]

Evidence indicates that managers are quite receptive to utility analysis when analysts present conservative estimates, illustrate the choices and their advantages and disadvantages, do not overload the presentation with technical details, and emphasize the same concerns managers of operating departments pay attention to (reducing the overall cycle time of the staffing process, reducing costs while maintaining the validity of the overall staffing process).[41] Clearly, the "framing" of the message is critical and has a direct effect on its ultimate acceptability.[42]

Employee Selection and the Talent Supply Chain

In the spirit of connecting selection utility analysis to the mental models that leaders already use, it may be useful to depict the staffing process as a supply chain and "retool" utility analysis within the language of supply-chain optimization.[43] Table 10-1 shows how the typical questions posed in supply-chain management can be translated to apply to employee recruitment, selection, and retention. These questions reflect the logical models in Chapters 8, 9, and 10, combined to reflect a comprehensive logical model for understanding and measuring the talent supply chain.

Table 10-1   How Supply-Chain Management and Employee Selection Share Business Logic

	Supply-Chain Management	Employee Selection
Demand Planning and Forecasting	Predicting future resource needs in terms of quality, quantity, cost, and timing, based on business activity and other factors. Planning approaches to better forecast or smooth demand levels for better planning.	Predicting the needed quantity, quality, and timing of future job openings and vacancies. Utility analysis can show where better performance has the highest payoff. Selection data can show where having a longer lead-time can improve selection validity or applicant quality.
Production Planning and Scheduling	Predicting and establishing future production schedules or inventory-acquisition schedules. Optimizing production to fit quality and quantity needs.	Predicting and planning future recruitment and staffing processes. Utility analysis can show the payoff from increased applicant "production" that produces lower selection ratios, and the impact of longer tenure among new hires that reduces turnover and increases the timeframe of the payoff from improved selection.
Distribution and Logistics	Planning how goods will move through space and time, identifying where to place warehouses and transportation channels, and determining how to optimize choices about which sources to use.	Planning whether to recruit locally or more broadly. Locating workplaces near applicant sources. Utility analysis can show the relative quality of applicants from different sources, and the relative predictability of applicant quality. Utility analysis can compare the payoffs and costs from different applicant sources.

continues

Table 10-1 Continued

	Supply-Chain Management	Employee Selection
Inventory Management	Planning how much and where to hold inventory of goods, where shortages and surpluses should be tolerated, and how to optimize the risks of being out of stock, having too much stock, against the costs of ordering and holding inventory.	Planning how far in advance to build inventories of applicants and potential applicants. Planning where to hold a surplus of job-holders and where to allow shortages to occur. Utility analysis captures the ordering costs of improved selection, as well as the potential quality improvements from anticipating job openings to attract better candidates or select more carefully.

These questions are illustrative, and many more parallel ideas exist between traditional supply chains and utility analysis for employee staffing. The point of these illustrations is to encourage HR and business leaders to explore how existing and proven business frameworks can be applied to talent and human capital decisions. The utility analysis framework can seem like a foreign language to most business leaders, but it is largely the same language they already apply to other decisions. It's just a matter of translation.

Exercises

Software that calculates answers to one or more of the following exercises can be found at http://hrcosting.com/hr/.

1. You are given the following information regarding the CAP test for clerical employees (clerk-2s) at the Berol Corporation:

   Average tenure as a clerk-2: 7.26 years

   Number selected per year: 120

   Validity of the CAP test: 0.61

   Validity of previously used test: 0.18

   Cost per applicant of CAP: $35

   Cost per applicant of old test: $18

   SR: 0.50

Ordinate at SR: 0.399

SD, in first year: $34,000

Use Equation 10-1 to determine (a) the total utility of the CAP test, (b) the utility per selectee, and (c) the per-year gain in utility per selectee.

2. Referring to Exercise 1, suppose that after consulting with the chief financial officer at Berol, you are given the following additional information: variable costs are –0.08, taxes are 40 percent, and the discount rate is 8 percent. Use Equation 10-2 in this chapter to recompute the total utility of the CAP test, the utility per selectee, and the utility per selectee in the first year.

3. The Top Dollar Co. is trying to decide whether to use an assessment center to select middle managers for its consumer products operations. The following information has been determined: variable costs are –0.10, corporate taxes are 44 percent, the discount rate is 9 percent, the ordinary selection procedure costs $700 per candidate, the assessment center costs $2,800 per candidate, the standard deviation of job performance is $55,000, the validity of the ordinary procedure is 0.30, the validity of the assessment center is 0.40, the selection ratio is 0.20, the ordinate at that selection ratio is 0.2789, and the average tenure as a middle manager is 3 years. The program is designed to last 6 years, with 20 managers added each year. Beginning in Year 4, however, one cohort separates each year until all hires from the program leave.

Use Equation 10-6 in this chapter to determine whether Top Dollar Co. should adopt the assessment center to select middle managers. What payoffs can be expected in total, per selectee, and per selectee in the first year?

References

1. Hansell, Saul, "Google Answer to Filling Jobs Is an Algorithm," *The New York Times* (January 3, 2007). www.nytimes.com/2007/01/03/technology/03google.html.

2. Tam, P. W., and K. J. Delaney, "Talent Search: Google's Growth Helps Ignite Silicon Valley Hiring Frenzy," *The Wall Street Journal* (November 23, 2005), A1.

3. Cascio, Wayne F., and John W. Boudreau, "Supply-Chain Analysis Applied to Staffing Decisions," in *Handbook of Industrial and Organizational Psychology,* ed. Sheldon Zedeck (Washington, D.C.: American Psychological Association Books, 2010).

4. Boudreau, John W., *Retooling HR* (Boston: Harvard Business Publishing, 2010).

5. Schmidt, F. L., J. E. Hunter, R. C. Mckenzie, and T. W. Muldrow, "Impact of Valid Selection Procedures on Work-Force Productivity," *Journal of Applied Psychology* 64 (1979): 609–626.

6. *Ibid.*

7. Inflation adjustments were made using the CPI inflation calculator from the U.S. Bureau of Labor Statistics, at http://data.bls.gov/cgi-bin/cpicalc.pl.

8. Boudreau, J. W., "Utility Analysis," in *Human Resource Management: Evolving Roles and Responsibilities,* ed. L. Dyer (Washington, D. C.: Bureau of National Affairs, 1988).

9. Boudreau, J. W., "Economic Considerations in Estimating the Utility of Human Resource Productivity Improvement Programs," *Personnel Psychology* 36 (1983a): 551–576.

10. Boudreau, J. W., "Effects of Employee Flows on Utility Analysis of Human Resource Productivity Improvement Programs," *Journal of Applied Psychology* 68 (1983b): 396–406.

11. Schmidt et al., 1979.

12. Boudreau, J. W., and C. J. Berger, "Decision-Theoretic Utility Analysis Applied to Employee Separations and Acquisitions," *Journal of Applied Psychology* Monograph 70, no. 3 (1985): 581–612.

13. Schmidt et al., 1979.

14. Boudreau, 1983b.

15. *Ibid.*

16. *Ibid.*

17. www.wholefoodsmarket.com/careers/hiringprocess.php.

18. De Corte, W., "Utility Analysis for the One-Cohort Selection-Retention Decision with a Probationary Period," *Journal of Applied Psychology* 79 (1994): 402–411.

19. Becker, B. E., "The Influence of Labor Markets on Human Resources Utility Estimates," *Personnel Psychology* 42 (1989): 531–546.

20. Murphy, K. R., "When Your Top Choice Turns You Down: Effects of Rejected Offers on the Utility of Selection Tests," *Psychological Bulletin* 99 (1986): 133–138.

21. Cascio, W. F., and H. Aguinis, *Applied Psychology in Human Resource Management,* 6th ed. (Upper Saddle River, N.J.: Prentice-Hall, 2005).

22. Schmidt, F. L., M. J. Mack, and J. E. Hunter, "Selection Utility in the Occupation of U.S. Park Ranger for Three Modes of Test Use," *Journal of Applied Psychology* 69 (1984): 490–497.

23. Sturman, M. C., "Implications of Utility Analysis Adjustments for Estimates of Human Resource Intervention Value," *Journal of Management* 26 (2000): 281–299.

24. Cascio, W. F., "Assessing the Utility of Selection Decisions: Theoretical and Practical Considerations," in *Personnel Selection in Organizations,* ed. N. Schmitt and W. C. Borman (San Francisco: Jossey-Bass, 1993).

25. Boudreau, J. W., "Utility Analysis for Decisions in Human Resource Management," In *Handbook of Industrial and Organizational Psychology* (Vol. 2, 2nd ed.), ed. M. D. Dunnette and L. M. Hough (Palo Alto, CA: Consulting Psychologists Press, 1991).

26. Weekley, J. A., E. J. O'Connor, B. Frank, and L. W. Peters, "A Comparison of Three Methods of Estimating the Standard Deviation of Performance in Dollars," *Journal of Applied Psychology* 70 (1985): 122–126.

27. Hoffman, C. C., and G. C. Thornton III, "Examining Selection Utility Where Competing Predictors Differ in Adverse Impact," *Personnel Psychology* 50 (1997): 455–470.

28. Sturman, 2000. See also Rich, J. R., and J. W. Boudreau, "The Effects of Variability and Risk on Selection Utility Analysis: An Empirical Simulation and Comparison," *Personnel Psychology* 40 (1987): 55–84.

29. Sturman, 2000.

30. Alexander, R. A., and M. R. Barrick, "Estimating the Standard Error of Projected Dollar Gains in Utility Analysis," *Journal of Applied Psychology* 72 (1987): 475–479.

31. Myors, B., "Utility Analysis Based on Tenure," *Journal of Human Resource Costing and Accounting* 3, no. 2 (1998): 41–50.

32. Alexander and Barrick, 1987.

33. Myors, 1998.

34. Latham, G. P., and G. Whyte, "The Futility of Utility Analysis," *Personnel Psychology* 47 (1994): 31–46; and Whyte, G., and G. P. Latham, "The Futility of Utility Analysis Revisited: When Even an Expert Fails," *Personnel Psychology* 50 (1997): 601–611.

35. Boudreau, J. W., and P. M. Ramstad, *Beyond HR: The New Science of Human Capital* (Boston: Harvard Business School Publishing, 2007).

36. Carson, K. P., J. S. Becker, and J. A. Henderson, "Is Utility Really Futile? A Failure to Replicate and an Extension," *Journal of Applied Psychology* 83 (1998): 84–96; Cronshaw, S. F., "Lo! The Stimulus Speaks: The Insider's View of Whyte and Latham's 'The Futility of Utility Analysis,'" *Personnel Psychology* 50 (1997): 611–615; and Hoffman and Thornton, 1997.

37. Sturman, 2000.

38. Boudreau, 2010.

39. Cascio, W. F., "The Role of Utility Analysis in the Strategic Management of Organizations," *Journal of Human Resource Costing and Accounting* 1, no. 2 (1996): 85–95; Florin-Thuma, Beth C., and John W. Boudreau, "Performance Feedback Utility in a Small Organization: Effects on Organizational Outcomes and Managerial Decision Processes." *Personnel Psychology* 40 (1987): 693–713.

40. Boudreau, J. W., "The Motivational Impact of Utility Analysis and HR Measurement," *Journal of Human Resource Costing and Accounting* 1, no. 2 (1996): 73–84; and Boudreau, J. W., "Strategic Human Resource Management Measures: Key Linkages and the Peoplescape Model," *Journal of Human Resource Costing and Accounting* 3, no. 2 (1998): 21–40.

41. Hoffman, C. C., "Applying Utility Analysis to Guide Decisions on Selection System Content," *Journal of Human Resource Costing and Accounting* 1, no. 2 (1996): 9–17.

42. Carson, Becker, and Henderson, 1998; and Hazer, J. T., and S. Highhouse, "Factors Influencing Managers' Reactions to Utility Analysis: Effects of SDy Method, Information Frame, and Focal Intervention," *Journal of Applied Psychology* 82 (1997): 104–112.

43. Boudreau, 2010; and Cascio and Boudreau, 2010.

11

Costs and Benefits of HR Development Programs

Organizations in Europe, the United States, and Asia spend billions each year on employee training—more than $125 billion in the U.S. alone. At the level of the individual firm, Google is exemplary. It offers each employee 100 hours of professional development training per year.[1] These outlays reflect the cost of keeping abreast of technological and social changes, the extent of managerial commitment to achieving a competent and productive workforce, and the broad array of opportunities available for individuals and teams to improve their technical skills and their social skills. Indeed, the large amount of money spent on training in both public and private organizations is likely to increase in the coming years as organizations strive to meet challenges such as the following:[2]

- **Hypercompetition:** Such competition, both domestic and international, is largely due to trade agreements and technology (most notably, the Internet). As a result, senior executives will be required to lead an almost constant reinvention of business strategies/models and organizational structures.

- **A power shift to the customer:** Customers who use the Internet have easy access to databases that allow them to compare prices and examine product reviews; hence, there are ongoing needs to meet the product and service needs of customers.

- **Collaboration across organizational and geographic boundaries:** In some cases, suppliers are colocated with manufacturers and share access to inventory levels. Strategic international alliances often lead to the use of multinational teams that must address cultural and language issues.

- **The need to maintain high levels of talent:** Because products and services can be copied, the ability of a workforce to innovate, refine processes, solve problems, and form relationships becomes a sustainable advantage. Attracting, retaining, and developing people with critical competencies is vital for success.

- **Changes in the workforce:** Unskilled and undereducated youth will be needed for entry-level jobs, and currently underutilized groups of racial and ethnic minorities, women, and older workers will need training.

- **Changes in technology:** Increasingly sophisticated technological systems impose training and retraining requirements on the existing work force.

- **Teams:** As more firms move to employee involvement and teams in the workplace, team members need to learn such behaviors as asking for ideas, offering help without being asked, listening and providing feedback, and recognizing and considering the ideas of others.

Indeed, as the demands of the information age spread, companies are coming to regard training expenditures as no less a part of their capital costs than plant and equipment.

Training and development entail the following general properties and characteristics:[3]

1. They are learning experiences.

2. They are planned by the organization.

3. They occur after the individual has joined the organization.

4. They are intended to further the organization's goals.

Training and development activities are, therefore, planned programs of organizational improvement undertaken to bring about a relatively permanent change in employee knowledge, skills, attitudes, or social behavior.[4]

The analytical tools that we present here apply to programs as diverse as providing learning through job experiences, coaching, mentoring, formal training, e-learning (online instruction, mobile learning such as podcasts, and virtual classrooms), and off-site classes or degrees. We focus our examples on training programs because that is where most of the research and discussion has occurred. In the area of training, topics range from basic skills (technical as well as supervisory skills) to interpersonal skills, team building, and decision making for individuals or teams. Technologies used run the full gamut from lectures to interactive video, to Internet-based training, intranet-based training, social software applications, Web 2.0 tools (technologies that enable user-generated content, such as blogs and wikis), and intelligent tutoring systems.[5]

Unfortunately, although billions may be spent providing training and development programs, little is spent assessing the social and financial outcomes of these activities. Consider leadership-development programs as an example. Despite the economic downturn that began in December 2007, firms such as Philips Electronics, Estée Lauder, and Canon continued to invest in such programs, hoping not to be caught short of strong managers when the economy recovers.[6] One thorough review estimated, however, that only 10 percent of leadership-development programs evaluated their impact on the actual behaviors of managers. Most consider only the satisfaction of participants as an indicator of the programs' effectiveness.[7] At a broader level, just 23 percent of companies in one recent survey reported that "measuring the impact of training" was a top priority.[8] The overall result is that little comparative evidence exists by which to generalize or to evaluate the impact of the various technologies. Decision makers thus remain unguided by systematic evaluations of past experiments and uninformed about the costs and benefits of alternative HRD programs when considering training efforts in their own organizations.

That said, meta-analytic evidence collected across many individual studies and in many different organizations does illustrate the positive benefits of different content, methods, and types of training, when designed and implemented properly, across different criteria, such as trainee reactions, substantive learning, behavior change, and organizational results.[9] The study we describe next asked a different question: Is there a relationship between firm-level investments in training and changes in those firms' stock prices?

The Relationship Between Training Expenditures and Stock Prices

At present, firms' investments in human capital—most notably, spending on employees' development—are treated as hidden costs that are buried in overhead, specifically in the accounting category "Selling, general, and administrative expenses," or SG&A. This treatment makes investments in human capital difficult to obtain.

Using a unique database, one study tested the hypothesis that firms that make unusually large investments in employee development subsequently enjoy higher stock prices than comparable firms that make smaller investments in employee development. To disentangle the effects of training, per se, from other potentially confounding variables, the authors deployed a variety of multivariate techniques and control variables.[10]

The research revealed that four portfolios of 575 publicly traded companies that invested in employee training and development at roughly twice the industry average outperformed the S&P 500 by 4.6 percentage points over a 25-month period, and outperformed it in the year prior to the study by 17–35 percent.[11] In 2009, the same authors demonstrated in a sample of 30 banks that training expenditures remain a powerful predictor of subsequent stock prices, even through the market turbulence of 2008.[12]

Moreover, some forms of training yield superior benefits, relative to others. Specifically, training in technical skills yielded an effect that was 3.5 times higher than the effect for all types of training and 6 times higher than that for general business skills.

To assess the direction of causality, the researchers examined the relationship between training expenditures and stock returns in various years. The only significant relationship they found was between training expenditures in year t-1 and stock return in year t. There was no significant relationship between training expenditures in year t-1 and stock returns in either year t-1 or t-2. This supports, but does not prove, that training investments help determine stock price performance, not the opposite.

In the absence of a true experimental design, however, it is impossible to rule out the possibility that the training measure is serving, at least in part, as a marker for other unmeasured, firm-level attributes that are correlated with a firm's long-term profitability (and thus equity market valuation). In other words, while on the surface it may appear that variables a and b are correlated, that relationship might be illusory, because both a and b are correlated with variable c, which is unmeasured in the study. As the authors noted:

> From the perspective of an individual investor, it is far less important whether the correlation between training and stock value represents a causal training effect on firm performance or whether training is instead simply a leading indicator for other productive firm activities or attributes. In the short run, so long as the underlying relationship between training and whatever firm characteristics that affect productivity continue to hold, investment portfolios that incorporate information about firm training expenditures will yield super-normal rates of return.[13]

While the researchers' analyses cannot determine *why* the relationship between training expenditures and stock price performance exists, three possible explanations seem plausible:

1. Training investments have their intended impact. Firms that make greater investments in this area subsequently perform better, as a result.

2. Training investments may well serve as a proxy for the degree to which a firm is willing and able to take a long-term perspective rather than focus excessively (and destructively) on quarterly earnings.

3. Expenditures on training (and, in particular, changes in those expenditures) may serve as a window into an organization's future financial health and prospects (or lack thereof).

Although the tools we describe in this chapter are certainly valuable for increasing the amount and effectiveness of development-program evaluation, the issue runs much deeper. Analytical decision tools are not just useful for evaluating programs after they are complete. The lack of evaluation in HR development is a symptom of a more fundamental issue: a lack of systematic logic to plan and refine such programs.

The Logic of Talent Development

Our intent in this chapter is not to present true experimental or quasi-experimental designs for evaluating HRD programs.[14] Instead, it is to illustrate how the economic consequences of HRD programs can be expressed. Let us begin, as we have in other chapters, by presenting the logic of talent development, as shown in Figure 11-1.

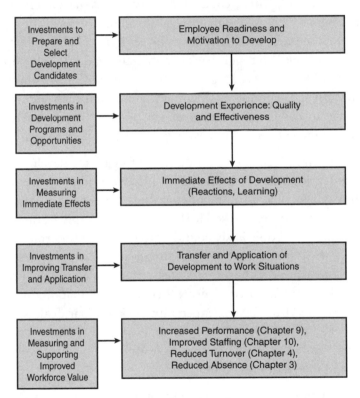

Figure 11-1 Logic of talent-development effects.

As Figure 11-1 shows, effectiveness of development is much more than sound design and effective implementation of HRD programs or experiences. These are necessary, but not sufficient by themselves, to ensure that what is learned in training is actually applied on the job.[15] For that to occur, other conditions must be satisfied. First, candidates for development must be prepared and motivated both to learn and to apply their learning at work. This requires investments by the organization both in the preparation of development candidates (for example, through challenging job assignments) and in careful selection of candidates for development experiences, such as jobs or training programs.

Second, after the development experience, there must be an environment that provides the opportunity and motivation for the newly developed individuals to apply or transfer their learning to their work. This second condition requires that supervisors and higher-level managers support employees' attempts to use on the job what they have learned in training or development. For example, if employees learn all about democratic leadership styles in training but then report back to autocratic leaders on the job, the effects of the training are not likely to have long-term effects. In addition, it is important to offer rewards and incentives to employees when they apply what they learned in training to improve their day-to-day job performance. This means that improved performance often carries with it increased costs of pay, incentives, or supervisory preparation.

The conditions shown in Figure 11-1 create "line of sight" for development candidates connecting their development, their on-the-job behaviors, improved unit performance, and the overall strategic success of the organization. Consider an illustrative example. In response to a shortage of trained service technicians, Caterpillar, Inc., partnered with a network of vocational schools in six countries to develop a Caterpillar-approved curriculum. This ties the training directly to important business processes that Caterpillar must execute well to achieve its business strategy. Students enter the vocational schools with dealerships already committed to hiring them upon graduation. In fact, the trainees spend up to half of their time in apprenticeships at Caterpillar dealers, learning on the job.[16] Dealer (that is, management) support, coupled with rewards for completing the training program (guaranteed jobs), provides the kind of "line of sight" that links strategy, execution, and motivation to do well in training.

At the bottom of Figure 11-1, we connect employee development to several other topics covered in this book. Although the vast majority of attention to valuing employee development has focused on its immediate effects or its effects on job performance, it should also be noted that when employees have more tools and opportunities to perform well, they are often more motivated and engaged with their work. This can lead to reduced turnover and absence. In addition, opportunities for development are increasingly an important part of the "total rewards" proposition that employers offer to the labor market.[17] For example, Procter & Gamble is globally known for its effective career and training programs to develop great marketers. GE is well known for the effectiveness of its career and management systems in developing future leaders. Not only do these programs improve the performance of those who directly participate, but they also are powerful attractors to external candidates. Thus, enhanced development can also lead to more and better applicants for employment, which, as you saw in Chapters 8, "Staffing Utility: The Concept and Its Measurement"; 9, "The Economic Value of Job Performance"; and 10, "The Payoff from Enhanced Selection," is one element of enhanced workforce value through staffing.

The remainder of the chapter focuses on two broad themes:

1. Developing a framework that extends the utility-analysis logic we applied to staffing in Chapters 8, 9, and 10 to the evaluation of HRD programs

2. Illustrating cost analysis, comparing offsite versus web-based meeting costs

Utility Analysis Approach to Decisions about HRD Programs

Faced with a bewildering array of alternatives, decision makers must select the programs that will have the greatest impact on pivotal talent pools—those where investments in HRD will have the largest marginal impact on activities, decisions, and ultimately, the value created for the firm. Recall that utility analysis specifically incorporates the idea of pivotalness by including the *quantity* of workers affected by an HR program, as well as SD_y, the pivotal value of enhanced worker *quality*. We saw in Chapters 8–10 that utility analysis is a powerful tool for staffing programs,[18] and now we show how it can be used to evaluate proposed or ongoing HRD programs.

The basic difference is that staffing programs create value through the quality of the choices they support regarding who joins. In contrast, programs such as HRD do not change the membership of the workforce. Instead, they change the quality of the intact pool of workers. So instead of deriving changes in quality based on who joins or leaves a workforce, we must derive changes in quality based on the direct effect of a program on the individuals who participate in it.

Modifying the Brogden-Cronbach-Gleser Model to Apply to Training

In the Brogden-Cronbach-Gleser model, the only difference between the basic equation for calculating staffing utility (Equation 8-17 in Chapter 8) and that for calculating utility from HRD programs is that the term d_t is substituted for the product $r_{xy} \times x$ (that is, the validity coefficient times the average standard score on the predictor achieved by selectees).[19] The resulting utility formula is as follows:

$$\Delta U = (N)(T)(d_t)(SD_y) - C \qquad (11\text{-}1)$$

Here, ΔU is the gain to the firm in monetary units (such as dollars, euros, or yen) resulting from the program, N is the number of employees trained, T is the expected duration of benefits in the trained group, d_t is the true difference in job performance between the trained and untrained groups in SD units, SD_y is the standard deviation of dollar-valued job performance among untrained employees, and C is the total cost of training N employees.

The parameter d_t is the effect size. It reflects the difference in job-relevant outcomes between those who participate in a development opportunity and those who do not. It is expressed in standardized units, just as Z-scores were in the selection utility equation.

To illustrate that idea graphically, we plot the (hypothetical) distribution of job performance outcomes of the trained and untrained groups on the same baseline (expressed in Z-score units, with a mean of 0 and a standard deviation of 1.0), as shown in Figure 11-2.

In Figure 11-2, d represents the size of the effect of the training program. How is d computed? It is simply the difference between the means of the trained and untrained groups in standard Z-score units. This might be the difference in average job performance, time to competency, learning, and so on. Therefore:

$$d = \overline{X}_t - \overline{X}_u / SD_x \qquad (11\text{-}2)$$

Here, d is the effect size. If the effect is expressed in terms of job performance, $\overline{X}_t$ is the average job performance score of the trained group, $\overline{X}_u$ is the average job performance score of the untrained group, and SD_x is the standard deviation of the job-performance scores of the total group, trained and untrained. If the SDs of the two groups are unequal, the SD of the untrained group should be used because it is more representative of the incumbent employee population.

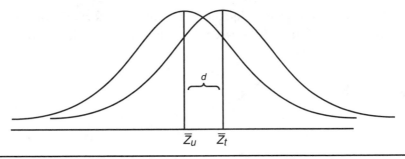

Note: $\bar{Z}_u$ is the average job performance score of the untrained group; $\bar{Z}_t$ is the average job performance score of the trained group; and d is the effect size.

Figure 11-2 Standard score distributions of job performance outcomes among trained and untrained groups.

Hypothetically, suppose that we are evaluating the impact of a training program for quality-control inspectors. Let's say that job performance is evaluated in terms of a work sample—that is, the number of defects identified in a standard sample of products with a known number (for example, 10) of defects. Suppose the average job performance score for employees in the trained group is 7 and for those in the untrained group is 6.5, and the standard deviation of the job-performance scores is 1.0. Equation 11-3 shows the effect size.

$$d = 7 - 6.5 / 1 = 0.5 \text{ SD} \qquad (11\text{-}3)$$

In other words, the performance of the trained group is half a standard deviation better than that of the untrained group. Because a perfectly reliable, objective measure of job performance was used in this case, the estimate of d need not be corrected for unreliability. In many, if not most, cases, managers will be using criteria that are less than perfectly reliable, such as supervisory ratings of the job performance of subordinates. In such cases, d must be corrected statistically for unreliability or measurement error in the criterion; otherwise, the estimate will be biased (too conservative).

If supervisory ratings are used as job-performance criteria, reliability probably will be estimated in terms of the extent of inter-rater agreement. A large-sample study that investigated the reliability of ratings of first-level supervisors found that average inter-rater reliabilities were 0.69 and 0.64, respectively, for ratings of supervisory abilities and ratings of the performance of specific job duties.[20] Regardless of how the reliability of job performance measures is estimated, Equation 11-4 shows the formula for computing the true difference in job performance between the trained and untrained groups.

$$d_t = d / \sqrt{r_{yy}} \qquad (11\text{-}4)$$

Alternatively, consider Equation 11-5:

$$d_t = (\overline{X}_t - \overline{X}_u) / (SD_y)(\sqrt{r_{yy}}) \qquad (11\text{-}5)$$

All terms are as defined earlier, and is the square root of the reliability of the job performance measure.

To express that difference as a percentage change in output, assuming that performance is measured on a ratio scale, it is necessary to multiply d_t by the ratio of the pretest standard deviation to the pretest performance mean (SD/M) × 100.[21] Thus, the percentage change in output equals this:

$$d_t \times 100 \times SD_{pretest} / \overline{X}_{pretest} \qquad (11\text{-}6)$$

Issues in Estimating d_t

If an organization already has conducted a training program and possesses the necessary data, it can compute d_t on the basis of an empirical study. Pre- and post-measures of job performance in the trained and untrained groups should be collected systematically, with special care taken to prevent the ratings or other measures of job performance from being influenced by knowledge of who has or has not been trained. These are the same kinds of problems that bedevil all HRD evaluation research, not just research on dt. Several thorough treatments of these issues are available.[22]

When several studies on the same topic have been done, or when d_t must be estimated for a new HRD program where there is no existing information, d_t is best estimated by the cumulated results of all available studies, using the methods of meta-analysis. We noted earlier that such studies are available in the literature. As studies accumulate, managers will be able to rely on cumulative knowledge of the expected effect sizes associated with proposed HRD programs. Such a "menu" of effect sizes for HRD programs will allow HR professionals to compute the expected utilities of proposed HRD programs before the decision is made to allocate resources to them.

Sometimes the results of evaluation research are presented in terms of statistics such as r, t, or F. Each of these can be transformed into d by means of the following formulas.[23]

When two groups are compared (and, therefore, $df = 1$), the F statistic is converted to a t statistic using Equation 11-7.

$$t = \sqrt{F} \qquad (11-7)$$

The t-statistic then can be converted into the point-biserial correlation (r_{pb}) between the dichotomous variable (training versus no training) and rated performance using Equation 11-8.

$$r_{pb} = t / \sqrt{t^2 + (N_t - 2)} \qquad (11-8)$$

Here, N_t is the total number of persons in the study, the sum of the trained and untrained groups.

To transform r_{pb} into d, use Equation 11-9.

$$d = \frac{1}{\sqrt{pq}} \sqrt{\frac{N_t - 2}{N_t}} \times \frac{r}{\sqrt{1 - r^2}} \qquad (11-9)$$

Here, p and q are the proportions of the total group in the trained and untrained groups, respectively.

For example, suppose that 100 employees are trained and 100 serve in a control group. Results of training are expressed as $F = 6.0$, using supervisors' ratings as criteria (assume that the reliability of the supervisors' ratings $r_{yy} = 0.60$). Using Equation 11-7,

$$t = 2.45$$

Using Equation 11-8,

$$r_{pb} = 2.45 / \sqrt{6.0 + (200 - 2)}$$

$$r_{pb} = 0.17$$

So,

$$d = 1/0.5 \ (0.9950)(0.17/0.985)$$

$$d = 0.34$$

Therefore, d_t is

$$0.34 / \sqrt{0.60} = 0.44$$

What If Training Covers Less Than the Full Range of Job Skills?

Different effect sizes can occur not because training is differentially effective, but because the evaluations differ in breadth of coverage of the outcomes. To be methodologically precise, evaluation should measure only training-related performance.[24] Training programs in first-level supervisory skills may encompass a large portion of the supervisor's job, whereas training programs designed to affect sales of a specific product may influence only a few tasks of a sales representative's job. In terms of impact, not all elements of the job are equally pivotal.[25]

Effect sizes measured using specific criteria will usually be larger than those based on a criterion of overall job performance because of the increased precision. When comparisons focus only on the elements that training affects, the observed effects are larger. However, there is a tradeoff. If the outcomes of training are very narrowly defined, a large effect size must be adjusted to reflect the fact that only part of the work outcomes are considered, so the proportion of total work value affected is smaller. At the limit, if training evaluations are so narrowly focused on esoteric training outcomes, even large training effects may be unimportant. Thus, it is vital to match the outcomes used to assess the effects of training to the decision context, and to ensure that training outcomes are comparable to allow meaningful comparisons of effect sizes.[26] The value of a change in performance will vary according to the percentage of pivotal tasks measured by criteria.

A large-scale study of the relative effects of HRD interventions in a major U.S.-based multinational firm adjusted overall utility estimates by recalculating the valuation base as the product of the percentage of job skills affected by training and the average full cost of employment. Thus, the utility estimates represented only the value of performance on specific job elements.[27]

Break-Even Analysis Applied to Proposed HRD Programs

Having determined an expected value of d_t, we can use the Brogden-Cronbach-Gleser model (see Equation 11-1 in this chapter) to compute a break-even value of SD_y (the value at which benefits equal costs and $\Delta U = \$0.00$; see Chapters 2, "Analytical Foundations of HR Measurement," and 10). For example, suppose that 300 employees are trained, the duration of the training effect is expected to be 2 years, $d_t = 0.55$, and the per-person cost of training is \$1,500. Setting $\Delta U = \$0.00$ yields the following:

$$\$0.00 = 2(300)(0.55)(SD_y) - 300\,(\$1,500)$$

$$SD_y = \$1,364$$

Even if d_t is as low as 0.10, the break-even value of SD_y is still only $7,500, well below the values of SD_y typically reported in the literature (for example, $28,000–$39,000 in 2010 dollars). To the extent that precise estimates of d_t and SD_y are unavailable, break-even analysis still allows a decision maker to use the general utility model to assess the impact of a proposed HRD program. If estimates of d_t and SD_y are available, utility can be computed, and the expected payoff from the program can be compared with the break-even values for d_t or SD_y. The comparison of "expected-case" and "worst-case" scenarios thus provides a more complete set of information for purposes of decision making.

Duration of the Effects of an HRD Program

A key parameter in Equation 11-1 is T, the duration of the effect of a training or HRD program. We know that the effects of development will not last forever because the relevance of the learning has a half-life due to changing work situations. In most cases, this parameter is difficult to estimate. One approach that has proven useful is the Delphi method, often used in long-range forecasting. With this method, a group of subject matter experts is asked to provide judgments about the duration of the training effect. Each expert responds individually and anonymously to an intermediary. The intermediary's task is to collect and summarize the experts' opinions and redistribute that information back to the experts for another round of judgment. The cycle continues until the experts reach a consensus, often after three or four rounds of judgments.

In practice, we have little knowledge about the duration of training effects. To deal with this issue in the large-scale study described in the previous section, researchers computed break-even values in terms of time. Such values represent the amount of time that the training effect must be maintained for the value of training outcomes to offset the training investment. Across 18 training programs (managerial, sales, and technical), they found great variability in results, with break-even periods ranging from a few weeks to several years. In the extreme, two management-training courses were never expected to break even or to yield a financial gain, because they produced slight decreases in performance; effect sizes were negative. The lesson to be learned from those results is that if we do not understand how long training effects last, we do not really understand the effects of training on organizational performance.

Economic Considerations and Employee Flows Applied to HRD Programs

Because training activities lead to diminishing returns over time (that is, training effects dissipate over time), a utility model that incorporates employee flows should be used to assess the net payoff of the program over time.[28] Beyond that, variable costs, taxes, and discounting must be considered to assess correctly the true impact of a proposed or ongoing HRD program. Because we considered these issues in Chapter 10, here we need consider only the summary model that incorporates all of these factors. Then we present a worked example to demonstrate how the utility analysis proceeds. Equation 11-10 shows the model. It is the same model used in Chapter 10, but here we have substituted the true effect size dt for the product of the validity coefficient and standardized average predictor score of selectees that we used in Chapter 10.

$$\Delta U = \sum_{k=1}^{F} \left[\sum_{t=1}^{k} (N_{a_t} - N_{s_t}) \right] \left\{ \left[1/(1+i)^k \right] \times (d_t)(SD_{sy})(1+V)(1-TAX) \right\} - \sum_{k=1}^{F} \left\{ C_k(1-TAX) \left[1/(1+i)^{(k-1)} \right] \right\} \quad (11\text{-}10)$$

For purposes of illustration, we adopt the d_t value we computed earlier, 0.44. Assume that 100 employees are trained each year for five years and that, for each cohort, the training effect dissipates gradually at the rate of 25 percent annually. No employees separate during this period (therefore, $N_{st} = 0$). That information allows us to compute a weighted average d_t value for the trained group each year, as a new cohort of trainees is added. Table 11-1 shows the weighted average d_t values.

Table 11-1 Diminishing Returns of an HRD Program over Five Years

Year	N_k	Weighted Average
1	100	(100(0.44)) / 100
2	200	(100(0.44) + 100(0.44 − .25d$_t$)) / 200
3	300	(100(0.44) + 100(0.44 − .25d$_t$) + 100
		(0.44 − .50d$_t$)) / 300
4	400	(100(0.44) + 100(0.44 − .25d$_t$) + 100
		(0.44 − .50d$_t$) + 100(0.44 − .75d$_t$)) / 400
5	500	(100(0.44) + 100(0.44 − .25d$_t$) + 100
		(0.44 − .50d$_t$) + 100(0.44 − .75d$_t$) + 100
		(0.44 − 1.00d$_t$)) / 500

Year	Weighted Average d$_t$ Values
1	0.44
2	0.385
3	0.33
4	0.275
5	0.22

Notes: d_t = The true difference in job performance between the trained and untrained groups in standard deviation units; HRD = human resources development; N_k = number of employees receiving training who remain in the workforce.

To use Equation 11-10, assume that SD_y = \$30,000, variable costs (V) = –0.10, the tax rate is 45 percent, and the discount rate is 8 percent. Because costs (\$1,000 per person) are incurred in the same period that benefits are received, we use k as the exponent in the cost term in Equation 11-10. The total payoff of the HRD program is the sum of the utilities of each of the five periods:

$$\Delta U_1 = 100(0.926)(0.44)(\$30,000)(0.90)(0.55) - \$100,000(0.55)(0.926)$$

$$\Delta U_1 = \$554,118$$

$$\Delta U_2 = 200(0.857)(0.385)(\$30,000)(0.90)(0.55) - \$100,000(0.55)(0.857)$$

$$\Delta U_2 = \$932,802$$

$$\Delta U_3 = 300(0.794)(0.33)(\$30,000)(0.90)(0.55) - \$100,000(0.55)(0.794)$$

$$\Delta U_3 = \$1,123,629$$

$$\Delta U_4 = 400(0.735)(0.275)(\$30,000)(0.90)(0.55) - \$100,000(0.55)(0.735)$$

$$\Delta U_4 = \$1,160,198$$

$$\Delta U_5 = 500(0.681)(0.22)(\$30,000)(0.90)(0.55) - \$100,000(0.55)(0.681)$$

$$\Delta U_5 = \$1,074,959$$

The sum of those one-period utility estimates is \$4,845,706. This is the total expected payoff of the HRD program over the five-year period.

Example: Skills Training for Bankers

The utility-analysis concepts discussed thus far were illustrated nicely in a study of the utility of a supervisory skills training program applied in a large commercial bank.[29] The study incorporated the following features:

- Training costs were tabulated using cost-accounting techniques.
- The global estimation procedure was used to estimate SD_y.
- Pre- and post-training ratings of the job performance of (non–randomly assigned) experimental- and control-group subjects were compared to determine d_t.
- Utility-analysis results that included adjustments for economic factors (discounting, variable costs, and taxes) were compared to unadjusted utility results.
- Break-even analysis was used to assess the minimum change in SD_y required to recoup the costs invested in the program.

- The effect on estimated payoffs of employee flows, decay in training effects, and employee turnover was considered explicitly.

Results showed that the training program paid off handsomely over time, even under highly conservative assumptions. Training 65 bank managers in supervisory skills produced an estimated net payoff (after adjustment for the economic factors noted earlier) of $79,000 (all figures in 2010 dollars), and $338,736 by Year 5. Not surprisingly, the reductions in value associated with adjusting for economic factors tended to become greater the farther in time they were projected. In general, however, utility figures adjusted for economic factors were 60–80 percent smaller than unadjusted figures.

When break-even analysis was used, even assuming a 25 percent yearly reduction in the strength of the training effect, break-even values of SD_y were still less than 50 percent of the values used in the utility analysis. Finally, in terms of employee flows, the economic impact of training additional groups was also considerable. For example, the estimate for the tenth year of the utility of training 225 employees in the first five years was more than $830,000 (in 2010 dollars), even after adjustment for economic factors. Information such as this is useful to decision makers, whether the focus is on the broad allocation of organizational resources across functional lines or on the choice of specific HR programs from a larger menu of possible programs.

Costs: Off-Site Versus Web-Based Meetings

Having illustrated methods and technology for assessing the value of employee-development efforts, this final section of the chapter focuses on identifying costs—specifically, the costs of offsite versus web-based meetings. Given the wide proliferation and continued growth of Internet-based technologies, many organizations have opted for a web-based or off-site approach to cut costs. What follows is a general costing framework that can be applied to many types of training and that can be used to compare relative costs.

Off-site meetings conducted away from organizational property are useful for a variety of purposes: for conducting HRD programs, for communicating information without the interruptions commonly found at the office, for strategic planning, and for decision making. In many cases, however, the true costs of an off-site meeting remain unknown because indirect attendee costs are not included along with the more obvious direct expenses. The method described here enables planners to compute the actual costs of each type of activity in an off-site meeting.[30] Then we consider web-based meeting costs.

We make the following assumptions about a hypothetical firm, Valco, Ltd. The firm has 500 employees, including 100 first-line supervisors and managers. Under the general planning and direction of Valco's training department (one manager and one secretary), Valco holds a total of ten days of off-site meetings per year (either training sessions or various types of meetings for managers). The firm retains outside speakers and consultants to develop and conduct the meetings. On the average, 20 managers attend each meeting, and the typical meeting lasts two full days.

Costs shown in Table 11-2 are based on those figures. The estimates we are using here are broad averages intended only to create a model for purposes of comparison. Note that, in this example, we make no attempt to place a monetary value on the loss of productive time from the job, although, if it is possible to estimate such costs reliably, do include them in the calculations. As with the illustrations in other chapters, we have attempted to make the numbers as realistic as possible, but the primary concern should be the methodology rather than the numbers.

As you can see in Table 11-2, the per-day, per-person cost of Valco's meeting comes to $2,969. Actually, that figure probably does not represent the true cost of the meeting, because no distinction is made between recurring and nonrecurring costs.[31]

During the development of a program, organizations absorb nonrecurring costs such as equipment purchases and training designers' salaries. Recurring costs absorbed each time a program is presented include session expenses, such as facilities and trainers' salaries, and costs that correspond to the number of participants in a program, such as training materials and trainees' salaries.

Separating costs into categories allows each set of costs to be incorporated into utility calculations for the time period in which each expense is incurred. Thus, the high initial expenses associated with a program may indicate that costs exceed benefits for some period of time or over a certain number of groups of trainees. However, at some point, an organization may begin to derive program benefits that signal the beginning of a payback period. Separating costs from benefits helps decision makers clarify information about the utility of HR programs and return on investment.[32] This is as important for off-site meetings as it is for web-based ones.

Web-based meetings incur all the costs shown in Table 11-2, with the exception of sleeping rooms (item 1a), the reception (item 1d), meeting charges (items 2a, b, and c), and transportation to the meeting (item 3). However, a premises-based license for web-based conferencing typically costs at least $1,000 per year for unlimited usage.[33] Moreover, the emerging generation of unified communications platforms featuring integrated instant messaging, e-mail, video, and audio tools is making it easier for geographically dispersed attendees to exploit the full range of media.[34]

Table 11-2 Costs of an Off-Site Management Meeting

Cost Element	Cost per Participant per Day	Total Cost
A. Development of programs (annual)		
Training dept. overhead		
Training staff salaries		
Outside consultants		
Equipment + meeting materials	$1,750[a]	$350,000
B. Participant cost (annual)		
Salaries and benefits (average)	$550[b]	$130,000
C. Delivery of one meeting for 20 people		
1. Facility costs		
a. Sleeping rooms	$220	$4,400
b. Three meals daily	$109	[c]$2,180
c. Coffee breaks	$30[d]	$600
d. Reception	$20[e]	$400
2. Meeting charges		
a. Room rental	$50	$1,000
b. Audiovisual equipment rental	$40	$800
c. Business services	$25[f]	$500
3. Transportation to the meeting	$175[g]	$7,000
Summary: Total cost per participant per day		
A. Development of programs	$1,750	
B. Participant cost	$550	
C. Delivery of one meeting (hotel + transportation)	$669	
	Total: $2,969	

Notes: Meeting duration: 2 full days. Number of attendees: 20 people. Costs do not reflect an estimate of the value of the lost productive time by the people in the program. Adding it would increase the costs dramatically.

[a] To determine the per-participant, per-day cost, divide $350,000 by the number of meeting days per meeting (2) times the number of managers attending all meetings (100) = $1,750 per day of a meeting.

[b] To determine the per-day cost, divide the total of $130,000 by 236 (average number of work days per year) = $550 per day of the work year.

[c] Assume the following daily costs per person: $20 for breakfast, $30 for lunch, $40 for dinner + 21 percent service fee/gratuity = $108.90.

[d] Assumes a total cost of $300 per coffee break, one morning + one afternoon = $600 per day, divided by 20 attendees = $30 per person per day.

[e] Assumes a charge of $100 to set up a bar + a $300 minimum total charge = $400 divided by 20 = $20 per person per day.

[f] Assumes a daily charge of $500 for Internet access, photocopying, and facsimile services.

[g] To determine the per-day cost, divide the group total ($7,000) by the number of participants (20); then divide the resulting figure ($350) by the number of meeting days (2) = $175 per day.

The very highest-level videoconferencing systems, such as Hewlett-Packard's Halo Collaboration Studio, Polycom's RPX product, and Cisco's Telepresence Meeting solution, include a set of technologies that allow people to feel as if they are present at a remote location, a phenomenon called telepresence.[35] To achieve the illusion that all attendees are in the same room, each vendor makes its videoconferencing rooms look alike, using the same semicircular conference tables illuminated by the same type of light bulbs and surrounded by identical wall colors. Participants appear as life-size images and sit at the table facing video displays, which have cameras set just above or around the screen.[36]

Telepresence systems are not cheap. HP's system can cost as much as $350,000, plus $18,000 a month per conference room for operating costs. Cisco's TelePresence System 3200 product costs $340,000 for the hardware itself (rich audio, high-definition video, and interactive elements), plus $40,000 for planning and design, plus $3,500 a month for maintenance. Those costs will likely limit the use of telepresence systems to large, deep-pocketed organizations. At the same time, however, IDC forecasts that the number of telepresence systems shipped annually will grow from 4,000 in 2009 to more than 49,000 in 2014 and will reach a global installed base of 127,000 systems by 2015.[37]

Why do so many meetings still occur in person all over the globe every year? Perhaps because 64 percent of communication is nonverbal,[38] and most lower-end web-based conferencing systems lose those cues. Hence, many organizations feel that there is no substitute for face-to-face contact and the opportunity for interpersonal interaction. The influence of the environment on training cannot be minimized. The task for decision makers is to consider whether facility costs or web-based conferencing costs as a percentage of the total of the true meeting costs identified will or will not be offset by a corresponding increase in learning effectiveness. Only by considering all the factors that have an impact on learning effectiveness—program planning and administration, the quality of the trainer, program delivery, and learning environment—can we derive the greatest return, in time and dollars spent, on this substantial investment in people.

Process: Enhancing Acceptance of Training Cost and Benefit Analyses

The total cost of evaluating 18 training programs in the multinational firm we described earlier in the chapter was approximately $765,000 (in 2010 dollars).[39] That number may seem large until you consider that, during the time of the study, the organization spent more than $368 million on training. Thus, the cost of training evaluation was roughly 0.2 percent of the training budget during this time period. Given expenditures of such magnitude, some sort of accountability is prudent.

To enhance managerial acceptance, the researchers presented the utility model and the procedures that they proposed to use to the CEO, as well as to senior strategic planning and HR managers, *before* conducting their research. They presented the model and procedures as fallible but reasonable estimates. The researchers noted that management preapproval prior to actual application and consideration of utility results in a decision-making context is particularly important when one considers that nearly any field application of utility analysis will rely on an effect size calculated with an imperfect quasi-experimental design. (See Chapter 2 for more on quasi-experimental designs.)

Conclusion

One of the important lessons to be learned from the material presented in this chapter is that methods are available now for estimating the costs and benefits of HRD programs (proposed, ongoing, or completed). Instead of depending on the power of persuasion to convince decision makers of the value of HRD programs, HR professionals can, by the use of cost-benefit models, join with the other functional areas of business in justifying the allocation of scarce organizational resources on the basis of evidence rather than on beliefs.

Exercises

Software to calculate answers to one or more exercises below is available at http://hrcosting.com/hr/.

1. Jane Burns, an HR analyst for Standard City, USA, knows that SD_y for firefighters in her city is $28,000. The fire department has asked the city to provide training in team building for 500 of its employees, at a cost of $2,500 per employee. The effects of this organization-development effort are expected to last for two years. Using Equation 11-1, compute the break-even value for d_t necessary for the city to recoup the costs of the program.

2. Suppose, in Exercise 1, that you have just read a meta-analysis of team-building studies and know that the cumulated estimate of d_t is 0.45. Compute an expected utility for the program and compare it to the break-even value you identified earlier. How might this affect the chances that the project will be funded?

3. With regard to Exercise 2, suppose that the discount rate is 10 percent and variable costs are –0.10. The city is not taxed. How do these factors affect the estimate of expected utility that you developed in Exercise 2?

4. Pilgrim Industries, a 2,000-employee firm with 400 managers, holds 40 days of off-site meetings per year. Outside consultants develop and conduct the meetings, and, on average, 20 managers attend each meeting. The typical meeting lasts two full days. Last year, total program-development costs consumed $350,000. The average attendee's salary (plus benefits) was $70,000. To deliver each two-day meeting for 20 people, sleeping accommodations, food, telephone, and a cocktail reception cost $10,000. In addition, transportation, business services, a meeting room, and audiovisual equipment rental totaled another $11,000. Determine the total per-day, per-person cost of one off-site meeting.

5. Pilgrim's CEO has heard about the remarkable quality of telepresence web-based conferencing systems, and she has asked you to prepare a per-person, per-day cost comparison of an off-site meeting versus a web-based conference for a two-day meeting. You calculated the per-person, per-day cost of an off-site meeting in Exercise 4. What costs must you consider with respect to a web-based system? Would you want any other information before recommending one alternative over the other?

References

1. Levering, R., and M. Moskowitz, "100 Best Companies to Work For," *Fortune* (February 2, 2009), 67–78. See also Cascio, W. F., and H. Aguinis, *Applied Psychology in Human Resource Management,* 7th ed. (Upper Saddle River, N.J.: Prentice Hall, 2011).

2. *Ibid.* See also Noe, R. A., *Employee Training and Development,* 5th ed. (Burr Ridge, Ill: McGraw-Hill, 2009).

3. *Ibid.* See also Goldstein, I. L., and J. K. Ford, *Training in Organizations: Needs Assessment, Development, and Evaluation,* 4th ed. (Belmont, Calif.: Wadsworth, 2002); and Kraiger, K., "Perspectives on Training and Development," in *Handbook of Psychology: Vol. 12, Industrial and Organizational Psychology,* ed. W. C. Borman, D. R. Ilgen, and R. J. Klimoski (Hoboken, N.J.: Wiley, 2003).

4. Cascio and Aguinis, 2011.

5. O'Leonard, K., *The Corporate Learning Factbook 2010: Benchmarks, Trends, and Analysis of the U. S. Training Market* (San Francisco: Bersin & Associates, 2010); Noe, R. A., *Employee Training and Development,* 5th ed. (Burr Ridge, Ill.: McGraw-Hill, 2009); Jana, R., "On-the-Job Video Gaming," *BusinessWeek* (March 27, 2006): 43; and Brown, K. G., and J. K. Ford, "Using Computer Technology in Training: Building an Infrastructure for Active Learning," in *Creating, Implementing, and Managing Effective Training and Development,* ed. K. Kraiger (San Francisco: Jossey-Bass, 2002).

6. Mattioli, D., "Training, Amid Cutbacks," *The Wall Street Journal* (February 10, 2009), 17.

7. Avolio, B. J., J. J. Sosik, D. I. Jung, and Y. Berson, "Leadership Models, Methods, and Applications," in *Handbook of Psychology* 12, ed. W. C. Borman, D. R. Ilgen, and R. J. Klimoski (Hoboken, N.J.: Wiley, 2004), 277–307.

8. O'Leonard, 2010.

9. Arthur, W. Jr., W. Bennett, Jr., P. S. Edens, and S. T. Bell, "Effectiveness of Training in Organizations: A Meta-analysis of Design and Evaluation Features," *Journal of Applied Psychology* 88 (2003): 234–245. See also Burke, M. J., R. R. Day, "A Cumulative Study of the Effectiveness of Managerial Training," *Journal of Applied Psychology* 71 (1986): 232–245; Guzzo, R. A., R. D. Jette, and R. A. Katzell, "The Effects of Psychologically-Based Intervention Programs on Worker Productivity: A Meta-analysis," *Personnel Psychology* 38 (1985): 275–291; and

Morrow, C. C., M. Q. Jarrett, and M. T. Rupinski, "An Investigation of the Effect and Economic Utility of Corporate-wide Training," *Personnel Psychology* 50 (1997): 91–129.

10. Bassi, L., P. Harrison, J. Ludwig, and D. McMurrer, "The Impact of U.S. Firms' Investments in Human Capital on Stock Prices" (June 2004), whitepaper downloaded from www.mcbassi.com, May 1, 2010.

11. Bassi, L., and D. McMurrer, "How's Your Return on People?" *Harvard Business Review* 82 (March 2004), downloaded from www.HBR.org, May 1, 2010.

12. Bassi, L., and D. McMurrer, "Training Investments As a Predictor of Banks' Subsequent Stock-Market Performance" (February 2009), whitepaper downloaded from www.mcbassi.com, May 1, 2010.

13. Bassi, Harrison, Ludwig, and McMurrer, 2004.

14. Cascio and Aguinis, 2011. See also Shadish, W. R., T. D. Cook, and D. T. Campbell, *Experimental and Quasi-Experimental Designs for Generalized Causal Inference* (Boston: Houghton Mifflin, 2002).

15. Boudreau, J. W., and P. M. Ramstad, *Beyond HR: The New Science of Human Capital* (Boston: Harvard Business School Publishing, 2007).

16. Coy, P., and J. Ewing, "Where are all the workers?" *BusinessWeek* (April 9, 2007), 28–31.

17. WorldatWork Total Rewards Model, downloaded June 11, 2010 from www.worldatwork.org/waw/aboutus/html/aboutus-whatis.html#model.

18. See, for example, Sturman, M. C., C. O. Trevor, J. W. Boudreau, and B. Gerhart, "Is It Worth It to Win the Talent War? Evaluating the Utility of Performance-Based Pay," *Personnel Psychology* 56 (2003): 997–1035. See also Mabon, H., "The Cost of Downsizing in an Enterprise with Job Security," *Journal of Human Resource Costing and Accounting* 1, no. 1 (1996): 35–62; and Mabon, H., and G. Westling, "Using Utility Analysis in Downsizing Decisions," *Journal of Human Resource Costing and Accounting,* 1, no. 2 (1996): 43–72.

19. Schmidt, F. L., J. E. Hunter, and K. Pearlman, "Assessing the Economic Impact of Personnel Programs on Workforce Productivity," *Personnel Psychology* 35 (1982): 333–347.

20. Rothstein, H. R., F. W. Erwin, F. L. Schmidt, W. A. Owens, and C. P. Sparks, "Biographical Data in Employment Selection: Can Validities Be Made Generalizable?" *Journal of Applied Psychology* 75 (1990): 175–184.

21. Sackett, P. R., "On Interpreting Measures of Change Due to Training or Other Interventions: A Comment on Cascio (1989, 1991)," *Journal of Applied Psychology* 76 (1991): 590, 591.

22. Cascio and Aguinis, 2011; Shadish et al., 2002; and Goldstein and Ford, 2002.

23. Schmidt et al., 1982.

24. Campbell, J. P., "Training Design for Performance Improvement," in *Productivity in Organizations,* ed. J. P. Campbell and R. J. Campbell (San Francisco: Jossey-Bass, 1988).

25. Boudreau and Ramstad, 2007.

26. Morrow et al., 1997.

27. *Ibid.*

28. Boudreau, J. W., "Effects of Employee Flows on Utility Analysis of Human Resource Productivity Improvement Programs," *Journal of Applied Psychology* 68 (1983): 396–406.

29. Mathieu, J. E., and R. L. Leonard, Jr. "Applying Utility Concepts to a Training Program in Supervisory Skills: A Time-Based Approach," *Academy of Management Journal* 30 (1987): 316–335.

30. The method is based on McKeon, W. J., "How to Determine Off-site Meeting Costs," *Training and Development Journal* 35 (May 1981): 126–122.

31. Mathieu and Leonard, 1987.

32. *Ibid.*

33. "Comparison of the Pricing and License Models for the 5 Best Web Conferencing Systems, *Online Meeting Tools Review,* downloaded June 9, 2010 from www.webconferencingtest.com/en/webconferencing_top5/webconference_pricing.html.

34. Murray, J. "Poor Comms Management Harms Virtual Teams," *IT Week* (September 20, 2006), downloaded from www.computing.co.uk/itweek/news/2164621/poor-comms-management-harmswww.itweek.co.uk.

35. Wikipedia, "Telepresence," 2010, at http://en.wikipedia.org/wiki/Telepresence.

36. "Polycom Delivers Lowest Telepresence Total Cost of Ownership Versus Competitors" (June 7, 2010), downloaded from www.polycom.com/products/telepresence_video/telepresence_solutions/index.html, June 9, 2010; "What's the Full Cost of Cisco Telepresence?" (May 19, 2008), downloaded from www.networkworld.com/community/node/27923, June 8, 2010; "Grappling with Cisco TelePresence, HP Halo Drops Pricing under Half a Million" (February 25, 2008),

downloaded from www.networkworld.com/community/node/25356, June 9, 2010; and Lee, L. "Cisco Joins High-End Videoconference Fray," *BusinessWeek* (October 25, 2006), www.businessweek.com/print/technology.

37. Edwards, J., "Understanding the Spectrum: Videoconferencing to Telepresence Solutions," IDC whitepaper (May 2010), downloaded from www.cisco.com/en/US/prod/collateral/ps7060/idc_vc_to_tp_spectrum.pdf, August 10, 2010.

38. Pearn-Kandola, *The Psychology of Effective Business Communications in Geographically Dispersed Teams* (San Jose, Calif.: Cisco Systems, 2006).

39. Morrow et al., 1997.

12

Talent Investment Analysis: Catalyst for Change

Chapter 1, "Making HR Measurement Strategic," noted that decision sciences evolve not simply when leaders within the profession develop logical and strategic models and measures, but when those models and measurement systems become integrated with the logical models and management systems that are used outside the profession. Finance and marketing frameworks are powerful because every business leader, regardless of professional background, is expected to understand basic financial or marketing logic. The ultimate test of any measurement and analysis system is simple: Does it improve decisions about vital resources where they matter most? Regarding talent, the decisions that matter often occur outside the HR function.

We envision a future in which leaders throughout organizations increasingly understand and are held accountable for the quality of their decisions about talent. They must have a sophisticated understanding of the connections between investments in HR programs and their effects on strategic success. Today organization leaders measure talent investments with a heavy reliance on accounting. As we have seen, accounting logic often provides valuable frameworks to track how traditional resources such as cash and time are spent on HR programs and employees. Unfortunately, however, this approach is often inadequate, and even dangerous, when it is the sole arbiter of HR investments. The increasing importance of talent resources to future strategic success means organizations that make better talent decisions will achieve their strategic missions more effectively.

This means that organizations must stop tolerating exclusive reliance on rudimentary cost-based frameworks for HR investments. Although this certainly presents an important challenge for leaders outside the HR profession, it also holds the HR profession to a high standard. If we expect leaders to act with more sophistication, we can help that process along by providing frameworks that enable more sophistication. The frameworks in this book provide HR leaders with ways to do that—and to demonstrate that the insights they provide often improve decisions, thereby improving organizational effectiveness.

Better Answers to Fundamental Questions

Recall the questions we posed at the beginning of Chapter 1. Remember that we challenged you to consider how well your organization could address the following questions or requests if they were posed by your CEO or other business leaders outside the HR function. Now that you've read this book, you can see that each question referred to one or more chapters, and those chapters have given you tools for a more sophisticated, logical, and analytical approach.

Absence Means More Than Just Getting the Work Done

> *I know that on any given day, about 5 percent of our employees are absent. Yet everyone seems to be able to cover for the absent employees, and the work seems to get done. Should we try to reduce this absence rate, and if we did, what would be the benefit to our organization?*

Chapter 3, "The Hidden Costs of Absenteeism," showed that although employees may be able to cover for absent employees and the work may be completed, much deeper issues must be considered. Chapter 3 showed how to calculate the costs of paying employees who aren't at work and uncovered the hidden costs of overtime or contract employees needed to fill in for the absent employees. We noted that even if the work is getting done, the extra cost of supervisory time managing absence may be substantial. Thus, a more reasoned approach would use the diagnostic elements in Chapter 3 to look beyond whether the work is getting done and ask whether it is being accomplished with the optimum level of human capital investment. As Chapter 3 showed, many strategies can reduce absence, such as providing absent employees with assistance to mitigate the causes of absence (such as the need to take time off to care for sick children or parents) and providing explicit incentives to encourage and reward attendance.

We also noted that the tools we provided to examine absence patterns and costs may produce counterintuitive insights. For example, we showed that increasing company payments for medications to treat chronic diseases might actually produce a net gain in workforce productivity, thereby reducing presenteeism (employees attending work when they are ill). In short, it isn't as simple as reducing absence whenever it occurs. Instead, a judicious approach focuses on where absence costs are highest and considers investments to both reduce absence and encourage employees to manage optimally their decisions on whether to attend work.

Turnover Isn't Always a Bad Thing

> *Our turnover rate among engineers is 10 percent higher than that of our competitors'. Why hasn't HR instituted programs to get it down to the industry levels? What are the costs or benefits of employee turnover?"*

As discussed in Chapter 4, "The High Cost of Employee Separations," the effects of employee separations, whether dictated by the employer (such as layoffs and dismissals) or by the employee (such as voluntary retirements or quits), carry an array of costs and benefits. Separations carry both obvious and hidden costs.

As discussed, the costs of processing employee separations are merely the tip of the iceberg. To appreciate the costs fully requires understanding not only the costs of separating employees, but also the costs of acquiring and developing their replacements. Moreover, instead of considering employee separations solely on the basis of costs, Chapter 4 provided a framework to examine how employee separations affect the quality of the workforce. Separations can increase workforce quality if replacements are of higher quality than those who left and if the costs of replacement don't overwhelm the increase in value that the replacements provide. We showed that fully accounting for turnover consequences requires looking beyond simply reducing turnover rates, even when the cost savings are significant. We also showed how organizations can move beyond simply assuming that turnover among high performers is dysfunctional and that turnover among low performers is functional.

The key is to consider employee separations as one of many processes that increase or decrease workforce quality, depending on how optimally they are managed. In many ways, employee separations are analogous to employee selection, except that the organization is "selecting" which of its current employees will remain. Organizations do this directly through their decisions about layoffs and dismissals, but they also do it more subtly through their decisions on how to encourage and reward employees for their decisions to stay or leave.

Layoffs Cut More Than Costs

> *Our total employment costs are higher than our competitors', so I need you to lay off 10 percent of our employees. It seems "fair" to reduce headcount by 10 percent in every unit, but we project different growth in different units. What's the right way to distribute the layoffs?*

Regarding layoffs, the implications are clear: Layoffs directed solely at labor cost reductions, particularly when they are arbitrarily spread evenly across the workforce, fall far short of the logical and systematic analysis required to optimize workforce quality.

Chapter 4 showed that the right answer to a CEO's request for blanket layoffs or turnover cost reductions is to step back and consider the full array of separation costs and consequences. Organizations that take that approach are likely to discover both hidden costs and potential benefits of employee separations. They are more likely to uncover differences in talent pools that are more pivotal with regard to the effects of separations. Turnover reduction will be directed where it has the greatest net effect on the future quality of the workforce.

When Everyone Is Reducing Employee Health Investments, Is It Smart to Invest More?

In a globally competitive environment, we can't afford to provide high levels of health care and health coverage for our employees. Many companies are cutting their health coverage, and so must we. There are cheaper health-care and insurance programs that can cut our costs by 15 percent. Why aren't we offering cheaper health benefits?"

Chapter 5, "Employee Health, Wellness, and Welfare," showed that employee health and welfare is more than just a source of increasing costs. The tangible effects of rising health-care costs are undeniable, and for many organizations, such costs have a significant effect on profits and financial returns. Yet the less tangible impacts of health and welfare investments on organizational productivity and resilience are equally important. Chapter 5 provided frameworks for estimating the costs of programs aimed at protecting employee health and caring for employee injuries and illnesses, and for estimating the effects of employee health and welfare on important organizational outcomes.

As discussed, employee health affects organizational performance through reductions in the costs of health care, but more subtly through reductions in absence and turnover, and through increases in productivity. Thus, by using combinations of techniques, as we described in our examples, organizations can analyze the effects of investments in employee health and welfare for their direct impact on costs and medical outcomes. In fact, they can go further to estimate the effects of changes in worker health on intermediate outcomes that also affect organizational performance.

The compelling and significant cost reductions that are often possible by reducing health insurance coverage or increasing employee health premium contributions must be tempered with an awareness of the powerful effects of improved employee health on organizational performance. A fixation on reducing the costs of insuring or caring for employees when they are ill may well obscure the significant benefits of investing more resources focused on improving employee health and productivity. Chapter 5 showed that organizations rarely systematically gather the data necessary to appreciate fully the effects of programs on worker health. In addition, it appears to be more effective to keep healthy employees healthy than to wait until they are ill and attempt to correct that. We also showed that the benefits of investments in employee health have proven to be significant in well-designed studies.

Only by understanding fully both the costs and potential benefits of proposed courses of action can organizations hope to optimize their decisions. As the question in this section suggests, business leaders all too often are understandably tempted by large and vivid cost levels to reduce health insurance and health-care programs. Organizations that take a more measured and analytical approach may well discover ways not only to achieve greater net productivity, but also to create more healthy workplaces in the process.

Why Positive Employee Attitudes Are Not Simply "Soft" and Nice to Have

I read that companies with high employee satisfaction have high financial returns, so I want you to develop an employee-engagement measure and hold our unit managers accountable for raising the average employee-engagement in each of their units.

Chapter 6, "Employee Attitudes and Engagement," showed tantalizing evidence that organizations with better employee attitudes and higher employee engagement are more likely to be rated as "great places to work"—and provide higher returns to their shareholders. However, before you conclude that investing in employee attitude enhancement is the path to double-digit growth and stock appreciation, Chapter 6 provides a framework for getting underneath the numbers. Indeed, under the right circumstances, there are logical and research-based reasons to expect that enhanced employee attitudes and higher employee engagement may lead to better customer service, higher customer loyalty, and improved profits. The popular press has provided many examples. However, the key is *the right circumstances.*

Chapter 6 showed that employee attitudes are actually a composite of several different elements, each measured in different ways and each affecting organizational outcomes differently. Employee job satisfaction differs from employee commitment, which, in turn, differs from employee engagement. Understanding the differences has proven key to dissecting the logical connections between attitudes and outcomes. Although commitment and satisfaction may drive employee retention, engagement and line of sight may be the key to improving employee service and production behaviors. Leaders who blindly pursue the goal of being rated highly in the "Best Places to Work" survey may miss more subtle opportunities to enhance attitudes and engagement where they matter most. The pivot points where enhanced attitudes and engagement make the greatest difference are not revealed by a blanket approach to enhance overall attitudes.

Chapter 6 also showed that the path from employee attitudes to organizational performance may be indirect. Employee attitudes may work because they lead to a more attractive workplace for high-quality applicants. Alternatively, they may produce their effects through the retention of high-performing and hard-to-replace employees. Or employee attitudes may have a direct effect on work behaviors when more satisfied or engaged employees demonstrate their attitudes to customers or other key constituents. Consistent with the idea of matching the measurement logic to the strategic situation, Chapter 6 showed how to measure the effects of employee attitudes through a behavioral-costing perspective and through a value-profit-chain perspective.

In the end, therefore, savvy HR and business leaders will look well beyond the typical focus on overall organizational attitudes, measures of engagement, or the ratings of "great places to work." The tantalizing correlation between those ratings and stock appreciation is just the beginning of a dialogue, one that is guided by principles developed over decades of research and analysis. The danger of equating a correlation with a cause is rarely illustrated more vividly than in the naïve mental models of business leaders who assume that the correlation between employee attitudes and stock performance means that the former *causes* the latter. Immense opportunities for improved decisions and organizational performance arise when the true power of employee attitudes and engagement is understood, and when they are approached with more "hard" science and less "soft" opinion.

Work-Life Fit Is Not Just a "Generational" Thing

I hear a lot about the increasing demand for work-life fit, but my generation found a way to work the long hours and have a family. Is this generation really that different? Are there really tangible relationships between work-life conflict and organizational productivity? If there are, how would we measure them and track the benefits of work-life programs?

Chapter 7, "Financial Effects of Work-Life Programs," showed that, for many workers, the days of passively accepting work demands that require 70 or even 100 hours per week may be fading. The desire to find a better fit between the demands and rewards of work and the demands and rewards of life outside of work are increasing not only for those with children or aging parents, but for virtually all members of the workforce. A strict accounting approach to talent might suggest that it is best to induce workers to devote as much time as possible to work. After all, how could greater work time be a bad thing?

Yet evidence increasingly suggests that employers that invest in programs to help workers find a better fit between work and life outside of work may reap great benefits.

Chapter 7 showed that work-life programs can include child and dependent care, flexible work conditions, options for work leave, information, and organization culture. The chapter also showed that an adequate analysis of such programs involves understanding that simply investing in the program is seldom sufficient. Work-life programs, like other HR programs, require communication, training, and the support of key leaders. The framework of Chapter 7 also showed that the effects of such programs can range from reduced stress to improved attitudes for current employees, which, in turn, lead to greater productivity and reduced turnover and absence. They also can lead to greater workforce quality because the company becomes attractive to whole new groups of job applicants: Increasingly, potential applicants are seeking an approach to work that satisfies their important nonwork goals and demands.

To answer the request for specific, tangible measures of the effects of such programs, Chapter 7 showed that it is often possible to estimate how such programs reduce time away from work by providing employees with ways to accomplish child- and elder-care tasks more easily and with greater advance planning. Naïve business leaders often frame work-life programs as a nice-to-have perquisite for employees, something that they do only when they can afford it, or something that panders to younger employees who lack sufficient work ethic. In reality, however, work-life programs can often be justified as logical investments that provide powerful business benefits in their own right. A correlation exists between enhanced work-life practices and organizational financial and stock performance. Unearthing whether your organization would benefit from improved work-life programs requires a deeper analysis within a framework such as Chapter 7 provides.

The Staffing Supply Chain Can Be As Powerful As the Traditional Supply Chain

We expect to grow our sales 15 percent per year for the next five years. I need you to hire enough sales candidates to increase the size of our sales force by 15 percent a year, and do that without exceeding benchmark costs per hire in our industry.

Is it worth it to invest in a comprehensive assessment program, to improve the quality of our new hires? If we invest more than our competition, can we expect to get higher returns? Where is the payoff to improved selection likely to be the highest?

Cost per hire and time to fill are two of the most frequent HR measures. It's often possible to save millions of dollars by managing staffing processes to lower such costs. However, it's also often possible to create multimillion-dollar problems when other factors go unmeasured and ignored. Focusing only on the number and cost of employees hired is seldom appropriate, because it ignores completely the effects of employee sourcing practices on workforce quality. No organization would manage the supply chain for its raw materials or unfinished goods based only on the cost of acquisition and the volume of goods acquired. Yet organizations often manage their talent supply chain based only on whether vacancies are filled and whether costs are kept at or below benchmark levels.

Chapter 8, "Staffing Utility: The Concept and Its Measurement"; Chapter 9, "The Economic Value of Job Performance"; and Chapter 10, "The Payoff from Enhanced Selection," collectively provided an alternative view. In combination, the chapters provided a logical framework for considering vital factors that determine not only the cost and quantity of talent affected by internal and external staffing, but also the quality of that talent over time. They showed that investments to enhance recruitment, selection, and retention can often pay off handsomely, even when they appear at first to be very costly. They also showed that the idea of simply duplicating the practices of others or setting benchmark cost levels based on what others do likely overlooks lucrative opportunities for unique competitive success through competing better in the market for talent. The frameworks provided in these chapters allow business leaders to integrate the effects of investments in higher-quality applicant pools with investments in more valid testing and with investments in enhanced retention of those hired. We saw that greater accuracy in selection does little good without a sufficiently large and high-quality applicant pool, and recruiting higher-quality applicants may do little good without sufficiently valid selection. Optimizing is the key, not maximizing the individual elements.

Moreover, these chapters showed that it is possible to estimate the amount of variability in job performance, and thus to translate the effects of programs to enhance performance quality directly into monetary units. The ability to estimate the relative value of performance differences across different roles and positions opens the door to systematic analysis of "pivotal" roles rather than a traditional focus merely on "important" or "critical" roles and competencies. As discussed, the focus on pivotal roles often uncovers hidden opportunities that traditional analysis misses.

Business leaders are seldom presented with an analysis of HR programs that is consistent with traditional financial investment models, but these chapters provided a framework to do just that. The chapters showed that investments in enhanced staffing can be analyzed for their impact on profits and discussed how to take into account standard financial considerations such as variable costs, discount rates, and taxes. Whereas every organization is concerned about potential talent shortages and enhancing its position in the "war for talent," Chapters 8, 9, and 10 showed that savvy organizations go much deeper, to determine where investments in improved staffing will and will not pay off. They do that with much greater sophistication and account for far more than simply whether positions are filled at a reasonable cost. Indeed, if other organizations are managing their staffing processes exclusively in terms of headcount and cost, more sophisticated organizations may well emerge as the victors in the more subtle game of talent management.

Taking HR Development Beyond Training to Learning and Workforce Enhancement

I know that we can deliver training much more cheaply if we just outsource our internal training group and rely on off-the-shelf training products to build the skills we need. We could shut down our corporate university and save millions.

As shown in Chapter 11, "Costs and Benefits of HR Development Programs," it is very dangerous to assume that all training has equivalent effects and that low-cost training is always better. Like other HR programs, some hidden effects of training are simply not apparent with the traditional accounting approaches. Leaders who fail to understand how training, development, and learning work together, and who fail to understand the factors that enhance their effects, risk investing in too much development where it is not needed and too little where it is desperately needed.

Chapter 11 provided a framework that embeds training within a larger concept of employee development. It showed that organizations must consider not only the development or learning experience, but also whether individuals are sufficiently prepared and ready to develop, and whether they have opportunities to transfer their learning back to the workplace. A significant implication of this model is that the investments that determine the effectiveness of development often extend well beyond the learning or training experience itself. Yet the vast majority of learning and training analyses focuses almost solely on the learning event. The framework also noted that improved work performance is only one outcome of enhanced development. In a world where job applicants increasingly regard development opportunities as a core element of the value proposition (particularly in economically developing regions), organizations that invest prudently in development have the potential for ancillary benefits through recruitment, retention, and reduced turnover.

As the chapter showed, the value of an investment in workforce development depends on the costs of that investment, the resulting quality of the workforce, and the impact of that quality improvement on the pivotal elements of the work. We presented analyses that found relationships (but not causal ones) between training expenditures and subsequent stock performance. We also saw that organizations often focus only on learning or performance as development outcomes, but that investments in workforce development may have important effects on employee attitudes, too.

Finally, Chapter 11 connected the earlier discussions about pivotalness and the value of variations in job performance to estimates of the payoffs from employee development. As discussed in that chapter, with a few simple modifications, the same formulas that enabled us to project the monetary value of staffing allow us to project the monetary value of development. Again, a vital factor to consider is the value of performance variability, what we have called the "pivotalness" of performance in a job or role. Better training is not equally valuable everywhere, and organizations that simply strive to enhance the skills of all employees will fail to optimize their investments. Using the frameworks of Chapter 11, organizations can apply the same rigor and logic to investments in workforce development that they apply to investments in other important resources.

Thus, when business leaders mistakenly focus only on the costs or even the learning outcomes of development, they miss opportunities and risk wasting significant resources. The development framework of Chapter 11 not only helps to estimate costs and learning outcomes more accurately, but it also embeds them in a broader and more appropriate investment framework.

Intangible Does Not Mean "Unmeasurable"

Accounting systems measure important costs, but effective talent decision frameworks go beyond costs to encompass "intangible" investments and value. As the chapters in this book have shown, *intangible* does not mean "unmeasurable," even if traditional accounting frameworks frequently overlook these "intangibles." The first step in improving talent decisions is often just to break through a traditional perception that decisions about talent cannot be systematic because talent measures are so "soft." Research shows that if managers perceive HR issues as strategic and analytical, they may simply not attend to analytical and numeric analysis. They seem to place HR in a "soft" category of phenomena that are beyond analysis and, therefore, addressable only through opinions, politics, or other less analytical approaches.[1]

An initial step in effective measurement is to get managers to accept that HR analysis is possible and could be informative. The way to do that is often not to present the most sophisticated analysis right away. Instead, the best approach may be to present relatively simple measures that clearly connect to the mental frameworks that managers are familiar with. As you have seen throughout this book, simply calculating and tracking the costs of turnover or absence, for example, reveals that millions might be saved with even modest reductions in employee turnover and absenteeism. Many organization leaders have told us that such a turnover-cost analysis was their first realization that HR issues could be connected to the tangible economic and accounting outcomes they were familiar with.

No one would suggest that measuring only the cost of turnover is sufficient for good decision making. As the frameworks in earlier chapters show, overzealous attempts to cut turnover or absence costs can lead to compromises in workforce quality or flexibility that have negative effects that far outweigh the cost savings. However, the change process toward more enlightened and logical decisions may require starting with costs before presenting leaders with more complete (and complex) analyses. An initial analysis that shows simple reductions in costs may create the sort of awareness among leaders that the same analytical logic used for financial, technological, and marketing investments can apply to human resources. Returning to the framework that we introduced in Chapter 1, HR measures in all three anchor points (efficiency, effectiveness, and impact) are useful. From a change-management perspective, efficiency measures may be the appropriate starting point to get broad acceptance of the idea of building measures that include effectiveness and impact.

The belief that something can't be measured is simply no excuse for avoiding logical analysis. As you have seen, it is possible to measure many aspects of talent that traditional systems seldom recognize. For example, there are several ways to measure the value of differences in performance, changes in employee attitudes, and the responses of employees to investments in employee health and welfare. Organizational leaders remain mostly naïve to these opportunities and, therefore, naïve to the significant opportunities they provide for enhancing their decisions. Even when perfect measures are unavailable, you have seen that solid logic can enhance decisions, using sensitivity analysis, simulation, and risk assessment to make up for measurement imperfections, just as these tools are used in other areas of management.

The HC BRidge Framework as a Meta Model

Figure 12-1 shows the HC BRidge framework. In Chapter 1, we introduced the anchor points of this framework: efficiency, effectiveness, and impact. Here we show the linking elements between HR investments and sustainable strategic success. We have not attempted to define measurements for every linking element, and more detail on the linking elements can be found elsewhere.[2] We have suggested that, when measuring the effects of HR investments, organization leaders should keep all three anchor points in mind.

Proceeding from the bottom-right side of Figure 12-1, we note that investments and policies and practices are perhaps the most prominent and tangible elements of the measurement frameworks we have described here. The chapters provided detailed frameworks for identifying both the tangible and intangible costs comprising HR investments, and they explained how to measure the frequency and use of HR policies and practices. Relying on those frameworks, HR leaders can estimate more accurately the full costs of programs such as training, health care, testing, recruiting, and communication, as well as the activity levels and use of such programs by employees and managers.

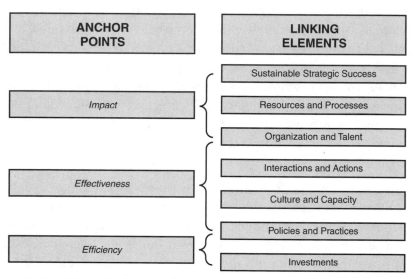

Figure 12-1 HC BRidge framework.

An important facet of our treatment of each HR program was to provide an overall logic model that showed the required conditions that must be achieved for the effects of the programs to offset their costs. These are "necessary and sufficient" conditions.[3] They comprise not only the elements that are necessary, but all the elements that are sufficient to achieve or explain program success. These conditions not only guide measurement, but they also become powerful frameworks for more sophisticated logical discussions about where and how HR programs work. Consider the supply-chain framework for staffing and the logical elements of the staffing-utility model. Chapters 8, 9, and 10 showed that, by combining powerful statistical assumptions with the simple concepts of cost, quantity, and quality, we can develop frameworks that predict when enhanced recruitment, selection, and retention will pay off, and how the three elements interact. More applicants are not always better, just as more valid testing and higher retention rates are not always optimal. The "necessary and sufficient conditions" depicted in the logic models in each chapter of the book allow leaders to go beyond simply recognizing the idea of optimization and instead actually strive to achieve it.

Culture emerged in a more subtle way. Looking back, virtually every chapter recognized the importance of a prominent "resource"—leadership support and engagement by key managers and supervisors—that is essential for success. This hidden resource is frequently the most vital requirement, and we have seen examples of its importance in areas as diverse as employee welfare, selection, and training. In addition, we have seen the importance of values, norms, and beliefs in driving sustained progress when the outcomes in question require long-term commitments, as in the case of employee development, health improvement, and better work-life fit. We have seen that although it is important to understand and track specific program investments and outcomes, contextual factors often are key determinants of the overall effectiveness of any given program.

Capacity has figured prominently in the frameworks we have described. Measuring the payoff of HR investments almost always includes assessing the effect of programs on the skill, knowledge, and capability of those who receive them. We have shown that knowledge and learning not only are measurable, but also often provide essential clues to understanding the mechanisms through which such programs eventually affect organizational performance. Moreover, we showed how to measure engagement and commitment, which represent important proxies for employee motivation. Measuring the combination of capability and motivation makes it possible to estimate the immediate return on investment (ROI) from HR programs using logic very similar to the ROI calculations that are so familiar in the context of other vital organizational investments. Indeed, as we have seen, cost-effectiveness analysis frequently provides valuable insights even when outcomes are not translated into monetary values. It is often quite valuable to estimate the cost of a particular increase in knowledge, learning, or engagement, particularly when comparing two or more programs designed to affect the same outcomes.

Actions and interactions have figured prominently because performance is usually observed through the specific actions or work behaviors of employees and their interactions both within and outside the organization. As Chapter 9 showed, deeply analyzing such performance elements often reveals unseen opportunities to create value by improving employee performance. The fundamental distinction between the average value of performance, or its "importance," and the value of performance differences, or pivotalness, is the key to understanding where improving investments in performance will pay off. We saw that traditional job descriptions often obscure pivot points, but that estimating the dollar value of performance differences often reveals pivot points and their associated opportunities. Once again, virtually all leaders recognize the principle of investing where there are large opportunities for gains. Chapter 9 showed how to find them, by considering the actions and interactions that make the biggest difference in key performance outcomes.

Resources and processes in the HC BRidge framework provide the connection points between the observable actions and interactions typically measured in performance assessment, and their effects on the sustainable strategic success of the organization. This kind of deep strategy analysis is a topic beyond the scope of this book,[4] but the importance of resources and processes in evaluating the effects of improved talent was still apparent. Often measures of the value of performance relied on an understanding of how performance affected processes such as sales or production.

As we have seen, although enhanced employee performance, engagement, health, knowledge, retention, and attendance are laudable goals, they are not uniformly valuable. We have seen how important it is to ask questions such as "learning for what purpose?" Often the answers require integrating the measurement of HR investments with strategy and planning processes outside the HR function. More precisely measuring the efficiency and effectiveness elements of such programs, which has been the focus of this book, provides a powerful platform for then engaging the question of how these outcomes really affect the business.

Lighting the LAMP of Organization Change

"Not everything that counts can be counted, and not everything that can be counted counts." This quote, often attributed to Albert Einstein, reflects some important conclusions and caveats as you begin to apply the frameworks we have described here. First, it is certainly true that we can't measure everything about talent and HR program effects. Many important elements of such investments remain relatively obscure and cannot be translated precisely into numbers. In particular, they remain outside the domain of traditional business measurement systems. That said, it is also apparent that the frequent failure to make systematic decisions about HR and talent investments is seldom due to the lack of measures. Indeed, advances in technology make it ever more possible to measure vital costs and effects that were once out of reach. Consider the ease with which data from organizational processes, such as supply chains and customer relationship management systems, can be accessed as those processes become more web enabled. Relating HR practices to these processes will be easier in the future. It is now feasible to connect customer reactions to particular call center or retail encounters with specific employees. Inexpensive and rapidly accessible data storage systems make it possible to archive information about employees at the time they are hired or promoted, and to use that information to determine what factors might be associated with their later success. Indeed, it is now quite feasible to evaluate business leaders on the accuracy and success of their decisions in hiring, promotion, layoffs, and performance assessment.

However, that brings us to perhaps the core dilemma facing future talent-measurement systems: Not everything that can be counted really counts. Some of the things that are easily measured may not be that valuable to decision makers. Information overload is a very real danger without logical frameworks that are capable of guiding leaders to the key relationships and measures that matter most to better decisions. That's why in this book we have emphasized logic and analytics over simply lists of measures or examples of scorecards. The measurement examples we have presented are meant to inspire and motivate future leaders to see beyond the limits of traditional data systems, but their more important purpose is to illustrate the logic of decision-based measurement. Replicating a particular cost calculation, or implementing a particular measure of engagement, is not the point. What matters is that you use these examples as templates and then develop the most valuable measures for your particular strategic and business situation, while at the same time considering the capacities of your measurement systems.

It is important to avoid the temptation to fixate only on the places where measures exist today. Even imperfect measures can prove extremely valuable if they illuminate vital factors that affect the outcomes of decisions. Logic and analysis are the tools that help take even imperfect measures and create tangible decision value.

In the end, the true test of talent and HR measurement is not its elegance, nor even its acceptance and use by members of the HR profession. These are important factors, but they are merely the intermediate steps to the larger goal: building more effective organizations by making better decisions about talent. We hope that this book will become one important tool in your journey to that important goal.

References

1. Johns, G., "Constraints on the Adoption of Psychology-Based Personnel Practices: Lessons from Organizational Innovation," *Personnel Psychology* 46 (1993): 569–592.

2. Boudreau, J. W., and P. M. Ramstad, *Beyond HR: The New Science of Human Capital* (Boston: Harvard Business School Publishing, 2007).

3. *Ibid.*

4. Strategy-analysis frameworks are covered in more detail in Boudreau and Ramstad (2007) and, more generally, in classic strategy works that are cited there.

Appendix A

The Taylor-Russell Tables

hese are tables of the proportion of employees who will be satisfactory among those selected (success ratio) for given values of the proportion of present employees considered satisfactory (base rate), the selection ratio, and *r*.

Source: H.C. Taylor and J.T. Russell, "The relationship of validity coefficients to the practical effectiveness of tests in selection: Discussion and tables," *Journal of Applied Psychology*, 23, 1939, 565-578.

Proportion of Employees Considered Satisfactory = 0.05

					Selection Ratio						
r	0.05	0.10	0.20	0.30	0.40	0.50	0.60	0.70	0.80	0.90	0.95
0.00	0.05	0.05	0.05	0.05	0.05	0.05	0.05	0.05	0.05	0.05	0.05
0.05	0.06	0.06	0.06	0.06	0.06	0.05	0.05	0.05	0.05	0.05	0.05
0.10	0.07	0.07	0.07	0.06	0.06	0.06	0.06	0.05	0.05	0.05	0.05
0.15	0.09	0.08	0.07	0.07	0.07	0.06	0.06	0.06	0.05	0.05	0.05
0.20	0.11	0.09	0.08	0.08	0.07	0.07	0.06	0.06	0.06	0.05	0.05
0.25	0.12	0.11	0.09	0.08	0.08	0.07	0.07	0.06	0.06	0.05	0.05
0.30	0.14	0.12	0.10	0.09	0.08	0.07	0.07	0.06	0.06	0.05	0.05
0.35	0.17	0.14	0.11	0.10	0.09	0.08	0.07	0.06	0.06	0.05	0.05
0.40	0.19	0.16	0.12	0.10	0.09	0.08	0.07	0.07	0.06	0.05	0.05
0.45	0.22	0.17	0.13	0.11	0.10	0.08	0.08	0.07	0.06	0.06	0.05
0.50	0.24	0.19	0.15	0.12	0.10	0.09	0.08	0.07	0.06	0.06	0.05
0.55	0.28	0.22	0.16	0.13	0.11	0.09	0.08	0.07	0.06	0.06	0.05
0.60	0.31	0.24	0.17	0.13	0.11	0.09	0.08	0.07	0.06	0.06	0.05
0.65	0.35	0.26	0.18	0.14	0.11	0.10	0.08	0.07	0.06	0.06	0.05
0.70	0.39	0.29	0.20	0.15	0.12	0.10	0.08	0.07	0.06	0.06	0.05
0.75	0.44	0.32	0.21	0.15	0.12	0.10	0.08	0.07	0.06	0.06	0.05
0.80	0.50	0.35	0.22	0.16	0.12	0.10	0.08	0.07	0.06	0.06	0.05
0.85	0.56	0.39	0.23	0.16	0.12	0.10	0.08	0.07	0.06	0.06	0.05
0.90	0.64	0.43	0.24	0.17	0.13	0.10	0.08	0.07	0.06	0.06	0.05
0.95	0.73	0.47	0.25	0.17	0.13	0.10	0.08	0.07	0.06	0.06	0.05
1.00	1.00	0.50	0.25	0.17	0.13	0.10	0.08	0.07	0.06	0.06	0.05

Proportion of Employees Considered Satisfactory = 0.10

					Selection Ratio						
r	0.05	0.10	0.20	0.30	0.40	0.50	0.60	0.70	0.80	0.90	0.95
0.00	0.10	0.10	0.10	0.10	0.10	0.10	0.10	0.10	0.10	0.10	0.10
0.05	0.12	0.12	0.11	0.11	0.11	0.11	0.11	0.10	0.10	0.10	0.10
0.10	0.14	0.13	0.13	0.12	0.12	0.11	0.11	0.11	0.11	0.10	0.10
0.15	0.16	0.15	0.14	0.13	0.13	0.12	0.12	0.11	0.11	0.10	0.10
0.20	0.19	0.17	0.15	0.14	0.14	0.13	0.12	0.12	0.11	0.11	0.10
0.25	0.22	0.19	0.17	0.16	0.14	0.13	0.13	0.12	0.11	0.11	0.10
0.30	0.25	0.22	0.19	0.17	0.15	0.14	0.13	0.12	0.12	0.11	0.10
0.35	0.28	0.2,4	0.20	0.18	0.16	0.15	0.14	0.13	0.12	0.11	0.10
0.40	0.31	0.27	0.22	0.19	0.17	0.16	0.14	0.13	0.12	0.11	0.10
0.45	0.35	0.29	0.24	0.20	0.18	0.16	0.15	0.13	0.12	0.11	0.10
0.50	0.39	0.32	0.26	0.22	0.19	0.17	0.15	0.13	0.12	0.11	0.11
0.55	0.43	0.36	0.28	0.23	0.20	0.17	0.15	0.14	0.12	0.11	0.11
0.60	0.48	0.39	0.30	0.25	0.21	0.18	0.16	0.14	0.12	0.11	0.11
0.65	0.53	0.43	0.32	0.26	0.22	0.18	0.16	0.14	0.12	0.11	0.11
0.70	0.58	0.47	0.35	0.27	0.22	0.19	0.16	0.14	0.12	0.11	0.11
0.75	0.64	0.51	0.37	0.29	0.23	0.19	0.16	0.14	0.12	0.11	0.11
0.80	0.71	0.56	0.40	0.30	0.24	0.20	0.17	0.14	0.12	0.11	0.11
0.85	0.78	0.62	0.43	0.31	0.25	0.20	0.17	0.14	0.12	0.11	0.11
0.90	0.86	0.69	0.46	0.33	0.25	0.20	0.17	0.14	0.12	0.11	0.11
0.95	0.95	0.78	0.49	0.33	0.25	0.20	0.17	0.14	0.12	0.11	0.11
1.00	1.00	1.00	0.50	0.33	0.25	0.20	0.17	0.14	0.13	0.11	0.11

Proportion of Employees Considered Satisfactory = 0.20

					Selection Ratio						
r	0.05	0.10	0.20	0.30	0.40	0.50	0.60	0.70	0.80	0.90	0.95
0.00	0.20	0.20	0.20	0.20	0.20	0.20	0.20	0.20	0.20	0.20	0.20
0.05	0.23	0.23	0.22	0.22	0.21	0.21	0.21	0.21	0.20	0.20	0.20
0.10	0.26	0.25	0.24	0.23	0.23	0.22	0.22	0.21	0.21	0.21	0.20
0.15	0.30	0.28	0.26	0.25	0.24	0.23	0.23	0.22	0.21	0.21	0.20
0.20	0.33	0.31	0.28	0.27	0.26	0.25	0.24	0.23	0.22	0.21	0.21
0.25	0.37	0.34	0.31	0.29	0.27	0.26	0.24	0.23	0.22	0.21	0.21
0.30	0.41	0.37	0.33	0.30	0.28	0.27	0.25	0.24	0.23	0.21	0.21
0.35	0.45	0.41	0.36	0.32	0.30	0.28	0.26	0.24	0.23	0.22	0.21
0.40	0.49	0.44	0.38	0.34	0.31	0.29	0.27	0.25	0.23	0.22	0.21
0.45	0.54	0.48	0.41	0.36	0.33	0.30	0.28	0.26	0.24	0.22	0.21
0.50	0.59	0.52	0.44	0.38	0.35	0.31	0.29	0.26	0.24	0.22	0.21
0.55	0.63	0.56	0.47	0.41	0.36	0.32	0.29	0.27	0.24	0.22	0.21
0.60	0.68	0.60	0.50	0.43	0.38	0.34	0.30	0.27	0.24	0.22	0.21
0.65	0.73	0.64	0.53	0.45	0.39	0.35	0.31	0.27	0.25	0.22	0.21
0.70	0.79	0.69	0.56	0.48	0.41	0.36	0.31	0.28	0.25	0.22	0.21
0.75	0.84	0.74	0.60	0.50	0.43	0.37	0.32	0.28	0.25	0.22	0.21
0.80	0.89	0.79	0.64	0.53	0.45	0.38	0.33	0.28	0.25	0.22	0.21
0.85	0.94	0.85	0.69	0.56	0.47	0.39	0.33	0.28	0.25	0.22	0.21
0.90	0.98	0.91	0.75	0.60	0.48	0.40	0.33	0.29	0.25	0.22	0.21
0.95	1.00	0.97	0.82	0.64	0.50	0.40	0.33	0.29	0.25	0.22	0.21
1.00	1.00	1.00	1.00	0.67	0.50	0.40	0.33	0.29	0.25	0.22	0.21

Proportion of Employees Considered Satisfactory = 0.30

	Selection Ratio										
r	0.05	0.10	0.20	0.30	0.40	0.50	0.60	0.70	0.80	0.90	0.95
0.00	0.30	0.30	0.30	0.30	0.30	0.30	0.30	0.30	0.30	0.30	0.30
0.05	0.34	0.33	0.33	0.32	0.32	0.31	0.31	0.31	0.31	0.30	0.30
0.10	0.38	0.36	0.35	0.34	0.33	0.33	0.32	0.32	0.31	0.31	0.30
0.15	0.42	0.40	0.38	0.36	0.35	0.34	0.33	0.33	0.32	0.31	0.31
0.20	0.46	0.43	0.40	0.38	0.37	0.36	0.34	0.33	0.32	0.31	0.31
0.25	0.50	0.47	0.43	0.41	0.39	0.37	0.36	0.34	0.33	0.32	0.31
0.30	0.54	0.50	0.46	0.43	0.40	0.38	0.37	0.35	0.33	0.32	0.31
0.35	0.58	0.54	0.49	0.45	0.42	0.40	0.38	0.36	0.34	0.32	0.31
0.40	0.63	0.58	0.51	0.47	0.44	0.41	0.39	0.37	0.34	0.32	0.31
0.45	0.67	0.61	0.55	0.50	0.46	0.43	0.40	0.37	0.35	0.32	0.31
0.50	0.72	0.65	0.58	0.52	0.48	0.44	0.41	0.38	0.35	0.33	0.31
0.55	0.76	0.69	0.61	0.55	0.50	0.46	0.42	0.39	0.36	0.33	0.31
0.60	0.81	0.74	0.64	0.58	0.52	0.47	0.43	0.40	0.36	0.33	0.31
0.65	0.85	0.78	0.68	0.60	0.54	0.49	0.44	0.40	0.37	0.33	0.32
0.70	0.89	0.82	0.72	0.63	0.57	0.51	0.46	0.41	0.37	0.33	0.32
0.75	0.93	0.86	0.76	0.67	0.59	0.52	0.47	0.42	0.37	0.33	0.32
0.80	0.96	0.90	0.80	0.70	0.62	0.54	0.48	0.42	0.37	0.33	0.32
0.85	0.99	0.94	0.85	0.74	0.65	0.56	0.49	0.43	0.37	0.33	0.32
0.90	1.00	0.98	0.90	0.79	0.68	0.58	0.49	0.43	0.37	0.33	0.32
0.95	1.00	1.00	0.96	0.85	0.72	0.60	0.50	0.43	0.37	0.33	0.32
1.00	1.00	1.00	1.00	1.00	0.75	0.60	0.50	0.43	0.38	0.33	0.32

Proportion of Employees Considered Satisfactory = 0.40

	Selection Ratio										
r	0.05	0.10	0.20	0.30	0.40	0.50	0.60	0.70	0.80	0.90	0.95
0.00	0.40	0.40	0.40	0.40	0.40	0.40	0.40	0.40	0.40	0.40	0.40
0.05	0.44	0.43	0.43	0-42	0.42	0.42	0.41	0.41	0.41	0.40	0.40
0.10	0.48	0.47	0.46	0.45	0.44	0.43	0.42	0.42	0.41	0.41	0.40
0.15	0.52	0.50	0.48	0.47	0.46	0.45	0.44	0.43	0.42	0.41	0.41
0.20	0.57	0.54	0.51	0.49	0.48	0.46	0.45	0.44	0.43	0.41	0.41
0.25	0.61	0.58	0.54	0.51	0.49	0.48	0.46	0.45	0.43	0.42	0.41
0.30	0.65	0.61	0.57	0.54	0.51	0.49	0.47	0.46	0.44	0.42	0.41
0.35	0.69	0.65	0.60	0.56	0.53	0.51	0.49	0.47	0.45	0.42	0.41
0.40	0.73	0.69	0.63	0.59	0.56	0.53	0.50	0.48	0.45	0.43	0.41
0.45	0.77	0.72	0.66	0.61	0.58	0.54	0.51	0.49	0.46	0.43	0.42
0.50	0.81	0.76	0.69	0.64	0.60	0.56	0-53	0.49	0.46	0.43	0.42
0.55	0.85	0.79	0.72	0.67	0.62	0.58	0.54	0.50	0.47	0.44	0.42
0.60	0.89	0.83	0.75	0.69	0.64	0.60	0.55	0.51	0.48	0.44	0.42
0.65	0.92	0.87	0.79	0.72	0.67	0.62	0.57	0.52	0.48	0.44	0.42
0.70	0.95	0.90	0.82	0.76	0.69	0.64	0.58	0.53	0.49	0.44	0.42
0.75	0.97	0.93	0.86	0.79	0.72	0.66	0.60	0.54	0.49	0.44	0.42
0.80	0.99	0.96	0.89	0.82	0.75	0.68	0.61	0.55	0.49	0.44	0.42
0.85	1.00	0.98	0.93	0.86	0.79	0.71	0.63	0.56	0.50	0.44	0.42
0.90	1.00	1.00	0.97	0.91	0.82	0.74	0.65	0.57	0.50	0.44	0.42
0.95	1.00	1.00	0.99	0.96	0.87	0.77	0.66	0.57	0.50	0.44	0.42
1.00	1.00	1.00	1.00	1.00	1.00	0.80	0.67	0.57	0.50	0.44	0.42

Proportion of Employees Considered Satisfactory = 0.50

						Selection Ratio					
r	0.05	0.10	0.20	0.30	0.40	0.50	0.60	0.70	0.80	0.90	0.95
0.00	0.50	0.50	0.50	0.50	0.50	0.50	0.50	0.50	0.50	0.50	0.50
0.05	0.54	0.54	0.53	0.52	0.52	0.52	0.51	0.51	0.51	0.50	0.50
0.10	0.58	0.57	0.56	0.55	0.54	0.53	0.53	0.52	0.51	0.51	0.50
0.15	0.63	0.61	0.58	0.57	0.56	0.55	0.54	0.53	0.52	0.51	0.51
0.20	0.67	0.64	0.61	0.59	0.58	0.56	0.55	0.54	0.53	0.52	0.51
0.25	0.70	0.67	0.64	0.62	0.60	0.58	0.56	0.55	0.54	0.52	0.51
0.30	0.74	0.71	0.67	0.64	0.62	0.60	0.58	0.56	0.54	0.52	0.51
0.35	0.78	0.74	0.70	0.66	0.64	0.61	0.59	0.57	0.55	0.53	0.51
0.40	0.82	0.78	0.73	0.69	0.66	0.63	0.61	0.58	0.56	0.53	0.52
0.45	0.85	0.81	0.75	0.71	0.68	0.65	0.62	0.59	0.56	0.53	0.52
0.50	0.88	0.84	0.78	0.74	0.70	0.67	0.63	0.60	0.57	0.54	0.52
0.55	0.91	0.87	0.81	0.76	0.72	0.69	0.65	0.61	0.58	0.54	0.52
0.60	0.94	0.90	0.84	0.79	0.75	0.70	0.66	0.62	0.59	0.54	0.52
0.65	0.96	0.92	0.87	0.82	0.77	0.73	0.68	0.64	0.59	0.55	0.52
0.70	0.98	0.95	0.90	0.85	0.80	0.75	0.70	0.65	0.60	0.55	0.53
0.75	0.99	0.97	0.92	0.87	0.82	0.77	0.72	0.66	0.61	0.55	0.53
0.80	1.00	0.99	0.95	0.90	0.85	0.80	0.73	0.67	0.61	0.55	0.53
0.85	1.00	0.99	0.97	0.94	0.88	0.82	0.76	0.69	0.62	0.55	0.53
0.90	1.00	1.00	0.99	0.97	0.92	0.86	0.78	0.70	0.62	0.56	0.53
0.95	1.00	1.00	1.00	0.99	0.96	0.90	0.81	0.71	0.63	0.56	0.53
1.00	1.00	1.00	1.00	1.00	1.00	1.00	0.83	0.71	0.63	0.56	0.53

Proportion of Employees Considered Satisfactory = 0.60

	Selection Ratio										
r	0.05	0.10	0.20	0.30	0.40	0.50	0.60	0.70	0.80	0.90	0.95
0.00	0.60	0.60	0.60	0.60	0.60	0.60	0.60	0.60	0.60	0.60	0.60
0.05	0.64	0.63	0.63	0.62	0.62	0.62	0.61	0.61	0.61	0.60	0.60
0.10	0.68	0.67	0.65	0.64	0.64	0.63	0.63	0.62	0.61	0.61	0.60
0.15	0.71	0.70	0.68	0.67	0.66	0.65	0.64	0.63	0.62	0.61	0.61
0.20	0.75	0.73	0.71	0.69	0.67	0.66	0.65	0.64	0.63	0.62	0.61
0.25	0.78	0.76	0.73	0.71	0.69	0.68	0.66	0.65	0.63	0.62	0.61
0.30	0.82	0.79	0.76	0.73	0.71	0.69	0.68	0.66	0.64	0.62	0.61
0.35	0.85	0.82	0.78	0.75	0.73	0.71	0.69	0.67	0.65	0.63	0.62
0.40	0.88	0.85	0.81	0.78	0.75	0.73	0.70	0.68	0.66	0.63	0.62
0.45	0.90	0.87	0.83	0.80	0.77	0.74	0.72	0.69	0.66	0.64	0.62
0.50	0.93	0.90	0.86	0.82	0.79	0.76	0.73	0.70	0.67	0.64	0.62
0.55	0.95	0.92	0.88	0.84	0.81	0.78	0.75	0.71	0.68	0.64	0.62
0.60	0.96	0.94	0.90	0.87	0.83	0.80	0.76	0.73	0.69	0.65	0.63
0.65	0.98	0.96	0.92	0.89	0.85	0.82	0.78	0.74	0.70	0.65	0.63
0.70	0.99	0.97	0.94	0.91	0.87	0.84	0.80	0.75	0.71	0.66	0.63
0.75	0.99	0.99	0.96	0.93	0.90	0.86	0.81	0.77	0.71	0.66	0.63
0.80	1.00	0.99	0.98	0.95	0.92	0.88	0.83	0.78	0.72	0.66	0.63
0.85	1.00	1.00	0.99	0.97	0.95	0.91	0.86	0.80	0.73	0.66	0.63
0.90	1.00	1.00	1.00	0.99	0.97	0.94	0.88	0.82	0.74	0.67	0.63
0.95	1.00	1.00	1.00	1.00	0.99	0.97	0.92	0.84	0.75	0.67	0.63
1.00	1.00	1.00	1.00	1.00	1.00	1.00	1.00	0.86	0.75	0.67	0.63

Proportion of Employees Considered Satisfactory = 0.70

					Selection Ratio						
r	0.05	0.10	0.20	0.30	0.40	0.50	0.60	0.70	0.80	0.90	0.95
0.00	0.70	0.70	0.70	0.70	0.70	0.70	0.70	0.70	0.70	0.70	0.70
0.05	0.73	0.73	0.72	0.72	0.72	0.71	0.71	0.71	0.71	0.70	0.70
0.10	0.77	0.76	0.75	0.74	0.73	0.73	0.72	0.72	0.71	0.71	0.70
0.15	0.80	0.79	0.77	0.76	0.75	0.74	0.73	0.73	0.72	0.71	0.71
0.20	0.83	0.81	0.79	0.78	0.77	0.76	0.75	0.74	0.73	0.71	0.71
0.25	0.86	0.84	0.81	0.80	0.78	0.77	0.76	0.75	0.73	0.72	0.71
0.30	0.88	0.86	0.84	0.82	0.80	0.78	0.77	0.75	0.74	0.72	0.71
0.35	0.91	0.89	0.86	0.83	0.82	0.80	0.78	0.76	0.75	0.73	0.71
0.40	0.93	0.91	0.88	0.85	0.83	0.81	0.79	0.77	0.75	0.73	0.72
0.45	0.94	0.93	0.90	0.87	0.85	0.83	0.81	0.78	0.76	0.73	0.72
0.50	0.96	0.94	0.91	0.89	0.87	0.84	0.82	0.80	0.77	0.74	0.72
0.55	0.97	0.96	0.93	0.91	0.88	0.86	0.83	0.81	0.78	0.74	0.72
0.60	0.98	0.97	0.95	0.92	0.90	0.87	0.85	0.82	0.79	0.75	0.73
0.65	0.99	0.98	0.96	0.94	0.92	0.89	0.86	0.83	0.80	0.75	0.73
0.70	1.00	0.99	0.97	0.96	0.93	0.91	0.88	0.84	0.80	0.76	0.73
0.75	1.00	1.00	0.98	0.97	0.95	0.92	0.89	0.86	0.81	0.76	0.73
0.80	1.00	1.00	0.99	0.98	0.97	0.94	0.91	0.87	0.82	0.77	0.73
0.85	1.00	1.00	1.00	0.99	0.98	0.96	0.93	0.89	0.84	0.77	0.74
0.90	1.00	1.00	1.00	1.00	0.99	0.98	0.95	0.91	0.85	0.78	0.74
0.95	1.00	1.00	1.00	1.00	1.00	0.99	0.98	0.94	0.86	0.78	0.74
1.00	1.00	1.00	1.00	1.00	1.00	1.00	1.00	1.00	0.88	0.78	0.74

Proportion of Employees Considered Satisfactory = 0.80

					Selection Ratio						
r	0.05	0.10	0.20	0.30	0.40	0.50	0.60	0.70	0.80	0.90	0.95
0.00	0.80	0.80	0.80	0.80	0.80	0.80	0.80	0.80	0.80	0.80	0.80
0.05	0.83	0.82	0.82	0.82	0.81	0.81	0.81	0.81	0.81	0.80	0.80
0.10	0.85	0.85	0.84	0.83	0.83	0.82	0.82	0.81	0.81	0.81	0.80
0.15	0.88	0.87	0.86	0.85	0.84	0.83	0.83	0.82	0.82	0.81	0.81
0.20	0.90	0.89	0.87	0.86	0.85	0.84	0.84	0.83	0.82	0.81	0.81
0.25	0.92	0.91	0.89	0.88	0.87	0.86	0.85	0.84	0.83	0.82	0.81
0.30	0.94	0.92	0.90	0.89	0.88	0.87	0.86	0.84	0.83	0.82	0.81
0.35	0.95	0.94	0.92	0.90	0.89	0.89	0.87	0.85	0.84	0.82	0.81
0.40	0.96	0.95	0.93	0.92	0.90	0.89	0.88	0.86	0.85	0.83	0.82
0.45	0.97	0.96	0.95	0.93	0.92	0.90	0.89	0.87	0.85	0.83	0.82
0.50	0.98	0.97	0.96	0.94	0.93	0.91	0.90	0.88	0.86	0.84	0.82
0.55	0.99	0.98	0.97	0.95	0.94	0.92	0.91	0.89	0.87	0.84	0.82
0.60	0.99	0.99	0.98	0.96	0.95	0.94	0.92	0.90	0.87	0.84	0.83
0.65	1.00	0'99	0.98	0.97	0.96	0.95	0.93	0.91	0.88	0.85	0.83
0.70	1.00	1.00	0.99	0.98	0.97	0.96	0.94	0.92	0.89	0.85	0.83
0.75	1.00	1.00	1.00	0.99	0.98	0.97	0.95	0.93	0.90	0.86	0.83
0.80	1.00	1.00	1.00	1.00	0.99	0.98	0.96	0.94	0.91	0.87	0.84
0.85	1.00	1.00	1.00	1.00	1.00	0.99	0.98	0.96	0.92	0.87	0.84
0.90	1.00	1.00	1.00	1.00	1.00	1.00	0.99	0.97	0.94	0.88	0.84
0.95	1.00	1.00	1.00	1.00	1.00	1.00	1.00	0.99	0.96	0.89	0.84
1.00	1.00	1.00	1.00	1.00	1.00	1.00	1.00	1.00	1.00	0.89	0.84

Proportion of Employees Considered Satisfactory = 0.90

						Selection Ratio					
r	0.05	0.10	0.20	0.30	0.40	0.50	0.60	0.70	0.80	0.90	0.95
0.00	0.90	0.90	0.90	0.90	0.90	0.90	0.90	0.90	0.90	0.90	0.90
0.05	0.92	0.91	0.91	0.91	0.91	0.91	0.91	0.90	0.90	0.90	0.90
0.10	0.93	0.93	0.92	0.92	0.92	0.91	0.91	0.91	0.91	0.90	0.90
0.15	0.95	0.94	0.93	0.93	0.92	0.92	0.92	0.91	0.91	0.91	0.90
0.20	0.96	0.95	0.94	0.94	0.93	0.93	0.92	0.92	0.91	0.91	0.90
0.25	0.97	0.96	0.95	0.95	0.94	0.93	0.93	0.92	0.92	0.91	0.91
0.30	0.98	0.97	0.96	0.95	0.94	0.94	0.94	0.93	0.92	0.91	0.91
0.35	0.98	0.98	0.97	0.96	0.95	0.95	0.94	0.93	0.93	0.92	0.91
0.40	0.99	0.98	0.98	0.97	0.96	0.95	0.95	0.94	0.93	0.92	0.91
0.45	0.99	0.99	0.98	0.98	0.97	0.96	0.95	0.94	0.93	0.92	0.91
0.50	1.00	0.99	0.99	0.98	0.97	0.97	0.96	0.95	0.94	0.92	0.92
0.55	1.00	1.00	0.99	0.99	0.98	0.97	0.97	0.96	0.94	0.93	0.92
0.60	1.00	1.00	0.99	0.99	0.99	0.98	0.97	0.96	0.95	0.93	0.92
0.65	1.00	1.00	1.00	0.99	0.99	0.98	0.98	0.97	0.96	0.94	0.92
0.70	1.00	1.00	1.00	1.00	0.99	0.99	0.98	0.97	0.96	0.94	0.93
0.75	1.00	1.00	1.00	1.00	1.00	0.99	0.99	0.98	0.97	0.95	0.93
0.80	1.00	1.00	1.00	1.00	1.00	1.00	0.99	0.99	0.97	0.95	0.93
0.85	1.00	1.00	1.00	1.00	1.00	1.00	1.00	0.99	0.98	0.96	0.94
0.90	1.00	1.00	1.00	1.00	1.00	1.00	1.00	1.00	0.99	0.97	0.94
0.95	1.00	1.00	1.00	1.00	1.00	1.00	1.00	1.00	1.00	0.98	0.94
1.00	1.00	1.00	1.00	1.00	1.00	1.00	1.00	1.00	1.00	1.00	0.95

Appendix B

The Naylor-Shine Table for Determining the Increase in Mean Criterion Score Obtained by Using a Selection Device

Using the Table

he following definitions are used in the table:

r_{xy} = Validity coefficient

Z_{xi} = Cutoff point (score) on the predictor in standard-score units

ϕ_I = Selection ratio

$\bar{Z}_{yi}$ = Mean criterion score (in standard-score units) of all cases above cutoff

λ_I = Ordinate of normal distribution at Z_{xi}

And the table is based upon the following equation:

$$\bar{Z}_{yi} = r_{xy}(\lambda_i / \phi_i)$$

Note: The use of the table may differ slightly in the case where r_{xy} is really a multiple regression coefficient. The major difference occurs in the Z_{xi} column. With a single predictor, there is no difficulty in expressing a cutoff score in terms of a particular value of X, the predictor variable (thus, we use Z_{xi}). However, in the case of multiple predictors, it is no longer feasible to do so because there are several X variables. The easiest procedure, therefore, is to reduce conceptually the multivariate case to the bivariate case by treating the multiple correlation coefficient as the correlation coefficient between the observed criterion scores (Z_y) and the predicted criterion scores (Z'_y). Thus, it becomes possible to talk about cutoff values for the multiple predictor case, but these cutoff scores are expressed in terms of Z'_{yi} values rather than Z_{xi} values. The only difficulty this creates is that $s^2_{z'y} \neq$ 1, but will always be equal to R^2_{xy}, the squared multiple correlation coefficient. Thus, to use the tables when r_{xy} is actually a multiple correlation coefficient, it is necessary to transform Z'_{yi} values by the following:

$$Z_{xi} = \frac{Z'_{yi}}{R_{xy}}$$

Table B-1 A Table for Computing the Mean Criterion Score (Z_{yi}) for the Group Falling above Some Cutoff Score (Z_{xi})

ϕ_i	Z_{xi}	λ_i	λ_i/ϕ_i	ϕ_i	Z_{xi}	λ_i	λ_i/ϕ_i	ϕ_i	Z_{xi}	λ_i	λ_i/ϕ_i
0.9987	−3.00	0.0044	0.00	0.9974	−2.79	0.0081	0.01	0.9951	−2.58	0.0143	0.01
0.9986	−2.99	0.0046	0.00	0.9973	−2.78	0.0084	0.01	0.9949	−2.57	0.0147	0.01
0.9986	−2.98	0.0047	0.00	0.9972	−2.77	0.0086	0.01	0.9948	−2.56	0.0151	0.02
0.9985	−2.97	0.0048	0.00	0.9971	−2.76	0.0088	0.01	0.9946	−2.55	0.0154	0.02
0.9985	−2.96	0.0050	0.01	0.9970	−2.75	0.0091	0.01	0.9945	−2.54	0.0158	0.02
0.9984	−2.95	0.0051	0.01	0.9969	−2.74	0.0093	0.01	0.9943	−2.53	0.0163	0.02
0.9984	−2.94	0.0053	0.01	0.9968	−2.73	0.0096	0.01	0.9941	−2.52	0.0167	0.02
0.9983	−2.93	0.0055	0.01	0.9967	−2.72	0.0099	0.01	0.9940	−2.51	0.0171	0.02
0.9982	−2.92	0.0056	0.01	0.9966	−2.71	0.0101	0.01	0.9938	−2.50	0.0175	0.02
0.9982	−2.91	0.0058	0.01	0.9965	−2.70	0.0104	0.01	0.9936	−2.49	0.0180	0.02
0.9981	−2.90	0.0060	0.01	0.9964	−2.69	0.0107	0.01	0.9934	−2.48	0.0184	0.02
0.9981	−2.89	0.0061	0.01	0.9963	−2.68	0.0110	0.01	0.9932	−2.47	0.0189	0.02
0.9980	−2.88	0.0063	0.01	0.9962	−2.67	0.0113	0.01	0.9931	−2.46	0.0194	0.02
0.9979	−2.87	0.0065	0.01	0.9961	−2.66	0.0116	0.01	0.9929	−2.45	0.0198	0.02
0.9979	−2.86	0.0067	0.01	0.9960	−2.65	0.0119	0.01	0.9927	−2.44	0.0203	0.02
0.9978	−2.85	0.0069	0.01	0.9959	−2.64	0.0122	0.01	0.9925	−2.43	0.0208	0.02
0.9977	−2.84	0.0071	0.01	0.9957	−2.63	0.0126	0.01	0.9922	−2.42	0.0213	0.02
0.9977	−2.83	0.0073	0.01	0.9956	−2.62	0.0129	0.01	0.9920	−2.41	0.0219	0.02
0.9976	−2.82	0.0075	0.01	0.9955	−2.61	0.0132	0.01	0.9918	−2.40	0.0224	0.02

Source: J.C. Naylor and L.C. Shine, "A Table for Determining the Increase in Mean Criterion Score Obtained by Using a Selection Device." Journal of Industrial Psychology, 3, 1965, 33–42. Used by permission.

0.9975	−2.81	0.0077	0.01	0.9953	−2.60	0.0136	0.01	0.9916	−2.39	0.0229	0.02
0.9974	−2.80	0.0079	0.01	0.9952	−2.59	0.0139	0.01	0.9913	−2.38	0.0235	0.02
0.9911	−2.37	0.0241	0.02	0.9834	−2.13	0.0413	0.04	0.9706	−1.89	0.0669	0.07
0.9909	−2.36	0.0246	0.02	0.9830	−2.12	0.0422	0.04	0.9699	−1.88	0.0681	0.07
0.9906	−2.35	0.0252	0.03	0.9826	−2.11	0.0431	0.04	0.9693	−1.87	0.0694	0.07
0.9904	−2.34	0.0258	0.03	0.9821	−2.10	0.0440	0.04	0.9686	−1.86	0.0707	0.07
0.9901	−2.33	0.0264	0.03	0.9817	−2.09	0.0449	0.05	0.9678	−1.85	0.0721	0.07
0.9898	−2.32	0.0270	0.03	0.9812	−2.08	0.0459	0.05	0.9671	−1.84	0.0734	0.08
0.9896	−2.31	0.0277	0.03	0.9808	−2.07	0.0468	0.05	0.9664	−1.83	0.0748	0.08
0.9893	−2.30	0.0283	0.03	0.9803	−2.06	0.0478	0.05	0.9656	−1.82	0.0761	0.08
0.9890	−2.29	0.0290	0.03	0.9798	−2.05	0.0488	0.05	0.9649	−1.81	0.0775	0.08
0.9887	−2.28	0.0297	0.03	0.9793	−2.04	0.0498	0.05	0.9641	−1.80	0.0790	0.08
0.9884	−2.27	0.0303	0.03	0.9788	−2.03	0.0508	0.05	0.9633	−1.79	0.0804	0.08
0.9881	−2.26	0.0310	0.03	0.9783	−2.02	0.0519	0.05	0.9625	−1.78	0.0818	0.08
0.9878	−2.25	0.0317	0.03	0.9778	−2.01	0.0529	0.05	0.9616	−1.77	0.0833	0.09
0.9875	−2.24	0.0325	0.03	0.9772	−2.00	0.0540	0.06	0.9608	−1.76	0.0848	0.09
0.9871	−2.23	0.0332	0.03	0.9767	−1.99	0.0551	0.06	0.9599	−1.75	0.0863	0.09
0.9868	−2.22	0.0339	0.03	0.9761	−1.98	0.0562	0.06	0.9591	−1.74	0.0878	0.09
0.9864	−2.21	0.0347	0.04	0.9756	−1.97	0.0573	0.06	0.9582	−1.73	0.0893	0.09
0.9861	−2.20	0.0355	0.04	0.9750	−1.96	0.0584	0.06	0.9573	−1.72	0.0909	0.09

(Continues)

Table B-1 (Continued)

ϕ_i	Z_{xi}	λ_i	λ_i/ϕ_i	ϕ_i	Z_{xi}	λ_i	λ_i/ϕ_i	ϕ_i	Z_{xi}	λ_i	λ_i/ϕ_i
0.9857	−2.19	0.0363	0.04	0.9744	−1.95	0.0596	0.06	0.9564	−1.71	0.0925	0.10
0.9854	−2.18	0.0371	0.04	0.9738	−1.94	0.0608	0.06	0.9554	−1.70	0.0940	0.10
0.9850	−2.17	0.0379	0.04	0.9732	−1.93	0.0620	0.06	0.9545	−1.69	0.0957	0.10
0.9846	−2.16	0.0387	0.04	0.9726	−1.92	0.0632	0.06	0.9535	−1.68	0.0973	0.10
0.9842	−2.15	0.0396	0.04	0.9719	−1.91	0.0644	0.07	0.9525	−1.67	0.0989	0.10
0.9838	−2.14	0.0404	0.04	0.9713	−1.90	0.0656	0.07	0.9515	−1.66	0.1006	0.11
0.9505	−1.65	0.1023	0.11	0.9192	−1.40	0.1497	0.16	0.8749	−1.15	0.2059	0.24
0.9495	−1.64	0.1040	0.11	0.9177	−1.39	0.1518	0.17	0.8729	−1.14	0.2083	0.24
0.9484	−1.63	0.1057	0.11	0.9162	−1.38	0.1539	0.17	0.8708	−1.13	0.2107	0.24
0.9474	−1.62	0.1074	0.11	0.9147	−1.37	0.1561	0.17	0.8686	−1.12	0.2131	0.25
0.9463	−1.61	0.1092	0.12	0.9131	−1.36	0.1582	0.17	0.8665	−1.11	0.2155	0.25
0.9452	−1.60	0.1109	0.12	0.9115	−1.35	0.1604	0.18	0.8643	−1.10	0.2179	0.25
0.9441	−1.59	0.1127	0.12	0.9099	−1.34	0.1626	0.18	0.8621	−1.09	0.2203	0.26
0.9429	−1.58	0.1145	0.12	0.9082	−1.33	0.1647	0.18	0.8599	−1.08	0.2227	0.26
0.9418	−1.57	0.1163	0.12	0.9066	−1.32	0.1669	0.18	0.8577	−1.07	0.2251	0.26
0.9406	−1.56	0.1182	0.13	0.9049	−1.31	0.1691	0.19	0.8554	−1.06	0.2275	0.27
0.9394	−1.55	0.1200	0.13	0.9032	−1.30	0.1714	6.19	0.8531	−1.05	0.2299	0.27
0.9382	−1.54	0.1219	0.13	0.9015	−1.29	0.1736	0.19	0.8508	−1.04	0.2323	0.27
0.9370	−1.53	0.1238	0.13	0.8997	−1.28	0.1758	0.20	0.8485	−1.03	0.2347	0.28

0.9357	-1.52	0.1257	0.13	0.8980	-1.27	0.1781	0.20	0.8461	-1.02	0.2371	0.28
0.9345	-1.51	0.1276	0.14	0.8962	-1.26	0.1804	0.20	0.8438	-1.01	0.2396	0.28
0.9332	-1.50	0.1295	0.14	0.8944	-1.25	0.1826	0.20	0.8413	-1.00	0.2420	0.29
0.9319	-1.49	0.1315	0.14	0.8925	-1.24	0.1849	0.21	0.8389	-0.99	0.2444	0.29
0.9306	-1.48	0.1334	0.14	0.8907	-1.23	0.1872	0.21	0.8365	-0.98	0.2468	0.30
0.9292	-1.47	0.1354	0.15	0.8888	-1.22	0.1895	0.21	0.8340	-0.97	0.2492	0.30
0.9279	-1.46	0.1374	0.15	0.8869	-1.21	0.1919	0.22	0.8315	-0.96	0.2516	0.30
0.9265	-1.45	0.1394	0.15	0.8849	-1.20	0.1942	0.22	0.8289	-0.95	0.2541	0.31
0.9251	-1.44	0.1415	0.15	0.8830	-1.19	0.1965	0.22	0.8264	-0.94	0.2565	0.31
0.9236	-1.43	0.1435	0.16	0.8810	-1.18	0.1989	0.23	0.8238	-0.93	0.2589	0.31
0.9222	-1.42	0.1456	0.16	0.8790	-1.17	0.2012	0.23	0.8212	-0.92	0.2613	0.32
0.9207	-1.41	0.1476	0.16	0.8770	-1.16	0.2036	0.23	0.8186	-0.91	0.2637	0.32
0.8159	-0.90	0.2661	0.33	0.7454	-0.66	0.3209	0.43	0.6628	-0.42	0.3653	0.55
0.8133	-0.89	0.2685	0.33	0.7422	-0.65	0.3230	0.44	0.6591	-0.41	0.3668	0.56
0.8106	-0.88	0.2709	0.33	0.7389	-0.64	0.3251	0.44	0.6554	-0.40	0.3683	0.56
0.8078	-0.87	0.2732	0.34	0.7357	-0.63	0.3271	0.44	0.6517	-0.39	0.3697	0.57
0.8051	-0.86	0.2756	0.34	0.7324	-0.62	0.3292	0.45	0.6480	-0.38	0.3712	0.57
0.8023	-0.85	0.2780	0.35	0.7291	-0.61	0.3312	0.45	0.6443	-0.37	0.3725	0.58
0.7995	-0.84	0.2803	0.35	0.7257	-0.60	0.3332	0.46	0.6406	-0.36	0.3739	0.58
0.7967	-0.83	0.2827	0.35	0.7224	-0.59	0.3352	0.46	0.6368	-0.35	0.3752	0.59

(Continues)

Table B-1 (Continued)

ϕ_i	Z_{xi}	λ_i	λ_i/ϕ_i	ϕ_i	Z_{xi}	λ_i	λ_i/ϕ_i	ϕ_i	Z_{xi}	λ_i	λ_i/ϕ_i
0.7939	−0.82	0.2850	0.36	0.7190	−0.58	0.3372	0.47	0.6331	−0.34	0.3765	0.59
0.7910	−0.81	0.2874	0.36	0.7157	−0.57	0.3391	0.47	0.6293	−0.33	0.3778	0.60
0.7881	−0.80	0.2897	0.37	0.7123	−0.56	0.3410	0.48	0.6255	−0.32	0.3790	0.61
0.7852	−0.79	0.2920	0.37	0.7088	−0.55	0.3429	0.48	0.6217	−0.31	0.3802	0.61
0.7823	−0.78	0.2943	0.38	0.7054	−0.54	0.3448	0.49	0.6179	−0.30	0.3814	0.62
0.7794	−0.77	0.2966	0.38	0.7019	−0.53	0.3467	0.49	0.6141	−0.29	0.3825	0.62
0.7764	−0.76	0.2989	0.38	0.6985	−0.52	0.3485	0.50	0.6103	−0.28	0.3836	0.63
0.7734	−0.75	0.3011	0.39	0.6950	−0.51	0.3503	0.50	0.6064	−0.27	0.3847	0.64
0.7704	−0.74	0.3034	0.39	0.6915	−0.50	0.3521	0.51	0.6026	−0.26	0.3857	0.64
0.7673	−0.73	0.3056	0.40	0.6879	−0.49	0.3538	0.51	0.5987	−0.25	0.3867	0.65
0.7642	−0.72	0.3079	0.40	0.6844	−0.48	0.3555	0.52	0.5948	−0.24	0.3876	0.65
0.7611	−0.71	0.3101	0.41	0.6808	−0.47	0.3572	0.52	0.5910	−0.23	0.3885	0.66
0.7580	−0.70	0.3123	0.41	0.6772	−0.46	0.3589	0.53	0.5871	−0.22	0.3894	0.66
0.7549	−0.69	0.3144	0.42	0.6736	−0.45	0.3605	0.54	0.5832	−0.21	0.3902	0.67
0.7517	−0.68	0.3166	0.42	0.6700	−0.44	0.3621	0.54	0.5793	−0.20	0.3910	0.67
0.7486	−0.67	0.3187	0.43	0.6664	−0.43	0.3637	0.55	0.5753	−0.19	0.3918	0.68
0.5714	−0.18	0.3925	0.69	0.4721	0.07	0.3980	0.84	0.3745	0.32	0.3790	1.01
0.5675	−0.17	0.3932	0.69	0.4681	0.08	0.3977	0.85	0.3707	0.33	0.3778	1.02
0.5636	−0.16	0.3939	0.70	0.4641	0.09	0.3973	0.86	0.3669	0.34	0.3765	1.03
0.5596	−0.15	0.3945	0.70	0.4602	0.10	0.3970	0.86	0.3632	0.35	0.3752	1.03

0.5557	−0.14	0.3951	0.71	0.4562	0.11	0.3965	0.87	0.3594	0.36	0.3739	1.04
0.5517	−0.13	0.3956	0.72	0.4522	0.12	0.3961	0.88	0.3557	0.37	0.3725	1.05
0.5478	−0.12	0.3961	0.72	0.4483	0.13	0.3956	0.88	0.3520	0.38	0.3712	1.05
0.5438	−0.11	0.3965	0.73	0.4443	0.14	0.3951	0.89	0.3483	0.39	0.3697	1.06
0.5398	−0.10	0.3970	0.74	0.4404	0.15	0.3945	0.90	0.3446	0.40	0.3683	1.07
0.5359	−0.09	0.3973	0.74	0.4364	0.16	0.3939	0.90	0.3409	0.41	0.3668	1.08
0.5319	−0.08	0.3977	0.75	0.4325	0.17	0.3932	0.91	0.3372	0.42	0.3653	1.08
0.5279	−0.07	0.3980	0.75	0.4286	0.18	0.3925	0.92	0.3336	0.43	0.3637	1.09
0.5239	−0.06	0.3982	0.76	0.4247	0.19	0.3918	0.92	0.3300	0.44	0.3621	1.10
0.5199	−0.05	0.3984	0.77	0.4207	0.20	0.3910	0.93	0.3264	0.45	0.3605	1.10
0.5160	−0.04	0.3986	0.77	0.4168	0.21	0.3902	0.94	0.3228	0.46	0.3589	1.11
0.5120	−0.03	0.3988	0.78	0.4129	0.22	0.3894	0.94	0.3192	0.47	0.3572	1.12
0.5080	−0.02	0.3989	0.79	0.4090	0.23	0.3885	0.95	0.3156	0.48	0.3555	1.13
0.5040	−0.01	0.3989	0.79	0.4052	0.24	0.3876	0.96	0.3121	0.49	0.3538	1.13
0.5000	0.00	0.3989	0.80	0.4013	0.25	0.3867	0.96	0.3085	0.50	0.3521	1.14
0.4960	0.01	0.3989	0.80	0.3974	0.26	0.3857	0.97	0.3050	0.51	0.3503	1.15
0.4920	0.02	0.3989	0.81	0.3936	0.27	0.3847	0.98	0.3015	0.52	0.3485	1.16
0.4880	0.03	0.3988	0.82	0.3897	0.28	0.3836	0.98	0.2981	0.53	0.3467	1.16
0.4840	0.04	0.3986	0.82	0.3859	0.29	0.3825	0.99	0.2946	0.54	0.3448	1.17
0.4801	0.05	0.3984	0.83	0.3821	0.30	0.3814	1.00	0.2912	0.55	0.3429	1.18

(Continues)

Table B-1 (Continued)

ϕ_i	Z_{xi}	λ_i	λ_i/ϕ_i	ϕ_i	Z_{xi}	λ_i	λ_i/ϕ_i	ϕ_i	Z_{xi}	λ_i	λ_i/ϕ_i
0.4761	0.06	0.3982	0.84	0.3783	0.31	0.3802	1.01	0.2877	0.56	0.3410	1.19
0.2843	0.57	0.3391	1.19	0.2090	0.81	0.2874	1.38	0.1469	1.05	0.2299	1.57
0.2810	0.58	0.3372	1.20	0.2061	0.82	0.2850	1.38	0.1446	1.06	0.2275	1.57
0.2776	0.59	0.3352	1.21	0.2033	0.83	0.2827	1.39	0.1423	1.07	0.2251	1.58
0.2743	0.60	0.3332	1.21	0.2005	0.84	0.2803	1.40	0.1401	1.08	0.2227	1.59
0.2709	0.61	0.3212	1.22	0.1977	0.85	0.2780	1.41	0.1379	1.09	0.2203	1.60
0.2676	0.62	0.3292	1.23	0.1949	0.86	0.2756	1.41	0.1357	1.10	0.2179	1.61
0.2643	0.63	0.3271	1.24	0.1922	0.87	0.2732	1.42	0.1335	1.11	0.2155	1.61
0.2611	0.64	0.3251	1.25	0.1894	0.88	0.2709	1.43	0.1314	1.12	0.2131	1.62
0.2578	0.65	0.3230	1.25	0.1867	0.89	0.2685	1.44	0.1292	1.13	0.2107	1.63
0.2546	0.66	0.3209	1.26	0.1841	0.90	0.2661	1.45	0.1271	1.14	0.2083	1.64
0.2514	0.67	0.3187	1.27	0.1814	0.91	0.2637	1.45	0.1251	1.15	0.2059	1.65
0.2483	0.68	0.3166	1.28	0.1788	0.92	0.2613	1.46	0.1230	1.16	0.2036	1.66
0.2451	0.69	0.3144	1.28	0.1762	0.93	0.2589	1.47	0.1210	1.17	0.2012	1.66
0.2420	0.70	0.3123	1.29	0.1736	0.94	0.2565	1.48	0.1190	1.18	0.1989	1.67
0.2389	0.71	0.3101	1.30	0.1711	0.95	0.2541	1.49	0.1170	1.19	0.1965	1.68
0.2358	0.72	0.3079	1.31	0.1685	0.96	0.2516	1.49	0.1151	1.20	0.1942	1.69
0.2327	0.73	0.3056	1.31	0.1660	0.97	0.2492	1.50	0.1131	1.21	0.1919	1.70
0.2296	0.74	0.3034	1.32	0.1635	0.98	0.2468	1.51	0.1112	1.22	0.1895	1.70

0.2266	0.75	0.3011	1.33	0.1611	0.99	0.2444	1.52	0.1093	1.23	0.1872	1.71
0.2236	0.76	0.2989	1.34	0.1587	1.00	0.2420	1.52	0.1075	1.24	0.1849	1.72
0.2206	0.77	0.2966	1.34	0.1562	1.01	0.2396	1.53	0.1056	1.25	0.1826	1.73
0.2177	0.78	0.2943	1.35	0.1539	1.02	0.2371	1.54	0.1038	1.26	0.1804	1.74
0.2148	0.79	0.2920	1.36	0.1515	1.03	0.2347	1.55	0.1020	1.27	0.1781	1.75
0.2119	0.80	0.2897	1.37	0.1492	1.04	0.2323	1.56	0.1003	1.28	0.1758	1.75
0.0985	1.29	0.1736	1.76	0.0618	1.54	0.1219	1.97	0.0367	1.79	0.0804	2.19
0.0968	1.30	0.1714	1.77	0.0606	1.55	0.1200	1.98	0.0359	1.80	0.0790	2.20
0.0951	1.31	0.1691	1.78	0.0594	1.56	0.1182	1.99	0.0351	1.81	0.0775	2.21
0.0934	1.32	0.1669	1.79	0.0582	1.57	0.1163	2.00	0.0344	1.82	0.0761	2.21
0.0918	1.33	0.1647	1.79	0.0571	1.58	0.1145	2.01	0.0336	1.83	0.0748	2.23
0.0901	1.34	0.1626	1.80	0.0559	1.59	0.1127	2.02	0.0329	1.84	0.0734	2.23
0.0885	1.35	0.1604	1.81	0.0548	1.60	0.1109	2.02	0.0322	1.85	0.0721	2.24
0.0869	1.36	0.1582	1.82	0.0537	1.61	0.1092	2.03	0.0314	1.86	0.0707	2.25
0.0853	1.37	0.1561	1.83	0.0526	1.62	0.1074	2.04	0.0307	1.87	0.0694	2.26
0.0838	1.38	0.1539	1.84	0.0516	1.63	0.1057	2.05	0.0301	1.88	0.0681	2.26
0.0823	1.39	0.1518	1.84	0.0505	1.64	0.1040	2.06	0.0294	1.89	0.0669	2.28
0.0808	1.40	0.1497	1.85	0.0495	1.65	0.1023	2.07	0.0287	1.90	0.0656	2.29
0.0793	1.41	0.1476	1.86	0.0485	1.66	0.1006	2.07	0.0281	1.91	0.0644	2.29
0.0778	1.42	0.1456	1.87	0.0475	1.67	0.0989	2.08	0.0274	1.92	0.0632	2.31

(Continues)

Table B-1 (Continued)

λ_i/ϕ_i	λ_i	Z_{xi}	ϕ_i	λ_i/ϕ_i	λ_i	Z_{xi}	ϕ_i	λ_i/ϕ_i	λ_i	Z_{xi}	ϕ_i
2.31	0.0620	1.93	0.0268	2.09	0.0973	1.68	0.0465	1.88	0.1435	1.43	0.0764
2.32	0.0608	1.94	0.0262	2.10	0.0957	1.69	0.0455	1.89	0.1415	1.44	0.0749
2.33	0.0596	1.95	0.0256	2.11	0.0940	1.70	0.0446	1.90	0.1394	1.45	0.0735
2.34	0.0584	1.96	0.0250	2.12	0.0925	1.71	0.0436	1.91	0.1374	1.46	0.0721
2.35	0.0573	1.97	0.0244	2.13	0.0909	1.72	0.0427	1.91	0.1354	1.47	0.0708
2.35	0.0562	1.98	0.0239	2.14	0.0893	1.73	0.0418	1.92	0.1334	1.48	0.0694
2.36	0.0551	1.99	0.0233	2.15	0.0878	1.74	0.0409	1.93	0.1315	1.49	0.0681
2.37	0.0540	2.00	0.0228	2.15	0.0863	1.75	0.0401	1.94	0.1295	1.50	0.0668
2.38	0.0529	2.01	0.0222	2.16	0.0848	1.76	0.0392	1.95	0.1276	1.51	0.0655
2.39	0.0519	2.02	0.0217	2.17	0.0833	1.77	0.0384	1.95	0.1257	1.52	0.0643
2.40	0.0508	2.03	0.0212	2.18	0.0818	1.78	0.0375	1.97	0.1238	1.53	0.0630
2.84	0.0167	2.52	0.0059	2.63	0.0297	2.28	0.0113	2.41	0.0498	2.04	0.0207
2.85	0.0163	2.53	0.0057	2.64	0.0290	2.29	0.0110	2.42	0.0488	2.05	0.0202
2.86	0.0158	2.54	0.0055	2.64	0.0283	2.30	0.0107	2.43	0.0478	2.06	0.0197
2.87	0.0154	2.55	0.0054	2.65	0.0277	2.31	0.0104	2.44	0.0468	2.07	0.0192
2.88	0.0151	2.56	0.0052	2.66	0.0270	2.32	0.0102	2.44	0.0459	2.08	0.0188
2.89	0.0147	2.57	0.0051	2.67	0.0264	2.33	0.0099	2.45	0.0449	2.09	0.0183
2.90	0.0143	2.58	0.0049	2.68	0.0258	2.34	0.0096	2.46	0.0440	2.10	0.0179

2.90	0.0139	2.59	0.0048	2.68	0.0252	2.35	0.0094	2.48	0.0431	2.11	0.0174
2.91	0.0136	2.60	0.0047	2.69	0.0246	2.36	0.0091	2.48	0.0422	2.12	0.0170
2.92	0.0132	2.61	0.0045	2.71	0.0241	2.37	0.0089	2.49	0.0413	2.13	0.0166
2.93	0.0129	2.62	0.0044	2.71	0.0235	2.38	0.0087	2.49	0.0404	2.14	0.0162
2.94	0.0126	2.63	0.0043	2.72	0.0229	2.39	0.0084	2.51	0.0396	2.15	0.0158
2.95	0.0122	2.64	0.0041	2.73	0.0224	2.40	0.0082	2.51	0.0387	2.16	0.0154
2.96	0.0119	2.65	0.0040	2.74	0.0219	2.41	0.0080	2.53	0.0379	2.17	0.0150
2.97	0.0116	2.66	0.0039	2.74	0.0213	2.42	0.0078	2.54	0.0371	2.18	0.0146
2.98	0.0113	2.67	0.0038	2.76	0.0208	2.43	0.0075	2.54	0.0363	2.19	0.0143
2.99	0.0110	2.68	0.003`1	2.76	0.0203	2.44	0.0073	2.55	0.0355	2.20	0.0139
3.00	0.0107	2.69	0.0036	2.77	0.0198	2.45	0.0071	2.55	0.0347	2.21	0.0136
3.01	0.0104	2.70	0.0035	2.79	0.0194	2.46	0.0069	2.57	0.0339	2.22	0.0132
3.01	0.0101	2.71	0.0034	2.80	0.0189	2.47	0.0068	2.57	0.0332	2.23	0.0129
3.02	0.0099	2.72	0.0033	2.80	0.0184	2.48	0.0066	2.60	0.0325	2.24	0.0125
3.03	0.0096	2.73	0.0032	2.82	0.0180	2.49	0.0064	2.60	0.0317	2.25	0.0122
3.04	0.0093	2.74	0.0031	2.82	0.0175	2.50	0.0062	2.61	0.0310	2.26	0.0119
3.05	0.0091	2.75	0.0030	2.83	0.0171	2.51	0.0060	2.61	0.0303	2.27	0.0116
3.23	0.0053	2.94	0.0016	3.14	0.0069	2.85	0.0022	3.06	0.0088	2.76	0.0029
3.24	0.0051	2.95	0.0016	3.15	0.0067	2.86	0.0021	3.07	0.0086	2.77	0.0028
3.25	0.0050	2.96	0.0015	3.16	0.0055	2.87	0.0021	3.08	0.0084	2.78	0.0027

(Continues)

Table B-1 (Continued)

ϕ_i	Z_{xi}	λ_i	λ_i/ϕ_i	ϕ_i	Z_{xi}	λ_i	λ_i/ϕ_i	ϕ_i	Z_{xi}	λ_i	λ_i/ϕ_i
0.0026	2.79	0.0081	3.09	0.0020	2.88	0.0063	3.17	0.0015	2.97	0.0048	3.26
0.0026	2.80	0.0079	3.10	0.0019	2.89	0.0061	3.18	0.0014	2.98	0.0047	3.26
0.0025	2.81	0.0077	3.11	0.0019	2.90	0.0060	3.19	0.0014	2.99	0.0046	3.27
0.0024	2.82	0.0075	3.12	0.0018	2.91	0.0058	3.20	0.0013	3.00	0.0044	3.28
0.0023	2.83	0.0073	3.13	0.0018	2.92	0.0056	3.21				
0.0023	2.84	0.0071	3.13	0.0017	2.93	0.0055	3.22				

[1] ϕ_i = Proportion above cutoff (selection ratio)

Z_{xi} = Predictor cutoff value in standard-score form

λ_i = Normal curve ordinate at Z_{xi}

Index

influence, HR analytics, 22

influencing senior leaders, work-life programs, 188-189

informational literature, costs, 100

insight, HR analytics, 22

integrating attitude-analysis systems into organizational systems, 162

Inter-Capital Limited, 75

interviews, entrance interviews, 95

involuntary turnover
    cost elements, 85
    versus voluntary, 83

J-K

job availability, communicating, 95

job offer rejections, effects of, 269-270

job outcomes, 145-146

job performance, 221
    Disney, 224-226
    estimating monetary value of variations in, 230
        cost-accounting approach, 230-233
    exercises, 249-250
    impact of work-life strains on, 174
    McDonald's, 227
    variances across jobs, 226-229

job satisfaction, 144-146
    OJS (overall job satisfaction), 153

JPMorgan Chase, child care, 180

L

LAMP, 10-11
    analytics, 13-14
    logic, 11-12
    measures, 12-13
    processes, 15-16

layoffs, 311-312
    cost elements, 85
    versus financial performance, 30

legal consideration, to modifying lifestyles, 122

levels of analysis, attitudes, 154-155

Lieber, Ray, 107

lifestyle discrimination, 122

lifestyles, modifying (legal considerations and incentives), 122

lift-outs, 101

line of sight, development candidates, 288

LISREL, 26-27

logic
    of health programs, 121
    investment value calculated using utility analysis, 257
    LAMP, 11-12
    talent development, 287-289
    utility analysis, 199-200
    of work-life programs, 172-174

M

MAUT (multi-attribute utility theory), 42

McDonald's
    job performance, 227
    turnover, 84-85

measures
    of absenteeism, 58
    behavior-costing approach, SYSCO, 158-159
    intangible does not mean "unmeasurable," 318-319

LAMP, 12-13
    WHP programs, 126-127

FINANCIAL TIMES

In an increasingly competitive world, it is quality
of thinking that gives an edge—an idea that opens new
doors, a technique that solves a problem, or an insight
that simply helps make sense of it all.

We work with leading authors in the various arenas
of business and finance to bring cutting-edge thinking
and best-learning practices to a global market.

It is our goal to create world-class print publications
and electronic products that give readers
knowledge and understanding that can then be
applied, whether studying or at work.

To find out more about our business
products, you can visit us at www.ftpress.com.